Curator, Editor and Layout Designer
Stephen Sadis

Writers
Dan Aznoff, Stephen Sadis, Marc Blau,
Charles Kapner, Eugene Normand, Todd Warnick,
Albert Israel, Mark Brunke, Joyce Dichkaut

Chapter Sponsors
Herman and Faye
Sarkowsky

Ken and Marleen
Alhadeff

Michele and Stan
Rosen

Generously supported by:

WSJHS

Washington State Jewish Historical Society

2031 Third Avenue, Seattle, WA 98121
(206) 774-2277

ISBN: 978-1-59849-162-3

Library of Congress Card Catalog Number: 2014931144

First printing: May 2014

Book Design, Layout and Graphics:

Stephen Sadis, Amy Vaughn (Soundview Design Studio), Nina Barnett

Published by:

Washington State Jewish Historical Society

Printed in China

Pictured on front cover (left to right, top to bottom):

Israel Halfon, Mike Sweeney, Dave Eskenazi, David Kosher, Rogers Hornsby, Addis Gutmann, Herman Sarkowsky, Ken Easley, Steve Bunin, Sue Bird, Abie Israel, Ben Mahdavi, Larry Sherry, Michael, Morrie and Ken Alhadeff, Dawn Trudeau, Ginny Gilder, Lisa Brummel, Anne Levinson, Sam McCullum, Adrian Hanauer, Dick Vertlieb, Lenny Wilkens, Bob Melvin. Spine: Joe Israel, Louis Sternberg

Pictured on back cover:

Sam, Jamien, Kathy and Justin McCullum, Sol Israel, Dave Mahler, Ken Griffey, Jr, Leon Grundstein, 1988 Maccabi Basketball Team, Ken Muscatel, 1902 Seattle Base Ball Club, Howard Cosell, Les Keiter, Naomi Weitz, Henry Prusoff, Jerry Belur, Karen and Dave Tarica, Charles Kapner, Howie Klein, Nate Ross, Rob Korman, Jimmy Rosenwald, Aaron Levine, 1984 ACJS Softball Team, Leo Dobry, Bob Moch

INTRODUCTION

In a classic scene from the satirical comedy film "Airplane!" a flight attendant
is distributing magazines to a passenger on board:

"Would you like something to read?" she asks.
"Do you have anything light?"
"How about this leaflet: 'Famous Jewish Sports Legends.'"

The Washington State Jewish Historical Society heard similar cracks soon after we
announced we were going to publish a collection of stories of the State's Jewish sports heroes:
"Thinnest book ever!"
"Will most of the pages be blank?"

Well, nobody is laughing now.

*   *   *

The Washington State Jewish Historical Society spent 2012 and 2013 honoring, remembering and celebrating our Jewish heritage in sport. We discovered what we long had suspected: Washington State is brimming with Jewish sports heroes.

The culmination of our two-year effort focusing on sport is this outstanding book: **Distant Replay! Washington's Jewish Sports Heroes**. And, Baruch HaShem, it's not as light as a leaflet. In fact, it is jam-packed with more than 180 fascinating stories of men and women, girls and boys, who personify the affirming values that sports can have on individuals and an entire community.

An estimated 45,000 Jews live in Washington State, amounting to less than 1 percent of the state's total population. And yet Jews in Washington have exerted a remarkable influence on the sports landscape in this state. In turn, sports have helped shape and define our Jewish community.

Jews in Washington have been professional athletes and amateur athletes. We have owned and operated professional sports franchises, and we have owned and bred Thoroughbred horses. We have been promoters, reporters, sports anchors, radio hosts, collectors, fighters, cheerleaders and daredevils.

You name the sport and Jews in Washington have made our presence felt. We've competed in football, baseball, basketball and soccer. We've been involved in running Longacres Race Track, Emerald Downs, the Seattle Seahawks,

Mariners, Supersonics, Sounders and even the Portland Trail Blazers. We have proudly donned the uniforms of the Mariners, Huskies, Cougars, Chieftains as well as the woolen jerseys of the Seattle Rainiers.

Like many immigrants in the early 20th century, we turned to boxing as a way to raise ourselves up and out of poverty and oppression. We built a track for horse racing and have won our state's pinnacle stakes race, the Longacres Mile, several times. We have also competed with Jews from around the globe in the Maccabi Games, the quadrennial Jewish Olympics, rewarding our state with a great sense of pride. We have played tennis and run track. We have piloted hydroplanes on Lake Washington. One of us even skates in the spectacle sport of roller derby.

Whether we play or spectate, sports stimulate- confidence and good will in us all – no matter whether the final result is triumph or defeat. "The interesting thing about sports is that it gives everyone in a community an emotional outlet, even when a team is going through hard times," said Walter Schoenfeld, a former minority owner of the Supersonics, Mariners and the original Sounders franchise. "And when you win, well, that really lifts the spirits of an entire group of people. It's just good for a community."

Civic leaders point to professional sports as a catalyst for community growth and a method for entering the national consciousness. Seattle may have had the Huskies and hydroplanes, but it was never considered a "major-league city"

until the Supersonics, Seahawks and Mariners took root in the Northwest. Each of those franchises grew out of the support of entrepreneurs who just so happen to be Jewish.

Herman Sarkowsky, who owned a piece of the Seahawks, Trail Blazers and Sounders, and owns horses that have won the Longacres Mile and the Breeder's Cup, feels the high number of Jews who have been involved in Seattle sports team front offices has little to do with religious background. "It's more by accident than anything else," he said. "Jews are entrepreneurial, I suppose, and you have to be entrepreneurial to start any type of professional franchise. But I don't apply any bigger meaning to it. It's just a matter of opportunities presenting themselves."

In addition to being entrepreneurial, Jews can be pretty competitive people. We even compete against one another – just for the sheer joy of it. Year after year, the Stroum Jewish Community Center softball league brings together a slapdash group of sports heroes who, by the end of the season, tend to have earned as many nagging injuries as they have game-winning hits. The games may not be elegant, but the SJCC softball league galvanizes the building of lasting friendships and even marriages – vital connections that fortify and strengthen our community for generations to come.

And isn't that really what sports are all about? Creating friendships. Building camaraderie. Sustaining community.

Stuart Eskenazi

FOREWORD

The Jewish community in Washington state boasts a dynamic and productive history. From Bellingham to Walla Walla, Spokane to Vancouver, and in Seattle, Tacoma and Everett, we have created our own communities while positively impacting the larger communities where we settled.

Our influence throughout the state covers many areas of daily life. Some are obvious. They include politics, the arts, medicine, law and business. Others are less so. One area of impact, which is the subject of this book, has long been deserving of more recognition.

Sports.

Jewish athletes, along with those in our community who have uplifted the sports scene, have helped shape the history of athletic achievement in Washington State for the last century. Whether those contributions occurred as a high school athlete, as a coach, as an owner of Thoroughbreds or as an individual who had the fortune of owning a sports team, we Jews have made a tremendous impact.

Distant Replay! is a collection of stories of Washington's Jewish sports heroes. The stories reflect just what we love about sports. They are full of intrigue and accomplishment. They are thrilling, surprising and moving.

As you will read, many of the stories illustrate how our local athletes have overcome competition and biases, feats that do not just require ability, but a strength of character as well.

We hope you enjoy the book and use the stories as inspiring examples of how Jewish children, teens and adults of all ages can embrace a goal, create a plan for achieving that goal, and foster that goal until it comes to fruition.

After all, these are the kinds of pursuits that make history.

Herman Sarkowsky

FOREWORD

CHRISTINE O. GREGOIRE
Governor

STATE OF WASHINGTON
OFFICE OF THE GOVERNOR
P.O. Box 40002 • Olympia, Washington 98504-0002 • (360) 753-6780 • www.governor.wa.gov

A Message from the Governor
Fall 2012

I am pleased to recognize *Distant Replay*, the Washington State Jewish Historical Society's new book showcasing the many significant sports accomplishments of Washington Jews.

Washington is privileged to have a vibrant Jewish community contributing to all aspects of our society, and this book provides a revealing look at an area of Jewish participation that many are unfamiliar with. Through photographs and compelling stories and people profiles, this volume will shed light not only on Jewish athletes, but also on many other positions of influence within the sports domain.

I applaud the Washington State Jewish Historical Society for its commitment to sharing the history and culture of the Jewish community in Washington. Our state's history is derived from a plurality of cultures and experiences, joined together by a common desire for opportunity and prosperity. When we celebrate the accomplishments of our Jewish community, we celebrate the importance of our diversity and enrich our collective experience.

Sincerely,

Christine Gregoire

Christine O. Gregoire
Governor

PREFACE

"WHAT WILL BE ON PAGE 3?"

When I was first approached to be involved with a book on Washington's Jewish athletes, admittedly I blurted out a variation of the same joke that everyone else had: "What will be on page 3?" Little did I know that I would spend the next year and a half proving myself and others wrong; a point made very clear when the book reached beyond 300 pages.

When the Washington State Jewish Historical Society kicked off its "Year in Sports" theme in 2012, it began the process by reaching out to the community and asking individuals to submit their stories or those of their family members or friends.

It wasn't long before the idea of a book materialized and a committee was organized to collect as many names of sports participants as possible. Our goal was to include as many men, women and children who have demonstrated an excellence in their achievements, at all levels of involvement, in the widest variety of sports, from all parts of Washington and from the earliest days to the most recent times. With some 300 names gathered, the committee - Ralph Maimon, Eugene Normand, David Eskenazi, Dan Aznoff and myself - prioritized which individuals we would pursue for stories and then began the process of researching, writing and preserving this history.

Though this book is voluminous, it is by no means complete. We know that we have missed a number of you and we gladly welcome receiving your stories for an updated edition in the future. We have also done our best to check and double-check all of the information to ensure accuracy but know that a few errors may have slipped through the cracks and we apologize for that.

For those of you who have helped sponsor this publication, you are the reason this history has seen the light of publication. This project demonstrates what is at the heart of why we exist as an organization; to collect, distill, preserve and make available the history of our people in this community. We are grateful to you for taking our calls, answering our emails, understanding our vision and entrusting us with your support.

As you read these stories and your mind is flooded with memories of individuals, incredible plays, moments of triumph and a number of things you had no idea about - remember that this is what preserving history is all about.

Stephen Sadis - Editor

ACKNOWLEDGEMENTS

TOUCHDOWN! MY OH MY! GOOOOOOAL!

The problem with writing a book, is that there is really nothing to scream when you're finished. I tried yelling "COMMAND S!" and "PRINT!" but that didn't seem to cut it. But that does not diminish the excitment of completing this project and the heartfelt appreciation I have for all of my teammates who have contributed so greatly to this book.

WSJHS Executive Director, Lisa Kranseler, was instrumental in seeing this project through to completion. WSJHS President, Albert Israel, was a constant support in my corner, continually coming through with whatever help was needed. Ralph Maimon's initiative to get the year of sports moving forward was invaluable. Past WSJHS President, Craig Sternberg, was a vocal and enthusiastic fan. Eugene Normand's contributions motivated the book project. And Dan Aznoff, who penned more than 100 profiles, was often in "beast mode" contacting individuals and churning out stories one after another.

David Eskenazi, Marc Blau and Charles Kapner provided dozens of photographs that brought these stories to life. Lori Ceyhun was very helpful organizing the materials submitted to the WSJHS office. Emily Keeler Alhadeff, Brad Spear, Eugene Normand, Steve Raskin, Betsy Schneier and Harold Sadis proofed these stories with dilligence and care. Elliott Wolf offered guidance in publishing this work. Amy Vaughn of Soundview Design created a layout that gave the book a wonderfully adaptive framework and Nina Barrett's design work added a beautiful aesthetic. Kyle Kegley helped keep my business running while I spent way too much time working on this side project and a special thanks goes to Cherie Singer, whose encouragment and patience were endless.

This book is dedicated to my Papoo Albert who inspired my love of sports and always told me to "keep my eye on the ball." And to my children, Sophia and Jaden, who remind me why sports are so much fun and why our history is so important to preserve for the generations to come.

Play Ball!

Stephen Sadis
Editor

SPORTS WRITERS

DAN AZNOFF

Kara Aborn
Barry Ackerley
Michael Alhadeff
Steve Altaras
Sylvia Angel
Morrie Arnovich
Dave Azose
Dave Baroh
Lou Baroh
Jim Brazil
Joel Brazil
Julie Brazil
Herb Bridge
Steve Bunin
Joel Buxbaum
Jerry Cohen
Warren Fein
Elliot Friedman
David Funes
Bruce Glant
Glendale CC
Bob Goldstein

Stan Golub
Matt Grogan
Dave Grosby
Leon Grundstein
Ben Harris
Hymie Harris
Joe Israel
Danny Jassen
Herb Karpel
Danny Kaye
Lester Kleinberg
David Kosher
Lisa Kranseler
Sandy Lederman
Aaron Levine
Ken Levine
Perry Levinson
Jacob Lunon
Ben Mahdavi
Dave Mahler
Joey Mayo
Taylor Mays

Jamien McCullum
Justin McCullum
Sam McCullum
Herb Meltzer
Jack Meyers
Morris Miller
Mike Morgan
Al Moscatel
Neiso Moscatel
Ray Moscatel
Ken Muscatel
Sid Nelson
Jay Posner
Terry Robinson
Greg Rosenwald
Jim Rosenwald
Todd Rubin
Beau Sadick
Michael Salk
Sam Schulman
Howard Schultz
The Seelig Brothers

Abe Sherman
Eddie Sherman
Jeff Solam
Elias Solomon
Mickey Soss
Marco Speer
Rudy Spring
The Staadeckers
Louis Sternberg
The Taricas
Stan Tobin
Zollie Volchok
Kim Waldbaum
The Warshal Family
Gertrude Wolfe
Aaron Wolff
Amy Wolff
Alan Woog
Hy Zimmerman

DAN AZNOFF and STEPHEN SADIS

Ken Alhadeff
Morrie Alhadeff
Sue Bird
Ely Caston
Marv Gilberg

Sonny Gorasht
Joseph Gottstein
Alex Grinstein
Addis Gutmann
Adrian Hanauer

Abie Israel
Charles Kapner
Les Keitner
Anne Levinson
Herman Sarkowsky

Walter Schoenfeld
Dick Vertlieb

SPORTS WRITERS

STEPHEN SADIS

Mark Alhadeff
Boxing intro
Jackie Caston
Sammie Caston
Jerry Cohn
Albert DeLeon
Trea Diament
Nate Druxman
Ralph S. Eskenazi
Glendale Country Club
Jordan Goldstein
Adam Gordon
Ari Grashin
Junior Sephardic League
Samuel Levine
Oscar Levitch
Paul Lowenberg
The Maccabees
Mark Maimon
Bob Melvin
Lee Mezistrano
Bob Moch
Moe Muscatel
Lipman Pike
Henry Prusoff
Harry Pruzan
Don Richman
Benjamin Roller
Jaden Sadis
David Schiller
Stan Sidell
Max Silver

Mike Silver
SJCC Softball
Harry Weinstone

MARC BLAU

Jerry Belur
Marc Blau
Michael Block
Bernie Brotman
Harold Brotman
Morley Brotman
Leo Dobry
David Eskenazi
Stan Farber
Dave Goodman
Jonathan Hurst
Sol Israel
Charles Littman
Louis Soriano
Harry Werbisky

CHARLES KAPNER

Al Federoff
Joe Ginsberg
The Grizwalds
Rob Kraft
Barry Latman
Jimmie Reese
Lawrence Sherry
Norm Sherry
SJCC Softball

EUGENE NORMAND

Jed Davis
Nate Druxman
Ari Grashin
Israel Halfon
Harry Schneiderman
Abe Spear
Sydney Thal
Naomi Weitz

TODD WARNICK

John Haas
Dave Haas
Mike Kahn
Bill Tone
Todd Warnick

ALBERT ISRAEL

Janet Esfeld Leopold
Mike Siegel
Howard Shalinsky

MARK BRUNKE

Jack Levy
Charles Schwartz

JOYCE DICKHAUT

Philip Sulman

TABLE OF CONTENTS

TABLE OF CONTENTS

FAN APPRECIATION

Where would we be without our supportive fan base? You are Jewish history's 12th Man and King Felix's Court all rolled into one. Your contributions cheer us on and we are very grateful to have all of you in our corner. With great appreciation - The Washington State Jewish Historical Society

4Culture
ABO Investments
Ken and Marleen Alhadeff
Emily Keeler Alhadeff
Morgan and Kathy Barokas
Jerry and Nancy Belur
Jerry Belur Family
Brazil, Cohn, Rosenbloom,
Sherman, Staadecker Family
Herb M. Bridge
Bob and Bobbi Bridge
Brumer Family
Joel Buxbaum
Jeff Coopersmith and
Stefanie Snow
Jed Davis
Irene Epstein
David Eskenazi
Glendale Country Club
Goldstein, Roberts Family
Jim and Erika Goldstein
Sonny and Gena Gorasht
The Grinstein Family
Leatrice Gutmann
Gutmann-Menashe, Kotzen,
Roberts Family
Jane Isenberg and
Phil Thompkins
Island Crust Cafe
Albert Israel

David Israel
Jewish Federation of
Greater Seattle
Charles and Betsy Kapner
Nick and Michele Keller
Keller Sulman Family
Kirkland Sports Cards
Larry Kleinberg
Kline Galland Center
Knopf Family
Kraft Palmer Davis, PLLC
Kenny and Lisa Kranseler
Krivosha, Sears, Caston Family
Steve and Cindy Linkon
Jeff and Julie Morris
Mark and Maggie Mosholder
Muscatel, McLeod Family
Eugene Normand
Pike Brewing Co.
Posner, Wolff, Muscatel,
Waldbaum Family
Fil and Janet Rose
Stan and Michele Rosen
Bette Rosenbloom
Greg and Jennifer Rosenwald
James Rosenwald
The Family of Nate Ross
Lawrence Ross
Rubin Family
Beau Sadick

Harold and Esther Sadis
Stephen Sadis
Herman and Faye Sarkowsky
Ruth Sassoon
David Schiller
Irwin and Babette Schiller
Mike and Dawn Schiller
Schneiderman Family
Jason and Betsy Schneier
Eddie Sherman
Stan and Iantha Sidell
Cherie Singer
Mike Silver
SJCC
Mickey and Lyn Soss
Charles and Bunny Staadecker
The Family of
Herb and Fern Meltzer
Craig Sternberg
Doris Stiefel
David and Marcie Stone
Stusser, Rosen Family
Temple B'nai Torah
Tobin, Katz Family
Irwin Treiger
Jack Warnick
Tony and Lynn Wartnik
Michael Wiviott
Sara Yashar

Washington State Jewish Historical Society

YESTERDAY'S MAVENS, TODAY'S FOODIES

For so many Jews, food is a connection to the many countries from which we have emigrated. Food offers a flavor of our past, it joins our families and communities in ritual and triggers childhood memories with the faintest aroma. The WSJHS has collected hundreds of delicious Ashkenazic and Sephardic recipes from our community's kitchens as well as the loving stories behind them. Learn the culinary secrets from some of the best Jewish cooks in Washington.

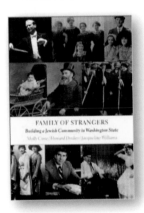

FAMILY OF STRANGERS

2004 Washington State Book Award Finalist

From the Ashkenazim who emigrated from central and eastern Europe to the Sephardim of the Mediterranean Basin to the American Jews who came westward in the postwar era, this is the story of our community's colorful beginnings and the vast number of civic and cultural contributions it has made to the Northwest. Stories of regional politics, congregational histories, burgeoning businesses and early philanthropies are all presented in the vibrant life stories of dozens of notable local individuals as well as through the voices of those who took part in the founding of our community.

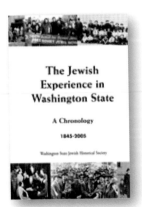

THE JEWISH EXPERIENCE IN WASHINGTON STATE

This 109-page sourcebook outlines the significant events, organizations and personalities that have contributed to Jewish communities throughout the state. Includes over one hundred photographs and copies of archival documents compiled by our archivist.

WSJHS
Washington State Jewish Historical Society

All titles are available through our website: WSJHS.ORG

BASEBALL

SEATTLE WASHINGTON

Proudly sponsored by
STAN AND MICHELE ROSEN

Steve Altaras

May 4, 1951, Seattle

It may have been a half-century ago, but Steve Altaras can still remember the frustration in the faces of his counselors at Camp Burton on Vashon Island when, as a 10-year old, he struck them out during the traditional softball game that matched counselors against the campers. "It was a long time ago, but those are the memories you savor forever."

The young hurler showed off his fastball at various levels of competition on the Eastside while growing up. In the late 1960s, he played first base and pitched for the varsity squad at Bellevue High School. His personal highlight was the afternoon he struck out 15 batters in a league game against Lake Washington.

During the winter months in high school, he worked as a ski instructor on Saturdays at Ski Acres near Snoqualmie Pass. "My parents allowed me to schedule my sports activities around my obligations at the synagogue," he remembered.

Altaras currently lives in Kenmore where he operates Altaras Insurance Services.

Steve Altaras, back row, eighth from the left, and his Bellevue High School team

Morrie "Snooker" Arnovich

November 16, 1910 – July 20, 1959, Superior, WI

Kosher outfielder assigned to Fort Lewis as player-coach

Morrie Arnovich first came up to the big leagues as a line-drive–hitting shortstop with Philadelphia in 1936. Known for his strict kosher diet, newspaper reporters often referred to him as the "Son of Israel" or the "Next Jewish Star." In 1939, the Phillies' right-handed left fielder hit a remarkable .324 — fifth best in the

National League — and was named to the All-Star team. Midway through the 1940 season, he was traded to the Cincinnati Reds where he hit .284 and helped his team defeat Hank Greenberg and the Detroit Tigers in the World Series.

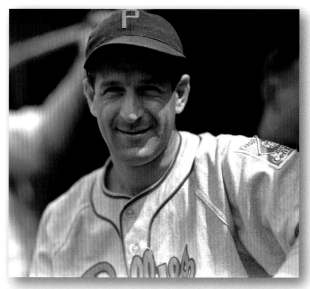
Morrie Arnovich played for the Phillies in the late 1930s

Arnovich was a two-time All-Wisconsin basketball star at the University of Wisconsin-Superior when he first tried to enlist in the US Army, but was turned down because he was missing a set of molars. Fitted with false teeth, he was finally accepted for duty after Pearl Harbor and spent the next four years on active duty.

Private Arnovich was assigned to Fort Lewis, where he quickly became the player-manager of the base's semi-pro team. The stocky outfielder guided the Fort Lewis Warriors to the state semi-pro championship in 1942. That same year he was selected to the All-Service team to play against a squad of American League All-Stars at Cleveland's Municipal Stadium. Arnovich's team of servicemen lost to the Major League players 5-0 in front of a crowd of 62,059 flag-waving fans.

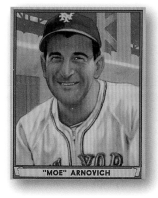
"MOE" ARNOVICH

Known to his teammates as "Snooker," Arnovich remained at Fort Lewis until early 1944, where he managed the baseball team each summer and coached the basketball squad in the Puget Sound League during the winter. The private was eventually promoted to acting staff sergeant for his leadership role on and off the field.

In 1946, at 35 years of age and out of shape after his time in the service, Arnovich attempted a comeback. He played in one game for the New York Giants before being sent down to their farm team in Jersey City. After going 5 for 25 in 10 games, he was released in June of 1946.

Arnovich returned to baseball in 1949 as a minor league manager in the Chicago Cubs organization. That same year he also signed on as a referee in the newly formed National Basketball Association. In 1959, at the young age of 49, the big leaguer died of a coronary occlusion in his home shortly after his third wedding anniversary.

Arnovich, Bill Kirk, Herm Reich in 1939 at Fort Lewis

David D. Azose

February 18, 1950, Seattle

Memories crumble along with demolition of Sick's Stadium

As a youngster, David Azose split his time between baseball and football at Lakewood Park and Rainier Playfield. He remembers scoring five touchdowns in one game, then having to ride home in his muddy uniform. When he got to Franklin High School, he was one of three sophomores called up to play with the varsity baseball team the year they played for the city championship at Sick's Stadium.

In his junior year, the 5'-7" first baseman was named to the All-City team, finishing the season with one of the top batting averages in the district. Azose admits that he did not swing with a lot of power, but managed to drive the ball and get on base any way he could.

Azose would wear his little league baseball uniform to Sephardic religious school at Ezra Bessaroth on Tuesdays and Thursdays after public school. He remembers Rabbi William Greenberg asking him which activity was more

David Azose during his Franklin High School years

important; Azose chose baseball, but his parents still required him to go to religious school — he just left early for his baseball games.

Azose also started as a junior on Franklin's football team as a linebacker and corner back, but almost quit when the new coach decided to go with younger players during his senior year. "It was a humbling experience to learn that I would not always be the star," Azose said. "Coach taught me the important lesson to never quit on myself or on my teammates and always do my best, even if that meant that I'd spend much of the year on the bench."

During the 1960s, children of Jewish families from Seward Park were a significant percentage of the diverse Franklin student body. "There were Filipinos, Italians, African Americans, Japanese and Chinese on the field together. Brennan King was our baseball coach while I was on varsity, and I believe he was the first black coach of a major sport in the Metro League," Azose recalls. (Azose noted that future Washington governor Gary Locke was also part of that Franklin Class of '68.)

Where a big-box hardware store now stands on Rainier Avenue, Azose's memories are bittersweet. Sick's Stadium was the site of the city baseball championships in which he helped turn a double play to shut down the opposing team's key rally. He also remembers mourning for the old wooden structure the day it was torn down in 1979. "It was like my glory days came tumbling down with that stadium," he said.

Azose's commitment to excellence he learned on the baseball diamond helped him build a career in the commercial real estate business. Azose is a co-owner of Morris Piha Real Estate Services, Inc. in Bellevue, a member of the board of the Samis Foundation and the Seattle Sephardic Brotherhood, and a past president of the Sephardic Bi-

David Azose and his son Michael

kur Holim congregation.

These days, the Mercer Island resident spends more time on a bicycle seat than he does at first base. He has completed the annual Seattle to Portland bike ride (STP) for over 20 years. He describes the event as the personal and athletic highlight of the year, because it gives him time on the road with his son, Michael, his son-in-law and his brothers. David and his wife, Terry, also have two married daughters, Sara and Debra, and seven grandchildren.

Mike Block

January 11, 1919, Bellingham – January 10, 1997, Tacoma

Mike Block's love of sports and strong community values led him to help save baseball in Tacoma. When the Chicago Cubs ended their relationship with Tacoma and the Pacific Coast League in 1971, Block was among the 22 investors who formed Baseball Tacoma, Inc. and brought the Minnesota Twins' Triple-A team to Cheney Stadium for six seasons.

Joel Buxbaum

July 1, 1929, Seattle

Painful moments from an exceptional athletic career

The athletic accomplishments of Joel Buxbaum stretched from the fields at Broadway High School to the base gymnasium at Ft. Lewis, but his dreams of a professional career as a ballplayer came to a painful end at home plate on a lonely baseball diamond in Wenatchee.

The Seattle native played baseball and basketball for the high school on Capitol Hill during the mid-1940s, before he took his glove and basketball shoes into the US Army. In between, he played semi-pro baseball during the summers for the Wenatchee Eagles.

"It's a moment and a pain that I'll never forget," Buxbaum remembers. "I was on second after hitting a double, and then tried to score on a hit by my teammate." The aggressive outfielder remembers how he dislocated his right shoulder when he reached out to tag home as he slid past the catcher. "The shoulder has never been the same since," he said with a grimace. "But more importantly...I scored on the play."

Buxbaum was a guard on the high school basketball teams at Broadway and the squads that represented Ft. Lewis, and he roamed the outfield for his high school and his Army base when he played baseball. He was also a standout for his AZA teams from Temple De Hirsch.

JOEL BUXBAUM

The most embarrassing moment for the young soldier took place on the basketball court during the early 1950s when the base team at Ft. Lewis hosted an exhibition game against the All-American Redheads, a traveling squad of women much like the Harlem Globetrotters.

LT. to RT.
NELSON, G. MYERS, D. MYERS, TOBIASON, M'ILLRAITH, TALLEKSON, DORAN, BUXBAUM.

"The gym was packed to see the game," said Buxbaum. "My assignment was to guard this little gal who had a flair for entertaining the audience. At one point I dribbled past her and thought I was on my way to an easy basket, but she reached into my shorts from behind and snapped my jock strap.

"That one really hurt in so many ways," he said.

Al "Whitey" Federoff

July 11, 1924, Bairdford, PA – August 2, 2011, Gilbert, AZ

Solid, speedy second baseman saves Trucks' no-hitter

Al Federoff spent his career in minor league baseball, except for 76 games spread over the 1951 and 1952 seasons, when he was a member of the Detroit Tigers. A second baseman, Federoff hit .238 in 235 major league at-bats, with no home runs and 14 runs batted in. He was a .279 hitter during his minor league career. After his playing days ended, Federoff managed for 10 seasons, ending his career in 1970 in the Pacific Coast League (PCL), where he had played the bulk of his minor league career.

While Federoff became known for mentoring successful Major League manager Jim Leyland, many are unaware that he was a sure-handed second baseman and was one of the fastest players in Major League Baseball. Batting right handed, from home plates to first he was clocked at 3.8 seconds, the sixth fastest time in Major League Baseball according to the 1952 issue of *The Sporting News*.

Federoff had a role in Virgil Trucks' 1952

AL FEDEROFF
Infielder

no-hitter at Yankee Stadium. Hank Bauer, the Yankees' strong leftfielder, stepped up to the plate with two outs in the 9th. Bauer squared up one of Trucks' fastballs right in the direction of Federoff. "I get my name mentioned in the paper every now and then when they recall Trucks' no-hitter against the Yankees. I made the last putout on a hard smash by Hank Bauer for the final out," said Federoff. He jokingly proclaimed, "I saved the no-hitter!" It should be noted that Joe Ginsberg was Trucks' catcher that day.

Federoff finished the season with a .242 average and did what he was expected to do: play good defense at second base. His fielding attracted the attention of another Hall of Famer, Tigers GM Charlie Gehringer. "He came to me personally and told me, 'You did damn good, your fielding was terrific,'" recalled Federoff. While his fielding impressed Gehringer, his overall play did not do enough to sway manager Fred Hutchinson to give him an extension for the 1953 season.

"I was disappointed when they sold me to San Diego in 1953," said Federoff, who thought he could add some youth to an aging ball club. "Johnny Pesky was a good ballplayer, but he was already in his mid 30s, [Billy] Hitchcock was in his mid 30s, and [Jerry] Priddy couldn't run after that broken leg. Hutchinson kept him, and he couldn't even run! I hadn't even hit my prime!"

Federoff began a long stretch in the PCL in '53; he sometimes formed a double-play tandem with another Jewish middle infielder, Moe Franklin. Federoff enjoyed four solid years with the Padres, helping to lead them to the 1954 PCL championship, walking 108 times against only 34 strikeouts. Even though he was no longer in the Major Leagues, Federoff, like many other veterans, enjoyed the comforts of playing on the West Coast. "In the PCL at that time, the playing conditions were better. We had a lot of good older players coming from the big leagues because the conditions were wonderful. A lot of great ballplayers finished their careers there and

they were paid better than the big leagues. We played a week at home and a week at each city. We flew by airplane, and the weather was wonderful, especially in San Diego," Federoff said.

But injuries finally caught up with Federoff. "During my last year in San Diego, I was over the hill. San Diego traded me to Seattle. I played a year-plus there. Then they sent me to Louisville; I played a half-year there. I was sold to Atlanta and that was the end of my career. At the end I was overcoming a broken leg; I lost a lot of my speed."

During Federoff's time with the Seattle Rainiers in 1957-58, he played in 129 games, batted just .229 in 402 at-bats, failed to hit any home runs and had just one stolen base.

Myron Nathan "Joe" Ginsberg

October 11, 1926, New York – November 2, 2012, West Bloomfield, MI

Batting left and throwing right, Myron Nathan "Joe" Ginsberg had a baseball career that spanned 19 years, playing catcher for seven different teams. At 18, he signed with Detroit and played in the Tigers' farm system for two and a half seasons before getting a shot at the big leagues late in 1948. In the early 1950s, he formed one of the few all-Jewish batteries with pitching teammate Saul Rogovin, and also caught for Seattle legend Fred Hutchinson. In 1955, he joined the Seattle Rainiers as the primary catcher, reuniting with

Hutchinson who was now the team manager. At age 28, Ginsberg was attempting a Major League comeback and furthered his cause by hitting .293 and helping the Rainiers to a Pacific Coast League championship. The next season, Ginsberg returned to the Major Leagues with the Kansas City Athletics and continued to play for another six seasons, mostly with the Baltimore Orioles.

1955, Seattle Rainiers

Bob Goldstein

October 8, 1927, Spokane

Spokane native rejects 'giant' offer

Bob Goldstein walked with a strut in his step as he crossed campus in the fall of 1945. Dressed in his royal blue sport coat, he was on his way to basketball practice at the University of Washington. The freshman had earned a spot in the starting lineup, and he was determined to make the most of the opportunity to play under the tutelage of Clarence "Hec" Edmundson. But fate had something else in mind for the confident teenager.

As he opened the door to the gymnasium, a near-empty pail of nails fell from scaffolding and hit Goldstein on the side of his head, opening an 8-inch gash in his scalp. The wound required 13 stitches and forced him to sit out the entire basketball season. The injury essentially cut the freshman from the Husky squad and ended his dream of playing basketball.

The wound was especially painful to Goldstein because he had just walked away from a lucrative contract that would have paid him the outrageous salary of $600 per month to play first base for the New York Giants. To the best of his memory, the agreement to play baseball also included a bonus of $50,000.

"That was as king's ransom in 1945," Goldstein said, settling back in the lounge chair in his son's backyard. "My father [Jack Goldstein] was upset that I did not take the money. But I was an idealistic kid. Playing basketball for Hec Edmundson is something I had always strived to do. Baseball was never in my long-range plans."

At almost 85 years old, Goldstein is just as confident today as he was when he graduated from Spokane's Lewis & Clark High School. The people he meets would never know that he suffered a stroke eight years ago. His thoughts are clear and his muscle tone looks as good as the day he took infield practice with the Seattle Rainiers in 1948.

"Sure, I was All-State in basketball," Goldstein said with a confident smile. "But I was an All-American in baseball."

★ BOB GOLDSTEIN, Seattle, Washington

On the West Coast they call this husky Jewish first-sacker another Hank Greenberg.

Selected by Seattle Post Intelligencer
Royal Brougham, Sports Editor

Goldstein attracted the attention of the Giants' scouts when he played at the Polo Grounds in New York as part of *Esquire's* All-American baseball game in August of 1945. One player from each state was selected based on recommendations from sports writers across the country. Goldstein was nominated by renowned Seattle newspaper reporter Royal Brougham.

The All-Stars were divided into two squads for an exhibition game. Players from the East were coached by the legendary Babe Ruth. Goldstein and the other ball players from the West played under the direction of Hall of Famer Ty Cobb.

The Spokane native remembers in vivid detail when a representative from the Giants stopped him after the game and invited him, his father, and Brougham to his office.

"It was already late August, but the Giants wanted me to play with the big league club through the end of the season," said Goldstein. "Royal Brougham thought I was crazy for turn-ing down the big league contract. My dad agreed. But his words were of the more colorful variety."

The pail apparently knocked some sense into the young ballplayer. After leaving the university following his freshman year in 1946 to join the Army, he returned to professional baseball after his discharge.

Goldstein played for 11 teams between 1948 until 1950. He compiled a career average of .280 with 78 doubles and 16 home runs over three full seasons. The scholar-athlete returned to college on the GI Bill after his playing days at the age of 23 to earn four post-graduate degrees, including a doctorate in history. He utilized his education as the basis for his career as an educator at private secondary schools in the Northwest and around the world.

Looking back, Goldstein has no regrets. He is still confident in the decisions he made during his lifetime. "I was lucky," he reasoned. "The bucket could have been full."

Dave Goodman

November 28, 1910 – July 2, 1998, Laguna Hills, CA

Dave Goodman played eight seasons of professional baseball in the minor leagues, highlighted by a pair of seasons with the Tacoma Tigers of the Western International League (WIL). The 5'-10" left-handed hitting outfielder batted .308 in 97 games with the Tigers in 1937, then improved to .337 in 135 games the next season. His average not only led the Tigers in 1938, but it was good enough to lead the WIL that season as well. Goodman came back to the Northwest to manage the Tacoma entry in the Shipbuilders League in the early 1940s.

Addis Gutmann

July 17, 1930 – September 2, 2006, Seattle

Sports fan and coach taught ball players about game and life

For Addis Gutmann, springtime in Paris would have to wait. He had two passions: he loved to travel with his wife, Leatrice, but he also cherished coaching PONY League Baseball. "Addis coached baseball for 25 years. So that was 25 springs when we did not travel," Leatrice remembers of the 51 years she spent with her husband.

Gutmann was a lifelong sports fan beginning from his earliest childhood days. In a documentary produced on the Seattle Rainiers baseball team, Gutmann reminisced about the players who seemed larger than life, the smell of the grass, and the feel of community at Sick's Stadium. When he had to go to bed before a Rainers game ended, he'd hide under the covers and listen to announcer Leo Lassen call the final innings on his transistor radio.

His parents also had box seats at Sick's Sta-

Addis Gutman (top left) and one of the 25 Pony League baseball teams he coached

dium, as did the parents of his then-girlfriend and eventual wife. "Some people accused me of dating her for those seats," Gutmann once said.

As a student at Seattle's Lakeside School, Gutmann was the chief editorial assistant of the school's newspaper, *Tatler*, and staffed the Numidian, the school's yearbook. For both he covered Lakeside's sports stories and earned a reputation for writing that was "unexcelled." "A caustic commentator on athletics and school life, Addis earned a reputation for his sense of humor," was how the yearbook described him, which remained an apt description his entire life. While at Lakeside, Gutmann could also be found on the sidelines as the manager and statistician for the baseball and football teams.

Growing up in Laurelhurst, so close to the University of Washington, Gutmann was a Husky fan from the earliest days he could remember. His neighbor was UW basketball coach Clarence "Hec" Edmundson, whom he greatly admired. So enamored with Edmundson and his teams that he and his teenage friends would often sneak in through the arena windows to watch games. Later, as a student at the UW, he became the coach's team manager.

After graduating from the UW, he eventually opened a travel agency and volunteered his time to the Rotary, NARAL, the UW and a number of organizations throughout the Jewish community. Addis and Leatrice were members of both Temple De Hirsch Sinai and Congregation Ezra Bessaroth in Seattle. "We tried to cover all the bases," she said.

Next to Judaism, sports were always a second religion to Gutmann — and truth be told, he would probably not argue if you said they were his first. He was a first season Seattle Supersonics ticket holder, with seats in the front row behind the basket. Over the years, he became close friends with the Sonics' first general manager Dick Vertlieb. He had season tickets to UW football and basketball games as well as the Mariners.

His knowledge of sports and memory of games and players often prompted him to write letters to the editor to debate or correct sportswriters. Over the seven decades of his life, Gutmann witnessed a number of Seattle baseball teams, players, and managers come and go, but the sport remained his big love.

With Gutmann's three daughters, Wendy, Lisa and Carolyn, showing little interest in playing sports, he stayed connected to athletics by volunteering to coach 13- and 14-year-old boys in PONY Baseball. Gutmann's record on the field was legendary. Under his direction, Team Totter Richfield captured the Pinto PONY championships in five of eight seasons beginning in 1964.

Leatrice said her husband was always calm while he was in the dugout as an example to his players. And while his goal was to prepare these boys for playing on North End high school baseball teams, he imparted a number of lessons that went beyond the baselines.

"He loved young people," she said. "But after 25 years, I made him retire," Leatrice recalls. Upon retiring, he combined his two passions traveling across the country with friends to visit nearly every Major League ballpark.

On a Saturday afternoon in September of 2006, the lifelong Seattle sports fan passed away in his Laurelhurst home while listening to a broadcast of a UW football game. "He passed away hearing the roar of the Huskies," she said.

It wasn't until he passed away that Leatrice truly realized the impact he had on the kids he coached. When word spread, she began receiving cards and letters from many players who remembered her husband as both an instructor on the field and as a mentor in life.

"Baseball Sol" Israel

June 15, 1922, Portland –- May 30, 2004, Seattle

Sol Israel graduated from Fremont High School in Los Angeles, before serving his country in the military during World War II. Upon his release, the Sephardic left-hander began a professional baseball career that lasted seven seasons.

Between 1946 and 1952, Israel spent time with 10 different minor league teams in six different minor leagues. The best season for the outfielder was in 1946 with the Wisconsin State League. In 107 games, he led the league with 135 hits, 24 doubles and 24 runs batted in while batting .326 with 18 home runs and 27 stolen bases.

Although he would never match those prolific numbers again, Israel continued to be an offensive threat. He played for the Spokane Indians and Tacoma Tigers in 1950 and with the Tigers again for the entire 1951 season. His offensive numbers were strikingly similar those two years, with 469 at-bats each year and averages of .292 and .277, respectively.

Israel batted at least .277 for seven of the 10 teams he played with, with a career-high 17 triples in 1951 while playing for Tacoma. The lefty settled in Seattle at the conclusion of his baseball career. An athlete to the very end, Israel was buried in the Sephardic Brotherhood cemetery, where his gravestone bears an etched baseball and his nickname, "Baseball Sol."

"Baseball Sol" Israel

Herb "Lefty" Karpel

December 27, 1917, Brooklyn – January 24, 1995, San Diego

Lefty had a cup of coffee with the '46 Yankees

Although he is listed along with Babe Ruth and Ty Cobb in the volumes of statistics preserved by Major League Baseball, the entry for the Jewish kid from Brooklyn covers only two games.

After 12 seasons of pitching for numerous teams in the minor leagues, Herb Karpel finally made his debut with the New York Yankees in the spring of 1946 at the age of 28. His big league career lasted exactly two games, giving up four hits and two earned runs, for a career ERA of 10.80.

In the language of baseball, Karpel was a career minor leaguer. He played in the Yankee farm system for a few years, coming up through the organization with many well-known players who went on to illustrious careers.

"When Dad was a rookie, his best buddy was [future Hall of Fame shortstop] Phil Rizzuto," said his daughter, Ronni Mayer. "Mom and Dad socialized with Phil and Cora. Phil and my dad were roommates while they were in the minors together and the families shared an apartment when the team was at spring training in Florida." Rizzuto and Karpel both learned to play baseball on the urban ball fields of Brooklyn. The shortstop made it to the big leagues first, earning his promotion to the Yankees in 1941. Karpel continued in the minors then served in the military during World War II from 1943 to 1945.

Mayer remembers that her father bought their first house in New Jersey after he returned from the war and made the big league club, but the family was forced to move again three months later when the Yankees sold his contract to the Seattle Rainiers.

Known as "lefty," Karpel found great success playing for the Rainiers from 1946 to 1950. In 1949, he led the Pacific Coast League with 14 wins and posted the lowest ERA in the league for three consecutive seasons. During the 1950 season, however, he was abruptly traded to the Hollywood Stars. In 12 minor league seasons, Karpel notched an impressive 124 wins against only 94 defeats with a minor league career ERA of 3.52.

Mayer still remembers the excitement of sitting in the stands behind home plate with the wives and families of the other players while her mother fed her peanuts in the first inning, hot dogs in the second, followed by ice cream and Cracker Jacks to keep her busy.

Mayer also recalled how she would wait anxiously for her father after the game while he signed autographs for fans outside Sick's Stadium. "It was probably past my bedtime and I just wanted to go home," she said. "My mother told me to be patient, because those fans paid my father's salary."

The Karpel family returned to Seattle when Herb retired as a player. He was active in the Jewish community as a coach for the Jewish baseball and basketball teams that played in church leagues throughout the city. He also coached a talented third baseman from Seattle, whom Karpel encouraged to pursue baseball as a career. That player was Ron Santo, who played 14 years with the Chicago Cubs and was inducted into the Hall of Fame in 2010.

Wherever they lived, the family was always affiliated with Conservative congregations, according to Mayer. The ex-ballplayer even served as the president of his congregation in Southern California.

"Lefty" Karpel pitching for the Seattle Rainiers

According to Mayer, her parents were married in an Orthodox wedding and maintained a kosher home until one eventful day. As her mother explained, Herb went to the butcher to buy something for dinner, but was surprised to learn they had sold out of kosher chickens. Not wanting to lose a sale, the butcher went into the back room and used a baseball bat to kill another bird, said a few prayers, then came back to the counter and charged Karpel twice as much as an ordinary fryer. Karpel reportedly stormed back into his house, threw the chicken into the sink and proclaimed, "We're not kosher anymore."

David "The Kid" Kosher

1925, Everett – July 1, 1996, Seattle

Toughness and smarts carried "the kid" to the Major Leagues

Despite a physical disability that kept him from playing his favorite sport, David Kosher developed an eye for talent that allowed him to become a respected talent scout for Major League Baseball.

The son of Russian immigrants, Kosher grew up in Everett and became involved in baseball during junior high school, in spite of an injury at birth that left him in a wheelchair with cerebral palsy. He battled his way out of his wheelchair after high school and became a fixture around Sick's Stadium, watching the Seattle Rainiers of the Pacific Coast League.

One day in 1951, Rainiers manager and Hall of Famer Rogers Hornsby noticed Kosher and called him over. "He told him to run around the field," said Mary Brown, Kosher's sister. "David said he couldn't, but the manager said, 'You can.' So David did. He came back and he was panting. The manager said, 'You have two minutes before you do it again.' And he did. And then the manager had the team trainer work on him," she said.

In a season when Hornsby and the Suds captured the PCL pennant, "The Raja" called Kosher his "good luck charm." When Hornsby accepted the job as manager of the struggling St. Louis Browns of the American League in 1952, he invited Kosher to accompany him. Newspaper articles at the time described Kosher as Hornsby's "personal bench confidant."

With an endorsement from Hornsby and other front office officials, the Everett native became a scout for young talent for the Los Angeles Angels, the Chicago White Sox and the Chicago Cubs. He was credited with signing future Hall of Fame third baseman Ron Santo out of Seattle's Franklin High School for the Cubs. "He was a good judge of talent. He had a good eye," said Edo Vanni, former outfielder and general manager

David Kosher with Seattle Rainiers manager Rogers Hornsby in 1951

of the Rainiers. "The handicap didn't bother him. Dave loved baseball. That was his life."

Brown said her brother "conquered some insurmountable odds" during his lifetime and remembered that Hornsby always referred to her brother as "the kid." "The players liked to be around him because Dave took personal pride in his players. He was a credit to any organiza-tion he worked for," said Vanni. Although his sister can't recall the circumstances, Kosher was awarded a World Series ring and a pass that allowed him free box seats at any profes-sional baseball game anywhere in the country. *(Details and quotes drawn from 7/2/96 Seattle Times story)*

Robert Kraft

1954, Seattle

Robert Kraft was drafted by the Atlanta Braves in the third round of the 1973 Major League Baseball winter draft out of Bellevue Commu-nity College. He played one season of minor league baseball as an outfielder for the Class A 1976 Seattle Rainiers. Rob hit .313 in 233 at-bats, with one home run and 25 stolen bases. In 1986 he played on the Temple De Hirsch team in the JCC's coed softball league. Kraft is

Robert Kraft played for the Seattle Rainiers in 1976

currently a personal injury lawyer with Kraft Palmer Davies, P.L.L.C. in Seattle.

Arnold (Barry) Latman

May 21, 1936, Los Angeles

Baseball career put on hold for Bar Mitzvah

When Barry Latman was 10 years old, his parents made him take a "sabbatical" from baseball for three years so he could study for his Bar Mitzvah. He started playing again at 13, and, as he put it, "never stopped until I retired from the Major Leagues."

In 1954, at the age of 18, Latman hurled a perfect game for Fairfax High School, the first one in a decade in the Los Angeles school sys-tem. Also on that Fairfax team was Larry Sher-ry, a fellow Jewish pitcher who would also make it to the Majors.

During that season, Latman began a five-year correspondence with the legendary Ty Cobb, who had seen him pitch on TV. After some time, the two met and Cobb watched Latman throw, telling him he had the stuff to pitch in the Major Leagues and sent him a series of encouraging letters.

As a senior that year, Latman was named the Los Angeles All-City Player by the Helms Athletic Foundation. His impressive pitching landed him a spot in the All-Star high school game in New York. Despite impressing Major League scouts and being offered bonuses by several clubs, Latman declined, accepting instead a baseball scholarship from the University of Southern California.

Latman was signed by the Chicago White Sox in 1955, making his debut in September of 1957. Two years later, he joined the Detroit Tigers in the World Series against the Los Angeles Dodgers. Coincidentally, pitching for the Dodgers was Larry Sherry, his former teammate from Fairfax High. The two would later become teammates on the 1967 Houston Astros team along with two other Jewish players, Bo Belinsky and Norm Miller.

Latman was an All-Star in both 1961 and 1962. In 1961 he had the fourth highest winning percentage (.722) in the American League, going 13-5 for the Cleveland Indians. Along with having his most successful season in 1961, Latman married Lynne Schwab in October of that year. She was the daughter of Leon Schwab, the owner of the famous Schwab drugstore chain in California. The newlyweds spent their honeymoon in Israel.

BARRY LATMAN   pitcher

In December 1963, the Indians traded Latman to the Los Angeles Angels for slugging outfielder Leon Wagner. When Latman heard the news, he told his father-in-law, "It's impossible; is that all they got for Wagner?"

In 1964, his first season with Los Angeles, Latman had his third straight losing season, going 6-10 with a 3.85 earned run average. He suffered a sore arm in 1965 and pitched in only 18 games for the Angels, all in relief, though his ERA was a fine 2.84. That June, the Angels sent him to Seattle to pitch in the Pacific Coast League, where he compiled a 7-6 record with a 3.09 ERA and 97 strikeouts in 99 innings. Latman pitched in the big leagues for 11 years. Appearing in 344 games including 134 starts, he went 59-68 with a career ERA of 3.91.

Jacob "Jack" Levy

1848, Sydney, Australia – April 29, 1913, Victoria, BC

The earliest known Jewish sports hero of Washington

1879, Seattle Alkis, Jack Levy in suit

Jack Levy has the distinction of being the earliest noted Jewish athlete in Washington that the Washington State Jewish Historical Society has discovered. Levy was an important early organizer and promoter of sports in Seattle. In addition to being president of Seattle's first organized Base Ball Club to play challenge matches, Levy would organize and promote the Seattle Rifle Team in international matches. The team Levy organized for a series of matches with the baseballers of Victoria developed over the following decade into an active semi-professional team. That team, the Seattle Reds, was the nucleus of baseball activity in Puget Sound prior to the advent of professional ball in 1890. Levy's efforts to promote dozens of games throughout the Northwest played a significant role in establishing organized baseball in Seattle.

Benjamin and Esther Levy were among the first Jews to emigrate from London to New Zealand in 1841. By 1848, they had settled in Sydney, New South Wales, Australia, and had given birth to their son, Jacob. In his 20s, Jacob, now known as Jack, and his brother Henry Emanuel were living in the Northwest and had established Levy Brothers' Seattle Soda Works, manufacturing ginger beer, sarsaparilla, and other beverages. Jack Levy also ran the Grotto Cigar Stand on Mill Street and was the correspondent for *The British Colonist* newspaper in Victoria.

In 1872, the game of "base ball" is mentioned for the first time in a Seattle periodical. The establishment of the Dolly Varden Base Ball Club was announced in the July 11 edition of the Puget Sound Dispatch. Four years later, the newspaper described a challenge issued by a baseball team from Newcastle, seeking to play any other team in the county. Levy is listed on the roster of the Seattle Base Ball Club, which accepted the challenge and beat the Newcastle Miners 51-0.

On May 18, 1877, *The British Colonist* published Victoria's challenge to the Seattle Base Ball Club to play a game for Queen Victoria's birthday. The Seattle nine accepted and beat the Victoria Club by a score of 15-7. Joshua P.

Davis umpired the game, and like Jack's brother's Aunt Elizabeth, he was a well-known leader of Victoria's Jewish community. Davis was also a founding director of the Olympic Base Ball Club of Victoria when it formed in 1866.

On June 1, 1877, the Seattle Base Ball Club voted to change its name to the Alki Base Ball Club and elected Jack Levy as its president. The members also voted to invite the Victoria Club to a game in Seattle on July 4th, which would also include a rifle match. Seattle beat Victoria by a score of 21-9, but Victoria redeemed itself with a victory in the rifle match. With Levy managing the ball club, the Alkis turned in their best season that year, going undefeated in front of crowds that reached several hundreds. Their home games were played in Georgetown, on the field of the Seattle Jockey Club's racecourse.

By 1879, Levy and nearly all his other Alki teammates had left the game. The team ultimately reorganized as the Seattle Reds, Seattle's first professional club in 1890. In 1897, Levy headed north to the Yukon. He prospected in Dawson for the next 12 years, with both the Seattle and Victoria papers reporting occasionally on his successes.

Robert (Bob) Melvin

October 28, 1961, Palo Alto, CA

Daunting start is just the beginning for two-time manager of the year

Bob Melvin began his short-lived managerial career with the Seattle Mariners with huge cleats to fill. His predecessor, Lou Pinella, had captained the team from 1993 to 2002, and in his first season had guided the Mariners to their second winning season in the 17-year history of the franchise. In 1995, the Mariners staged one of the greatest late-season finishes in Major League Baseball history, making the playoffs for the first time ever. In 2001, Pinella's Mariners tied the 1906 Chicago Cubs with the most wins (116) by any team in MLB history. In the final three years under Pinella, the team won an average of 100 games each season.

Despite collecting 93 wins in Melvin's first season with the Mariners in 2003, the team finished second in the American League West Division and did not make the playoffs. The following season, the team lost 99 games and

Melvin's contract was not extended.

The California native bounced back as the 2005 manager of the Arizona Diamondbacks. In his third season there, he led the Diamondbacks to 90 wins and the National League West title. Nicknamed "The Mad Scientist" for the chemistry he found in the myriad lineups he employed, Melvin was named the National League and MLB manager of the year in 2007 and remained in Arizona for the next two seasons.

In 2011, he took over as the Oakland Athletics' interim manager, and by September he was given a three-year contract. In his first full season, the Athletics won 94 games, 20 more than the previous year, and clinched the Western Division of the American League. It was the A's first playoff appearance in five years. The turn-around Melvin brought to Oakland earned him the 2012 American League Manager of the Year Award.

During his 10-year playing career, from 1985 to '94, the backup catcher donned seven different MLB uniforms. He finished his career with a .233 batting average and 35 home runs.

While his managing debut with the Mariners was a daunting situation to step into, Bob Melvin's perseverance has been rewarded with victories and honors. With only 30 managerial positions in Major League Baseball, to be selected for that role is an accomplishment in and of itself. But to be honored not once, but twice, as the best among your peers is a legacy Melvin will leave behind along with some pretty big cleats to fill.

Lee Mezistrano

February 17, 1982, Bellevue, WA

Lee Mezistrano was an athletic force at Newport High School in Bellevue. For three years he lettered in basketball and did the same for two years in football and baseball. While playing on the diamond for the Knights, Mezistrano helped lead his team to a district championship in his junior year. As a senoir, he captured the King County batting title.

At Bellevue Community Col-

Lee Mezistrano hit 17 RBI during an 11-game stretch

lege, he batted .317 with 28 RBI and 22 runs scored in 104 at-bats as a freshman. He helped Bellevue to a 34-14 overall record, and a 26-4 conference mark in the North Division of the Northwest Athletic Association of Community Colleges (NWAACC). He was named first team All-NWAACC North Division and second team All-NWAACC, and was also was named to the NWAACC's all-tournament team.

During the summer, he played for the semi-pro Seattle Cruisers in 2001, batting .370 and

Mezistrano played for NC State

Mezistrano played for the Kalamazoo Kings in 2005-06

junior season hitting .407 after 10 games, and .352 after 20 contests. During one 11 game stretch, he drove in 17 runs. While playing against Virginia that March, Mezistrano hit his first homerun - a grandslam that put the nail in the coffin of a 12-1 rout. Two weeks later, he had a career-high four hits in six at-bats against Florida State.

After graduating in 2005, the southpaw joined the Kalamazoo Kings in the Frontier League. After two seasons of hitting under .250, the Bellevue native decided to put his baseball career on hold to earn a law degree from Seattle Univeristy. Mezistrano currently lives in Seattle and works for Starbuck as a content manager.

earning a berth on the Pacific International League All-Star team.

He went on to enroll at North Carolina State, where he became the Wolfpack's regular right fielder. In 2004, Mezistrano began his

Lipman "Iron Batter" Pike

May 25, 1845, New York City – October 10, 1893, Brooklyn

First professional baseball player and first home run king is also first Jew in baseball

Special consideration is being given to Lipman Emanuel Pike for inclusion in this book. Though he may have never stepped foot in the Pacific Northwest, technically speaking, his 22-year baseball career all occurred before

Washington had even achieved statehood. Pike is credited as not only the first Jewish baseball

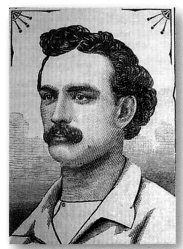

player, but when he accepted $20 a week to play third base for the Philadelphia Athletics in 1866, he became baseball's first professional player.

Immigrating from the Netherlands, the Pike

family settled in New York, where "Lip" was born in 1845. He began playing baseball a week after his Bar Mitzvah, ultimately becoming one of the premier players of his day.

On the list of firsts, Pike's name can also be added as baseball's first home run champion. Nicknamed the "Iron Batter," from 1871 to 1877, he led the league in home runs four times. In one game in July 1866, he sent six dingers over the wall, the final score totaling 67-25. His slugging prowess was so well known that stories were recounted for years after he stopped playing.

Since all players of the day were amateurs, many followed Pike's lead and accepted money under the table. The practice grew so common that a hearing was scheduled by the sport's governing body, the National Association of Base Ball Players'. When no one showed up, the matter was dropped. Pike's hearing, or lack thereof, seemed to pave the way for professionalizing baseball. By 1869, the Cincinnati Red Stock-ings became the first openly professional team, with players earning as much as seven times the pay of the average working man.

Primarily an outfielder, Pike played every position, hitting and throwing left-handed. His career spanned the years 1865 to 1887 as a play-er, player-manager, and manager of numerous teams in six different leagues.

In 1871, the National Association was formed as the first professional baseball league, and Pike joined the Troy Haymakers for its inaugural sea-son. He quickly became the star of the team, bat-ting .377 (sixth best in the league) and hitting a league-leading four home runs. He also led the league in extra base hits (21), and was second in slugging percentage (.654) and doubles (10), fourth in RBIs (39), fifth in triples (7), sixth in on-base percentage (.400), ninth in hits (49), and tenth in runs (43).

Pike's athletic career was not confined to baseball. Known for his remarkable speed, he ran competitively, often for cash prizes in chal-

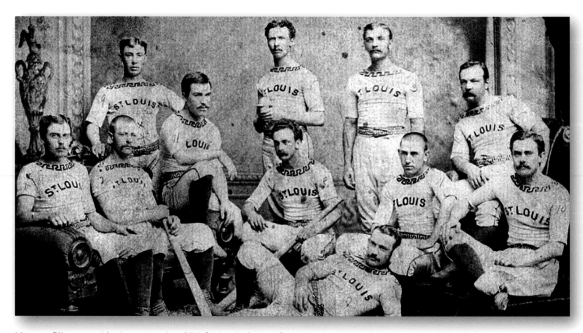

Lipman Pike seated in the center in 1875 St. Louis Brown Stockings team photo

lenge races. He once raced and beat a famous trotting horse in a 100-yard sprint, winning by four yards in 10 seconds flat, earning a $250 prize ($4,850 today).

Pike never seemed content to stay on one team too long. Over his career, he played for the Philadelphia Athletics, the New York Mutuals, the Lord Baltimores, the Hartford Nutmegs, the Brooklyn Atlantics, the Baltimore Canaries, the Hartford Dark Blues, the St. Louis Brown Stockings, the Cincinnati Red Stockings, the Providence Grays and the Worcester Ruby Legs. In the waning years of his career, his numbers began to fall. Between 1878 and 1881, Pike's batting average dropped from .311 to .111. Arousing suspicions that he was fixing games, he was "blacklisted" and banned from the National League. He joined his father in the haberdashery business while continuing to play another six years of amateur baseball. In 1883, the ban was lifted and he was reinstated by the league.

In 1887, the New York Metropolitans, of the American Association, gave Pike one last shot. At 42, he was the oldest player in baseball. And though he only played in one game, it was a chance for fans to give him the send-off he deserved. Many years later, *Sporting Life* magazine chose Lipman Pike as one of the top three outfielders of the 1870–80 decade.

In 1893 Pike died suddenly of heart disease at the age of 48. The Brooklyn Eagle reported, "Many wealthy Hebrews and men high in political and old time baseball circles attended the funeral service."

Jimmie Reese

1901, New York – 1994, Los Angeles

Yiddish-speaking Yankee spent lifetime in baseball

James "Hymie" Herman Solomon was born to Russian Jewish immigrants in New York City, but grew up in Los Angeles. Jimmie had a lifelong career in baseball beginning at age 16 as a batboy for the Pacific Coast League's Los Angeles Angels. He later returned to the Angels as a player and spent time with the PCL's Oakland Oaks and San Diego Padres. From 1930 to 1932 he played in the Majors with the New York Yankees and St. Louis Cardinals. He was known as one of the best fielding second basemen and finished his

career with a respectable .278 batting average.

Playing alongside Tony Lazzeri, Bill Dickey and Lou Gehrig in 1930 and '31, Jimmie also roomed with baseball legend Babe Ruth. But as Jimmie recounted, he really roomed more with Ruth's suitcase, since the Babe was often out late into the night.

Jimmie's Jewish background served him well in a player/celebrity ballgame in the 1920s. On the mound pitching against his team was the great songwriter Harry Ruby. His catcher was Ike Danning, who had a two-game "cup of coffee" with the St. Louis Browns in 1928. Since Ruby and Danning were both Jewish, they decided to communicate their pitch selection in Yiddish. Jimmie took it all in and went 4 for 4 that day.

Seattle Angels coach Jimmie Reese

Ruby congratulated him after the game, telling him that he hit as if he knew what pitch was coming. That was when Jimmie Reese told Ruby his real last name.

Jimmie moved on to coaching with stints in Portland, Hawaii, and San Diego, where he also managed. From 1965 to 1968, Jimmie was invited by manager Bob Lemon to help coach the Seattle Angeles, which won the PCL Championship in 1966.

Jimmie was famous for his fungo hitting.

Longer and thinner than a normal bat, with one flat side, Jimmie made his own fungo bat and used it to hit balls to fielders in practice. Jimmie's fungo hitting was so uncannily accurate, Hall of Fame pitcher Nolan Ryan said, "He could knock a grasshopper off a leaf." On occasion, Jimmie would stand on the mound and use his fungo to "pitch" to batters. While in Seattle, he was challenged to hit a flagpole 150 feet away and nailed it on his first try. He even played rounds of golf using only his fungo bat and a putter.

Jimmie was well loved throughout baseball and had an especially close friendship with Nolan Ryan. The bond was such that Ryan honored Jimmie by naming his son Reese.

In 1972, at age 71, Jimmie asked the Angels for a job, and was hired as a conditioning coach. He continued to be listed as an Angels coach until his death 22 years later on July 13, 1994. To honor his memory and his service, the club retired his uniform #50. Jimmie Reese is believed to be the oldest person ever to regularly wear a uniform in an official capacity in the history of organized professional baseball in North America. To cap a nearly lifelong career in baseball, Jimmie was inducted into the PCL Hall of Fame in 2003.

Jaden Sadis

May 1, 2003, Seattle

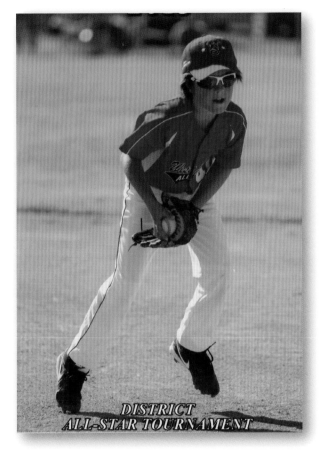

At the young age of ten, Jaden Sadis has demonstrated a love, talent and head for baseball that goes well beyond his years. During the 2013 season, he played for the White Sox in the West Seattle Little League and was the dominant pitcher in the minors division. Of the 223 batters he faced, he struck out 122.

At the plate, the young slugger had 33 hits and 14 walks in 65 at bats for a blistering .647 batting average and .723 on base percentage. The White Sox finished the season 10-5, placing second in the end of season tournament.

Selected to play for the West Seattle All-Star team, Jaden had nine hits in 11 at bats. His .818 batting average helped the team take the District 7 Championship and advance to the state tournament. Jaden's favorite player is Seattle Mariners pitcher Felix Hernandez and hopes to follow in his footsteps all the way to the big leagues one day.

Charles Schwartz

February 25, 1877, Romania – July 4, 1936, Seattle

From his baseball card: "1902 marks the fourth year at professional base ball for Chas. Schwartz, captain and second base. He was in London, Ont., in the Canadian league in 1899, and San Francisco, Cal., had him in the two succeeding years, winning the pennant both times.

This year he came to Seattle, playing star ball up to his last week in August, when an injury to the knee put him out of the game. Batting average .275, fielding average, .941."

From 1900 to 1908, Schwartz played for 11 teams in seven different leagues, including the

Seattle Clamdiggers in 1902 and the Seattle Siwashes in 1903. Schwartz's last pro skipper, upon introducing him to the local press, said, "The kid is a middling batsman and so-so fielder, but boy howdy, can he fill a suitcase." Schwartz was born in Romania and resided in Seattle for 36 years.

1902 Seattle Base Ball Club, Schwartz, 2nd row, far left

Lawrence Sherry

July 25, 1935, Los Angeles, CA

BROTHER BATTERY
Norm Sherry • Larry Sherry

Dodger had challenging first steps to 1959 World Series MVP

Larry Sherry and his older brother, Norm, formed the first and only Jewish brother battery in Major League history. But life did not begin easily for Sherry. Born with a clubfoot, doctors had to break his legs and reset them. He had severe trouble walking until he was about 12 years old. After a series of operations, and outfitted with special shoes, Sherry went on to overcome this disability.

Larry Sherry is best known as the MVP of the 1959 World Series as a reliever for the Los Angeles Dodgers. Sherry was the winning pitcher in two of the World Series games against the Chicago White Sox and had saves in the other two, posting an unbelievable 0.71 ERA. As one Talmudic saying goes, "Some win eternity after years of toil, others in a moment." This was Sherry's moment and it gave the Dodgers their first championship since relocating from Brooklyn two years earlier.

Sherry retired with a record of 53-44, 606 strikeouts, 82 saves and a 3.67 ERA in 416 games and 799-1/3 innings.

In 1958, Sherry was up with the Dodgers, but was wild and ineffective. Sent down to Spo-

LARRY SHERRY, Pitcher   SEATTLE **ANGELS**

kane, he won six and lost 14. Over the winter of 1958, he worked with his brother Norm to develop a slider. Playing in the Cuban League, he used his new pitch and performed well enough to return to the big leagues. In 1959, he was with St. Paul using his fastball and slider to good advantage. On Independence Day of 1959, the Dodgers called up Sherry.

Sherry last appeared in the Major Leagues for three games in 1968. Most of that season was spent in the minors where he was a pitcher and the pitching coach for the Seattle Angels. He had a 6-6 win-loss record and a very commendable 2.86 ERA in 88 innings. Always a good hitter, Sherry even sported a .381 batting average for Seattle.

Norm Sherry

July 16, 1931, New York City

Backup catcher molds ace out of Koufax

After a five-year career as a catcher for the Los Angeles Dodgers and the New York Mets, Norm Sherry began his second career in coaching, which eventually led him to manage the Class-A short-season Everett Giants of the

Northwest League in 1992 and 1993.

But Norm Sherry's biggest contribution to baseball transcended his career as a player and even as an official coach. He is best known as the man who, while still an active player and the second-string catcher for the Dodgers, helped transform Sandy Koufax from a wild "thrower" into one of the most dominant hurlers of all time — and ultimately a member of the Baseball Hall of Fame.

Sherry was born July 16, 1931 in New York City. His family soon moved to Los Angeles, where he attended Fairfax High School. Norm was signed by the Brooklyn Dodgers as a free agent in 1950, just as his younger brother, Larry, would be three years later. Their other brother, George, also signed with the Pittsburgh Pirates. Norm Sherry went off to serve two years in the military during the Korean War, returning to baseball in 1954. He spent many years working his way through the Dodgers' farm system. By the time he reached the Dodgers in 1959 for a two-game "cup of coffee," he was 28 years old and the team was based in Los Angeles.

Norm Sherry, 1992 Everett Giants Manager

Sherry made the team as second-string backstop behind John Roseboro from 1960 through 1962. Early in that tenure, he took aside the young Koufax — who was struggling to become a consistent winner in the Majors despite possessing a blazing fastball and one of the best curveballs of all time — and convinced him to take something off his fastball to get better control. The results were astounding. Koufax dominated the National League from 1962 through his 1966 swan song, winning three Cy Young Awards and leading the Dodgers to three NL championships and two World Series titles in 1963 and 1965.

In 1965, Sherry began his managerial career in the Dodger organization, and switched to the California Angels system in 1969. He coached for the Angels in 1970 and 1971, and returned to the minor leagues to manage their AA and AAA affiliates from 1972 to 1975. The following year, he rejoined the California coaching staff under manager Dick Williams. When Williams was fired, Sherry managed the club in the second half of 1976 and the first half of 1977, and had a 76-71 record. He later served as a Major League pitching coach with the Montreal Expos, San Diego Padres, and San Francisco Giants.

Jeffrey Solam

January 11, 1962, Seattle

Pitcher's no-hitter was a tribute to his father

A jubilant Jeffrey Solam sprinted off the mound into the waiting arms of his proud parents after pitching a complete game no hit shutout. It was the first high school no-hitter that year in the state of Washington.

The game itself was a one-sided affair, with the highly touted Islanders of Mercer Island blanking their KingCo league rivals, the Wolverines from Bellevue, by a score of 10-0 on April 13, 1979 at the Hidden Valley Baseball Field in Bellevue.

For Morris Solam, his son's historic accomplishment was the culmination of hundreds of hours of hard work and determination. But there was more to the game for Jeff than just the final score.

"My father was diagnosed with terminal lung cancer about three months prior and this was at the forefront of my mind during each inning," Solam remembers. "Especially the final three outs. I wanted him to know how much I appreciated all he had done for me."

Anticipation of the no-hitter began to build midway through the game as the Mercer Island players and their fans watched as the high school pitcher continued to add zeros to the scoreboard. Morris rushed to the bench after each half-inning to check on his son.

Everybody was aware of what Solam was accomplishing on the field, and were respectful of the baseball tradition of never uttering the term no-hitter when talking with the pitcher.

Solam relied on his pinpoint accuracy to keep Bellevue runners off balance through the first few innings. While opposing players were having a difficult time getting their bats on the ball, Solam's Mercer Island teammates had little to do other than watch in awe as their ace mowed down batters one after the other.

As the game progressed and Solam began to tire, Bellevue players started to put the ball in play. But by that time, the Islanders were so invested in the game that they were ready for anything. The Islander defense made stop after stop, from diving plays by infielders to shoestring catches by outfielders.

The tension mounted as each inning passed. Solam finished the last inning by retiring the final three batters in a row, and the game was history. The Mercer Island team ran onto the field and surrounded Solam jumping, cheering and celebrating.

The winning pitcher walked off the field and into the arms of his father and mother. "My father was beaming with pride. He was so happy and yet so sick at the same time." It was one of the last games Morris Solam would see his son play. He passed away eight months later.

"The no-hitter game was special, but mostly what I remember were the exchanges I had with my dad," Solam said. "The looks, the glances, and the strategy he gave me between innings is something I will never forget. He loved me so much."

Jeff Solam pitched a no-hitter for MIHS in 1979

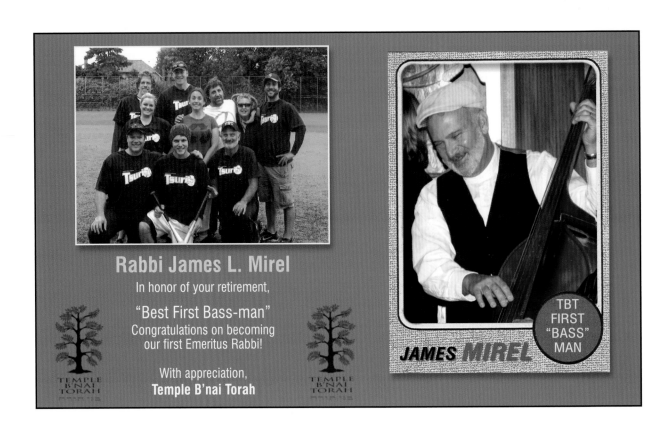

Rabbi James L. Mirel

In honor of your retirement,

"Best First Bass-man"
Congratulations on becoming
our first Emeritus Rabbi!

With appreciation,
Temple B'nai Torah

JAMES *MIREL*

TBT
FIRST
"BASS"
MAN

We love baseball!

**Bob and Bobbi
Bridge
and family**

Go Mariners!!!

Greetings from a sports-loving family.

The Treigers

Back row, center: **Beau's grandfather, Bill Sadick**
Front row, far left: **Beau's father, Arnold Sadick**
Front row, far right: **Beau's uncle, Lawrence Sadick**
Front row, center: **Beau's aunt, Sylvia Sadick, circa 1940s**

Cousins Leslie (Sadis) Huppin, Albert Israel,
Stephen Sadis and David Israel
playing baseball in the backyard

What a fabulous community
treasure this book is.

Congratulations to
Stephen Sadis
for this wonderful
work of art.

Albert Israel
President,
Washington State
Jewish Historical Society

Addis Gutmann

For his 50th birthday, Addis threw out the
ceremonial first pitch at a Mariners game in the
Kingdome on July 17, 1980

With love,
from his daughters, **Wendy, Lisa, Carolyn** and
grandchildren, **Adina, Chantal, Hannah** and **Leila**

Addis Gutmann

**Champion baseball coach
from his #1 fan,
Leatrice Gutmann**

Karli Schiller

You show us all The Love of the Game.

Love,
Mom, Dad and Uncle David

Marcus Schiller

Your passion and desire are amazing to witness.

Love,
Mom, Dad and Uncle David

The Schiller Family

Congratulations to all the athletes.

**Dawn, Karli, Marcus
and Michael Schiller**

Congratulations!

Very happy to "play it forward."

Babette and Irwin Schiller and Family

Sophia Sadis

A great fan of all sports and the loudest supporter from the bleachers!

With much love,
Stephen Sadis

Jaden Sadis

A sports fan and an athlete who always amazes me on the diamond, court and field.

With much love,
Stephen Sadis

David Eskenazi

David Eskenazi was honored by the Seattle Mariners with the ceremonial first pitch on May 2, 2009 in recognition for his many years collecting and preserving Northwest baseball history and for his contributions to the many historic displays and details utilized at Safeco Field.

Dan Aznoff

Dan with legendary LA Dodgers pitcher Fernando Valenzuela

Thanks Dan for all your incredible efforts writing stories for Distant Replay!

The Washington State Jewish Historical Society

Lester (Larry) Kleinberg

1947 Seattle Times photo of Larry Kleinberg at bat as player in grade school interfaith baseball team

Rob Kraft

1976 Seattle Rainiers - Rob Kraft, front row, third from left

Rob Kraft is part of another great team

Kraft Palmer Davis PLLC
Lawyers for the injured

BASKETBALL

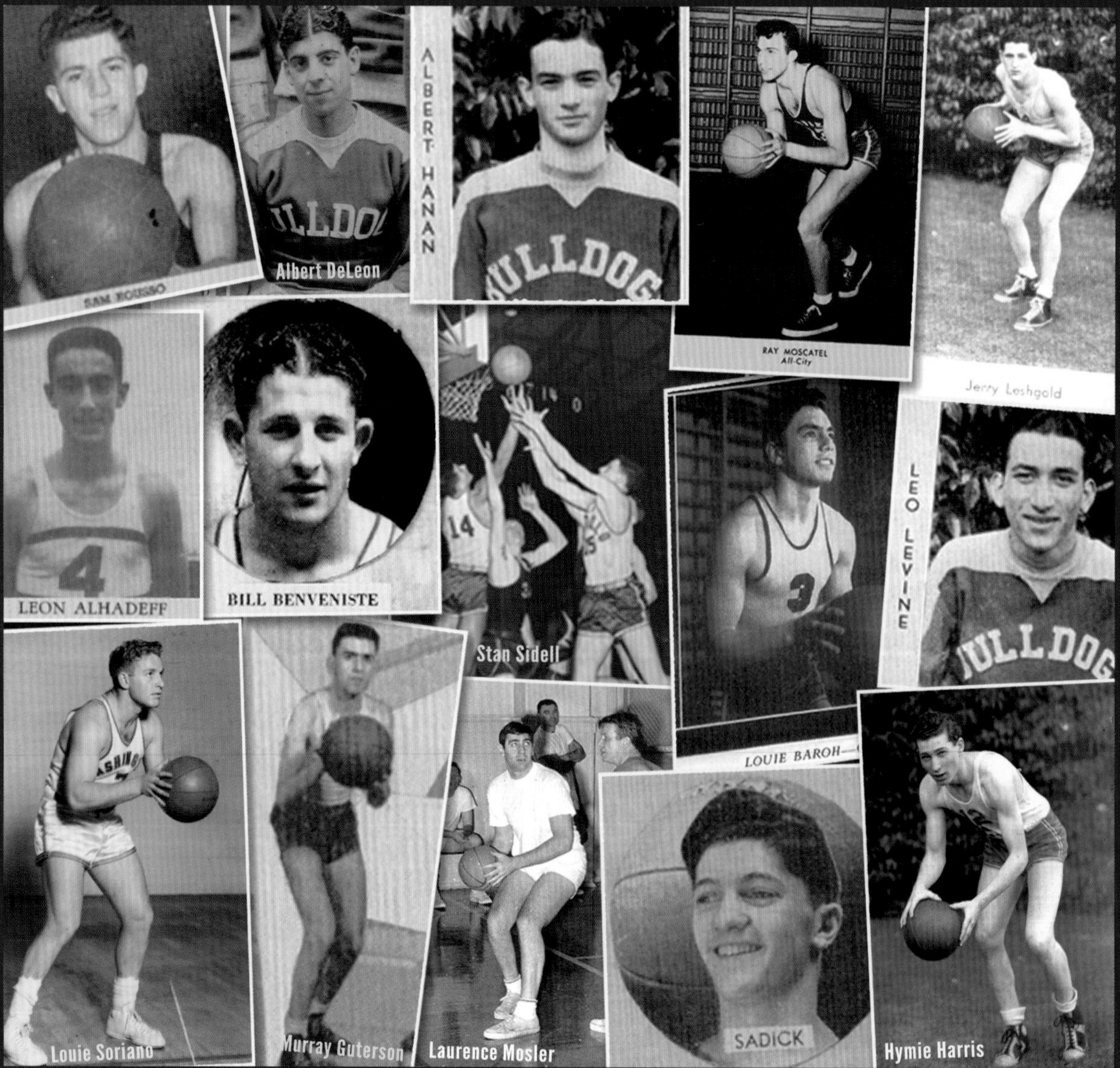

SAM ROUGGO

Albert DeLeon

ALBERT HANAN

BULLDOG

RAY MOSCATEL
All-City

Jerry Leshgold

LEON ALHADEFF

BILL BENVENISTE

Stan Sidell

LEO LEVINE

BULLDOG

LOUIE BAROH

Louie Soriano

Murray Guterson

Laurence Mosler

SADICK

Hymie Harris

50

Suzanne Brigit 'Sue' Bird

October 16, 1980, Long Island, NY

Bird leads Seattle to WNBA title twice and the US to gold thrice

Growing up in Oyster Bay, Long Island, Sue Bird had all the comforts of suburban New York. But the youngest daughter of a Jewish father of Russian descent had a competitive drive and a calling that made her feel at home on basketball courts around the world.

The dark-haired, ponytailed point guard excelled on the court from an early age and was quickly a magnet for attention. She recalls that when she was just 11, while playing during the halftime of a St. John's University basketball game, a security guard was so impressed with her skills he asked the pre-teen for her autograph.

Sue Bird drives to the hoop (Scott Engelhardt)

Bird's decision to transfer from her hometown high school to a prestigious basketball program at a Catholic school was the first step in one of the most successful women's basketball careers in history. In Bird's second season playing at Christ The King Regional High School in Queens, the Royals took the New York State championship and the high school national title. She was selected as the player of the year by the city, the state, and the *New York Daily News*.

Sidelined with a torn ACL her freshman year at the University of Connecticut, Bird returned the next season and led the Huskies to a 36-1 record, the Big East championship and the 2000 NCAA national title. When Bird was a junior, UConn went 32-3. That season Bird hit a last-second shot in what is regarded as "the best women's basketball game ever played." The Huskies' defeat of Notre Dame was immortalized in the book *Bird at the Buzzer*. In her senior year, UConn went undefeated 39-0 and again won the NCAA title, with Bird capturing the Wade Trophy and Naismith College Player of the Year Award. In the 118 college games in which Bird played, the Huskies won 114.

In 2002, she arrived in Seattle as the overall No. 1 pick in WNBA draft and quickly led the Storm to its first playoff appearance. Over the next eight years Bird brought Seattle two national championships, beating the Connecticut Sun in 2004 and the Atlanta Dream in 2010. She has twice led the league in assists and became just the third player in WNBA history to reach 3,000 career points and 1,000 assists. In 2011, fans across the country voted her as one of the top 15 players in the 15-year history of the WNBA.

In the WNBA's off-season, Bird's Jewish roots allowed her to claim Israeli citizenship to qualify for the Russian team in the European professional league, which limits the number of Americans on a roster.

Selected to play on the women's Olympic basketball team, Bird continued to feel at home on the court in Athens in 2004, Beijing in 2008 and London in 2012, bringing back gold to the United States each time.

Not many players, male or female, in any sport have a resume that's quite like this:

- 1998 high school state and national championship
- State player of the year
- 2000 and 2002 NCAA national championship
- College player of the year
- 2004, 2010 WNBA national championship
- 2004, 2008, 2012 Olympic gold medal
- Seven-time WNBA All-Star

Hopefully, Sue Bird will never need to update her WNBA resume. When asked to weigh the options of playing out her current contract and becoming a free agent, Bird said Seattle "is the place where I started my career. Hopefully it's the place where I'll end it."

Jed Davis

March 3, 1952, Cleveland, OH

Four-time coach of the year brought philosophy and wins to NYHS

As an outstanding basketball and tennis player at Cleveland's Beachwood High School, Jed Davis knew athletic talent when he saw it. It was a skill that lay dormant until he witnessed a girls' high school basketball team play in Seattle. In his mid-40s, he left behind the business he founded and pursued a brand new career in coaching, a move that has benefited hundreds of Jewish girls and boys in the Seattle area.

From the time he held a fishing rod at age 2 1/2, Davis was an avid fisherman. Over time, he developed an understanding  of what made artificial lures attractive to fish. With a partner, he founded Pen Tac Corp. to manufacture and sell high quality spinners and spoons. The company became very successful, and in 1996 the partners sold the business, leaving Davis ready for a new challenge.

In December 1998, while watching an intramural basketball game at Northwest Yeshiva High School (NYHS), he was struck by the abundance and strength of talent on the girls' team. He thought they should be playing inter-scholastic high school basketball. Prior to that, his only experience was coaching his son's Little League team and the JCC basketball team.

He submitted a 14-page proposal to NYHS, offering to serve as the school's athletic director and coach. He offered to work as a volunteer the first year, but if he succeeded and the school wanted him to continue, he would receive a salary. The proposal was accepted and he has never looked back.

Davis began a long and determined journey to create a culture of excellence in which the players were expected to make a full commitment to playing on the team, attending every practice and continuing to improve their skills in their own time. In exchange, he would teach strategies he remembered from his high school days and show players how to develop as a unified team.

Initially, some parents did not embrace the commitment Coach Davis required of his students, thinking the emphasis on athletics would detract from their studies. But Davis stuck to his game plan, and over time parents saw that excelling in academics and athletics could go hand in hand. "The cumulative GPA of the girls' basketball team is always higher than the combined GPA of the entire school," said Davis. The SHA and NYHS community also learned,

Coach Jed Davis with SHA Girls Basketball 2012

as Davis explained, "that athletics have a way of breaking down social barriers among students as they come together on a team."

In 2000, the NYHS women's basketball team was invited to Miami to play in the Hillel Invitational Girls' Basketball Tournament, featuring the top girls' basketball teams from Jewish high schools across the country. In only their first season under Coach Davis, the team known as the 613s climbed all the way to the finals, but finished second. A year later, they returned to the tournament and won the 2001 championship against schools that were two to six times larger than NYHS.

Although the victorious 613s drew wide acclaim, Davis wasn't satisfied. As a member of the WIAA, Davis single-handedly, organized and led the fight to change the by-laws, such that, in the post-season, the WIAA would accommodate schools celebrating a Saturday Sabbath. Approved in August 2002, now nothing stood between NYHS and the state championship.

In order to be successful at the high school level, Davis established a feeder program at the Seattle Hebrew Academy (SHA). When SHA needed a physical education instructor in 2001, Davis was hired and was later also given the job as the school's athletic director. Working two full time jobs as AD and coach at SHA and NYHS, he also started the Stars of David program for boys and girls, grades 3-5.

Under Davis' guidance and intense focus on fundamentals, his teams had established a winning tradition for good by 2006. As a testament to his success, he was named the SeaTac 1B Coach of the Year in 2009, 2010, 2011 and 2012. In 2010, he was nominated for athletic director of the year in Washington State.

The 2010 NYHS girls' basketball team was the first Jewish girls' team in North America (in any sport) to qualify for a state tournament berth. Their first appearance, however, was marred by controversy. The second day of the tournament took place on the Fast of Esther. Though game time was set for 12:15pm, the girls could not eat or drink until 6:30pm. The WIAA would not alter the schedule, claiming that the 2002 Sabbath Accommodation amendment did not include fast days. National and local television coverage of the event showed NYHS walking on the court to forfeit game two and then congratulating their would-be opponent, St. John-Endicott.

In 2012, the 613s once again made it to the state tournament and had no intervening issues. Despite being eliminated after their second game, the team, their parents and the entire school celebrated the astonishing achievement. "It was a great affirmation for all the years of sacrifice, hard work and dedication that these girls put in. I am the coach but really, I am the student who learned so much from them," reflected Davis. Davis vows that his team will return to the state tournament again and again. "My best teams are yet to come - and perhaps a state championship will be part of the package."

Albert DeLeon

July 28, 1908, Seattle - April 15, 1971, Seattle

Son of a cantor sang the praises of sports

He wasn't blessed with the ability to chant like his father Haim, Congregation Ezra Bessaroth's first cantor, but his ability to play defense earned him a spot on a championship basketball team.

Born in 1908, Albert DeLeon attended Garfield High School from 1923-26. In his senior year, he was captain of his soccer team and was part of the Bulldogs sec-

Albert DeLeon, front row far right, and the Garfield High School 1926 city championship second team

DeLeon during his UW years

ond team basketball squad that captured the city championship in 1926.

After graduating from the University of Washington with a Pharmacy Doctorate, he moved to Bremerton in 1941. It wasn't long before he traded his skills for mixing pills for mixing drinks, opening two taverns near the Bremerton ferry dock.

While living on the Kitsap Pennisula, he became a co-owner of the Bremerton Blue Jackets, a semi-pro baseball team in the Western International League. "The team was an interesting mix of Major Leaguers trying to extend their careers and up-and-comers looking for a chance to get noticed," said Bremerton resident and baseball fan Louie Soriano.

The Blue Jackets played at Roosevelt Field and according to Soriano, "They packed the stadium every night." Soriano also recalled that if a Blue Jacket player hit it over a particular merchant's sign on the outfield wall, the slug-

ger would get $100 and everyone in the stands would get a hot dog and a bag of popcorn. Between innings, DeLeon seemed to take part in some version of "Donkeyball," playing for the local Jaycees.

During the late 1940's, DeLeon, would travel from Bremerton every week to coach the Junior Sephardic League softball team. Sam Angel, who played second base, remembered DeLeon as "calm, cool and collected." "He knew the game well and was an effective strategist," recalled Angel. "He was a natural leader and liked by everyone on the team."

DeLeon playing "Donkeyball" in 1944

Warren Fein

April 13, 1959, Seattle

Lakeside players got lessons in small-town prejudice

As a backup shooting guard at The Lakeside School, Warren Fein remembered how shocked he was by the ugly comments from spectators aimed at minority members of his team. Many of the Single-A schools, with enrollments comparable to Lakeside at the time, were located in rural communities as far away as Darrington and Langley. As the only Jew on the Lakeside squad, Fein said he took racial comments directed at his black teammates personally.

"None of the abuse was ever directed at me," said Fein, "but I heard the comments being made about the four or five black players on our team." Fein thinks that Lakeside may have been the only team in the league with minority players. "There was taunting and blatantly bad calls by the referees at those small town schools. It was a new experience for me. This was the mid-'70s. I mistakenly believed that Washington residents had grown past racial slurs by then." The Seattle native did admit that part of the hostility directed toward Lakeside could also have been attributed to their undefeated record over two consecutive years.

While playing football at Lakeside, Fein was surprised that his coach did not understand why he elected to skip a game that conflicted with Yom Kippur. "Apparently he had never heard of Sandy Koufax," Fein said. Fein said his parents accommodated his dedication to sports

Warren Fein scores for Lakeside

by temporarily suspending Shabbat dinners during football and basketball season.

During the 1976 basketball season, Fein had difficulty focusing on the game knowing that his every move was being judged by referee Todd Warnick, who was dating his sister. But Fein had the last laugh; he married the ref's sister.

That season continues to provide a long-running debate at Fein-Warnick family gatherings. "Todd claims that he charged me with a technical foul," Fein said. "I will not deny that I received some calls in high school for my reactions. But I don't think Todd ever blew the whistle on me."

A favorite memory from his time at Lakeside was when they defeated a powerful squad from Roosevelt. The public high school had an enrollment four times larger than Lakeside. "Roosevelt was literally in a different league," recalls Fein. "They had better players overall. They even had better Jewish players, like my friend Josh Schorr."

Fein graduated from medical school at the University of Washington in 1985 and is now the executive medical director of the Primary

Care Group at the Swedish Physicians Ballard Clinic. He and his wife, the former Lisa Warnick, have two sons, Sam and Jacob. Sam followed in his father's athletic footsteps, playing basketball at Lakeside for three years.

Warren's son, Sam, played for Lakeside as well

Marv Gilberg

February 3, 1921, Boise, ID – June 8, 2002, Ross, CA

Sixth man helps 1941 Cougars to NCAA finals

Throughout the 1941 season, Marv Gilberg was consistently tapped by coach Jack Friel as the first man off the bench. In game after game, the 6'-2" sophomore breathed new life into a Washington State College basketball team that had been written off before the season began.

After losing its two big men to graduation, coaches and sportswriters predicted that the team would finish at the bottom of the Pacific Coast North Conference, which included Washington, Oregon, Oregon State and Idaho. But the Cougars bolted from the gate, surprising everyone by winning their first six games.

By the halfway mark, they brought a 16-3 record to the University of Washington Pavilion for two consecutive games against their cross-state rivals. The Cougars took both games and with the final two of the series in Pullman the next weekend, the idea of a sweep against their rivals was in reach. In front of a crowd of 5,300 at Bohler Gym in Pullman, the Cougars took

Marv Gilberg, back row, third from left.

the first game 50-38 and broke out the brooms in the second game for a decisive 69-47 victory and the series sweep.

Playing forward, Gilberg tied three starters with a game-high 10 points. It was the first time the Cougars had swept their intrastate rivals since 1917, which was also the last year the Cougars played for the NCAA championship title.

Gilberg and the Cougars took the Pacific Coast North Conference and went on to defeat Stanford, winner of the Pacific Coast South Conference, in a

NATIONAL RUNNER-UP

For the first time in the history of Washington State College, a basketball team soared to stellar heights to win national recognition as Pacific Coast champions, Western champions, and National runner-up.

three-game playoff for an automatic berth to the NCAA tournament. In the West Regional bracket, Washington State swept past Creighton and Arkansas for the right to play for the title against the University of Wisconsin. The Badgers, however, inched past the Cougars in the final quarter, taking the national championship 39-34. While Gilberg drained his only shot, his teammate Kirk Gebert had 21 of Washington State's 34.

Ari Grashin

October 10, 1985 – September 23, 2002, Seattle

From promising athlete to symbol of courage

At a time when Ari Grashin was just realizing his potential as a basketball player, he developed brain cancer. He was 16. Grashin faced cancer like he was driving the lane, with strength and a focus that were part of his character. His family, friends, teammates, and especially his coach were always there to help the promising athlete shake his opponent. His fight to survive engendered an outpouring of support from the sports community and beyond, and inspired others with similar medical challenges to find their own strength.

It was clear to his parents, David and Debbie, that from the time he was 2 years old Ari was in love with sports. He would grab the TV remote and surf the channels until he found a game. Growing up he bowled, played baseball, soccer, and his favorite, basketball.

At Northwest Yeshiva High School (NYHS) on Mercer Island, he became a standout on the basketball team. *Seattle Times* sports columnist Steve Kelley got to know Ari and wrote of him on several occasions. "He was the best shooter" on his team, remarked Kelley. "He was a zone buster. He knows the game, knows how to find his shot and had that quick, Dell Curry, finger-in-the-cookie-jar release. He was pure as bottled water."

During a preseason practice in 2001, Ari noticed something was off with his jumper. He became tired more quickly, and by the opening game of the season, he pulled himself out after playing for two minutes.

In December, an MRI confirmed a brain tumor and surgery was scheduled. One of Grashin's friends, Abby, sent an email to Howard Schultz, owner of the Seattle SuperSonics, telling him the situation and asking if a Sonics players could visit him in the hospital. Abby was very persistent.

SuperSonic Desmond Mason and Ari Grashin

On the day before his surgery, Schultz and star forward Desmond Mason visited Ari at his parents' home and showered him with Sonics paraphernalia. Schultz asked Grashin for his opinion of the Sonics, and he responded with his usual frank honesty. The visit made Ari's heart soar and left a grin on his face the entire day.

Kelley was also familiar with Ari's honesty. "He was sharply opinionated," he reported. "When he didn't like something I wrote, he didn't hesitate to tell me. I liked that about him. He was honest. He told you what he was thinking. His friends came to expect that from him."

The surgery went well, but the doctors found that the cancer was malignant, requiring future treatments. Grashin's parents, his three brothers and his many friends created Team Ari, a network of people who wanted to help him get through his ordeal.

While Ari was recuperating at Children's Hospital, Desmond Mason and a few other Sonics, including Gary Payton, came to the hospital to visit him. Grashin was overwhelmed.

About a month later, a Jewish organization called Chai Lifeline, which assists families of children who are very ill, arranged for a trip to the Super Bowl in New Orleans. Ari asked Steve Bunin, his good friend and former NYHS basketball coach, to accompany him.

Bunin, who was a sportscaster on ESPN and now works for Comcast SportsNet Houston, credits his young player and friend with giving him courage when he applied for the national broadcast position. Through Ari, Bunin also met his wife Viviane, a physician who was part of Grashin's large support group.

Following a Mariners game, Kelley escorted Ari in his wheelchair to the clubhouse to introduce him to manager Lou Piniella. Piniella took the time to answer questions, then interrupted pitcher Joel Pineiro's postgame interview to have him to sign a baseball for Ari.

Grashin was also introduced to Mariners

pitcher Rob Ramsay, who had been diagnosed a year and a half earlier with brain cancer and was in remission until the cancer returned. The two would talk baseball over the phone for a while and then Ramsay would finally ask him how he was doing. Ari seemed to open up to the pitcher and would talk about his fatigue and frustration. Ramsay reassured him that he had felt that way as well. His words gave Ari some momentary peace in the weeks before his passing on September 23, 2002.

A close friend of Grashin's, Jason Okrent, wrote to *The Seattle Times* to express his gratitude to the sports community for their support. "The Thursday before Ari passed away, Mason came to the Grashin house a second time. He came and held Ari's feeble hand for almost three hours. Although Ari was oftentimes unresponsive, Mason chatted with Ari's friends and family. He brought warmth and comfort to a house that needed a lot of both. His presence that day is one of the classiest things I have ever been witness to. He made a complete stranger's problems his own, and that takes a lot of courage. Both Mason and Schultz attended Ari's funeral. They offered their shoulders to cry on and shared in our grief. If only the NBA had more men like these two distinguished people. Desmond Mason is a true difference maker and an asset to not only the Sonics but the entire community."

Before a Sonics game, Mason wrote "In

Ari Grashin with former coach Steve Bunin at the Super Bowl

memory of Ari Grashin" on the side of his basketball shoes. "I wanted to do something special," Mason said. "And most of all I know Ari will be happy knowing [he's by my side]."

Grashin's story is one that reminds us of the deeper relevance of sports in our lives. For Ari, it taught him the value of a caring coach, loyal teammates and supportive fans. It gave him moments to feel the glory of winning and to face defeat. Basketball allowed a young boy shooting hoops in the gym to daydream about playing in the NBA. And during the remaining months of his life, when those sports heroes he grew up cheering for stood by his bedside, it gave Grashin the gift of being so very close to that dream.

The story of Ari's courage left an indelible mark on the community. For years after his passing, his friends hosted the Ari Grashin Basketball Tournament at the SJCC to raise funds for children with illnesses. The Seattle Hebrew Academy named their sports facility the Ari Grashin Memorial Gymnasium and retired his jersey #42. And in 2005, King County's Paul Robeson Scholar-Athlete Program created the Ari Grashin Memorial Award to honor scholar-athletes who demonstrate exceptional leadership and determination. Despite all that still remained for Ari to accomplish, with the short life he was given, he left a legacy that will long be remembered.

Israel Halfon

August 24, 1914 – December 3, 2001, Seattle

Sephardic multi-sport star found sweet spot

Israel "Izzy" Halfon grew up among the large Sephardic community in the Central District of Seattle. Though his grandfather was the first rabbi of Sephardic Bikur Holim Congregation, Izzy was hooked on sports.

While attending Garfield High School from 1929 to '33, he was a starter for both the varsity basketball and football teams along with Homer Harris. On the court, Halfon played guard while Harris was the team's center. On the gridiron, Halfon was a running back while Harris was an end. The two became

"Huff" played halfback for the Bulldogs

good friends, which wasn't unusual, except that Harris was black. Bigotry was prevalent in the 1930s, and many white players were not very eager to play with or against black players. Despite the slights and jeers, their friendship through sports endured long after high school. Halfon's children remember Harris visiting their father and explaining to them how much he appreciated him, because he loved playing with him.

During the 1931-32 school year, Halfon — who also earned the nickname "Smiling Huffard," shortened to "Huff" — helped the Bulldogs bring home the city championship. The following season, Huff served as captain but graduated before the season was finished. That year he had the fourth highest scoring average among all players in Seattle's high schools.

For those two seasons, six to seven of the eight players were Jewish and included: Halfon, Gerald Mandell, Al Franco, Edmund Shupack, Ezra Rose, Vic Calderon and Sam Ziegman.

Israel Halfon played guard and forward for Garfield HS

Champions! After five long, lean years of working and striving, the Garfield basketeers are once more the proud possessors of this impressive title.

"Hearty are the men.
Who wear the purple and the white."

Gerald Mandell
Forward. Considered the cleverest player on the squad. His smooth floor-work and clever passing were outstanding.

Al Franco
Forward. Although small and inexperienced, his exceptional speed and shooting ability marked him as first team timber.

Edmund Shupack
Forward. A sophomore. His uncanny ability to hit the basket will make him a real threat in future years.

Israel Halfon
Guard and Forward. A former "super" who blossomed into a first team star. His scoring spree in the Ballard game was a sensation.

Vic Calderon
Guard and Forward. Tall, fast, and aggressive. He excelled in every department of the game. His close checking baffled opposing forwards.

Ezra Rose
Guard. Speedy, colorful, and a good shot. Another sophomore who succeeded in breaking into the "big-time."

Al Flett
Guard. The smallest player in the league, and one of the best. He leaves a vacancy hard to fill.

Captain Pete Gray
Center. A leader of champions; ace of the city's hoopsters. He holds the record for points scored in one game.

Huff attended the College of Puget Sound in Tacoma, but looked elsewhere to participate in sports. For football, the best venue was the Puget Sound Football Conference, which was stocked with some of Seattle's best former high school football players and a few former UW players. For basketball, Huff found the community league and played on a team sponsored by the Order of DeMolay. Some of Huff's Garfield teammates also played on that team, which captured the championship in 1932. During the summer season, Huff was a star baseball player on the Seattle Jewish Athletic Club team that competed in the Commercial Playground Baseball League.

From his playing days at Garfield, Halfon became the closest of friends with Ezra Rose, who was later killed while fighting in World War II. Halfon kept a photo of his teammate Ezra in his wallet until the day he himself passed away.

In 1946, Halfon founded the Halfon Candy Company. He began his business with his two brothers, selling confectionaries and bags of locally made popcorn to movie theaters. Halfon Candy has continued to expand over its 67 years, and is now run by Halfon's youngest daughter and son-in-law, Marie and Alan Scharhon.

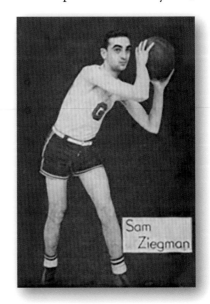

Sam Ziegman was a landsman and teammate of Halfon's in 1933

Ben Harris

August 22, 1916 – December 31, 2012, Seattle

Harris had a lifetime love of sports

When interviewed for this profile, Ben Harris was almost 96 years old, but he could still remember every second of the 1934 basketball playoff game in which he and his Garfield teammates faced West Seattle.

Down by one point (29-28) with only a few seconds left to play, Garfield guard Mordo Barlia intercepted a pass and immediately called for a time-out. Guard Leo "Lapo" Levine threw the inbound pass to Harris, who was standing on the opposing team's foul line. Harris turned, dribbled the ball once and launched a set shot that traveled three-quarters of the length of the court and swished through the net. "I could have tried that shot 1,000 times and probably would not have made the shot again," said Harris. The victory was especially meaningful to Harris because the West Seattle team had taunted the Garfield starting five before the game with chants of "Let's beat those Jew boys."

Enlarged images of his 1934 basketball team from the Garfield Arrow were displayed proudly in Harris' apartment at The Summit senior living facility in Seattle. His adult children had heard the stories dozens of times, but still leaned for-

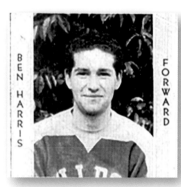

ward to hear the tales retold at family gatherings.

"Sports have always been important to me," said Harris. "Sports and music." At 6'-2" in high school, Harris towered over his teammates and excelled at both basketball and tennis. He taught himself to play tennis by spending hours hitting balls against the wall at a park near his home. Another Jewish athlete, Henry

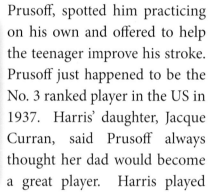

Prusoff, spotted him practicing on his own and offered to help the teenager improve his stroke. Prusoff just happened to be the No. 3 ranked player in the US in 1937. Harris' daughter, Jacque Curran, said Prusoff always thought her dad would become a great player. Harris played doubles, but preferred the singles game because "there was nobody there to blame for my mistakes except me."

Tennis also provided Harris with an important lesson in life when he was invited to play singles with Ward Beecher, the heir to the famous Seattle cheese makers, at the Seattle Tennis Club. Beecher had his personal driver pick up Harris and escort him to the private club. The two teenagers first matched up when the Lakeside team played against Garfield. After being beaten soundly on the court, Beecher invited Harris to have lunch with him in the private dining room at the club. "It was not until we were halfway through our meal that I realized that Jews were normally not permitted to even play at the Seattle Tennis Club, let alone eat in their dining room," said Harris. "I just smiled."

In 1934, Harris was paired with fellow Jewish athlete Harry Kessler in a doubles match against Broadway High School. The pair won their match and with the victory captured the high school city championship.

Baseball was another favorite sport of Harris', and at age 15 he was the batboy for the Seattle Indians. Harris vividly remembered his walk home from the ballpark on Independence Day, 1932. He watched as fire trucks raced past him only to learn later that they were heading to Dugdale Park to fight the flames that consumed the Indians' wooden stadium.

Harris joined a AAA team after high school, leading the club to a No. 1 ranking in the state and an invitation to the national championships in New Orleans. Harris did not realize he was the only Jew on the team until they stopped for a roadside meal in Spokane.

Harris took one look at his plate, and then looked up to ask the waiter to help him identify the piece of meat. When he was told it was pork, Harris began to barter for something else

to eat. "I had never seen a piece of pork before," Harris remembered. "Several of my teammates offered to trade me their potato. So I had potato for dinner that night. Lots of potato." According to Harris, the team from Washington eventually made it down to Louisiana and reached the semi-finals before being eliminated.

Ben Harris in 2009

The blue-eyed athlete did not retire from sports for several more decades. In the interim, he established Harris Furniture, a successful retail furniture store in Bellevue. Harris was well known at the Glendale Country Club for carrying his own clubs around the 18-hole course, refusing to use a golf cart until the age of 90. His son, Bill Harris, added that his father came extremely close to shooting his own age on the course until a stroke forced him to hang up his golf bag.

GARFIELD WINS PREP NET TITLE OVER BROADWAY

PREP TENNIS
(Final Standings)

	W.	L.	Pct.	Points For	Agst
Garfield	7	0	1.000	49	11
Broadway	6	1	.856	45	15
Franklin	5	2	.714	39	19
Queen Anne	4	3	.571	29	34
Lincoln	3	4	.428	32	25
Roosevelt	2	5	.286	16	46
Ballard	1	6	.143	21	42
West Seattle	0	7	.000	13	51

At last! Garfield wins the 1934 high school tennis championship.

After four postponements, that critical second doubles between the Broadway and Garfield sextets was finally completed yesterday at the Tennis Club with the Bulldog pair of Ben Harris and Harry Kessler coming from behind to take the final set of a closely contested three-set duel, 6-3, 4-6, 6-4. This match gave the Garfield outfit the deciding point in the team match which stood at 4-all when rain intervened on May 10.

From the Seattle Times, May 24, 1934

Mark Maimon

May 8, 1978, Seattle

Point guard gave mother last-second gift

Basketball was Mark Maimon's first love growing up. Maimon developed his skills while playing at the Seattle Hebrew Academy (SHA), where he was the team's leading scorer his 9th-grade year. He later played on the basketball team that represented Seattle in the 1977 Maccabi games in Detroit and on Mercer Island High School's junior and varsity teams.

Maimon immersed himself (and his family) in the game and was part of an SHA team in 8th grade that went undefeated and is still referred to as the school's "dream team." Under the direction of legendary coach Ed Pepple, Maimon played

Maimon takes it to the hoop for MIHS

point guard on the Islanders' varsity squad, where he was the team captain and wore the No. 3 jersey of prior MI point guard standouts. The team that year was unranked statewide — and at one point lost an unprecedented three games in a row — but they quickly reestablished themselves, making the playoffs in true Mercer Island style.

In the qualifying game for the 3A state championships, MI played Redmond High at the UW's Hec Edmundson Pavilion. At the close of the game, Mercer Island was up by 3 points, but Redmond tied the score with a 30-foot jumper. With 6.6 seconds left, Pepple called time-out and pulled Maimon from the game in favor of a faster guard. Maimon protested, and Pepple, feeling Maimon had earned the chance to bring the ball down court, reconsidered.

Maimon inbounded the ball to a teammate who passed it back to him. Running in, out, and between a stifling defense he reached the foul line. With the clock ticking to zero, Maimon put up a shot that bounced on the front of the rim. The crowd gasped as it hit the backboard, then rolled around for what seemed like an eternity, until it finally dropped through the hoop. The roaring MI crowd leapt from their seats as the team pig piled on Maimon. In the stands, Maimon's mother Esther, who was celebrating her birthday, got the most exciting present ever. The shot sent the unranked Islanders to the 3A state championships, where they advanced as far as the semifinals. At the end of the season, Maimon was honored with the team's Most Improved and Most Inspirational Player awards.

Jack Meyers

May 10, 1920, Seattle

Three-sport letterman served his country and his community

Seattle native Jack Meyers was a big man on campus at Garfield High School in the late 1930s. It was more than the fact he stood 6-foot-4 and wore size 14 shoes. Meyers was the center on the high school basketball team, ran track for the Bulldogs and helped lead Garfield to an undefeated City football championship in 1939.

"Sports and school took up every day," Meyers remembered. "If I was not at practice or playing in a game, I was probably studying. It was important to keep up your grades so that you'd be eligible to play on game day."

The school newspaper reported that Meyers was not a flashy player on the basketball court, but provided his team with solid defense in the middle and controlled the rebounds on both ends of the court. The former center said games during that era were usually low scoring affairs, so defense was as important as scoring when he played in the post position.

On the gridiron, Meyers played tight end on offense and defensive end on defense in an age when most players played both ways. He remembered protecting the quarterback on the play when Garfield scored its only touchdown of the game against their rival Roosevelt in a 7-0 victory for the City Championship. The winning pass was caught by Coach Leo Brigham's son.

Brigham was also Meyers' coach for basketball and track. The tall teenager competed in the high jump and ran one leg of the high hurdles relay team that took first place at the City Championships his senior year.

After graduating from Garfield, the three-sport star went to work on the production line at Boeing for a year. To subsidize his $25 weekly salary, he played on Boeing's semi-pro football

Jack Meyers, back row, fourth from left, on the 1939 Garfield baskebtball team with Mike Ovadia, front row, far right

and basketball team on Sundays.

Meyers still regrets ignoring his mother's wishes in 1941 when chose to play football one Sunday instead of attending Yom Kippur services. He cracked his knee cap that day and ended up in the hospital. The injured teen was still in the hospital in December when the Japanese attacked Pearl Harbor.

The start of the war would later mean that he would have to decline the Whitman College football scholarship, to serve as an airplane mechanic in the Army Air Corps.

Meyers was stationed in New Mexico as part of the top secret Manhattan Project that developed the atomic bomb. The enlisted man still remembers being knocked out of his bed from the blast of the first bomb tested near the desert outpost.

Returning to his roots after the war, Meyers used the GI Bill to attend the University of Washington and played intramural sports for his ZBT fraternity

Meyers was a track star as well

and with his AZA chapter. He remained active in recreational leagues through the Jewish Community Center in Seattle and coached the Biddy Youth Basketball program there for 10 years.

His son Marv, and Jack's wife Betty still laugh when Meyers retells the story of his transcontinental flight to Europe during the war. When his B-29 stopped to refuel in Kansas, an officer boarded the transport and ordered Meyers off the plane. Somehow, an Army Air Corps general had discovered that Meyers was aboard the military flight. The general wanted Meyers to suit up for a basketball game being staged against a team from another camp. The game was apparently scheduled as a grudge match between the two generals.

"When you think about the waste of equipment and manpower diverted for that one game," said Meyers. "It's a wonder we won the war at all!"

Meyers served as a mechanic in the Army Air Corps

Albert Moscatel

March 7, 1964, Seattle

Heartbreaker separates family from long-sought state title

Loud crowds and high-pressure situations on the basketball court never made Al Moscatel nervous. But his hands were sweating when he knelt down on one knee to propose to Rebecca while they were in Haifa for the World Maccabiah Games. Besides being anxious about her answer, Moscatel needed to remember the Hebrew phrase to propose he had just learned from the concierge at his hotel. Rebecca had her answer ready the moment she saw the beads of sweat on his forehead.

Born to former Garfield basketball star and furniture retailer Neiso Moscatel, it's hard to say which has had the most influence on Al's life, nature or nurture. By the early 80s, Moscatel was a 6'-2" guard and was named to the All-State high school basketball team twice. Playing for the powerful Mercer Island High School team, he helped the squad reach the state's 3A championi-

Al Moscatel, front row, fourth from left, was two-time All-State

onship games twice. The 1981 title game ended with one of the most controversial calls in the state's playoff history. Officially, Mercer Island came out on the short end of a 66-65 final score. But many Islander fans believe to this day that the winning shot by Shadle Park came after the final buzzer. Mercer Island returned to the championships but lost by six points to Roosevelt in Moscatel's senior year.

Three decades later, the fiery shooting guard can only laugh at the irony of playing in back-to-back title games. "You can add up the Moscatel legacy," he said with a smile. "Between my father, my brother Sam, and my uncle Ray, we played for the Washington State championship five times and we lost every time."

Despite a stellar prep career, Moscatel did not draw a lot of interest from Division I universities. He joined the basketball squad at Mesa College in San Diego, where he was honored as male athlete of the year. The next year he transferred to the University of San Diego and helped the Toreros qualify for the NCAA tournament in 1984.

Determined to prove college recruiters wrong, Moscatel returned home to join the

University of Washington team as a walk-on. As a junior, he was named the Pac-10's sixth man of the year, helping the Huskies to a berth in the NCAA tournament. Given a scholarship for his senior year, Moscatel continued his personal post-season run when Washington was invited to play at Madison Square Garden in the National Invitational Tournament.

Moscatel emphasized that the college spotlight did not compare to the memories he brought home along with one gold and two silver medals from Israel, when he played for the US team at the World Maccabiah Games. The awards still remind him of the lifelong friendships he created with players on the US squad and with Jews around the world.

Moscatel chases down a loose ball for the Huskies in 1986

"We were as close as people can be," said Moscatel. "We were much more than teammates. We were all Jews who played an active role in our own history." The chants of "USA! USA!" that echoed in the gym 30 years ago continue to make him smile today.

Basketball at its highest level, said Moscatel, has given him the strength to flourish in two of the most competitive arenas of business: restaurants and retail furniture. "Basketball taught me how much a business and a family can thrive when you stick together during the hard times," he explained. "My mother, Arlene, taught us to never give up. My father taught me how to listen, how to really listen. Because if you listen long enough, you'll eventually find the solution that provides a win-win for everybody."

Neiso Moscatel

August 21, 1936, Seattle

Business before basketball happened for a reason

Like his older brother Ray, Neiso Moscatel was selected to the All-City team during his high school playing days at Garfield High School. And like Ray, Neiso played a vital role when the Bulldogs went to the state basketball championship. Neiso also envisioned himself wearing a Seattle University jersey just like his brother.

Neiso Moscatel shoots a jumper for Garfield HS

In 1953, the Seward Park, Seattle native joined the varsity basketball squad at Garfield High School. The Bulldogs fell to fourth place early on in the season, but turned it around to go 8-5 and nearly take the city crown.

During Moscatel's senior year, the squad finished with three more wins finishing second in the city to Franklin. Their momentum carried over to the state tournament in which Garfield won all three games to advance to the finals. Again they met Franklin and again they suffered defeat, losing the state championship 46-42.

Moscatel remembers dozens of Jewish families at the high school on 23rd Avenue, but the Moscatels were the only Jewish family — and Sephardic Jews at that — who tried out for basketball at that time.

While Moscatel envisioned joining his brother on Seattle University's basketball team and follow in the footsteps of the O'Brien brothers as sibling teammates, their father, Al, became ill and passed away. The younger brother was forced to abandon his plans for college to run the family business.

"Dad passed away in '53 and we did not want Ray to give up college so close to graduation," Moscatel remembers. "I've always regretted not going to college and not continuing to play basketball. But everything happens for a reason. And things have turned out pretty well."

While Ray went on to open his medical practice in California, Neiso expanded the family business from the original Continental Furniture store in Belltown to specialty home and office outlets in Seattle, Bellevue and Tukwila. Moscatel then delved into commercial real estate, developing projects throughout the Puget Sound region.

Moscatel's sons, Albert and Sam both played varsity at Mercer Island High School. Al, his grandfather's namesake, helped the team to the state championship twice during the 1980s, and went on to play in college before joining the family business.

While the Seward Park teenager had to put work before basketball, the decision allowed Neiso Moscatel to pass down both his family business and his love of the sport to his sons.

Front Row: (l to r) Paul Dammkoehler, Rob Mitchell, Brian Schwabe, Scott Lammers, Jorgan Light, Mike Hubbard. Back Row: Coach Pepple, Sam Muscatel, Scott Norwood, Peter Lyon, Laszlo Hedeus Quin Snyder, Rick Hodge, Tom Spencer.

Neiso's son Sam, back row, second from left

Ray Moscatel

April 26, 1931, Seattle

Sephardic guard was a standout at Catholic university

Like most of the teams from Garfield High School, the 1949 basketball squad that played for the city championship was the definition of diversity. Ray Moscatel was the starting center on a team with Chinese, African-American and Irish players. When the Jewish kid was invited to play ball at a private Catholic university, he didn't hesitate.

Moscatel had been All-City and All-State his senior year at Garfield and saw the potential to play on another good team at the Seattle University, located only a few blocks from his neighborhood. The opportunity to play with Johnny O'Brien and his twin brother Eddie made it an even easier decision.

"Seattle U had never been ranked in the top 20 before I arrived with the O'Brien twins. But we were ranked all three years I played with the varsity," Moscatel said with a sly smile. "We were a small school and our schedule was filled with games against other small schools, like Gonzaga, before it became a national powerhouse."

The Garfield grad said he never had a problem being the only Jewish player on his college team. "In fact," he said, "the Catholic players were sometimes jealous of me because I was allowed to eat meat on Fridays." Since several of his teammates wore crosses and Moscatel wore his Star of David, the players would put the two together before each game for luck.

The players were not accustomed to blatant examples of prejudice in Seattle, but Moscatel clearly recalls one incident on a road trip when his black teammates were denied entry to a movie theater. The team, he remembers, left the theater to find an activity they could all do together.

In Moscatel's sophomore year, the Chieftains went 32-5 under coach Al Brightman. Seattle U's student newspaper, The Spectator, noted after one game, "Ray Moscatel's fine board work and 15 points were the backbone that kept the Chieftains in contention." A year later,

Ray Moscatel made All-City and All-State playing for Garfield High School in 1949

the team did what hundreds had tried but only a rare few had accomplished. The private little Catholic college beat the famous Harlem Globetrotters. The 1952 exhibition match was played as part of a three-game tour the Globetrotters scheduled to raise money to send the US Olympic team to Helsinki. In less than 48 hours, all 12,500 tickets for the game at the UW's Hec Edmundson Pavilion had sold out.

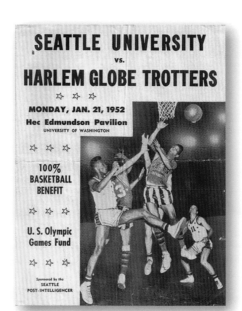

Johnny O'Brien scored 43 points to lead SU past a stunned Globetrotter team, 84-81. Globetrotter owner Abe Saperstein was reportedly so upset that he canceled the balance of the benefits scheduled

round.

As a senior, Moscatel and his squad returned to the Garden in December of 1952 where they faced NYU for a regular season game in front of a crowd of nearly 13,000. The two teams lit the net on fire with the Chieftains emerging with a stunning 102-101 victory. It was the first time opposing college teams both broke 100 points in a game.

After Seattle U posted a 29-4 record, they were ranked 14th in the country and landed a berth in the 1953 NCAA tournament. After defeating Idaho State in the first round, they faced the No. 2 ranked University of Washington in the Regional Semifinals. Though the two schools were separated by just a few miles, they had never played each other. The match-up brought a jolt of basketball electricity that surged through the entire city, and forced family and longtime friends to cheer from opposing sides. In the end, the crowd of 10,000 watched the Huskies defeat the Chieftains, 92-70.

Ray's achievements on the court set the tone for his brother Neiso and his nephew, Albert, who both followed in his footsteps - but perhaps too closely. Together, the three Moscatels played for the Washington State high school basketball championship five times, and lost all five. According to Ray, all five losses in the state finals were by a total of six points.

Moscatel, far left, and his Seattle U teammates dash through New York City

that year. The Chieftains finished the season by playing in the National Invitational Tournament in New York's Madison Square Garden, but were defeated by Holy Cross in the first

Don Richman

1931 – November 8, 1986, Los Angeles

University of Southern California graduate Don Richman partnered with fellow alumnus Dick Vertlieb in 1967 to orchestrate Seattle's effort to land its first modern professional sports franchise, the Seattle SuperSonics. The two brought in California businessmen Eugene Klein and Sam Schulman to underwrite the deal. A toss of the coin determined that Richman would be the general manager and Vertlieb the business manager.

Richman hired Al Bianchi as the team's first head coach, chose Al Tucker as the team's first college draft pick, and from the NBA expansion draft selected Tom Meschery from the San Francisco Warriors, Walt Hazzard from the Los Angeles Lakers, Bob Weiss from the Philadelphia 76ers, and Rod Thorn from the St. Louis Hawks.

Richman launched the team's first booster club, "The UltraSonics," and created its first publicity campaigns. He even coaxed some media outlets into reporting the scores of "horse" games played by the Sonics at practice. Richman was loved by the media for spouting a stream of one-liners, once referring to Seattle as a "24-hour car wash." But Richman lasted only 16 months on the job, returning to L.A. to write scripts for "Mod Squad" and "FBI," assignments that made him a lot more money than he could earn as the Sonics GM.

Nate Ross

1924, Seattle

JCC is boyhood dream for lifelong athlete

Born in Seattle in 1924 to Polish immigrants, Nate Ross first set eyes on a Jewish Community Center when he traveled to Portland as a teen with his AZA chapter of BBYO. He was immediately jealous. Seattle had nothing like it but the thought stuck in his mind for decades.

After going to the University of Washington and serving in the United States Navy, Ross returned to Seattle

and got a job in the insurance industry. Outside of work, he played basketball at the downtown YMCA at lunchtime and served on the board of the JCC, which officially organized in Seattle in April, 1949.

In those early years, the JCC rented meeting rooms in buildings downtown, mostly for adult programs. In 1959, the JCC purchased the Elks Building on 4th Avenue and Spring Street and finally had a place to call home. For Ross though, it still did not offer all the amenities of the JCC in Portland.

As a board

Charles Kapner, Howie Klein, Nate Ross, Rob Korman, Jimmy Rosenwald

member, Ross worked closely with businessman and community leader Sam Stroum in the 1960s to organize the resources to build an improved facility. Nate's wife, Judy, remembers the day her husband told her the news of a new JCC. "We were so excited at the prospect!" Judy recalled. "A Jewish Community Center where Jewish kids could play with other Jewish kids!"

In 1968, their dream was realized when the J opened its doors on Mercer Island. Ross immediately suited up to play basketball in the new gym and would continue playing there until he turned 82.

"It meant more to him than just playing basketball," said Nate's son, Neil Ross. "The vision of the Jewish Community Center was that this would be the center of the Jewish community."

"My dad provided financial support and leadership for many years," he continued. "But he's gotten so much more back from the JCC. It's given him the physical exercise which has allowed him to maintain good health, friendships, and relationships formed over the years."

Ross' daughter, Bobbi Chamberlin, said, "Playing basketball gave him a tremendous sense of community and accomplishment, to be with these younger guys and still be able to play. And although he couldn't run down the court the same way, he was a tremendous inspiration for his teammates."

"I quit playing without a reason," said Nate, "because I felt it was time. I understand Larry Barokas is 72 and still playing," he said with a competitive smile. "He has another 10 years to go."

Nate continues to be a presence at the J, working out regularly by speed walking the track and then lifting weights with trainer Jared Matson. "Nate is an icon at the J and an inspiration to everyone who comes to work out at the fitness center," said Matson. *(Details and quotes drawn from a story in The Mercer Island Reporter, 2011)*

Todd Rubin

June 29, 1982, Bellevue

"Hebrew Hammer" nailed his chance to coach at Christian college

Most people see the basketball court as a field of play. For Todd Rubin, the hardwood provides a classroom to teach the intricacies of the game he loves.

There was never a doubt that Rubin would spend his adult life at the coach's end of the bench. The only question was whether that bench would be inside a gymnasium or in a dugout.

"Baseball is a game of percentages. I understand how it works and the coaching skills that are needed to put together a winning team. But baseball does not provide the same mental challenge as basketball," Rubin explained. "The truth is, I was a better baseball player, but basketball has always been my favorite sport and courtside is where I wanted to be."

Rubin was the captain of both his varsity baseball and basketball teams at Redmond High School in 2000, then went on to play four years of college baseball at Linfield College in McMin-

Todd Rubin pitching for Linfield College

nville, OR. His college coach transformed the center fielder/shortstop into a power pitcher. After not allowing an earned run as a starter for much of his sophomore year, the scrappy ballplayer became the team's closer and earned the nickname, "The Hebrew Hammer."

"Being Jewish was not a negative. It was a badge of honor that I wore proudly at the small liberal arts college," he said. But Rubin does remember a time when his own commitment to athletics conflicted with his religion. That was when he was 13 and begged his parents to allow him to skip Bar Mitzvah classes so he would not miss practice. "I'm sure it drove my parents crazy," he said with a smile.

An injury to his pitching arm derailed any dream Rubin had of playing professional baseball. The setback allowed him to focus on his goal of becoming the head basketball coach at a major university.

Following graduation, Rubin taught health at Sammamish and Bellevue high schools, then stayed after school to assist with the baseball and basketball teams. He then moved on to Seattle Prep in 2004, where he spent four years as the junior varsity head coach as well as the assistant coach to the varsity team that won the state championship in 2006. A high school in Edmonds then provided him with his first chance to become a basketball head coach. He guided the Edmonds-Woodway Warriors to three consecutive appearances in the playoffs.

Rubin moved one step closer to his dream of becoming a head coach in the college ranks after accepting an offer in 2012 to serve as an assistant coach at NW University in Kirkland. In his first two years there, the Eagles made it to the National Tournament twice and went as far as the "Elite 8."

Rubin as the head coach of the Edmonds-Woodway Warriors

"Religion was apparently not a factor to the staff at this Christian college. Morally, the college is in line with the way I was raised as Jew. Our faith may be different, but that does not mean we cannot work together," Rubin said with confidence. "Coaching young people is judged with how well you help the players mature as human beings, and not just wins and losses on the schedule."

Rubin prides himself on being a "player's coach" who can provide friendship and serve as an example to young players. He said that role may change when he becomes a head coach and his job will require him to provide more leadership and discipline. He went on to explain that the role of a coach makes it difficult to interact with students as their teacher in an ordinary classroom.

"The basketball court is my classroom," he said. "The dedication and commitment I ask of my team goes far beyond what is required as homework."

Rubin did say that his greatest athletic accomplishment did not come on the field as a player. It was the life-changing steps he witnessed his student-athletes achieve in the classroom and at home to improve their lives that made him proud.

Rubin resides with his wife, Andrea, in Redmond.

Stan Sidell

June 22, 1937, Seattle

Stan Sidell played forward for the most successful varsity basketball squad in Garfield High School history to that point. The 1955 Bulldogs won 13 and lost 1, tying Lincoln High School for first place, and were declared city co-champions. The one loss by each team came at the hands of the other. Garfield finally distanced itself from Lincoln when Sidell and the Bulldogs won the state championship by defeating the O'Dea Irish.

STAN SIDELL
Forward

Mike Silver

November 6, 1949, Seattle

Mike Silver played center for Garfield's varsity basketball team in 1967. That year, the Bulldogs won the Southern Division of the Metro League, lost to Ballard in the city championship, and beat No. 1-ranked Puyallup in the first game at State, but lost in the next round, finishing fifth. As a member of Garfield's golf team, Silver remembers the team throwing their coach in the pond to celebrate their second-to-last-place finish — their best showing in three years!

Louie Soriano

September 19, 1929, Bremerton

Bremerton basketball star called the shots for 24 years

Louie Soriano was a basketball star at Bremerton High School and the University of Washington before enjoying a lengthy and successful officiating career. Soriano was a two-time All-State honoree at Bremerton before graduating in 1947. During his three varsity seasons at UW, he was selected to the All Pac-Eight team and that All Coast team as a junior and helped lead the Huskies into the NCAA tournament as a senior.

Following a stint in the Navy during the Korean War, Soriano put together his own insurance agency in Bremerton in 1955. While working his day job, he also officiated college basketball games for 24 years. Soriano had the opportunity to work big-time matchups that ranged from a North Carolina/UCLA preseason game in 1969 to the 1975 NCAA regional final between Kentucky and an unbeaten Indiana. Following the latter game, Indiana coach Bobby Knight confronted Soriano in the dressing room about the loss, but NCAA officials walked in

Louie Soriano during his UW days

Soriano called the shots for 24 years as a basketball ref

prompting the hot-tempered coach to leave. It was then that the NCAA officials honored Soriano with his selection as an official for the Final Four series.

After retiring as a referee in 1977, Soriano signed with the NBA to work as an official observer. He evaluated referees for the league in an effort to improve officiating, serving in this capacity until health issues forced his retirement in 2001. In his hometown, he assisted in the formation of the Bremerton Athletic Roundtable and was a member of the Olympic College Board and the Olympic College Boosters.

Zalmon Marcola "Zollie" Volchok

September 22, 1916, Salem, OR – February 26, 2012, Seattle

Sonics GM put showtime into halftime

University of Oregon graduate "Zollie" Volchok owned and operated Northwest Releasing from 1953 to 1969. The entertainment impresario built the company into the largest talent-booking agency in America, handling clients such as Lena Horne, Louis Armstrong, Jack Benny, George Burns, Sammy Davis, Jr., Frank Sinatra, the Beatles and Elvis, to name a few. When Sonics owner Sam Schulman approached his friend with an offer to be general manager of Seattle's NBA team, Volchok had only one response: "I don't know anything about basketball." "That's alright," said Schulman. "Neither do my players."

Born to Jewish parents who had fled Russia, first

to England and then to Canada before landing in the United States, young Zollie got his start in show business as a teenager as the master of ceremonies for a weekly live variety show for local children called *Zollie's Mickey Mouse Club Matinee*. With show biz in his blood, Volchok managed movie houses in Portland before he joined the Navy during World War II to serve as an entertainment booker for the Pacific Fleet.

Schulman was savvy enough to know that the Sonics needed marketing help and convinced Volchok that his vaudeville and entertainment roots would bring imagination to the team's marketing efforts. At age 61, Volchok came out of retirement and

Coach Lenny Wilkens and guard Fred Brown hoist 1978-79 NBA championship trophy (seattlepi.com)

served as general manager from 1977 to 1983, with a promise that the team would have assistants and coaches to handle the personnel side of the business, while his job would be simply to fill seats at the Seattle Center Coliseum.

Volchok brought back former player/coach and future Hall of Fame legend Lenny Wilkens, who was handed a team that started the season 5-17. Under Wilkens, the Sonics went on to win 11 of their next 12 games, finished the season 47-35, won the Western Conference title, and led the Washington Bullets three games to two in the 1978 NBA Finals before losing in game seven.

Seattle had been averaging fewer than 6,000 fans at home games before Volchok arrived. Under his direction, the Sonics became the first NBA team to provide halftime acts and live music to add entertainment value to each game. He turned player introductions into theater. Seattle was also the first professional basketball franchise to offer special events to the game-day program, including kids nights, ladies nights, and senior nights.

With crowds growing beyond all expectations, the following season the team moved to the cavernous Kingdome, where attendance at Sonics games broke all NBA records. Volchok sold tickets in the 300-level for a dollar. He wanted people to see the games. "I remember one night we ran out of tickets for the upper deck," said Dave Watkins, who worked in the Sonics public relations office at the time. "I mean we physically ran out of tickets, so we just let people in. That's the way Zollie was." During that 1978-79 season, an average of 21,725 screaming fans cheered the Sonics to their first and only NBA championship, defeating the Washington Bullets in five games.

When Schulman sold the team to billboard baron Barry Ackerley in 1983, Volchok ended his tenure with the team, leaving on a high note with the NBA Executive of the Year Award.

Volchok lived on Mercer Island with Sylvia, his wife of 73 years. They were longtime members of Temple De Hirsch Sinai in Seattle.

Rod Waldbaum

November 20, 1944, Seattle

Court is where taxman takes best shot

When the IRS attempted to disallow the Seattle SuperSonics' federal tax write-off of 90 percent of the $1.75 million original 1967 purchase price paid for the NBA franchise and all of the player rights and TV rights that came with it, the Sonics turned to Rodney J. Waldbaum and his partner, Woolvin Patten, of LeSourd & Patten.

In a case of national significance, the IRS argued that what the Sonics acquired was an indivisible mass asset, which could not be deducted or amortized. At that time, the NBA had each new team allocate 10 percent of the purchase price to the franchise rights and 90 percent to the player draft rights granted to new teams. The Sonics then deducted that 90 percent over the first five years of the franchise.

Waldbaum quickly recognized that the player rights acquired were not worth 90 percent of the purchase price. However, in a three-week US Tax Court trial, Waldbaum convinced the court that almost all of the $1.6 million originally placed on the player rights was de-

ductible, some as player rights amortizable over five years, some as TV revenue rights, some as imputed interest expense, and some as part of the franchise rights transferred as new teams were subsequently added to the NBA.

Two weeks of the trial were held in Seattle, which were covered each day in *The Seattle Times* and the *Seattle Post-Intelligencer*, and one week was held in Washington, D.C. to accommodate the fragile health of then-NBA Commissioner Walter Kennedy.

Waldbaum traveled the country meeting such basketball greats as Kennedy; Boston Celtics coach Red Auerbach; Ned Irish, who brought the New York Knicks to Madison Square Garden; Kansas City Kings owner Joe Axelson; Marty Blake, a national basketball scout; Sonics coach Bill Russell and owner Sam Schulman; and many others who testified during the trial.

Later, Waldbaum represented the Sonics in Thurston County Superior Court, successfully getting the court to agree that the Sonics' $2 million sale of Spencer Hayward's contract rights was a casual and isolated sale and, therefore, exempt from the Washington business and occupation tax. That sale, at the time, was the highest in NBA history.

Todd Warnick

August 8, 1955, Tacoma

Tacoma native calls the shots around the globe

From an early age, Todd Warnick had an affinity for refereeing, especially basketball. He began his career as a referee when he was just 18 years old and attending the University of Washington as a student. He served as a referee for both basketball and football. Two years later, he went on to officiate at basketball games for Seattle-area high school varsity teams, the Amateur Athletic Union and local junior colleges.

In 1979 Warnick made aliyah, finding a home in Jerusalem. From 1979 to 2004, he refereed at the professional level for the Israel Basketball Association, including officiating in the finals of the Israeli playoffs for approximately 20 years and in six state cup finals games. For many years, he was considered as one of the top

three referees in Israeli basketball, and he became a well-known fixture at games in all of the major sports competitions in Israel.

Between 1984 and 2003, Warnick refereed at the top levels of European professional basketball games, including many playoff and finals games. He retired from active officiating in 2004.

Warnick is currently the head trainer for the referees in Israel's professional league, and is also a referee instructor for the European section of the International Basketball Federation, traveling to games and tournaments around the continent.

HARRY WERBISKY
"Guard"
"Whisky" was drafted from the Midgets at the close of their schedule to fill the hole at guard caused by the injuries to Scott. Although handicapped by his lack of height, Harry showed well in the last Lincoln game and at the state meet. He will not be back next year.

Harry Werbisky

October 16, 1919 – December 27, 1940, Tacoma

Harry Werbisky was a four-sport star at Stadium High School in Tacoma, and was destined to become one of the University of Puget Sound's greatest athletes when he enrolled in 1939. Werbisky served as captain of the UPS basketball team, was selected to the All-Northwest Conference, and led the Loggers to their first Northwest Conference championship in school history during his only full season with the team. Tragically, in his sophomore year, he died suddenly from an infection. Werbisky was inducted into the University of Puget Sound Athletic Hall of Fame in 1974. An award named in his honor is presented annually to a student-athlete who demonstrates scholarship, skill and determination.

Aaron J. Wolff

May 25, 1973, Seattle

Wolff demonstrates skills on and in court

Basketball is more than a sport to Aaron Wolff. The game has helped mold him into the person he is today. Wolff played for legendary coach Ed Pepple at Mercer Island High School, was a member of the Seattle team that played in the North American Maccabi Youth Games, returned to the Games as an assistant coach, suffered through Sonics games inside the cavernous Kingdome, and sold tickets for the Atlanta Hawks. He has even taken one team owner to court.

Wolff dedicated hundreds of hours of his time pro bono as an attorney during the two years he served as co-legal counsel to the grassroots organization Save Our Sonics beginning in 2007. Wolff used public disclosure laws and cited specific performance guarantees in his arguments to try and keep the NBA franchise in Seattle. Ultimately, Oklahoma City businessman Clay Bennett prevailed in breaking his lease with the city and moved the franchise to his hometown.

"It was just a thrill to be part of the effort,"

Wolff said proudly. "And I will support every effort to bring the NBA back to Seattle. Sure, it's selfish, but it's also good for the city and great for the economy."

Growing up, Wolff said he studied the nuances of basketball to offset his "limited" phys-

ical skills. "Basketball was always the sport I played the most, even as a kid. But when I was told that I was not good enough to be on the elite teams, my parents quickly found the equivalent program for me at the JCC," he said. These days, he has returned to the J to coach his own children in the Dinky Dunkers program.

The attorney also has basketball to thank for helping him meet his wife, Amy Posner. At 6'-5", Wolff earned a spot as the center on the Seattle basketball team at the North American Maccabi Youth Games in 1988. He had no way of knowing that the woman he would eventually settle down and raise a family with was a member of the same delegation of athletes that represented the local Jewish community in Chicago that summer.

When Wolff returned to the Maccabi Games as an assistant coach to David Schiller six years later, he decided it was time to pursue the track star with the beaming smile.

"Funny thing. We belonged to the same congregation [Temple De Hirsch Sinai] and knew each other from the games in Chicago," said Wolff. "But there was something different when we were together again in Philadelphia. We had the chance to get reacquainted and there was a spark, a very special spark."

The father of three remains active in his community. He practices law as a criminal defense attorney with a firm in Kirkland. Wolff has taken up skiing and golf to supplement the occasional pick-up game of basketball he still plays at the JCC.

He did admit that one of his three children has the potential to become a skilled basketball player. But, like any wise attorney, he declined to identify which one.

SuperSonic Tom Meschery, far left, and Al Hairston, center, chat with fans at the JCC, circa 1969

SuperSonics play at the JCC against members. Dorie Murray, far left, coach Al Bianchi driving to the hoop, chased by Moe Muscatel, Sonic Al Hairston, far right in back.

Marc Blau, far left in back, Jerry Rosenthal with ball, Dan Pease #24, ?, Eddie Rose #15, far right in back in an AZA game

Stan Sidell

Garfield

Bulldogs

Garfield High School
Seattle, Washington

Purple and White

Bob Tate, *Coach*

No.		Pos.	Age	Ht.	Wt.	Class	Pts.*	Avg.
6	Lewis Coaston	G	18	5-9	134	Senior	35	2.5
10	Jim Crutchfield	G	17	5-7	150	Soph.	4	1.0
11	Eddie Jordan	G	18	5-10	165	Senior	16	1.3
13	Dave Holden	F-C	17	6-2	186	Junior	142	10.1
14	Doug Smart (Capt.)	C	18	6-6	203	Senior	374	26.7
15	Stan Sidell	F	17	6-3	182	Senior	63	4.9
20	Carl Cady	F	17	6-2	168	Senior	19	1.7
21	Len Peterson	G	18	5-10	175	Senior	89	6.4
25	Dave Miller	F	16	6-4	182	Junior	56	4.7
30	Al Pembleton	G	18	5-10	140	Senior	72	5.1

Richard Ball, *Manager*

*Total for regular season; average indicates points per game.

SEASON RECORD

Won 13, Lost 1

Garfield....	63	Queen Anne ..	57
Garfield....	48	Franklin	44
Garfield....	52	Roosevelt	37
Garfield....	63	West Seattle ..	47
Garfield....	78	Ballard	52
Garfield....	68	Cleveland	35
Garfield....	49	Lincoln	52
Garfield....	68	Queen Anne ..	43
Garfield....	70	Franklin	57
Garfield....	60	Roosevelt	48
Garfield....	73	West Seattle ..	48
Garfield....	73	Ballard	47
Garfield....	67	Cleveland	46
Garfield....	51	Lincoln	49

From left: Asst. Coach Frank Inslee, Coach Bob Tate, Richard Ball, manager, Jim Crutchfield, Lewis Coaston, Al Pembleton, Ed Jordan, Len Peterson, Carl Cady, Dave Holden, Stan Sidell, Dave Miller, Doug Smart.

Stan, Dad, Papa

We are so proud that you are part of Washington's Jewish sports history.

Iantha
Mark, Leslie, Leah & Hannah
Scott, Pam, Sydney & Emma
Ben, Brooke & Ella

Albert DeLeon

My Papoo Albert passed down his love of baseball and basketball to me. A gift that has given me countless memories and inspired my devotion to this book.

Stephen Sadis

Albert DeLeon, front row, far right, was a member of Garfield High School's 1926 championship 2nd team.

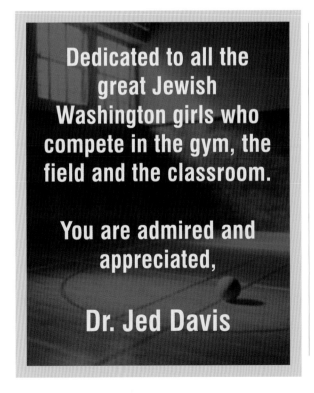

Dedicated to all the great Jewish Washington girls who compete in the gym, the field and the classroom.

You are admired and appreciated,

Dr. Jed Davis

Al Warnick

Al is one of 15 Warnicks to graduate from Stadium High School from 1922-1994. Varsity letters have been awarded to Warnicks in football, basketball, tennis, golf, girls' swimming and track.

In honor of the
2009-10 and 2011-12

Northwest Yeshiva High School "613's" girls' basketball teams:

Laurel Aaronson, Grace Almo,
Marissa Almoslino, Milana Davydov,
Halle Friedland, Ilana Greenberg,
Elana Hasson, Julia Owen, Makena Owens,
Dena Phillips, Sophie Price, Zelle Rettman,
and their coach, Dr. Jed Davis.

The 613's are the first girls' team from a
Jewish school in North America to go to a
state championship in any sport!

Ruth Sassoon

Nate Ross

With Love and Admiration,

Judy Ross
Liz Davis and **Neil Ross**
Bobbi Chamberlin and **Don Shifrin**
Alexis Chamberlin and **Max Shifrin**

Congratulations and thank you to the WSJHS and Stephen Sadis for turning Distant Replay into a reality.

Mike Silver

Jewish Federation
OF GREATER SEATTLE

BOXING

NATE DRUXMAN *presents*
15 ROUNDS AT 160 POUNDS FOR THE
WORLD'S MIDDLEWEIGHT CHAMPIONSHIP

FREDDIE

Al Hostak

SEC.			TUESDAY — 8:30 P. M. — JULY 26, 1938
7			SEATTLE CIVIC STADIUM--3rd No. and MERCER
ROW M			ADMISSION - - $5.00
SEAT 2			Gov't Tax - - - 50c
			State Tax - - - 25c
			TOTAL - $5.75

Boxing history packs a Jewish punch

As difficult as it may be to believe, Jews were at the forefront of the sport of boxing from its earliest days to its golden era.

Daniel Mendoza was England's Heavyweight Champion from 1792-1795

From 1792 to 1795, Daniel Mendoza, who proudly billed himself as "Mendoza the Jew," was England's 16th Heavyweight Champion. With a frame that measured only 5'7" and 160 pounds, Mendoza had developed a variety of defensive techniques that so confounded his opponents, he could defeat boxers from much heavier weight classes. His book, The Art of Boxing would forever revolutionize the sport.

Fighting in the early 1800s, Jewish lightweight boxer Samuel "Dutch Sam" Elias, is credited with inventing the uppercut punch.

During the 1920s and 30s

Samuel Elias invented the uppercut

in the US, almost a third of all professional boxers were Jewish. Twenty thousand Jews at that time fought for some kind of purse – and between 1910 and 1940 there were 27 Jewish world champions.

1939 edition featured 1934 Jewish World Heavyweight Champion Max Baer

The Ring magazine, regarded as "The Bible of Boxing," was first published by New York Jew Nat Fleisher in 1922. Everlast, the biggest manufacturer of boxing equipment, was started by Bronx Jew Jacob Golumb in 1910. As boxing historian and author, Mike Silver put it, "If there is any sport that can be describe as 'a Jewish sport' it is the sport of boxing." (Quotes and information drawn from documentary, "A Star in the Ring")

Herbert "Herb" Bridge

March 14, 1925, Seattle

From boxing ring to diamond rings

Better known as the Seattle businessman who helped turn one small jewelry store into 75 locations nationwide, Herb Bridge honed his toughness as a welterweight pugilist in the Navy in 1942 and then as a member of the boxing team at the University of Washington.

Following in his father's footsteps, Herb Bridge was only 17 when he joined the Navy. During boot camp in San Diego, he slipped on a pair of boxing gloves to face his first opponent in the ring. "I liked hitting people," Bridge remarked. "And I apparently enjoyed getting hit too."

Bridge was a natural, scoring knockouts over all recruits on board and winning the title in his weight class before being shipped off to the Pacific. Bridge remembers one particular fight with a recruit from Louisiana that was refereed by former heavyweight champ Joe Louis.

"All I can remember was that he put his hands on our heads and told us to have a clean fight. I knew right away that I did not want to do anything wrong to make the champ mad," said Bridge. "My commander must have thought that I was pretty good because I never lost a fight."

With Bridge handily beating the novice boxers in the Navy, officers set up a fight be-

1947 UNIVERSITY OF WASHINGTON

Herb Bridge, back far right, with his UW boxing teammates

tween the young seaman and the reigning AAU champion, Dale Redfern. "It was a total mismatch," he said, smiling. "The guy had a three-inch reach advantage. He could have destroyed me. But he was nice enough to carry me through three rounds so I would not be humiliated in front of the rest of the base. Although, my mother thought I won the fight."

Bridge hung up his gloves when he earned his commission as an officer in 1945 and served on the escort carrier USS Breton for a year before being discharged. After the war, Bridge returned to the ring at the University of Washington. While earning his liberal arts degree, he found enough time between classes to win the intramural senior welterweight boxing title. Bridge promoted his image on campus to match the nickname the "ZBT Destroyer" given to him by his fraternity brothers.

Bridge said his experiences boxing taught him how to take a punch, and had his nose broken "several times," but was never harassed or singled out for being Jewish.

"People don't mess with a guy who can fight, even though my fighting weight as a senior welterweight was always between 145 and 155 lbs.," he said.

"I wish my weight was closer to that today," he added.

Ely "The Newsboy" Caston

November 25, 1900, Tekirdag, Turkey – January 31, 1961, Seattle

Boxing matchmaker staged "smokers" at White Center Arena

Ely Caston was the oldest of four Sephardic brothers who fought professionally in the Seattle area. Nicknamed "The Newsboy" and "Battling Ely," the lightweight fighter had a brief career in the ring and then went on to become a boxing promoter.

Caston was born in Turkey in 1900 and came to Seattle at the age of 9. His younger brothers, Jackie and "Sammie," were boxers as well. As a kid, Ely peddled newspapers downtown, earning him his early boxing nickname. From 1917 to 1921, the lightweight fought in 16 professional bouts, winning eight (one by knockout) and losing three, and with five draws.

A few years after graduating from Broadway High School in Seattle, Caston hung up his gloves and pursued a career as a promoter. By the mid-1920s, he operated the White Center Arena, a barn-like structure with a ring and

enough bleachers to seat 1,200. During the day it served as a gymnasium for boxers to workout and spar, but at night, once a week, the venue transformed into the site of boxing events known as "smokers." Serving as matchmaker, Caston's job was to arrange six or seven bouts that prom-

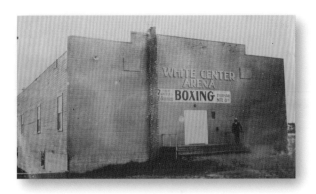

ised the thrill of a good fight and would draw boxing fans willing to shell out 75 cents to sit ringside, 50 cents for general admission. In his book, *A Dream, A Buck, an Era,* author Robert Jepperson captures the character and color of a White Center smoker:

The barn carried a proper name, the White Center Arena, splashed across the wall that faced 16th Avenue SW; and it was a proper place, largely for males to gather every Thursday evening to spit tobacco and to smoke and holler a mix of insightful and crude comments at the ring, the altar where men and a few boys worshipped an ancient contest of will and strength and speed, the altar upon which men pitted all their power and resolve and savvy against other men — winner take all. Like it or not, no one could ignore the weekly goings-on at the barn. Although the structure squatted on a large piece of land, nearby residents, some as close as directly across 16th Avenue SW, heard the roar of the Thursday night crowds, especially at punctuated moments when

Ely Caston (far left) and his championship soccer team

the drama in the ring grew intense, and while those more distant may not have heard all the frequencies of the crowd's noise, they felt the collective, deep tones of the throbbing arena, and wondered what sort of magic makes men revel that way.

In the early 1930s, when the economy was still in the throes of the Great Depression and other boxing venues were failing, Caston was able to keep his arena afloat by frequently trading boxers back and forth with Bremerton promoter and fellow ex-boxer Bud Ridley. Since the former Pacific Coast featherweight champion ran the Navy Yard Athletic Club, sailors stationed in Bremerton were frequently on the White Center's boxing card, as well as the occasional shipyard worker.

Perhaps sensing a need to diversify, Caston also invested in a professional soccer team that captured the Northwest Championship in 1929.

At the age of 45, Caston was approved as a judge by the Washington State Boxing Commission. His biggest scorecard was the 1960 12-round clash between heavyweight future champ Sonny Liston who beat Eddie Machen by a unanimous decision at Sick's Stadium. Records indicate that Caston judged 17 fights over 15 years, mostly at the Seattle Civic Auditorium.

Ely was a member of Sephardic Bikur Holim synagogue.

Jackie Caston

May 10, 1910 – October 20, 1952, Seattle

"Spanish Jumping Bean" adds Sephardic flavor to local boxing

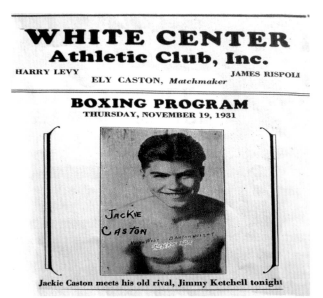

WHITE CENTER
Athletic Club, Inc.

HARRY LEVY   ELY CASTON, *Matchmaker*   JAMES RISPOLI

BOXING PROGRAM
THURSDAY, NOVEMBER 19, 1931

Jackie Caston meets his old rival, Jimmy Ketchell tonight

Known as the "Spanish Jumping Bean," Jackie Caston became one of the most popular fighters in the Seattle area, fighting in Wenatchee, Vancouver, Everett, Bremerton, Tacoma, and as far away as Hollywood.

In 1920, *The Seattle Daily Times* featured a story on Jackie Caston and his younger brother, Sammie:

Fifty-five pounds in weight, 10 years old, claimant to the coast fleaweight title and willing to defend his laurels against all comers. This is Jackie Caston, Seattle newsboy, who, together with his 9-year-old brother, Sammie, has been entertaining local ring fans as the curtain raiser to many recent shows. "I'll meet any boy my weight in the world," says Jack, "even if he's Jack Dempsey's son."

In that first "official" fight with his brother, the younger Sammie beat him in four rounds at the Pavilion in Seattle. A month later, the two were at it again at the Elks Club in Bremerton, with the four-round bout ending in a draw. After a five-year break, Caston jumped back in the ring in 1926 winning his first eight fights. In one match in 1928 at the Greenwich Coliseum in Tacoma, Caston knocked his opponent

out so early in the first round, he agreed to fight another opponent that same night, which went four rounds and ended in a draw.

At the Crystal Pool in Seattle, local Jewish promoter Nate Druxman staged the Pacific Coast bantamweight title fight in the fall of 1929. Caston squared off against Tommy Gardner of Walla Walla, who was coming off victories in his last six fights. *The Everett Daily Herald* reported: "[Caston] displayed plenty of nerve. Time after time he rushed in on his foe who stood a head taller and whose reach bested his by several inches. Gardner waited for Jackie to come in milling. He never had long to wait. A right to the head sent Caston to the canvas in the second round." Though he pulled himself back up, Caston lost the title on points.

In another bout held in January of 1932 at White Center Arena, a venue his older brother

Ely operated, Jackie was pitted against Roy Goodman, who grew up just down the street. *The Seattle Daily News* reported: "Goodman dropped Caston in the second round, but Jackie came back strong to win four of the six rounds scheduled. It was a hard, fast bout with Caston clearly entitled to the nod."

Over a career that spanned 1921 to 1933, the bantamweight pugilist fought in 83 bouts, won 46 (three by knockout), lost nine (none by knockout), and had 27 draws.

Jackie Caston and his wife, Jean, had three children, Mark, Beverly and Linda. He passed away in 1952 at the very young age of 42.

Solomon "Sammie" Caston

September 22, 1912 – October 24, 1979, Seattle

The youngest of the fighting Caston brothers, "Sammie" fought his first match at 9 years of age against his older brother Jackie at the Pavilion in Seattle in 1921. The younger Caston was declared the winner in the four-round bout. The two "flea-weight" boxers would often square off in exhibition fights before the curtain was raised for the main bouts at the White Center Arena. Sammie continued to box as a bantamweight until 1932 and remained undefeated after 12 matches, with 10 wins (three by knockout) and two draws.

Jackie and Sammie Caston at age 10 and 9

"Natty Nate" Druxman

March 25, 1892 – November 20, 1969, Seattle

Seattle's preeminent ringleader brought world-title bouts to town

Known as "Natty Nate," Nate Druxman was a larger-than-life character who became Seattle's leading boxing promoter from the 1920s to the 1940s.

Born in Seattle in 1892 to Ukrainian Jewish immigrants, Nate's family made its home above his father's furniture store near Yesler Way and Second Avenue. Early in the 1900s, Nate and his brothers, Harry and Leo, changed their family name from Druxinman to Druxman. Nate attended South School in Seattle, where he became a champion marble player. "I came up the hard way," Druxman told a Seattle Daily Time reporter in 1964. "Quit school after the eighth grade and went to work for the Schwabacher Brothers." He remained there for 19 years.

As a young man, he was good at a number of sports: baseball, boxing and even hockey. "Baseball was my first love," said Druxman, "and for a while, I thought I was going to be a big-league player." While playing for the local Elks Club team, Druxman met his future wife, Jessie Simmons, granddaughter of early Seattle settler and alderman Moses Korn. Though talented enough to play at the semi-professional level, he wasn't able to advance much further.

In 1910, he began fighting professionally, competing in five bouts, which kindled his great love for the "sweet science of boxing."

In the 1920s, efforts across the nation by boxing promoters like Tex Rickard prompted media interest in the sport, bringing in new audiences and a sharp rise in its popularity, ushering in the golden age of boxing.

Ironically, during this time professional boxing was illegal in Washington, but state law allowed "sparring or fencing amongst members of private clubs…for the enjoyment of their fra-

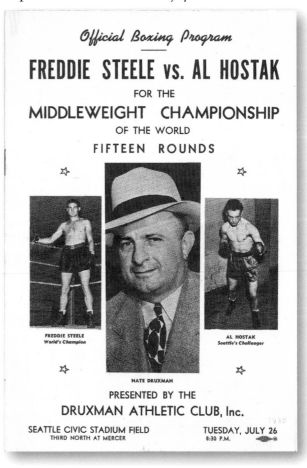

Official Boxing Program

FREDDIE STEELE vs. AL HOSTAK

FOR THE

MIDDLEWEIGHT CHAMPIONSHIP

OF THE WORLD

FIFTEEN ROUNDS

FREDDIE STEELE
World's Champion

NATE DRUXMAN

AL HOSTAK
Seattle's Challenger

PRESENTED BY THE

DRUXMAN ATHLETIC CLUB, Inc.

SEATTLE CIVIC STADIUM FIELD
THIRD NORTH AT MERCER

TUESDAY, JULY 26
8:30 P.M.

ternal brothers." Boxing shows called "smokers" were staged at various fraternal orders such as American Legion Posts, Eagles Aeries and Elks Lodges, and were packed with fans paying $1 per head. Boxing's growing popularity allowed this thinly veiled system to work, gaining further advantages from dedicated boxing fans such as *Seattle Daily Times* publisher Alden Blethen.

Druxman began his career as a boxing promoter during this time. Having been a fighter, he knew the kinds of matches that would interest

Nate Druxman promoted boxing matches known as "smokers" throughout the Northwest

fans the most: pitting two fighters with different styles against each other, such as a boxer against a puncher or an up-and-coming fighter against a seasoned pro on the decline. The trick was matching the fighters to make for a long and entertaining bout, and at that Nate excelled. So much so, that he was able to quit his job at Schwabacher Brothers to promote boxing full time.

Boxing became a family business for the Druxmans. Harry tried his hand at promoting as well and with Nate ran the Druxman Athletic Club, while Leo took to managing fighters. In 1925, Nate also opened his own club at the Crystal Pool on Second Avenue and Lenora Street.

Druxman promoted fights at Seattle's Elks Lodge, Dugdale Field (later Sick's Stadium), Civic Ice Arena, Civic Auditorium and Civic Stadium. In August 1931, he brought former heavyweight champion Jack Dempsey to Seattle for three exhibition bouts, each of which filled Civic Arena.

After countless efforts through the intervening years, many of which were stalled by incidents of boxers dying from injuries, professional boxing was legalized in Washington on June 8, 1933. Three weeks later, Druxman staged the first legal bout and the first world-title fight ever held in Seattle. The featherweight champion Freddie Miller defended his title, knocking out local Jewish favorite Abie Israel in four rounds.

On July 26, 1938 Druxman staged what is regarded as one of the top sporting events in Seattle history. Held at Seattle Civic Stadium Field, the National Boxing Association's middleweight title fight brought together two locals, reigning champion Freddie Steele, the "Tacoma Assassin," and the "Savage Slav" of Seattle, Al Hostak.

The national title fight between cross-town

rivals sold 30,000 tickets in a matter of hours. In cardrooms throughout downtown Seattle, over $25,000 had been wagered. With the match held outside, Druxman grew anxious when rain clouds appeared on the horizon. Not taking any chances, he moved up the starting time and notified Hostak's manager. When Druxman arrived at Steele's dressing room, two Tacoma policemen were guarding the door and wouldn't let him in. Druxman didn't have time to waste, so he decked one officer with a left and felled the other one with a right hook. He broke one of his hands, but walked in and informed the Steele camp of the new start time.

Despite Steele's 120 victories over just four losses, Hostak dropped the champion with a left hook in the first round. Referee Jack

Dempsey ruled the match over one minute and 43 seconds after it began. Between 1933 and 1940, Druxman promoted 11 world title fights in Seattle.

Nate and his wife, Jessie, had four sons and were married for 51 years until Jessie's passing in 1965. Nate passed away four years later.

Abie Israel

1913–1972, Seattle

Seattle's Sephardic southpaw pugilist

In April 1933, Abie Israel squared off against Freddie Miller, the reigning featherweight champion in an exhibition fight, and won. The match prompted *The Ring* magazine to rank him as the nation's No. 3 flyweight. Three months later, after professional boxing was legalized in Washington, Israel entered the ring for the first world-title fight ever held in the state. Israel again went toe to toe with Miller, going four rounds before a knockout punch

ended his quest for the featherweight title.

Born in the Yesler Way district, young Abie began his career as a professional boxer at the age of 10 when the well-known trainer Spider Roach took him under his wing. Under Roach's guidance, Israel converted from a right-hander to a southpaw with an orthodox stance.

In 1926, at the age most Jewish boys were becoming bar mitzvah, Israel boxed in two amateur fights against fellow Sephardic Sammy Caston of Seattle. With Israel's family from the Island of Rhodes and Caston's from Turkey, the fights were immensely popular in the local Jewish community as they drew out the rivalry among the Sephardim. Israel lost the first bout held at the Arena Athletic Club in Everett and battled to a draw in the second at the Eagles Auditorium in Seattle.

"He boxed continually from that time on, coming to Portland, where it wasn't long before he was lord of the little fellows," reported the *Portland Oregonian* on June 16, 1929. "(Israel) is only 16 years old, but special dispensation has been secured for him, permitting him to appear as a professional. He is now a flyweight and a finished performer." In his professional boxing debut, Israel took the bout.

Between 1929 and 1938, Israel fought up and down the West Coast against boxers whose names suggested the color of the sport: Young Pancho, Pee Wee Gale, Nutzie Luizza, Panama Kid, Battling Zoro, Speedy Dado, Baby Palmore, Little Dempsey and Midget Wolgast. The reporting was equally as rich:

Associated Press, April 1932: "They put on a fierce slugging match in the first canto but a terrific left to the stomach in the second sent

Abie Israel beat the reigning featherweight champion in 1933

Freddie down for the count."

Everett Daily Herald, August 1932: "Israel handed out a lacing to McArdle. [He] made it interesting for three stanzas, but was on the receiving end most of the time. Although he lost, the little Vancouverite drew quite an ovation for his gameness."

For the Northwest featherweight title held at the Crystal Pool in Seattle, the *Everett Daily Herald* reported in October 1932: "Bundy floored Israel with a sharp left hook in the opening session. The Portland boy, although shaken a few times by stiff lefts and rights, had the top hand most of the way. Israel opened a slight cut over Bundy's left eye in the third, and put out some valiant opposition in the fourth, but the effort was outclassed when the Negro put on a whirlwind finish to wind up the scrap."

For the National Boxing Association World Featherweight Title held at the Civic Ice Arena in Seattle, the *Associated Press* reported in July 1933: "The closest the Seattle youngster came to the N.B.A. championship was his claim to a foul in the third when he was flattened with a left uppercut to the body. He writhed and rolled on the canvas while many of the approximately 7,000 fans yelled 'foul,' but Referee Tommy McCarthy ruled otherwise and ordered Israel to continue after a six-minute rest."

In December 1933, the Washington State Athletic Commission named Israel the state's featherweight champion. He held on to the title for three years, remaining a top attraction for Jewish

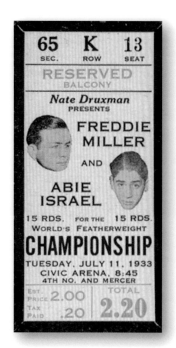

boxing promoter Nate Druxman. In 1937, Israel lost the title to Billy Buxton, getting knocked out in the third round. Over the next 15 months, he won his next bout in a technical knockout, but lost the next three. After 28 years in the ring, Israel quit fighting and became a boxing matchmaker in Vallejo, CA.

Abie Israel finished his boxing career with 92 professional fights, 59 wins (26 by knockout), 24 defeats, and 10 draws. He was knocked out only six times.

Oscar Levitch

1900, Portland – April 7, 1952, Spokane

A Spokane sports gem

While most kids were still working on their bar mitzvah thank you notes, at age 14 Oscar Levitch was acting as manager for a Coeur d'Alene boxer. The experience cemented a lifelong association with sports.

Born in Portland, Levitch and his family moved to Spokane in 1906 when he was six. As a young boy, Levitch stood on street corners shouting out the day's headlines to sell newspapers. He realized then that the sporting news was his favorite.

Oscar Levitch, left, with 1935-37 heavy weight boxing champion James Braddock

By the time he was in his 20s, he organized the Levitch Sparklers, a top independent basketball team that scored victories over college teams and other independent clubs. Before he was 30, golfers competed for the Oscar Levitch Trophy at Downriver Golf Course.

After a brief stint in New York, where he learned the jewelry trade, he opened his own store in downtown Spokane in 1935. While growing his business, he was active in the boxing circles, managing some of the best-known Spokane battlers of the day, two of which were contenders for the world light heavyweight title.

While Levitch was busy promoting fights at the old Alan race track near Post Falls, he used sports to promote his jewelry store. Calling it, "The Meeting Place of Champs," the jewelry store on North 10 Howard Street hosted dozens of national sports celebrities including boxers Joe Louis and James Braddock.

A March 21, 1972 article in the Spokane Daily Chronicle claimed, "Levitch probably knew more nationally famed athletes during his day than any other Spokane sports fan. His place of business was for years the meeting place of athletes moving in and out of Spokane."

In addition to sports celebrities, autographed baseballs Levitch collected were also on display at the jewelry store. One signed ball, was the one Detroit Tiger Hank Greenberg hit over the wall in the fifth game of the World Series. Another was signed by all the members of the World Series contending 1940 Tigers.

Levitch was an ardent supporter of the Spokane Indians baseball team and often employed players at his jewelry store during the off-season. "Spokane's leading credit Jeweler" also used the proceeds from his business to sponsor several semi-pro baseball and basketball teams, invest in Playfair Race Course, underwrite purses there and sponsor dozens of other sports-related awards.

Ever the promoter, in 1945 Levitch put together an all-star quintet to play against the Harlem Globetrotters on their tour through Spokane. Olympian Jesse Owens was on hand at the event. In 1951, Cleveland Indians general manager and former Detroit Tigers home run king Hank Greenberg, a friend of Levitch's, appointed him the Inland Empire scout for the team.

Shortly after his passing in 1952, Playfair named a Handicap race in his honor. Currently, Levitch is the only Jewish individual to be inducted into the Inland Northwest Sports Hall of Fame.

Sidney Nelson

December 12, 1915, Seattle – May 15, 1984, Hawaii

'Let the *goyim* be the fighters'

Sid Nelson was the definition of an all-around athlete during his days at the University of Washington. He went out for football in 1937 and was considered for the varsity basketball team in 1939. He enlisted in the Army shortly after the beginning of the war and met his wife on the train ride between Seattle and Chicago. His connection to sports continued after his stint in the service, when he took on the role of manager and sparring partner for the notorious Jewish boxer Barney Ross.

Dina Tanners remembers her father as a gentle man who rarely spoke about his past, but does recall that when she was a child her father would squat down to her level to demonstrate boxing techniques.

Sid Nelson on left

"We had all heard the stories about the colorful figures our dad had associated with, but he never let on to what an exceptional athlete he was," said Tanners. "He lived to ski. I can still remember the smile on his face when he heard the weatherman predict snow in the mountains."

As a young man in the '30s, Nelson was responsible for arranging sparring partners for Ross, who held championships in the lightweight, junior welterweight and welterweight divisions at different

Barney Ross, world champion boxer in three weight divisions

points in his career. Finding people to get in the ring with a world champion was not always easy, so Nelson was often forced to put on the gloves himself to help the champ prepare for a bout. Ross went on to become a war hero and gained notoriety by socializing with mobsters and shady characters, such as Jack Ruby.

Tanners remembers her father recalling the words of the champ, who quoted his own father by saying, "Let the *goyim* be the fighters — we are the scholars." She also remembers her father boasting how Ross maintained his strict kosher diet, even while training, and how Ross proudly wore tallit katan in the ring under his boxing shorts.

Tanners describes how her father lived his life to the fullest until the very end, explaining that he learned to swim late in life just so that he could participate in the annual public swim for enthusiasts on New Year's Day.

Jim Rosenwald

June 19, 1943, Seattle

Lightweight champ cleaned clocks and teeth

The basketball court was not where Jim Rosenwald wanted to start his dental practice, but he was forced to do his first extraction on his friend after the two scuffled while he was still in his first year of dental school.

The fight ended quickly. After dodging two sucker punches, the 135-lb. dental student dropped his opponent with a quick counter punch. Rosenwald looked after his friend on the court and continues to be his dentist to this day.

On his first attempt trying out for Franklin High School's football team, Rosenwald did not meet the minimum weight requirement. He had filled out by the next season, but his father convinced him that playing football would give his mother "another heart attack." Still interested in "hitting people," Rosenwald turned his energy toward boxing.

"My uncle called his friend, the legendary boxing trainer George Chemeres," Rosenwald recalls. "Chemeres was one of the top 10 boxing trainers in the country. Everybody figured I'd quit and come home after getting whipped around the ring by real boxers."

But the determined teenager proved them wrong. Chemeres liked something about the Jewish boxer and invited him to train at the gym as the only amateur among a stable of contenders, including light heavyweight Eddie Cotton. Rosenwald remembers attracting curiosity one day when he used a technique he picked up from Chemeres to stagger a heavyweight opponent during a sparring session.

The pint-sized pugilist competed in the 1963 Golden Gloves tournaments in Seattle and Tacoma. He went the distance in both fights, but lost in close decisions to the more experienced boxers. Over time, Rosenwald earned the respect of the professionals at the gym, remembering proudly that he was never knocked down.

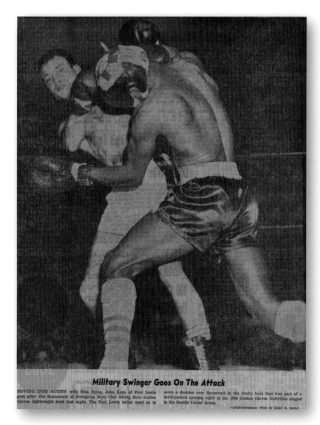

Military Swinger Goes On The Attack

MOVING INTO ACTION with fists flying, John Keys of Fort Lewis goes after Jim Rosenwald of Evergreen Boys Club during their Golden Gloves lightweight bout last night. The Fort Lewis belter went on to score a decision over Rosenwald in the lively bout that was part of a thrill-packed opening night of the 1963 Golden Gloves festivities staged in the Seattle Center Arena.
—(Post-Intelligencer Photo by Elmer E. Harris.)

Rosenwald had far more success boxing at the University of Washington than in Golden Gloves, becoming the Huskies' 1961 undefeated lightweight champion. When he was offered $425 to make his professional debut at Madison Square Garden in 1964, Jim chose to stay home to work in construction and enroll in dental school. "Probably the best decision I ever made," he said.

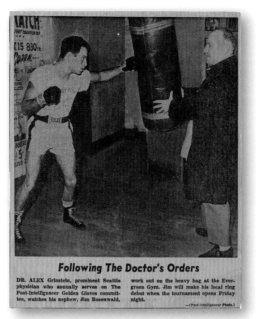

Following The Doctor's Orders

DR. ALEX Grinstein, prominent Seattle physician who annually serves on The Post-Intelligencer Golden Gloves committee, watches his nephew, Jim Rosenwald, work out on the heavy bag at the Evergreen Gym. Jim will make his local ring debut when the tournament opens Friday night.

—(Post-Intelligencer Photo.)

After graduating from dental school at the University of Washington and honing his skills for two years with the Marines, the Mercer Island resident returned home in 1970 to open his practice in Bellevue.

Jim and his wife, Vivian, have two sons, Paul and Greg, and several grandchildren. The former boxer now gets his thrills from fast cars, motorcycles and competitive tennis. When Rosenwald finally decided to take up golf, his friend Mo Muscatel had only one comment on the subject: "Rosie, golf is much better for a nice Jewish boy than boxing."

As far as his religion playing a role, Rosenwald said he mostly prayed "not to get hit" before every fight. "There was nothing unusual about a Jewish boxer. There have been a number of very good ones over the years," he said.

Harry "Scotty" Weinstone

1905, Glasgow, Scotland – September 21, 1983, Tacoma

Harry Weinstone chaired the Golden Gloves boxing competitions in Tacoma for more than 25 years and was a member of the Tacoma Athletic Commission. Born in Glasgow, "Scotty" and his family moved to the US in 1911. A graduate of Stadium High School, Scotty's boxing career lasted just two bouts before he chose to devote his time to the sport outside the ring.

In short time, there was probably no one who knew more about the Northwest's pool of boxing talent than Weinstone. He spent countless hours scouting Puget Sound gyms for talented fighters to fill the cards of the dozens of boxing classics he organized over the decades.

Herb M. Bridge
"The ZBT Destroyer"

HERBERT M. BRIDGE
General Studies
Zeta Beta Tau

1947 UNIVERSITY OF WASHINGTON

"I liked hitting people and I apparently
enjoyed getting hit too. People don't
mess with a guy who can fight."
Herb Bridge

Miriam R. Stiefel

Cappy's Boxing Gym, Seattle: 2005 to Present
USA Amateur Boxing Association:2008

Love,
Doris "Oma" Stiefel

The Rubin Family

**Marc, Kayla and Max
Steven, Lara and Beia
Todd and Andrea**

A stout supporter of Washington's Jewish history

Capturing great stories
since 1992

FOOTBALL

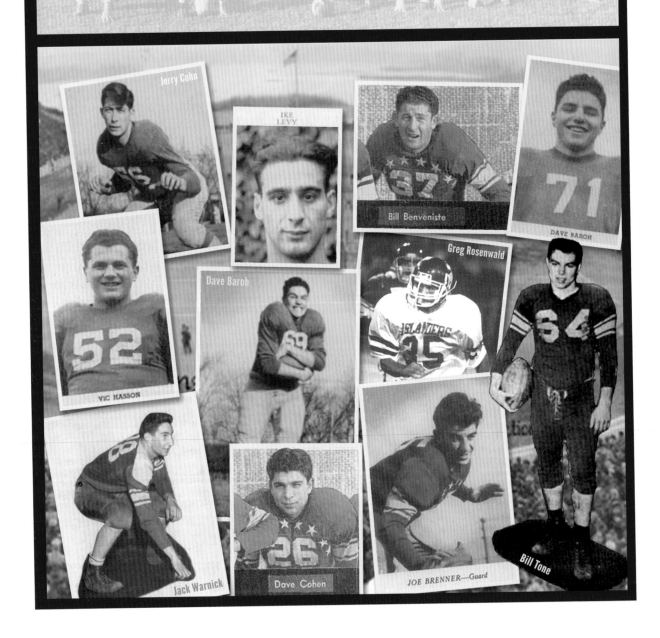

Jerry Cohn

IKE LEVY

Bill Benveniste

DAVE BAROH

Greg Rosenwald

Dave Baroh

VIC HASSON

Bill Tone

Jack Warnick

Dave Cohen

JOE BRENNER—Guard

Lou Baroh

July 11, 1925, Seattle - September 12, 2013, Seattle

Baroh brothers were Bulldogs on the gridiron

For the two sons of Turkish immigrants, early childhood began with a tough blow when Lou and Dave Baroh lost their father at just 11 and 8, respectively. The brothers immersed themselves in sports and played with such heart, it seemed that if the cheers were loud enough, they would gain the attention of someone far away.

LOUIE BAROH—Fullback

Lou was a running back for Garfield High School for two seasons beginning in 1941. At the start of his senior year, Lou was replaced in the starting lineup by highly acclaimed running back Art Harris. But "Louie" was soon back in the headlines after his performance in the team's victory over their cross-town rivals in the second game of the year.

Garfield's newspaper, *The Arrow*, reported: "Showing a powerful running attack, Garfield continued its offensive wave by defeating Roo-sevelt 20-0. Little Louie Baroh took over without any letdown after Art Harris was lost from action with a leg injury in the second quarter."

The next game's story was equally telling:

Six more points for Louie!

"Coming from behind with a brilliant second half rally, the fighting men of Coach Brigham overcame the West Seattle Indians 19 to 13. Louie Baroh's accurate spot passing, Darrell Anderson's receiving and the line's hard blocking led to a victory for the Bulldogs."

Baroh capped his senior season by being the only Garfield player named to the second team All-City roster. Lou was also a guard on the Bulldogs' varsity basketball team.

Here comes Baroh!

Dave Baroh

February 22, 1928, Seattle - October 15, 2008, Seattle

CAPTAIN DAVE BAROH

Dave Baroh followed his brother's illustrious footsteps on the football field by playing under Brigham and his successor, Don Burnet, for three years, from 1943-45. He also excelled in spring sports as a hurdler on the track team.

According to his daughter, Toni, Dave had a great passion for football and waited patiently on the sidelines as an underclassman for his turn to contribute. When the starting linebacker failed to make the tackles needed, the frustrated coach grabbed Dave by the jersey and yelled, "Baroh, get out there!"

Baroh sprints the end in the Kuay fray.

On the first play, Baroh tackled the running back so hard that he knocked himself unconscious. After that, Brigham promoted Baroh to first-string linebacker. In another memorable play, Dave took a pitch from the quarterback at the five-yard line and galloped to the outside, found a seam in the defense and turned upfield 95 yards for a touchdown.

Dave Baroh goes for a long gain against West Seattle.

His mother — who rarely attended games and knew little about football — happened to be there. Experiencing the commotion of Dave's run, she stood up and screamed to everybody within earshot, "That's my son!" While she still had no idea what her son had actually accomplished, she knew that Dave was a hero and she beamed with pride.

During the 1945 season, Dave was elected captain of the squad and was also awarded the fullback position on the All-City second team. Dave and his teammate were also the high-point leaders with three touchdowns apiece that season.

Hymie Harris

April 3, 1920 – May 29, 2010, Seattle

Garfield graduate returned to gridiron in Oregon as a war hero

Hymie Harris and his older brother Ben were batboys for the Seattle Indians when an aging Babe Ruth came to town in 1934 for an exhibition game at Civic Field. After swinging at and missing three consecutive pitches, the Babe turned to the Harris brothers and said, "You can't hit it if you can't see it."

The Babe's words rang true for Hymie Harris in May of 1942 when he was an officer aboard the USS Lexington aircraft carrier during World War II. Japanese Kamikazes flew directly out of the sun to avoid detection and crashed into the Lexington, sinking the Essex-class carrier during the Battle of Coral Sea. Harris told his family that he and hundreds of his crewmates were forced to abandon ship into the shark-infested ocean and tread water for several hours until they could be rescued.

The tall and lanky teenager made the varsity squad as the starting wide receiver at Garfield High School during his freshman year and was the featured wide out for the Bulldogs on the gridiron for four years. In 1937 and 1938, Harris also found a spot on Garfield's basketball squad.

He graduated in 1939 and accepted an invitation to attend the University of Oregon on a football scholarship. Harris made the starting lineup as a wide receiver for the Oregon Ducks as a sophomore before he enlisted in the Navy. During his sophomore season, the Ducks finished with a 3-5-1 record, highlighted by a 38-0 romp over Washington State.

The official media guide for the university listed Harris as a 6'-2", 185-lb. right end who wore No. 21. His coaches praised the native Washingtonian for his "brilliant play" during spring practice, earning him a starting role in the Ducks' season opener against USC. He came home to Seattle after his first year of college in 1940 to play with the West Seattle Yellowjackets of the Northwest Football League. The semi-pro team posted a 5-3-1 record with five shutouts during the only year Harris was on the roster.

Harris' daughter, Nina Mason, said her father returned to school in Eugene after World War II to finish what he had started, both in the classroom and on the football field. The war hero led Oregon to a 4-5 finish in the Pac-10 during his final year of eligibility, including lopsided wins over Idaho and Montana.

"My grandfather was an amazing man who accomplished so much in his life," said his granddaughter, Alexandra Mason. "He met many famous people and became a very well-known football player."

Harris spent his first year after college teaching math and coaching basketball in Portland before deciding to go back to Eugene to earn his master's degree. But instead of an advanced degree, Harris accepted a job selling furniture in

Hymie Harris was a wide receiver for Oregon University

Albany, OR. He moved back to Seattle one year later so that his wife, Frances Pearl, could be closer to her family, and opened Harris Brothers Furniture with his big brother. They quickly outgrew the store on Main Street in Old Bellevue and moved to a larger location in the Eastgate area.

The Harris brothers were both members of the Glendale Country Club. Hymie joined Temple De Hirsch for his family, but attended services at Herzl-Ner Tamid near his home on Mercer Island.

Nina Mason remembers the furniture store very well and the television in the back room that was always tuned to whatever game was being broadcast that day. "Business always came first," said Nina with a sly smile. "But sports came in a close second."

Joe Israel

June 4, 1913 – April 21, 2003, Seattle

Israel lent a hand on and off the field

The stout and sturdy Joe Israel was one of the many successful Sephardic athletes to emerge from the Yesler community. He stood only 5'-5", but went on to earn All-City honors from a Garfield football team that finished in last place.

Israel's heart and power were best described by teammate Brennan King who related a story to Joe's children 30 years later.

It was during the team's first full day of workouts with pads in 1931 when one play and one individual made a lasting impression on King. On the first play of scrimmage, King rolled to his left to meet the running back coming out of the backfield when the sophomore linebacker noticed an undersized guard pulling around the end as the ball carrier's only protection.

As King lowered his shoulder to meet the running back, he suddenly found himself knocked backward and staring up at the sky. It took King

Joe Israel during his days playing football at Garfield High School

a moment to collect his thoughts to realize that little offensive guard had cleaned his clock. Before he could get up, the senior guard was standing over King asking if he was all right. He then extended his hand to help King to his feet, and said, "Hi, my name is Joe Israel. What again was your name?" King never forgot that name or that meeting. In the 1932 Garfield yearbook, Israel's determination on the gridiron was aptly noted: "At his best when the going was tough-

est, [he's] every inch a fighter."

Israel was one of three freshmen invited to practice with the University of Washington varsity squad, but decided to hang up his cleats after one season to focus on his studies and fulltime job.

With a degree in pharmacy, Israel worked for 10 years behind the counter before opening a pharmacy of his own in Ballard. Israel remained there until he "retired" in 1980. At the age of 67, he started a real estate practice and took great satisfaction brokering the purchase of homes for people with special needs on behalf of various organizations.

"Dad would first have to find a home that met that agency's needs, and then took it upon himself to meet neighbors," said his son, Moe Israel. "After going through all that, Dad would donate his commission to the organization that bought the home." From his children's perspective, their father was a strong and tough athlete, a devoted husband and father, and a person of integrity that truly enjoyed helping others.

"Football was his passion; righteousness his legacy," said Moe.

Sandy Lederman

1934, Santa Monica, CA

Controversial Husky QB recorded more headlines than touchdowns

After the first four games in 1955, senior quarterback Sandy Lederman and the University of Washington football team was undefeated and had jumped to No. 12 in the national rankings. After that fourth game, Lederman skipped a practice to protest his lack of playing time and was then suspended by Coach John Cherberg.

In front of a crowd of 42,000 at Husky Stadium, the dogs fell to Baylor 14-7 in an upset that rippled through the rest of the season. Without a passing attack, Washington failed to win another game that season. By the time the dust had settled, the coach had been fired, rehired and then fired again. The athletic director resigned, leading to an investigation that revealed a slush fund for players. As a result of the inquiry, penalties were levied against 27 Husky players, and the team was banned from bowls for two seasons.

The coach had his own explanation for the controversy when he was interviewed about his dismissal by *Sports Illustrated*.

"I found out," said Cherberg, "that Lederman was trying to persuade the most promising young quarterback on the squad to leave school. I bounced Lederman off the squad. But I wound up taking him back. So I took him back, after he apologized to the squad, but he went right on spreading dissension."

In high school, Lederman earned All-America prep honors in 1950 and 1951. When his high school coach, Jim Sutherland, took the Huskies' backfield coach position in 1952, Lederman followed him, breaking the UW freshman record by throwing nine touchdowns in his first year, upstaging the legendary Don Heinrich. The Jewish quarterback went on to set varsity records as a sophomore by completing 92 passes in 189 attempts for 1,157 yards and eight touchdowns.

THE ARLINGTON TIMES, ARLINGTON, WASH

READY FOR PASSING DUEL

Sandy Lederman, sophomore University of Washington quarterback, will match passes with one of the best T-formation QB's in the business—Utah's Jack Rydalch—on October 31 in Seattle, when the Huskies and Utes tangle in a tough intersectional battle. Lederman, a left-hander, will have to be at his best to outpoint the veteran Rydalch and his Utah teammates, as the Rocky Mountain team is rated as one of the top 20 in the nation.

Lederman's claim to fame was a 69-yard touchdown pass completion to George Black against Utah in 1953. It was one of eight completions on the day and one of two tosses for touchdowns. That year he also completed a 57-yard touchdown pass to Mike Monroe against Colorado. During his sophomore season, Washington finished with three wins, six losses and one tie, which included a loss to Colorado by a point and a victory over Utah by a touchdown.

In his junior year, the 5'-11", 185-lb., left-handed quarterback was leading the nation with 35 completions and only one interception when he broke his leg in the third game against Oregon State.

Ben Mahdavi

February 27, 1980, Mercer Island

UW walk-on named football captain and MVP

The Washington State high school wrestling championships were a microcosm of the athletic career of Mercer Island native Ben Mahdavi. After battling his way to the championship match, he took the mat against an opponent who outweighed him by 50 lbs. Mahdavi used his agility and explosiveness to defeat his opponent and take the wrestling title. After graduating, Mahdavi would use those same skills and determination to earn his football scholarship at the University of Washington.

The coaches at Washington apparently did not witness Mahdavi's heroics that day, because they declined to offer a scholarship to the undersized linebacker. Instead, he accepted a football scholarship with the University of Utah and quickly made others realize

he had the ability to play — and start — with any Division One program. He made the decision to transfer to Washington to be closer to his family and try out for the Husky team as a walk-on.

Mahdavi explained that his Judaism and his family were the two elements from his childhood that have impacted every aspect of his life, adding that family remains his top priority. Playing high school football on Friday nights and college football on Saturdays was a decision he made with the support of his mother.

"Playing in Utah did not seem right," he said. "We were not an overly observant Jewish family and only went to shul two or three times every month. But my mom knew how important football was to her youngest son. What else could she do?"

No scholarship meant Mahdavi's single

mother, Julie, needed to generate additional income to pay tuition. She had worked at the JCC for 14 years, but took on the additional task of coordinating the concessions at Husky Stadium to help make up the difference.

Transferring schools also meant that Mahdavi would lose a year of his eligibility.

He was the youngest of three siblings who were in college at the same time. "Coming home [and playing for Washington] meant I could be there for my mom. That was the overwhelming factor."

Mahdavi not only made the team in 1999, he scored the team's first touchdown of the season on a recovered fumble in the opener against BYU. He went on to earn a full scholarship the next year.

"It's almost embarrassing when I go back to campus now," said Mahdavi with a wide grin. "Coaches come up to me to apologize for not recruiting me out of high school. One of them called it one of the biggest mistakes of his career."

Mahdavi scored the Huskies' first touchdown of the season for the second year in a row in 2000, when he scooped up a fumble and rambled 35 yards into the end zone against Idaho. Mahdavi led Pac-10 that season with four fumble recoveries and was named to the conference's All-Academic second team and to the Jewish All-American first team, selected by the

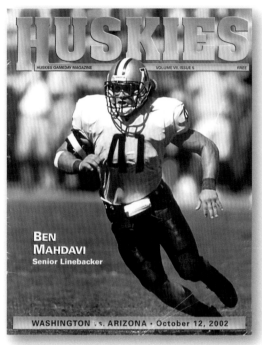

HUSKIES

HUSKIES GAMEDAY MAGAZINE   VOLUME VII, ISSUE 5   FREE

BEN MAHDAVI
Senior Linebacker

WASHINGTON vs. ARIZONA • October 12, 2002

Ben Mahdavi had a team leading 85 tackles in 2001

Jewish Sports Review.

Mahdavi was also chosen as the team captain and defensive MVP, and capped his collegiate career with 14 tackles in a triple overtime win in the Apple Bowl matchup against the No. 4-rated Washington State Cougars. "I can still remember the huge adrenaline rush from stopping the Cougs on a fourth-and-one at the goal line," he said.

Mahdavi ranks being honored by his teammates with the Guy Flaherty Award as the team's most inspirational player and the Chuck Niemi Big Hit Award as his personal highlights from his time playing at the UW.

The determined Mercer Island grad proved the so-called experts wrong again when the undrafted free agent was signed with the Atlanta Falcons. But his time in the NFL was cut short. While chasing a quarterback out of the pocket on the first day on contact drills, Mahdavi suffered a stress fracture to his foot and missed the entire 2003 season. Mahdavi said the best part of his 18 months in Georgia was studying with a rabbi in suburban Atlanta who inspired him to pursue his education and "work my tail off to be the best player I could be."

With his clean bill of health, Mahdavi signed his second free agent contract with the Indianapolis Colts, who sent him to Europe to play linebacker for the Amsterdam Admirals.

While there, Mahdavi was also selected to play with the Berlin Thunder in the World Bowl.

His football career came to an abrupt end the following summer when he ruptured a disc in his back at a pre-season practice with Indianapolis. Mahdavi choose to exit gracefully when faced with surgery and several months of rehabilitation with no guarantee he'd ever play again. A family friend convinced him to go back to business school rather than become a coach. "He said coaches are hired to get fired," Mahdavi remembered. "But there would always be a need for people with level heads."

Julie Mahdavi passed away in 2008, but

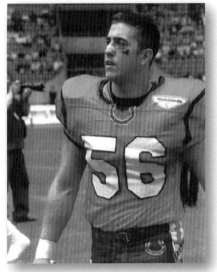
Mahdavi signed with the Indianapolis Colts

not before instilling a work ethic in her son that he carries to this day. "She was my inspiration and the reason I worked so hard to succeed," he said. "Both at football, and now in business."

After some soul searching, Mahdavi went back to Washington to earn his MBA from the Foster School of Business. His network of friends from college and sports helped him secure a position with Lehman Brothers in New York and then in San Francisco. After Lehman Brothers, Ben joined a similar division at Barclays. He credits the team approach he learned on the football field as the key to his success in business.

Taylor Mays

February 7, 1988, Seattle

NFL Bengal was tailor-made for safety

Born in Seattle and raised in the Magnolia neighborhood, Taylor Mays began playing football in the 7th grade and continued all four years at O'Dea High School. As the son of former University of Washington and NFL defensive lineman Stafford Mays and Nordstrom executive Laurie Black, Taylor turned down scholarship offers from his father's alma mater and the Fighting Irish of Notre Dame to join the Trojans football squad at the University of Southern California.

As a youngster, Taylor and his brother were raised in their mother's religion and were each called to the Torah as a bar mitzvah. "I don't think at the time I really understood what it meant," Mays told a reporter. "Now, looking back on it, I feel like I have come a long way in regards to maturity and becoming an adult. I think [Judaism] helped me do that." As a pre-teen, Mays attended Hebrew school twice a week in the years leading up to his 13th birthday and demonstrated to his family and friends his love of sports by having a football-themed event at his bar mitzvah.

He may have received his religious direction from his mother, but his bulk and speed came from his father. Mays was always larger than most of the other students in school and excelled in both soccer and track. In the spring of 2004, he etched himself in the history books by winning the 3A state championship titles in both the 100-meter and 200-meter dash.

Taylor Mays at USC was Pac-10 co-freshman of the year

On the gridiron, Mays was named to the Student Sports Junior All-American team as a defensive back, wide receiver and quarterback during his junior year at O'Dea. As a senior, he compiled 166 tackles, five interceptions and five pass deflections as a safety and caught 36 passes (15 for touchdowns) as a wide receiver for the Fighting Irish.

At USC he became a starter in the second game of his freshman year. With many of his friends and family watching back home, he picked off his first interception in the fifth game against Washington State. His 62 tackles in 12 games helped him earn Pac-10 co-freshman of the year. He returned for his sophomore year in 2007 at an imposing 6'-3" and 230 lbs. and the fastest player on the Trojans squad. He was immediately named the team's starting strong safety.

Expectations were high for the Seattle native in 2008 when he was named to the preseason All-American team. He did not disappoint. Although he didn't register an interception during his junior season, Mays had a team-leading eight pass deflections, with four of them coming in the matchup against California. The junior was named a finalist for the Jim Thorpe Award for his dominance on the defensive side of the ball.

The defensive back shocked pro scouts when he announced his decision to return for his senior year to develop his skills and to complete his education at Southern California. He explained that graduating was important to his parents and he wanted one last shot at leading USC to a Bowl Championship Series National

Championship. He did his best to reach his goal by leading the 2009 Trojans with 96 tackles and with one interception.

With his college coach, Pete Carroll, moving to Seattle to coach of the Seahawks, Mays was understandably disappointed when the Seahawks selected another defensive back in the first round of the NFL draft. Mays was eventually drafted in the second round (49th overall) by the San Francisco 49ers and signed a four-year contract. The news of his selection splashed across the *San Francisco Sentinel*:

"SAN FRANCISCO 49ERS SELECT JEWISH SAFETY TAYLOR MAYS."

As a professional, Mays began his rookie season with San Francisco on special teams, but he was promoted to the starting lineup at free safety after scoring a touchdown in the fourth game of the season against Atlanta on a deflected punt. Mays was traded to the Cincinnati Bengals in 2011, that same year he was inducted into the Southern California Jewish Sports Hall of Fame.

Jamien McCullum

July 11, 1979, Mercer Island

Scholar athlete ranks playing with brother above game-winning touchdown

The oldest son of former Seattle Seahawk receiver Sam McCullum and big brother of Carolina Panther Justin McCullum, Jamien was a PrepStar All-Pac-10 region selection his senior season at Mercer Island High School in 1999 when he recorded 24 receptions for 315 yards and three touchdowns to go along with one rushing TD and one interception. His scholastic prowess also earned him membership into the National Honor Society.

Every kid who ever tossed a football around in the backyard has fantasized about winning the game with an amazing last second catch. Jamien McCullum realized that dream while playing for Stanford University. In the 2000 homecoming game against a highly ranked USC, the Cardinal team was behind most of the game, but managed to drive the ball to the Trojan 20-yard line with only four seconds left on the clock.

"The coaches sent in the play from the sidelines, wanting me to run a corner pattern into the end zone," McCullum recalled. "Our quarterback, Chris Lewis, had ice in his veins. He threw me a perfect pass. I remember making the catch then just being swarmed by my teammates. I looked up at the scoreboard to double-check that we had actually won the game."

McCullum had always wanted to play football like his father, but his parents had encouraged him to play sports that were "less dangerous." He excelled at basketball, baseball and soccer before his parents finally relented and allowed him to try out for football in high school. He excelled as both a flanker and defensive back at Mercer Island. After red shirting his first year at Stanford, the coaches switched him to free safety. He responded to the challenge with 14 tackles, one interception and one fumble recovery that season.

He moved back to offense for his final two years of eligibility, averaging 16 yards per reception on 17 catches, including a 75-yard touchdown pass that still stands as one of the longest scoring plays in Cardinal history.

Even though the McCullum brothers are less than three-and-a-half years apart in age, Jamien's senior season at Stanford was the first time the brothers had played together. "His presence on the field and in the locker room made me a better player and a better teammate," Jamien said. "Sharing that one year with Justin was my own very personal highlight. Even better than beating SC."

With a BA in International Economics and a Masters in Business, McCullum walked away from an NFL free agent contract to accept an offer to become an analyst with the Royal Bank of Canada. "I was tired," he laughed. "It was time to try something new and become an adult."

Jamien McCullum at DoctorBase

Jamien became a bar mitzvah and treasures the teachings of his Jewish faith. "Judaism provided me with a blueprint on how to live my life and gave me reason to work hard," he said. "I believe that being a Jew helped me to better understand people. I am more compassionate and more accepting of how others may believe, both in business and with another person's personal philosophy."

McCullum remained in the San Francisco Bay area. He is currently the vice president of business development at DoctorBase.

Justin McCullum

October 5, 1982, Seattle

Record-setting MI receiver discovered religion of football

Son of former Seattle Seahawk receiver Sam McCullum and younger brother of ex-Stanford wide out Jamien McCullum, Justin was a consensus prep All-American at Mercer Island High School in 2000. He set school records with 103 receptions, 1,700 receiving yards, and 15 touchdowns while being ranked as the No. 14 receiver in the country by SuperPrep his senior year. His accomplishments on and off the field earned him a scholarship to Stanford. Justin also led the MI basketball team to the state championship in 1999.

Growing up in a house filled with talented athletes in the predominantly Jewish community on Mercer Island did not prepare McCullum for the challenges he would face on the football field. He was proud of the Jewish heritage his parents brought to the family, so he was understandably uncomfortable when his teammates in college gathered to recite the Lord's Prayer at the 50-yard line after each game. He was unsure how to react when his team gathered for Bible study after practice. "Fans and players realize that football is like its own religion," said McCullum. "But I was not prepared for the intense [Christian] overtones that dominate every locker room."

Mercer Island was the only team McCullum played with that did not bring religion into the huddle. He was respectful of his teammates at Stanford and stood to the side while his teammates prayed before and after each game. He said the overt religion he experienced in college was amplified once he reached the pros.

"Prayer has its place in sports if you're asking the Lord to watch over you and your teammates to get through the game without injury. And I don't have a problem asking that you perform up to your ability," he explained. "But it does not seem right to pray for victory. That's not why we pray. God has more important

matters to deal with."

McCullum redshirted his freshman season at Stanford, and was forced to sit out the next season with an injured knee. His college career took off during his redshirt sophomore year when he finished with seven catches for 64 yards. He was also a perfect one for one in pass attempts. He caught passes in all nine Cardinal games in 2005, with a career-best nine grabs against USC for 138 total yards. His 36 catches that year included five for touchdowns.

"I'd always been a perfectionist, so there was pressure on me to live up to the standards set by my dad and my brother," he explained. "It was not until my first healthy year in college that I put all those worries away and just became the best player I knew how to be. Everything worked out like it should."

After graduation, McCullum was signed to the practice squad with Carolina Panthers in the NFL, and then traveled across the Atlantic to play with the Amsterdam Admirals in NFL Europe. He returned to the Panthers in 2007, but leg injuries ended his comeback.

McCullum parlayed his Stanford connections into an opportunity to work in the computer software industry in the San Francisco Bay area. He currently works in business development at Box, the leader in cloud content management.

The bonds of friendship McCullum created on the football field in Palo Alto and on Mercer Island, remain the highlight of his career.

Samuel Charles McCullum

November 30, 1952, McComb, MS

Wide receiver christened Kingdome then converted to Judaism

Sam McCullum was brought up to fear the threat of hell and damnation as a strict Southern Baptist. The further his athletic career took him from the Bible Belt days of his youth, the more he distanced himself from religion.

His father's military career took the McCullum family to several posts while Sam grew up. He spent his high school years in Kalispell, MT and stayed close to home during college by playing for Montana State.

"We had experienced the prejudice that comes from pure ignorance," McCullum said. "College gave me the opportunity to learn about different people and many different religions. College was a time of true soul-searching for me."

By the time he was catching passes from Jim Zorn at the Kingdome, McCullum had married a Jewish woman who encouraged him to live his life and to not fear what may come next. Having two young sons inspired him to convert to Judaism.

McCullum said he was content with his own concept of religion, but made the decision to convert to Judaism to shelter his two boys, Jamien and Justin, from the negative aspects of faith he had experienced while growing up. He credits his own father for providing him with the confidence to search for answers beyond the walls of the church.

"Just sitting in the stands as a fan watching football with my sons, I could see the religion that was being forced on the players on the sidelines and even in the middle of the huddle," he said. "Prayer is a good thing at the right time and in an appropriate place. I wanted my sons to be aware that there is so much more to living

Sam McCullum made historic reception at Kingdome

your life to its fullest every day. That is what being Jewish means to me."

McCullum was selected by the Seattle Seahawks in the 1976 veteran allocation draft. Playing for Minnesota the previous two seasons, McCullum had been drafted by the Vikings in the ninth round out of Montana State in 1974.

He started opposite future Hall of Fame receiver Steve Largent in the Seahawks' inaugural season in 1976. McCullum made history when he caught Jim Zorn's first touchdown pass at the Kingdome, in preseason and during the regular season.

As the team's union representative, the fan favorite found himself at the center of controversy during the weeks and months leading up to the 57-day work stoppage in 1982. Players and supporters were outraged when the Seahawks, who claimed McCullum was washed up, released him just prior to the start of the 1982 season, just one year removed from career highs in receptions (62), receiving yards (874) and touchdowns (6).

He returned to the Vikings to play in six of the nine games that season and again in 1983, before he decided to hang up his helmet and cleats on his own terms. In 1992, McCullum was eventually awarded $250,000 from the Seahawks for being illegally let go in 1982 because of his activities as the team's union representative.

After 129 games — including an appearance in the Super Bowl his rookie season with Minnesota — McCullum's most vivid memory of football was before a pre-season game broadcast on *Monday Night Football*. He remembers walking past the broadcast trio of Howard Cosell, "Dandy" Don Meredith and Keith Jackson. "I'll never forget the voice of Howard Cosell calling out to me, 'Have a nice game Sammy.' Howard Cosell knew me by name. He called me Sammy. That's when I knew I had arrived."

McCullum finished his career with 274 receptions for more than 4,000 yards and 26 touchdowns. He also excelled at returning punts and kickoffs, ending up with an average of almost 25 yards per return on 21 kickoffs and 107 yards returned on 24 punts. He averaged

35 catches and over 500 yards over the six years he spent with the Seattle Seahawks.

Sam, his wife, Kathy, and his sons, Jamien and Justin

Jay Posner

June 9, 1979, Bellevue

Kirkland quarterback parlayed athletic skills into Ivy League diploma

It was obvious after his first day on campus: Jay Posner was more comfortable under center than he was walking across campus at Cornell. He stuck out like a sore thumb — a tall blonde

thumb with a Jewish Afro.

"I did not look like everybody else," he remembers. "Sure, I was 6'-4" and weighed about 220 lbs. But it was the tan and curly hair that threw everybody for a loop when I first arrived in upstate New York. Everybody just assumed I was a surfer straight from the beaches in California."

Despite setting records for pass completions and total yardage at Lake Washington High School in Kirkland, Posner knew after his first day of practice at Cornell that he did not possess the physical tools to play professional football. His goal was to do his best for four years and stay healthy while he enjoyed the benefits of an Ivy League university.

"The difference is speed. I thought the game was fast in high school, but it's twice as fast in college, even at a smaller program like Cornell," he said. "The Ivy League will never be confused with powerhouse conferences like the SEC or the Pac-12."

Posner was one of nine quarterbacks competing for playing time when he arrived as a freshman. He quickly worked his way up to No. 3 quarterback as a freshman, and served as the primary backup during his last three years. "My job was to be ready in case the other quarterback was injured. Turns out both of us stayed healthy all four years."

The versatile athete

Jay Posner played quarterback for Cornell

played in every game as a member of the special teams for punts and kick-offs and also played tight end for Cornell's Big Red. After being picked to finish last, Posner said his teammates "played above their heads" to finish second in the conference during his sophomore and junior years (1999 and 2000). "We overachieved thanks to some clutch play and great coaching."

The backup quarterback did have his moment of glory when he threw his first pass in the second game of the season his sophomore year. The coaches called for a "pump and go" route on his first play from scrimmage. Posner responded with a 50-yard strike that turned out to be the longest completion of his collegiate career.

Posner's connections at Cornell helped him land his first job with a firm on Wall Street. He received his job offer on Sept. 9, 2001. "Firms up and down Wall Street rescinded job offers after the tragic events and the fallout from 9/11," he said. "Apparently, I made a good enough impression during my interviews, because it was the Jewish connections from Cornell alumni who convinced my firm to hire me anyway. That made my four years of playing back-up worth every second on the sidelines." The Cornell grad has spent the past four year as director of bond trading for Citi in Chicago.

Growing up, Posner and his sister, Amy (Wolff), traveled to Chicago for the Maccabi Games in 1988. Jay was only 8, but was there to cheer for his sister when she competed in the hurdles. He later represented Seattle at the games in Cleveland and Los Angeles, and was part of the first basketball team to defeat the team from Israel during the American version of Maccabi. The Maccabi Games also helped strengthen Posner's friendship with Mercer Island grad Ben Mahdavi. The pair shared a studio apartment while the linebacker was practicing with the Atlanta Falcons. "We were joined at the hip and ate almost every meal together for 6-7 months," Posner remembers. "Ben honored me by asking me to sign the ketubah at his wedding. The Games were much more than athletic competition. They also helped create lifelong friendships."

The quarterback's father, Terry Posner, spearheaded the effort to raise funds and recruit athletes to send the first Seattle Maccabi team to Chicago in 1988.

Greg Rosenwald

January 27, 1972, Seattle

MI athlete rushed and raced through childhood

The same passionate drive that inspired an undersized Greg Rosenwald to become an all-conference fullback in football and goalie in soccer at Mercer Island High School have helped propel him to a successful career in residential real estate.

The coaching staff at Mercer Island High School was too busy winning league championships to notice that Rosenwald was too small to line up at fullback on the varsity football team or defend the home team goal in soccer.

Greg Rosenwald was a fullback for MIHS

At 5'-8" and only 160-lbs, Rosenwald was named the KingCo 3A all-conference fullback as a junior when he helped lead the Islanders to an undefeated season in 1989. He broke the mold again during spring sports when he protected the Mercer Island goal during the prep soccer season in 1990.

"The coaches told me that I played large," Rosenwald said with a smile. "It was all about contact for me. My quickness helped me overcome my lack of speed. I would hit the hole and just keep driving my legs until the officials blew the whistle to end the play."

The Mercer Island native often carried the ball 20 or more times from his position as the only back in a spread offense, averaging more than 4.5 yards per carry during high school. His personal highlight was scoring the winning touchdown against Inglemoor on a 14-yard burst during the Islanders undefeated season. Rosenwald gained 117 yards on a rain-soaked field the night Mercer Island was eliminated from the state playoffs.

With varsity football games on Friday nights, Rosenwald was forced to decide at an early age between his love of sport and his commitment to Shabbat. He made the decision to participate in Friday night football with the full endorsement from his family.

"I'm sure there was probably a Jewish holiday or two during my playing days in high school too, but there was never any pressure from my family not to play," he said.

His drive to finish first began at the tender age of 8 when Greg and his father were introduced to midget racing cars at an auto show.

"It was love at first sight," Greg remembered. "My dad was a car buff, so he was all in favor of getting me behind the wheel at an early age. Racing was a thrill. But winning was an addiction."

Rosenwald had immediate success on the track and eventually moved up to stock cars and open-wheel competition. He was honored

Rosenwald behind the wheel of his Quarter Midget race car

twice as Sportsman of the Year as a teenager in a vote by his fellow drivers.

The father and son team traveled together to compete at tracks in Canada and throughout Western Washington. Rosenwald remembered very clearly that he was often the only Jewish driver at an event and that many of the young drivers had probably never met a Jew before.

He laughed, because years later he realized that one of the drivers he competed with at an early age was racing legend Jeff Gordon.

The dedicated athlete made the very practical decision to give up the expensive participation in motor sports to focus his attention—and finances—on a college education. "That decision was probably influenced by being Jewish."

Even though he was disappointed that he was not recruited to play football at the University of Washington, Rosenwald remains a dedicated alumnus and loyal Husky fan who attends every home football game and as many road games as possible every year. He admits he is still the same height that he was in high school, but probably not the same weight.

Greg still lives on Mercer Island and is a real estate broker at Coldwell Banker Bain. He and his wife, Jennifer, have three girls, Rainey and twins Natalie and Emily.

Harry Schneiderman

1906, Ukraine – January 13, 1990, Seattle

Newsboy excelled on the gridiron

The Schneiderman family, with five sons and four daughters, fled czarist Russia and landed in Portland, OR in 1907 when the youngest son, Harry, was just six months old. While still in the first years of elementary school, Schneiderman was expected to help earn money for the family. Following in his brothers' footsteps, he began working as a newsboy in Portland at age seven, selling day sheets. By the time he was 14, he graduated to "night newsie," which allowed him to make better money "owning" his own street corner to sell the evening papers.

Also like his older brothers, Schneiderman loved football and played all four years at Commerce High School, and was named team captain his senior year in 1925. But playing football was a heated family issue. His older brother, Marcus, who also played football at Commerce, broke-

his foot during a game and continued to play, resulting in a permanent injury. Though his parents questioned his decision, Schneiderman convinced them and excelled as a lineman and center. For three years in a row he was selected to Portland's All-Star team. In his senior year, several colleges pursued him, but he chose the University of Washington.

Schneiderman played on Husky teams coached by Enoch Bagshaw and was named team captain of the freshmen 11. On offense he played center, moving up each year within the full football squad. He also backed up the defensive line.

In his senior year in 1928, he lettered, starting in games for a Husky team that went 7-4. Two of his teammates later made names for themselves off the field, future senator Warren Magnuson and future King County prosecutor Charles Carroll. Carroll was a great All-American running back who was later inducted into the Football Hall of Fame. After Schneiderman graduated, a college in Oregon tried to woo him back to coach their football team, but he declined.

Schneiderman was UW team captain in 1925

When Carroll was named King County prosecutor, he needed staff people he could trust and hired his former teammate, Schneiderman. The football connection carried on for another generation as Schneiderman's son, Barry, worked for Carroll as deputy prosecutor. Schneiderman also owned a service station in Pioneer Square during the Depression and World War II. According to his daughter, people would come into the station and if they were short on money, would ask Harry for a couple of dollars' worth. They promised to pay him back, and always did. In later years, Schneiderman became a bailiff in the King County Superior Court until he retired in 1982.

Abe "Iron Man" Spear

October 14, 1912, Mirgorod, Ukraine – November 1, 1986, Seattle

"Strauss Boy" became "Iron Man" at UW

Abe Spear was born in 1912 in the city of Mirgorod, then within Russia but currently in the Ukraine. He was eight years old when his parents immigrated to the US, settling first in South Bend, IN, where they had relatives. The family then moved to nearby Chicago where Abe spent the next eight years.

Spear played lineman on his high school football team and received citywide recognition for his talents. His team won the local championship, received national recognition and an invitation to play in a championship game in Florida.

Spear was recruited to play for the University of Washington by Dr. Alfred Strauss, known

as "Doc Strauss," a UW alumnus and football scout living in Chicago. Strauss was so successful luring Chicago-area players to Seattle, these recruits were referred to as the "Strauss Boys," or sometimes as the "Chicago Gangsters."

Spear played on offense and defense every minute of every game in 1935 for the UW

Under the leadership of legendary UW coach Jim Phelan, Spear and a few of his teammates earned the nickname the "Iron Men." by playing the entire 60 minutes of the game - on offense and defense - of every game of the 1935 season. That year he was named to the All-Coast team and was invited to play in the East-West Shrine Game. His teammates also selected him to receive the highest honor given to a UW football player, the Guy Flaherty Most Inspirational Player Award. That same year, Spear was named to *American Jewish World*'s Jewish All-America team.

After graduation in 1936, coach Phelan hired Spear to be an assistant coach. That season, the Huskies earned a spot in the Rose Bowl, but fell to the University of Pittsburgh. Spear continued as an assistant coach until 1940. The young coach married Sonia Wachtin in 1938. They had two sons, Bradley and Jeffrey, and a daughter, Sandra.

Bill Tone

April 18, 1933, Tacoma - October 26, 1998, Tacoma

BILL TONE

Growing up in Tacoma, Bill Tone played halfback for Stadium High School between 1948 and 1950. As the captain of the sophomore squad in 1948, Stadium's yearbook summed up Tone's talents best: "Led by the outstanding playing of Bill Tone, the young Tigers fought their way through a good season taking five out of eight games to win the city championship."

The following year, Tone was involved in what was nominated "the play of the year;" as described in the yearbook, "Bill Tone swept around right end with the ball and would have been away for a TD if an English bulldog hadn't run in his way and 'tackled' him. Apparently thinking he hadn't done enough, the dog took the ball from Tone and started to run away with it."

The Tigers came roaring back during Tone's senior year, going undefeated in nine games and capturing both the city and cross-state league titles. Tone was honored as a first-string selection to the All-City and cross-state team and selected to play in the Washington State High School All-Star Game.

"Three generations of Husky fans!"

From the
Keller Sulman Family

Happy 80th Birthday

Alan Knopf

from your
loving family and children,

Howard, Vikki and Curtis

Thanks for being such a great
coach, father and sportsman
for all these years.

Alan Knopf, Rutgers University, 1952

Harry Schneiderman

The family of Harry Schneiderman salutes his life and legacy as a
University of Washington varsity football player, respected
professional and a very good friend and family member to many.

We appreciate the efforts of the WSJHS to preserve
this slice of local Jewish history,

**Israel Rabinowitz
Judy Schneiderman Rosen
Stuart and Mirle Bussell,
great-grandchildren Dalia and Noah
Joshua and Alix Rabinowitz,
great-grandchildren Jessica, Rachel and Ari
Paul Schneiderman
Leah and Tim Snyder,
great-grandchildren Cassidy and Stella**

Members of ZBT Fraternity playing football at Montlake Field in 1940.
Back row: l to r, Stan Tobin, Marlowe Goldsby, Frank Friedman, Red Lachman
Front row: ? , Norton Schaeffer, ? , Herb Lipman, Alan Lurie, ?

Remembering
Stan Tobin
who enjoyed an active participation and love of sports.
As sports editor of the UW Daily, he covered the campus sports beat and remained a lifelong devoted Husky fan.

**Goldie Tobin
Brian Tobin
David Tobin
Marcy Tobin & Dan Katz**

In honor of
Our Favorite Team

—⋘—

Abe and Sonia Spear

—⋘—

from your children,
grandchildren
and great-grandchildren

Elliot Yashar
Redmond High School
Mustangs, Varsity 2010

Michael Yashar
Redmond High School
Mustangs, 2012

In Loving Memory

Irving Epstein

Outdoorsman, Garfield High football player,
hydroplanedriver, target shooter and
Husky football fan

The Epstein Family

HORSE RACING

Proudly sponsored by

KEN AND MARLEEN ALHADEFF

Ken Alhadeff

August 15, 1948, Seattle

From yell king to the sport of kings

Kenneth Alhadeff

He was not gifted with the ability to hit a 90-mph baseball or sink an 18-foot jump-shot, but Kenny Alhadeff proudly boasts that as a yell king he took part in more athletic events during his tenure at Franklin High School than any other student in his graduating class.

As a sports fan throughout his life, Alhadeff used his yell leader talents cheering on the Seattle Supersonics in their championship playoff run and as a season ticketholder to the Seahawks and Mariners.

As the grandson of Joseph Gottstein, the man who built Longacres racetrack, Alhadeff grew up surrounded by some of the world's greatest four-legged athletes. According to an article in the *Seattle Post-Intelligencer*, Kenny and his older brother Michael "followed their grandfather around Longacres like proud puppies." Alhadeff recalls pitching pennies with a variety of characters with names like Boxcar and Whistling Harry and walking along the railroad ties with track steward, Buster Wiles, a former stunt double for Errol Flynn.

Kenny and Michael were required to work in the family business as soon as they celebrated their bar mitzvahs. Michael eventually succeeded his father, Morrie, as president, and Kenny became the senior vice president of track operations.

Today, Alhadeff's office in downtown Seattle is a personal sports museum of sorts. The original glass panel from the Washington Jockey Club (the corporate umbrella for Longacres) is displayed near the entrance. Ken's high school letter is in the same trophy case as a basketball signed by the 1978-79 championship Sonics team, a Mariners batting helmet signed in 2001 by all the players of that 116-win team, and a football autographed by the Seahawks who played in Super Bowl XL in 2006.

The rest of his office is filled with pieces of family history that date back to the early days

Ken Alhadeff with son Aaron and wife Marleen at the Turf Club

of Longacres, including the family's riding silks of Elttaes Stable (Seattle spelled backwards). Next to it is the harness worn by Elttaes Slew, the only Washington-bred offspring of Seattle Slew, and a horse many thought would take the Kentucky Derby.

The harness is a tragic reminder to Ken of the fleeting dreams inherent in Thoroughbred racing. While working out on the backstretch at Emerald Downs, Elttaes Slew spooked, broke loose from her groom and hit a retaining wall at full speed. The horse died instantly and the entire racing community was struck by the loss. After the death of Elttaes Slew, Alhadeff questioned his involvement in the sport, but Margo, an "honorary daughter" of his family, convinced him to attend that year's breeders auction.

Despite his reservations, Alhadeff spotted a yearling and couldn't shake his hunch. He purchased "Margo's Gift," and trainer Doris Harwood began exercising the Thoroughbred. In May of 2007, he won his maiden race at Emerald Downs and two stakes races thereafter — one by disqualification. Alhadeff entered Margo's Gift in the Gottstein Futurity, a race named in honor of his grandfather. He told a *Seattle P-I* reporter at the time, "It's no secret

26-1 longshot Margo's Gift takes the Breeders' Cup Stakes

that I want to win my grandfather's race more than the Longacres Mile. My grandfather Joe taught me to love this game."

But Alhadeff would have to wait on that dream as Margo's Gift finished third. The winner of the Futurity, Smarty Deb, was also trained by Harwood and set the trainer on a course for the Breeders' Cup at Monmouth Park in New Jersey. With room on the plane for another horse, Harwood asked Alhadeff if she could take Margo's Gift. He thought it was crazy, but agreed.

Harwood entered Margo's Gift in the Favorite Trick Breeders' Cup Stakes, a six-furlong, $250,000 race. On October 26, 2007, the rain had not let up all day. The track was a sloppy soup and Margo's Gift went off at 26-1. The horse broke from the gate and languished in the back of the pack. Trailing seven other horses with only two furlongs left, jockey Ricky Frazier let his ride loose and guided the 2-year-old through a crowd on the inside rail. The improbable longshot snatched the victory by one and a half lengths.

With his enthusiasm restored, Alhadeff purchased a colt at the September 2011 sale and named him Music of My Soul, named for a song from Memphis, the Tony-award-winning musical produced by Alhadeff and his wife, Marleen. Music of My Soul was winless in three starts, but captured his maiden victory in the Dennis Dodge Stakes at Emerald Downs on September 9, 2012. The next race Alhadeff set his sights on was two weeks later, the elusive Gottstein Futurity.

The race was filled with an unbelievable slew of coincidences. It was scheduled on September 23, three years to the day that Memphis opened on Broadway. The musical began touring the country and just happened to return to Seattle's Fifth Avenue Theatre, where the show was first workshopped, with its run overlapping the Gottstein Futurity. And who were the race's honorary stewards that day? None other than Joe Gottstein's grandson, Kenny, and Marleen. It would be too cliché to write a screenplay in which the dark bay 2-year-old wins, but that's just what happened. And it wasn't just any win, it was a victory the demonstrated the incredible heart of this race horse.

In the one-mile race, Music of My Soul went out to the front early on, racing head to head with Mike Man's Gold, four and five lengths ahead of the rest of the pack. At the three-quarter mark, Mike Man's Gold began to fade while FinallyGotaBentley made a hard-driving move in the final turn, taking a one-length lead. Down the stretch, Music of My Soul continued

Music of My Soul captured the 2012 Gottstein Futurity for Alhadeff

to fight back, gaining on the lead horse in the last 100 yards. As he crossed the finish line, the track announcer shouted, "Music of My Soul. What a tough winner!"

As the honorary steward, Alhadeff handed the trophy with his grandfather's name on it to himself. Music of My Soul went on to be honored as the Washington Thoroughbred Breeders & Owners Association and Emerald Downs' top 2-year-old of 2012.

Harwood, who also trained Music of My Soul, and is the leading stakes winner at Emerald Downs with 56 victories, called the most important race of her career. To *The Seattle Times* she said, "I wanted to win for this man," poking Alhadeff in the chest. "I wanted to give him his first win in his grandfather's race."

Winning, of course, is important to Alhadeff. But his interest in the local longevity of the sport is demonstrated in his actions. Of the more than 100 Thoroughbreds he has owned over the years, nearly all of them have been Washington-bred. This, more than anything, reflects his commitment to a sport and an industry that was brought back to life by his grandfather. "We could have walked away," said Alhadeff, "but we stayed in it because we love the sport and it's part of who we are."

Mark B. Alhadeff

June 9, 1950, Seattle

While most racing fans at Longacres were focused on one or two horses, Mark Alhadeff had to keep all of them in focus. From 1966 to 1970, the Sammamish High School graduate worked for Criterion Films, which provided filming services for racetracks. Starting as a "film runner" whose job it was to deliver the exposed film to the processing lab, he steadily progressed to head cameraman. In Ben Mitchell's "There They Go" column published in the 1970s in a South Seattle newspaper, he described the perks of Alhadeff's job: "High atop the grandstand on the highest building at Longacres you will find the outsized and overgrown camera operated by Mark Alhadeff. His position gives him an unsurpassed panoramic view of the entire track and the race in progress." Mark's job was to capture every horserace in order to give the racing stewards the ability to judge any infractions that might occur. During Longacres' off-season, Alhadeff would capture the action at Yakima Meadows and Santa Anita Race Track.

Michael Alhadeff

March 8, 1945, Seattle

Alhadeff inherited grandfather's passion for horse racing

There was never any doubt what Michael Alhadeff would do when he grew up. The older grandson of Longacres founder Joe Gottstein was drawn to the competitive nature of Thoroughbred racing and enjoyed the intricacies of orchestrating the racing conditions to put on a good show.

"Racing is in my blood," Alhadeff said in a very matter-of-fact way. "From the time I played tennis in high school, to softball games in the Longacres league, I inherited the need to

Michael Alhadeff

excel in everything. Some things don't always turn out as well as possible. But never because of a lack of effort on my part."

Michael Alhadeff with jockey Gary Stevens and father Morrie

His competitive nature lured him to the four-legged athletes on the backstretch. When he was given charge of the track's operation, his familiarity with the racing end of the business led to his overseeing the condition book for the season, setting the types of races and the purse amounts. The process found Alhadeff striking a balance between creating races for the horses stabled at the track and those that would attract the West Coast's best runners.

While Michael Alhadeff handled the horse-racing end of the business, his father, Morrie, was the front man who added a sense of style to the track. His younger brother, Kenny, handled the concessions and restaurants. "Kenny, my dad and I made a great team," said Michael. "We really balanced each other out and worked well together. Those were some very special days we had at Longacres."

Alhadeff's favorite memory from his 16 years as general manager (1972-1988) was the 1981 Longacres Mile. Washington-bred Troop-er Seven won the previous year's one-mile race, and his entry attracted a slate of legendary jockeys and the best horses on the West Coast. Willie Shoemaker, Laffit Pincay, Jr. and Sandy Hawley all made their way to the Northwest that summer with the same goal in mind — prevent Trooper Seven from becoming the first back-to-back Mile winner.

"The race attracted a record crowd at Longacres of more than 25,900," remembers Alhadeff. "And just like in the movies, Trooper Seven, ridden by local jockey Gary Baze, beat all those more famous horses and big-time jockeys."

Trooper Seven wins the 1981 Longacres Mile

Another memory Alhadeff recalls was when Seattle Slew made his first and only appearance at Longacres. As the only undefeated Triple Crown of Thoroughbred Racing winner in history, Seattle Slew arrived in Renton with tremendous fanfare for an exhibition called the Golden Gallop.

"Horses are smart, but Seattle Slew was special. He knew what was going on that day and played his part perfectly," Alhadeff remembers. "At one point, he walked past the crowd, turned

Table 15 wins the 1990 Independence Day Handicap

his head to look back and then arched his back so everybody could see him in all of his glory. He loved the spotlight."

Throughout his tenure at the track, Alhadeff always made it a point to be at the yearling sale, but mostly watched from the sidelines. In 1986 when a colt came on the block, he was standing next to trainer Howard Belvoir and they liked what they saw. Three thousand dollars later, Take Me Back became his first horse and the winner of its first two races. Alhadeff was hooked. Since then, he and his wife Marjorie have owned some 35 to 40 Thoroughbreds. Table 15 won two stakes races as a 3-year-old and the Independence Day Handicap at 4, beating the venerable Captain Condo. Spite & Malice, named for his mother Joan's favorite card game, won two stakes races and placed in another.

In 2002 though, Sundance Circle was the horse that began the backstretch whispers. After breaking the track record for six-and-a-half furlongs at Emerald Downs as a 2-year-old,

early talk of competing in the Kentucky Derby was becoming prophetic. Sundance Circle, however, needed surgery to remove bone chips and never fully recovered. "It was sad he never came back, but he's probably my most special horse," said Alhadeff.

Though there may have never been any doubt what Michael Alhadeff would do when he grew up, his passion for Thoroughbreds and his commitment to racing in Washington go beyond family responsibilities and speak more about his desire to fan the flames of his competitive spirit.

Sundance Circle wins the 2003 NWSS Strong Ruler Stakes

Morrie Alhadeff

November 14, 1914 – November 8, 1994, Seattle

Radio personality brought charm, style and popularity to Longacres

With a flair for the dramatic, Jerry Morris was building a promising career in radio and television. After time spent as a news reporter, sports commentator and disc jockey for various Seattle radio stations, his big break came in 1945 when he was assigned to cover the United Nations conference for network television. Among family, Jerry Morris was better known as Morrie Alhadeff, and his father-in-law, the founder of Longacres racetrack, had other plans for him.

Joe Gottstein was not one to mince words and in 1947 suggested that his son-in-law take charge of public relations at the track. Alhadeff

Morrie Alhadeff was better known as "Jerry Morris" on the mic in 1945

described the conversation with the *Seattle Post-Intelligencer* in 1978: "He was a very outspoken fellow. He asked why I didn't come out and give him a hand. I pointed out that I didn't know anything about racing. He said I did know something about public relations and said, 'Come on out and try it for three months.' That was the longest three months in history." For the next 41 years, Alhadeff used his media savvy and passion for the arts to bring even more success to the Renton oval than his father-in-law could have ever envisioned.

Morrie's son, Ken, said that his father's greatest contribution was introducing horse racing to an entire generation in the Puget Sound area. In 1956, Alhadeff created and hosted a live television show called "This is Longaces" on KING 5. It is believed to be the first weekly television show in the country devoted exclusively to horse racing. Viewers who knew nothing about Thoroughbred racing were now growing familiar with the sport of kings. "He really was a great promoter and brought a lot of attention to Longacres," said Morrie's son Michael.

As this new audience ventured to the track, they were greeted with an unexpected elegance. Little by little, Alhadeff had filled the track with one of the largest equestrian art collections in the country. Paintings and sculptures by Eustace Ziegler and Kenneth Callahan adorned the

Longacres Race Track, circa 1950

Turf Club, clubhouse, and throughout the betting areas, adding a style matched by few other racetracks. The dining experience was also important to Alhadeff. "Dad was a gourmet cook," said Michael, "and he would be very involved with that operation, bringing in new recipes to the track's kitchen." At one point, the Turf Club was considered by many to be one of the best restaurants in the Seattle area.

The more he added his own touch to Longacres, the more successful it became. Said Alhadeff to the *Post-Intelligencer* in 1978, "You learn this business by walking and touching and doing. You can't read a book on how to run a racetrack. It's a unique

Alhadeff with PI Sports Editor Royal Brougham

business, and certainly one of the most exclusive in the world. I learn something every place I go. If you are willing to see as well as look, you have to learn."

Alhadeff's marketing skills brought "Derby"-themed fashion shows to Frederick & Nelson, sponsorships of Little League teams and radio campaigns on rock-and-roll stations. A television campaign featuring local celebrities and the song "Camptown Races" brought the catch phrase "doo dah" to Longacres as well as bigger and bigger crowds. Alhadeff doubled Longacres' seating capacity with the construction of the Paddock Club, North Grandstand and Gazebo. Attendance reached a peak in the early 1980s with the Longacres Mile race attracting more than 20,000 fans year after year. In 1981, a record crowd of 25,900 racing fans watched Washington-bred Trooper Seven become the first horse to win consecutive Longacres Miles. With $2,770,179 bet on that one day, it was the largest handle ever in

Alhadeff with sons Michael, left, and Ken, right

Washington and was never exceeded.

Alhadeff was equally attentive to the backstretch, home to the hundreds of horsemen that worked at the track. As noted in an interview with the *Post-Intelligencer*, "He put in long, hands-on work days to maintain the success of the track. He made early-morning visits to the barn area. He was a tough negotiator with horsemen and union representatives and took a close personal interest in upgrading the track."

With horse racing's integrity often questioned, Alhadeff installed one of the world's most sophisticated, state-of-the-art television centers at the track's finish line, plus nine cameras placed at various positions around the track. Each captured the race at angles that could reveal infractions and grounds for disqualification.

From his first earliest days in publicity to his 17 years as president beginning in 1971, Alhadeff oversaw Longacres' most profitable era. In 1974, he was honored with the Thoroughbred Racing Association of North America's Distinguished Service Award. And, in an unprecedented move, the Association named

Alhadeff the president in 1983. Ken compared the executive position to the commissioner of Major League Baseball or the National Football League. He said TRA presidents were normally chosen from among horse owners and racetrack operators from just a few states — Kentucky, Florida and occasionally California.

Along with his wife Joan, Morrie Alhadeff owned some 50 Thoroughbreds over his lifetime. Different Beat was easily the most accomplished, winning multiple stakes races throughout its career in the 1980s. Alhadeff used his stable and the track's spotlight to raise awareness as well. As part of a ballot campaign to fund emergency medical services in King County, he named one horse Medic One and gave all the proceeds to the effort.

In 1988, Alhadeff was named Longacres' chairman of the board and passed the day-to-day responsibilities to his sons, Michael as president and Kenny as vice president of track operations.

As Seattle's appetite for other professional sports grew and other gambling opportunities were introduced, track attendance began to steadily decline in the late '80s. "You have to

Joan Alhadeff, wife of Morrie and daughter of Joe Gottstein

remember," Kenny Alhadeff explained, "at one time, Longacres was the only game in town. It was part of Seattle long before the Seahawks, before the Mariners and before there was any kind of lottery. There is only a limited amount of money available for gaming and recreation. Longacres was leaking money faster than we could plug the holes."

Alhadeff and his sons announced the sale of the property to Boeing in 1990, with the track operating for two additional years. The Alhadeff family continued to provide assistance to the Longacres family and funded purses for Thoroughbred races throughout the state. Feelings for Longacres ran deep among devoted fans and horsemen, and there was nothing the charismatic son-in-law could do to remove the pain of selling the track. At the annual *P-I*

Alhadeff during the last years at Longacres

Sports Star of the Year banquet, Alhadeff was booed so badly he had to leave the building.

"People did not understand that we loved Longacres as much, or more, than anybody," said Kenny. "[The sale] was more than a painful business decision. It was something we had to do."

The ponies found a new home in 1996 when Emerald Downs opened in Auburn. There the Longacres Mile still continues to beckon the fastest horses in the country and fans can still enjoy a majority of Alhadeff's art collection on display.

Morrie Alhadeff died on November 8, 1994. Governor Mike Lowry proclaimed November 14, 1994 "Morrie Alhadeff Day" in recognition of his lifelong contributions to the public good. It would have been his 80th birthday.

Mervin "Sonny" Gorasht

December 1, 1937, Calgary, Alberta

Canadian architect built stable of Thoroughbreds

When Mervin "Sonny" Gorasht is called to the Torah on Shabbat morning at the Capitol Hill minyan, after the completion of the aliyah he makes a Mi Sheberach - a personal appeal for the well being of those dear to him. He includes his wife Gena, his daughters and their families, the entire Congregation, and often, at the very end, he asks on behalf of his "soosim", his horses. Maybe that is why he has enjoyed great success for his almost twenty years of involvement in the racing and breeding of Thoroughbred horses.

The second child of immigrant parents from Poland and Romania, Sonny Gorasht grew up on the prairies of Alberta where, at that time, farming and ranching were the economic engine of the province and Calgary was the commercial heart of the region. Horses and cattle were an everyday part of the landscape. The world-renowned Calgary Stampede, an annual, week-long celebration honoring the native tribes that first roamed the prairies, was best known for its international caliber rodeo competition. Everyone looked forward to Stampede week; everyone wanted to be a "cowboy", including the young, impressionable Sonny Gorasht.

Hockey season was over and the warming

Sonny Gorasht, 3rd from left, in winner's circle with legendary jockey Laffit Pincay, Jr.

spring air was full of promise when the natural curiosity of the 15-year-old took Sonny to the barns at the Calgary Stampede grounds, where Thoroughbred horses were stabled for the spring race meeting. Seeing an eager kid who was just the right size, Joe Holden, a trainer with three horses in his barn, gave Sonny a job exercising his horses each morning before the high school bell rang.

As a result of that initial exposure, Sonny fell in love with the horses, the sensory stimulation and all of the culture related to Thoroughbreds and racing. He still remembers the hot coffee in a paper cup that warmed his hands in the pre-daylight hours of the cold spring mornings, the smells of clean straw and fresh hay and liniments and saddle leather mixed with all the other natural barn odors. Vivid too were the sounds, the heavy, rhythmic breathing of working horses whose warm breath was condensed by the cool early morning air, the thumping

Gorasht's Bay Street Blues winning the Washington Thoroughbred Breeders' Association Lads Stakes on August 31, 1997

sound of hooves digging into a freshly graded dirt track. Also imprinted in his memory is the lithe, loping yet elegant way that the horses moved as they walked around the shed row, cooling down after their morning's workout.

Forty years later, in the offices of his Seattle architectural firm, Sonny took a call from his cousin, Allen Mendelman. Allen had owned and successfully raced Thoroughbreds in Canada for a few years and was at the breeding farm of his friend, Ernie Braithwaite on Whidbey Island, buying two yearling colts for racing. Without a lot of forethought, Allen asked Sonny if he would like a piece of the action with two horses, Arctic Sunrise and King Bernsie. And without a lot of thought, Sonny agreed to get in the game. It was the beginning of a long racing partnership between Sonny and Braithwaite, a continuing relationship that has gone into the record books of horse racing in the northwest as winning owners and breeders of champion runners.

Arctic Sunrise provided Sonny and Gena with their first visit to the winner's circle when the two-year-old colt broke his Maiden at Yakima Meadows. "Even though the race was anything but the caliber of a 'Kentucky Derby', the victory provided an adrenalin rush unlike any other," said Sonny. There have been many more visits to the winner's circle at race tracks in the

Gorasht and his granddaughter Ella Endres at Emerald Downs with Lasting Rose.

Pacific Northwest, California and Canada since that day in Yakima, but "the thrill of victory remains undiminished and the adrenalin rush is renewed every time."

Optimism is the key personality trait necessary for anyone involved in horse racing. To emphasize the point, Sonny likes to tell of a recent lunch he had with Herman Sarkowsky, who loves horse racing and has enjoyed great success with it at the highest levels. At 85 years of age Herman had recently completed his annual physical check-up. When Sonny asked, "How's your health, Herman?", Herman replied, "Well, I'm still buying yearlings!"

Looking back, Sonny remembers meeting friends years ago and their greeting was invariably, "Hi Sonny, how are Gena and the girls?" Today, almost everyone greets him with, "Hi Sonny, how are the horses?" That question really means "Are you making any money?" For those who are involved with racing horses, if you are making money, it's a business. If not, it can be an expensive hobby. To insure that his passion for breeding and racing Thoroughbred horses tilts to the business side of the ledger, it's a sure bet that whenever Sonny is called to the Torah, he will continue to ask for a blessing for his "soosim."

Dr. Alex Grinstein

October 5, 1900, Denver – December 24, 1984, Seattle

Ringside, courtside, sideline, diamond, winner's circle: sports doctor was a Seattle fixture

Chicago was a tough city in 1921. Surviving as a professional boxer at the time was even tougher. Mixing it up in the ring was how Alex "Skelly" Grinstein not only paid for his medical school tuition at Northwestern University, but it also provided the sturdy flyweight with an athlete's perspective that served him throughout his career.

Dr. Alexander Grinstein's boxing background and medical skills made him uniquely qualified to be selected as the ring physician for the Washington State Athletic Commission in the 1930s. "He was required to examine every boxer before each fight," said Bill Grinstein, the doctor's younger son. "He was also the ring doctor who stopped the fight if somebody was cut or injured."

In the early '60s he was called into the ring of a professional fight when both boxers went to the mat. According to *Sports Illustrated*, he called the first double TKO in boxing history. The relationships he nurtured with fight pro-

moters and local dignitaries opened the doors for Grinstein to spend his life surrounded by collegiate and professional athletes at virtually every sports venue in Seattle

A 1916 Franklin High School graduate, Grinstein began boxing while completing his pre-med studies at the University of Washington. When he finished medical school at Northwestern, the young doctor returned home to open his practice. In 1925, one of Grinstein's first patients was theater owner and sportsman Joe Gottstein. The two became fast friends, and when Gottstein opened Longacres racetrack in 1933, Grinstein served as the track physician.

Dr. Alex Grinstein was the track physician at Longacres

"My father was one of several community leaders who backed Joe to establish Longacres in 1933," said Grinstein. "Dad was on call for the jockeys, the trainers, the patrons and the owners."

Beginning in 1956, when the horse-racing season ended in the summer, Grinstein spent his fall and winter serving his alma mater as the Huskies' team physician. He worked from the sidelines, helping battered football players get back on the field. "My father was a magician with the use of cortisone," said his son, Bill. Loyal Washington fans still talk about the time Grinstein stitched a deep gash in the leg of Husky halfback Don McKeta during the 1960 Apple Cup game. McKeta returned to the game in the second half and caught the 2-point conversion pass that sealed the 8-7 victory over Washington State.

Grinstein is honored by the UW football team

His passion for college football — and his beloved Huskies — superseded the team doctor's apprehension about working on Shabbat afternoons. The High Holy Days were different. Bill said his father would ask other doctors to fill in for him on the rare occasion Yom Kippur conflicted with game day.

Off the field, Grinstein also served as the surrogate father for several of the football team's out-of-state players, and helped dozens of others get jobs at Longacres during the summer. Grinstein also played an instrumental role in recruiting the first black athletes to the university.

Grinstein's older son, Jerry, recalls an incident when his father was a team physician for the Seattle Rainiers. During a Triple-A Pacific Coast League game with Sacramento, he was called to second base to examine an injured Sacramento baserunner who had injured his ankle on the slide. Upon hearing the name of the injured player, Grinstein began speaking Yiddish to him. The player looked up at him and said his nickname "Katz" was short for Katsopolous, and he was Greek!

Through the '60s and into '70s, his UW medical responsibilities also included track and basketball. Despite his busy schedule, an introduction to Don Richman and Sam Schulman led Grinstein to be named team physician for the Seattle SuperSonics franchise when it was established in 1967.

Dr. Grinstein was a sportsman at his very core. At the family ranch in Snohomish County, Grinstein would often take friends to fish for steelhead and hunt duck and pheasant. His sons, Jerry and Bill, considered their father "the finest Jewish duck hunter in Washington."

Grinstein's circle of friends extended beyond the world of sports, including many prominent local politicians, especially those who matched the socially progressive values he admired. His guest list often included mayors, governors, congressman and US senators. The most prominent name on the list was his life-long friend and patient, Senator Warren Magnuson.

At the tail end of his medical career, Grinstein moved on from his work at the UW and with the Sonics, but he remained the Longacres track physician until the day he died in December of 1984.

In 1992, the Alexander Grinstein Endowed Fellowship Fund was established to honor his memory and provide financial assistance to medical students at the UW. At Longacres, the Skelly Award was presented to the outstanding jockey of the year.

"My dad loved sports and worked hard to create opportunities for deserving athletes," said Bill. "He was an important piece of the fabric that made Seattle a great city."

Irv Levine

June 7, 1912 – September 24, 1986, Seattle

Liquor distributor poured himself into Thoroughbred lifestyle

Longacres was more than just a place where people gathered to bet on horses. For Irv Levine it was the highlight of his social calendar. It afforded him a unique stature in the community and it gave him a reason to be in Renton before sunrise.

Thoroughbred horses were as much a part of Irv Levine's identity as his seat at the synagogue during the High Holy Days or the empire he built as a distributor of beverages and spirits throughout Western Washington. "Dad loved to be at Longacres by 5 a.m. during the season to watch his beloved Thoroughbreds breeze around the track during their morning workout," Mark Levine remembers fondly. "My father had a special relationship with everybody at the track, from the trainers to the kids who cleaned out the stalls. And that included the man upstairs: Joe Gottstein."

According to his son, Irv Levine prospered by emulating the man who built Longacres. Gottstein taught his friend how to properly entertain clients, where to buy his custom-

1958 newspaper ad

made shirts, and who the important players were in the business community. Gottstein also introduced Levine to the friends he would need in Seattle politics.

Levine's passion for horses was not limited to Western Washington. His son, Mark, remembers celebrating birthdays and family milestones while attending the races at Playfair in Spokane and at Yakima Meadows. "[He] poured himself completely into the glamorous lifestyle that people associate with Thoroughbred racing. My parents entertained at the Turf Club [at Longacres] like it was their own living room," Mark recalls. "They loved the white tablecloths and everything that came along with the lifestyle of Thoroughbred racing. It was only a matter of time until he became one of the owners."

As the "L" in K & L Beverage Co., Levine quenched the thirst of Longacres' patrons from the day it opened in 1933 until the track closed its doors in 1992. The beverage distributor became one of the track's most ardent supporters, sponsoring a KOL radio show in the 1940s that featured racing highlights and news from the track.

Levine's relationship with Gottstein ex-

Irv Levine, far left, in the winner's circle with Amble In, winner of the 1946 and 1948 Longacres Mile

tended beyond their business ties. While the two men were traveling together in Portland, it was Gottstein who introduced Irv to his future wife, Sally. The families spent holidays together and their children grew up as *mishpocha* (family). Though he convinced many other local businessmen to do so, it took Gottstein several years to convince Levine to purchase a racehorse. No longer satisfied with simply betting on them, Levine finally made his first four-legged investment in 1946.

Once he made up his mind to become an owner, Levine was determined to become one of the best. He traveled to Santa Anita racetrack early in the season and returned home with a chestnut colt named Amble In that he claimed for $8,000. The first thing Levine did when he returned home was to sell Amble In to his wife for the grand sum of $1. Eager to put their newest investment to the test, Irv and Sally entered their colt in the Longacres Mile. While most owners needed to establish their horse to be considered for the Mile, the Levines had an inside track.

The early favorite to win the Mile that year was a horse shipped in from Ireland named Mafosta, who had established a Longacres track record when he won the speed handicap a few weeks earlier. The Irish import had been the national champion on his home turf as a 2-year-old in 1944, and had collected victories and prize money during his journey across America. While every newspaper predicted Mafosta would outrun all others, Levine's horse went off as a 14-1 long shot. But Amble In and his jockey, "Specs" Richardson, were not intimidated by the foreign import. Amble In did not just win the race, he won by six lengths, the widest margin of victory in the history of the Mile, and broke the track record by two-fifths of a second.

went on to break numerous track records and quickly established Levine as a formidable owner. The following season, however, a severe case of arthritis sidelined the colt after winning his only race. At one point, Levine's prized possession was so ill that "The horse was down on the ground dying," Levine said. "The vet gave him 24 hours to live, but his heart carried him through."

When the 1948 season came around, Amble In showed no signs of his ailment and the 5-year-old began to race again. By August, he was the odds-on favorite to win the Mile. With a crowd of 10,500 cheering on the chestnut Thoroughbred, Levine's horse became the first ever to win the Mile twice, a record that stood for 33 years until Trooper Seven captured the Mile back to back in 1980 and '81.

With two Mile victories to his name, Levine's stature among the owners who gathered at the Turf Club had risen dramatically. His early taste of success boosted his confidence, and soon enough, he owned one of the largest stables on the backstretch. At one time, according to Mark, more than 40 Thoroughbreds wore the silks that represented K&L Stables, with two or three horses entered at Longacres on any given day of the season. Mark emphasized that his par-

AMBLE IN WINS LONGACRES MILE

Allen Drumheller Entry Runs One-Two-Three

SEATTLE, Aug. 29. (AP)—Amble In, chestnut son of Fighting Fox, repeated his 1946 triumph in the Longacres mile today, winning the $20,000 feature by a neck over Minstrel Boy. The time was 1:35 3/5.

Minstrel B[...]
Hank H—t[...]
third, making[...]
for the ent[...]
Drumheller o[...]
The entry[...]
$2.50.
Jockey No[...]
5-year-old A[...]
Mrs. I. J. L[...]
his second v[...]
stake of the [...]
net to the wh[...]
Packing [...]

Amble In wins second Lomgacres Mile in 1948

Mafosta finished the race 16 lengths back in sixth place. The $57,200 wagered on that race set a new record for the track. Amble In

ents reinvested every penny they earned from purses back into the stable.

Perry Levinson

August 9, 1910 – June 14, 1991, Seattle

Levinson made day at the races a family affair

If you ask any of his grandkids, the horses that Perry Levinson entered at Longacres won every race. He thrived on the energy at the racetrack and loved to share his affection for the sport of kings with his family. If his horse finished in the money, he shared the winnings with each grandchild. But he was just as excited when his horse crossed the finish line several lengths behind the winners.

There were only two things Perry Levinson loved more than owning racehorses. That was his family and his religion. And he always made his best effort to combine all three passions.

"My father was always active and involved, whether he was an owner at the track, as a concerned grandfather or on the board at the shul," Marcia Mayo remembers. "Horse racing was an expensive hobby. But he wanted the family to share in the excitement he felt every time we went to the track."

His daughter recalls how happy her father was during the "heydays" at Longacres, entertaining his family and business associates in the Turf Club. Levinson's son David said they would visit the track in Renton together an average of three to four afternoons every week during the racing season.

Levinson named several of his horses after members of his family. His horse MayJo combined the names of his daughter and her husband, Joey. He honored their children Stacy and Mark with a Thoroughbred named Stamark Judge. The proud grandfather named other colts after David's children, Joshua, Elicia, Jessica and Abby. The Mayo family includes two other sons, Michael and David.

The elder Levinson housed as many as 35 horses in his stables during the '90s, with four to six horses racing every week during seasons at Longacres, Santa Anita, at Golden Gate and Bay Meadows in Northern California and at Del Mar near San Diego. His horses occasionally ran at Portland Meadows and Playfair in

The Levinson family and friends with Hoist the Silver, 1978 Longacres Derby winner

Spokane as well.

Mayo said it was not unusual for her father to fly down to California to watch his horse in a race and fly home the same day. However, his religion was always his top priority. If one of his horses was entered in a race that happened to fall on a Jewish holiday, Mayo had no doubt that her father would be in his regular seat at Herzl-Ner Tamid Conservative Congregation on Mercer Island. Levinson played a key role in securing land on Mercer Island in 1970 for the construction of the new synagogue.

Born and raised in an Orthodox home, Levinson attended Garfield High School and later married Beatrice Slotnick in 1940. The young family joined the Herzl congregation in the 1950s, where Perry went on to serve as president 10 years later. His contribution to his community and his congregation were honored with an award presented by the University of Judaism. "Being Jewish was my father's identity," said Mayo. "Everything else either fit in or took a back seat. He loved his religion."

The unquestioned highlight of Levinson's tenure as a horse owner took place in 1978 when his horse, Hoist the Silver, was invited to run in the Kentucky Derby. The 3-year-old qualified for the annual pageantry at Churchill Downs with victories in several high-profile events, including stakes races at Longacres and other prominent tracks on the West Coast. The Derby that year was won by Affirmed, who went on to win the Triple Crown of horse racing in dramatic style. Hoist the Silver finished a respectable eighth in a field of 11 entries.

David Levinson said his father had horses entered in several stakes races every year, but especially enjoyed his role as an owner at Santa Anita. His son remembers his father claiming an outstanding prospect named Gardening Girl after one dramatic race at Bay Meadows. The father and son shared ownership of the dark brown stallion.

Levinson was a Thoroughbred owner, but did not breed horses for racing. Mayo said her father and brother took pride in studying the pedigree of colts with their trainer before each auction to determine if any might be worthy of an investment. She also noted that Levinson often utilized the talents of former NFL and Washington Huskies running back Junior Coffey as his trainer.

News Flash wins at Longacres in 1987

Levinson and his son worked side by side for 35 years at Oversea Casing Co. in Seattle. They were partners in the business as well as in several promising Thoroughbreds. David said his father did not get involved with owning horses until 1972, at the age of 62, when he was encouraged to buy a share of a promising colt by an associate in the meat packing business — and by his wife.

David said it was no surprise that his mother supported the idea of his father becoming involved with racehorses because her own father, Samuel Slotnick, had a reputation as an excellent handicapper. The younger Levinson is certain that his father's involvement with Thoroughbred racing extended his life by several years. The past president also shared ownership of several horses with fellow congregants at Herzl.

"My father loved to discuss the horses with members of the congregation after services on Shabbat and any chance he had," David said with a smile. "We would go to lunch three-four times every week and he would always have a racing form under his arm." The family eventually sold off the horses in Levinson's Washington Stud stables after Levinson's passing in 1991.

Herb Meltzer

October 5, 1913 – October 19, 1978, Seattle

Horses were serious business for fun-loving family

Herb and Fern Meltzer did not need an excuse to fly down to California if one of their horses was entered in a race at Bay Meadows or Santa Anita. Some people referred to their lifestyle as "jet setting," but Herb was quick to identify himself as part of the "manure set."

According to his son Eric, Herb Meltzer threw himself completely into everything he did, believing that "the harder you work, the luckier you get."

Eric said his father's dream was to operate a successful little stable. Meltzer wanted his horses to be competitive with stables that had more horses and abundant resources. Metropole Stables, according to Eric, never had more than seven horses and limited its entries to two horses in a single day. "My dad's philosophy was that every horse has a shelf life. He treated the horses like retail merchandise," said Eric. "If it doesn't move, get rid of it and put something on the shelf that will move. Our dad did not get into Thoroughbred horses as just an expensive hobby. He wanted his participation to be a profitable business."

Bobbie Stern remembered her parents' involvement with Thoroughbreds from a different perspective. The eldest daughter has fond memories of the happy hours the family spent together with friends in the Turf Club at Lon-

Red Wind captures the 1972 Longacres Mile and sets record

gacres, with her parents in the center of the festivities. "Sure, Daddy ran the business side of horse racing as a business," said Stern. "But I always thought he owned horses as an excuse to provide good times for his friends and family. He brought laughter and excitement to whomever was within earshot."

The Meltzers bought their first four-legged investment at the annual Spokane Sale based on advice from their friend and trainer, Glen Williams. Later, the Meltzers had high hopes for the yearling Aegean Star until the horse

The Meltzer family in winner's circle with 1972 Longacres Mile winner, Red Wind

was injured on a loading platform while being transported. Aegean Star eventually returned a profit as a broodmare at the Rainier Stables. Determined to get right back in the saddle, the Meltzers purchased the yearling Red Wind at the Longacres sale in 1969. The small investment they made began to pay dividends after only two races. The Thoroughbred turned out to be the Meltzer's best investment and one of the greatest stories from the 59 years of racing at Longacres.

Eric and Bobbie remember vividly the Longacres Mile on August 27, 1972, a race that featured Red Wind against the Canadian standout Briartic. Red Wind was rated (held back) early by jockey Tex Hollingsworth to save his energy for the long race. Coming out of the final turn, there was an opening in the cluster of 12 horses. Miraculously, Red Wind and Briartic broke through the gap together and raced eyeball-to-eyeball toward the finish line. The two horses crossed the finish line ahead of the pack in a memorable photo finish. "We held our breath, then screamed hysterically when the results were posted and Red Wind was declared the winner!" Eric exclaimed.

Red Wind set a track record in the Mile that year, breaking the mark that had been set in 1955 by two-fifths of a second. The wagers placed that day marked the first time in state history that betting topped $1 million for a single race.

In addition to winning The Mile in 1972, the prized Thoroughbred ran to victory in both the Independence Day Handicap and the British Columbia Handicap that season. He returned to the winner's circle again the next year in the 1973 Washington Championship. Red Wind won 16 races and finished in the money 23 times during his illustrious career. Invigorated by the success of Red Wind, the Meltzers purchased another Washington-bred yearling, Silky Wind. The newest occupant of the Metropole Stables finished in the money 14 times in 31 starts, with three wins over his career.

Herb Meltzer was not only successful in the horse racing business, but more importantly, according to Bobbie, he was brilliant in the people business as well. "Everybody knew he was a fantastic salesman," Stern said proudly. "Daddy parlayed his natural skill into becoming a compelling storyteller who delighted children by entertaining them with his jokes and tall tales." Stern went on to describe her father as the quintessential dreamer who kept everybody mesmerized to the point they would follow him around just to hear the next chapter of whatever saga he was making up at the moment. His friends referred to him as the Pied Piper, or simply Happy Herbie. "Children of all ages wanted to be transported to his imaginary lands and faraway kingdoms," said Stern. "Daddy would create stories that kept his audience entranced for hours. He was a wonderful father and an incredible grandfather."

Like many of his friends who lived around Cherry Street in Seattle during the Great Depression, Herb Meltzer dreamed of a better life. The only son of a Russian immigrant married Fern Rosenfeld from Portland in 1941 and worked side by side with his bride in the jewelry business. The Meltzers eventually opened their own store, Herbert's Jewelers in downtown Seattle. "Our father worked tirelessly in order to provide a lifestyle for us that he could only imagine as a child," said daughter Patti Newby. "His hard work and determination provided that better life for his family."

Stern admired her parents' ability to balance their social life with their business activities by giving back to the community. The Meltzers were original members of Temple B'nai Torah in Bellevue. They also volunteered together to develop a new location for the Jewish Community Center on Mercer Island. Herb served on the acquisition committee for the JCC, while Fern coordinated the groundbreaking ceremonies as committee chair and served for several years on the center's board of directors. All three Meltzer children agree that their parents left them with a legacy of love and laughter, as well as an obligation to serve their community.

Red Wind wins mile at 'Acres

RENTON (Wa)—The records tumbled at Longacres as lightly regarded Red Wind won the 37th running of the Longacres Mile Sunday.

Red Wind, the $5,700 auction block bargain with a reputation for kicking anyone nearby, broke the track record for a mile in winning the race. The colt's time on the fast track was 1:34 flat—two-fifths off of a track record set in 1955.

The audie[...] ing the race[...] mark for cr[...] wagered $[...] time more [...] lars has b[...] Washington

Crowds wager over $1 million for the first time on 1972 Mile Day

156

Herman Sarkowsky

June 9, 1925, Gera, Germany

From sport of kings to king of sports

Herman Sarkowsky is considered by many to be one of the most influential individuals in Northwest sports history. Over a period of 30 years, Sarkowsky brought the Trailblazers to Portland, the Seahawks to Seattle, invested in the Sounders (NASL), kept the Mariners from fleeing, and helped resurrect Washington's horse racing industry. While his ownership ties to other sports have loosened, his love of Thoroughbreds continues to get his blood racing.

Herman Sarkowsky and his wife Faye

After graduating from the University of Washington in 1949, Sarkowsky was given a make-or-break deal to develop 25 homes on 80 acres of land in Tacoma. By 1969, he was the largest residential developer in the Puget Sound region.

It was during that rise that Herman took a stab at horse ownership, purchasing Forin Sea for $1,200 in a Longacres claiming race in 1968. After five races of moderate success, the horse was claimed from him for $2,000. But that was all it took.

"Horse racing and breeding is my passion," he said. "The Seahawks and the Trail Blazers were certainly unique sports ventures, but the business side of it is tedious. There's just something more special about breeding and racing horses; just the people involved, it's a circus on the backside most days and it gets my blood going. It's a tonic for the mundane tasks a businessman in my position has to endure. It's a love affair that gets in the blood."

For Northwest racing fans, the Longacres Mile has long represented the pinnacle of racing, and it looked like Sarkowsky would reach that peak just three years into the sport. Titular II had just won the 1971 Governor's Handicap and entered the Mile as a 5-2 favorite.

Moving down the backstretch, Titular II had taken a commanding three-length lead and was turning for home. "I was on the way to the winner's circle," Sarkowsky recalled. With less than a furlong to go, Titular II became confused when he saw the starting gate parked in the infield, a practice not normally done at the time, and simply stopped running.

Sarkowsky tried him again in the Mile in

1972 and 1974, but to no avail.

Dick Mandella, who's been training for Sarkowsky since the '70s, explained, "You know, Herman's a quiet guy, intense but even-keeled, lets you train without much interference. Well, for some reason he liked to call in the a.m. Bad timing: I've got some 30-50 horses on the track at any given time. I guess I was a little short at times because he suggested I might go to charm school. I'd call him back and someone would always answer 'Seahawks Inc.' Now who in the hell were the Seahawks? Hell, I didn't know he bought a football team...that's how out of the loop I was.

"Over the years he's been a prince of a fellow, a gentleman and a true student of the game," Mandella said. "You've got to go a long way to find a better human being."

When Longacres racetrack closed in 1992, Sarkowsky joined the Northwest Racing Associates, a group of investors dedicated to the return of Thoroughbred racing in Western Washington. In June of 1996, Sarkowsky and 18,000 other fans were on hand to witness the return on his investment. Set in the shadow of Mount Rainier, Thoroughbred racing was given a new home at Emerald Downs in Auburn.

Sarkowsky invested in Emerald Downs which opened in 1996

Sarkowsky's interest in horse racing began to include breeding as well. One foal that surprised everyone was Phone Chatter.

Phone Chatter wins at the 1993 Breeders' Cup

"You know, when that horse was vanned down to my barn, she was a great big gangly thing and me and the boys figured she'd be the last one ready to run," said trainer Mandella. "I was dead wrong. Something you should know about that filly that might be of interest: the horse was all heart."

Sarkowsky's chestnut racehorse won $838,742, three stakes races and was voted the 1993 American Champion Two-Year-Old Filly. But the race that remains etched in Sarkowsky's mind was the 1993 Breeders' Cup Juvenile Fillies. Phone Chatter broke fifth from the gate and stayed there for all but the last three furlongs. Phone Chatter bore down on the lead horse, and the two were matched stride for stride in the final yards. With inches to go, Sarkowsky's runner bobbed her nose forward while the TV announcer screamed, "Phone Chatter prevails in a stiff drive to the finish!"

"Here's the remarkable thing," said Mandella. "As Phone Chatter was being cooled down after the race, one of my grooms discovered severe heat on her hind leg. She ran the last third of that race with a fractured cannon bone, ran down the stretch on pure adrenalin and will. She was a champion through and through, and I will never forget her. What she did in the Breeders' Cup was heroic."

But the race that still eluded Sarkowsky was the Longacres Mile, a tradition that continued at Emerald Downs. After four more tries over 34 years, Sarkowsky still yearned to win the biggest prize at his hometown track. No Giveaway was yet another attempt in the 2005 Mile, and at 60-1, not a very likely

60-1 Longacres Longshot

No Giveaway captured the 2005 Longacres Mile in dramatic fashion

one. The Washington-bred horse was the product of a dam and sire also bred by Sarkowsky, and was 20½ lengths behind the leaders at the halfway mark. But around the final turn, No Giveaway moved up along the inside rail and caught the lead horse in the final yards to win by three-quarters of a length. No Giveaway was the biggest long shot in the 70-year history of the Mile, paying $122 for a $2 ticket.

"Winning the Mile was a bigger thrill than any other race for me, including the Breeders' Cup," said Sarkowsky.

"This is my home here," he said in *The Seattle Times*, August 22nd, 2005. "It's the thrill of winning here and doing it with a Washington-bred…It's important to the people involved that the horse is local. It's great for the breeders of the State of Washington."

When asked whether he stayed in his seat this time, Sarkowsky said, "You better believe it."

His stable continues to grow in both number and

reputation. He sells off Thoroughbreds from his herd each year, including the 11 new foals born in 2012. By his own assessment, Sarkowsky is now a full-time horse breeder.

Faye and Herman in the winner's circle in 2005

"Breeding is not a science, nor is it random selection," Sarkowsky said. "Luck and circumstance play a role. Intuition plays a role in each pairing, and always will. Nature is a wild card in racing, and will not be tamed by human ambition or financial acumen alone.

"What I love about the sport is this: there's always something new to learn," he added. "Horse breeding is endlessly fascinating. Winning matters to me; I don't deny that a bit."

To *The Seattle Times* he reflected, "I think that you learn some great lessons in this business, and one of them is to accept the disappointments as part of the game. I think I've learned that over the years very well. The highs are really high. If you can cope with the lows, you can have a ball. I'm very passionate about racing."

Abe Sherman

1881, Poland – December 17, 1956, Seattle

New life, fortune and passion all riding on the muscle of horses

In the early 1900s, at the age of 16, Abe Sherman escaped forced service in the Imperial Russian Army by fleeing to Europe. The young refugee drove a horse and buggy in Paris to pay for his passage across the Atlantic, then guided a carriage through the streets of New York to earn enough money to get him to Seattle.

Once he arrived in the Northwest, Sherman began driving his horse and buggy around Seattle. But instead of transporting people, the Polish immigrant canvassed the city for salvage materials that could be reused and recycled. His most notable project was dismantling the barracks at the abandoned navel training facilities at Ft. Farragat in Idaho and then reassembling them on the corner of Seventh Avenue South and South Lander Street, where they still stand.

Sherman Supply and Salvage grew during the Depression and thrived after World War II by turning war surplus into building materials for a booming construction industry. The business was doing so well that Abe turned the operations over to his nephew, Marvin Federman, so he could focus on his real love, Thoroughbred horses.

"My grandfather bought a horse ranch near Olympia, complete with horses that he entered in races at Longacres," said Diane Cohn. "He was funny. He named all the horses based on what men might say to their wives after coming home from a day at the track, like 'Forgive Me' and 'For You Dear.'"

Sherman would visit the stable in rural Thurston County to check on his horses and to get away from the city, said Cohn. The Sherman stable never housed more than six or eight horses, but Abe tried his hand at breeding Thoroughbreds by inviting his friends to bring their promising colts and mares to the peninsula for conjugal visits.

Cohn described her grandfather as eccentric. In the late '20s, he built a home in the Mount Baker community that was out of place with its Southwestern design and red-tiled roof. "Grandpa did everything in a big way," Cohn remembers. "All he ever wanted was to be a real American."

Abe Sherman in the winner's circle with his granddaughter Diane Cohn, left, and his daughter Rose Goldstein, right

Eddie Sherman

February 29, 1936, Seattle

Looking for winners all of his life

Discarded tickets scattered on the floor at Longacres were like buried treasure for young Eddie Sherman and his brother Ernie. After a trip to the track with their father in the 1940s, the boys would compare the tickets they collected with the results in the newspaper the next morning to see if someone threw away a winner. "We'd pick up $10 or $20 every time we went with our dad," Eddie remembers. "Two or three tickets with a horse in the money made our day."

The rewards of horse racing stuck with Eddie Sherman as an adult. He would study bloodlines and examine the horses entered in

Lilly Fa Pootz drives to the finish at Emerald Downs in 2008

claims races for potential winners. He would walk through the paddock before the first race to look for subtle signs in the horses before he'd ever wager on an entry. Winners, he said, are made from a combination of ability, determination, and the physical state of the horse on the day of the race.

In 2002, Sherman bought his first horse, Tejati, for $12,000 after a claiming race at Golden Gate Fields based on the advice of his trainer. Tejati was a hard-driving closer that won several races and earned more than $100,000 in his lifetime.

After a few more experiments with horses from claiming races, the Garfield grad went to Kentucky to select a yearling he lightheartedly named Lily FaPootz (Yiddish for "all dressed up"). Even though the horse's dam and sire had performed better on grass than on the dirt tracks she'd be racing on in Northwest, Sherman liked the horse's strong bloodlines.

Others saw her potential as well, and Sherman lost his prized Kentucky-bred filly in a claiming race. The new owner took her to California to race on turf, where Lily FaPootz eventually earned more than $300,000. Later on,

Sherman would always make an effort to visit Lily in her stall if they happened to be at the same track.

"Lily was special. Discovering a winner at a sale of yearlings is like finding a needle in a haystack," said Sherman. "You have to read books, study the charts and compare a horse's tendencies. And even if you have the professionals in Kentucky providing advice on each horse, you still need a great deal of good luck on your side."

Eddie's older brother Ernie became a much bigger player as a horse owner, with six to 10 Thoroughbreds entered at tracks up and down the West Coast every season.

In 1951, after their father died, Eddie and Ernie transformed Pacific Plumbing Supply into a major player in the plumbing industry. Continuing his love of sports, Eddie later became a fixture on the links at Glendale Country Club. Despite all his success, the little boy in Eddie Sherman can still remember the thrill of peering through the fence at Longacres as the horses thundered past him on their way to the finish line. "Even now, the excitement of watching those beautiful horses in full stride takes my breath away."

Eddie Sherman, far left, in winner's circle in 2008

Elias Solomon

August 27, 1908, Calcutta, India – January 19, 1991, Seattle

Day at the races began with 'Papa's wild ride'

Brothers Lewis and Edward Malakoff knew they were in for an adventure every time their grandfather picked them up in his Rolls Royce for a day of watching the ponies run at Longacres. Their mother — Elias and Ruth Solomon's daughter Jennifer Malakoff — described the 20-minute journey from Mercer Island to Renton as "Papa's wild ride."

Elias Solomon hung up his ledgers and picked up his gold watch from his high-pressure career as a merchant banker at the age of 45, determined to discover greener pastures as the owner of Thoroughbred race-horses. His decision led to a life filled with actual green pastures, the smell of hay and dozens of trips to the winner's circle.

Born in Calcutta and raised in England, Solomon received a first-hand education in the fine art of Thoroughbred racing from his cousin, Sir Victor Sasson. His banking career had

Elias Solomon, seventh from left, in the winner's circle

moved him and wife Ruth to New York, but it was too hot and humid for their taste. Elias and Ruth decided to spend their new life in Seattle, where the weather was more like the cloudy days he remembered fondly from his youth in the British Isles.

Retirement allowed Solomon to focus on the business side of Thoroughbred racing. He became close friends with Longacres founder Joe Gottstein and was a regular at the track. "Papa loved the races and all the traditions of the track," Malakoff remembers. She also recalled how her father would pour over the daily racing form each evening to be ready for the next day's bets. He was a real character."

"He didn't just bet on any old horse," said son-in-law Paul Malakoff. "Elias wanted to pick horses that he thought could beat the favorite." He continued with an impression of his father-in-law with a proper British accent: "Anybody can pick the favorite, my boy. It takes faith and knowledge to bet your money on a horse with long odds."

Solomon was not just an expert at handicapping, said Malakoff. As an owner, he won most of the stakes races for colts and geldings held at the Renton track over the years. "Other owners may win races, but Elias was lucky enough to win multiple stakes races," said Malakoff. "And stakes races are what really count."

Solomon also enjoyed the prestige that went along with being an owner in the sport of kings. Even parking his car at Longacres became a tradition. The parking attendants were aware that nobody was allowed to

Proud Admiral wins the Washington Futurity in 1968

drive the Rolls Royce. Solomon would pull "the Silver Shadow" into the lot adjacent to the entrance, head directly to the only reserved spot in the lot and then back the opulent vehicle into the space next to the one reserved for Gottstein.

The most thrilling victory Jennifer can remember was her father's horse, Proud Admiral, coming from behind on the outside in the home stretch to win the Washington Futurity in 1968. Her $2 bet paid the happy daughter $127. Malakoff remembers that Solomon was forced to

Full Regalia, 1963 Longacres Mile winner

import a jockey from Vancouver, B.C. and pay him an extra share of the purse because none of the jockeys at Longacres wanted to ride the 63½-to-1 long shot.

Elias and Ruth traveled to California in 1956 to witness their horse Battle Dance win the San Pasqual Handicap at Santa Anita, and later posed for photos in the winner's circle at Longacres with Full Regalia after wins in the Longacres Mile and the Seattle Handicap in 1963. The happy couple returned to the winner's circle with Philatelist when the colt won both the Juvenile Mile for 2-year-olds and the Boeing Stakes. They were joined by Perry and Bea Levinson after Hoist the Silver won the Longacres Derby in 1978.

Malakoff recalls that many of the mares and fillies that raced for the Solomon stables over the years wore the orange and black silks that represented Ruth Solomon as the owner. Her horse Princess Quilla captured numerous stakes races at Longaces, and Rachel's Excalibur found her way to the winner's circle at Santa Anita in the time-honored handicap.

Elias and Ruth were lifelong members of Temple De Hirsch Sinai in Seattle.

Like many of her contemporaries, Malakoff remembers the festive atmosphere in the Turf Club on Sundays for the families of owners at Longacres. At the height of their involvement, the Solomons were at the track every Friday, Saturday and Sunday.

And those weekend visits to the track often began with Papa's wild ride.

Phreda and Joel Staadecker

October 4, 1913 – August 10, 2001, Seattle   November 5, 1908 – February 2, 1964, Seattle

Nation's first female horse racing commissioner

The call from Governor Albert Rosselini came as quite a surprise to Phreda Staadecker. Her husband Joel had finished serving a six-year term as Washington's horse racing commissioner and was appointed to serve another when he passed away suddenly in 1964. Phreda's passion for horse racing and her ability to navigate through an up-till-then exclusive men's club gave the governor all the confidence he needed to appoint her to the position.

At the age of 48, when most women at the time were firmly settled in their child-raising

Phreda and Joel Staadecker and daughter Bonnie in the winner's circle with Happy Valley at Longacres in 1949

responsibilities, Staadecker stepped in to become the nation's first female horseracing commissioner. As a constant companion to her husband Joel, Phreda attended all the meetings and conventions, had visited dozens of tracks around the country, and was well known and immensely liked among the nation's horse racing circles.

Happy Valley wins by a neck at Longacres in 1949

Her tenure as Washington State horseracing commissioner required Staadecker to administer operations at Longacres in Renton, Playfair in Spokane, and Yakima Meadows, while simultaneously serving on numerous national horse racing committees that ensured the integrity of the industry.

Her new responsibilities were a natural fit. Staadecker's father, Abe Sherman, was one of the pioneer Thoroughbred breeders in the state. She always loved horses and grew up watching her father buy and sell Thoroughbreds and race his stable at tracks across the Northwest. Shortly after Phreda and Joel were married, they built a small stable of their own that included Ambolero, a cherished horse that won the 1956 Washington Futurity.

"It's impossible to describe the thrill when a horse you have bred and raised stands in the winner's circle — best of his age in the state," she once said. The family even traveled with their champion to California racetracks, enrolling their two boys and one daughter in nearby schools for the racing season.

Staadecker was also a competitor and an athlete in her own right, winning three golf championships at Glendale Golf Club, and had a 14 handicap. She was a charter member of the Bellevue Club and would arrive every morning at 5 o'clock, read the business page and then hit the Nautilus weight machines. On a typical Saturday, her son Charles remembers, she would play a set of tennis, hit a bucket of balls, walk nine holes of golf, then go for a swim.

David and Karen Tarica

February 24, 1929, Seattle   December 8, 1936 – March 30, 2007, Seattle

Taricas were the 'daily double' at Longacres

The Club House dining room at Longacres was where David and Karen Tarica would gather with friends before the first race. The staff knew many of the owners and regular patrons by name, but they reserved a special title for Karen. She was known as "The Exacta Queen" for her uncanny ability to pick the first- and second-place horses in a race.

Seattle native David Tarica has his wife to thank for introducing him to the excitement of Thoroughbred horse racing. The smells of the track and the sounds of laughter are what help him remember the best of times with his loving wife. "Karen brought me to Longacres to introduce me to the sport of kings," he said. "It wasn't long before she convinced me to spend our money on a four-legged investment."

Karen and David Tarica at Longacres

The Taricas enjoyed playing the ponies, but their perspective changed when the two went in on their first horse, Patient Patrick, with Ray Galante and Bill Benveniste. "Patient Patrick was a perfect name for the horse, because you had to be really patient if you wanted to see him ever win a race," said David. Patient Patrick finally won his first race when the optimistic owners shipped him to Spokane to race at Playfair. "We owned a fair number of horses over the years," he said. "A few good ones and a lot of *really* bad ones."

David and Karen were regulars at Longacres, with seats in the grandstands or standing along the rail two or three days every week before they bought their first horse and moved upstairs to the Turf Club. David commented that the club often resembled the gathering of Sephardic brothers from Congregation Ezra Bessaroth.

"I know it wasn't always kosher," he said with a smile. "But it was not unusual for some of the regulars to be missing from shul if one of the High Holy Days happened to fall on a day one of them had a horse entered in a race."

The Taricas bought a special horse in 1988 for their granddaughters, Molly and Anna Goren, and named her MollyAnna. The 2-year-old broke her maiden in her first race and turned out to be "a fine investment." MollyAnna won five races in her career, and finished in the money in 16 of 18 races she ran.

The Taricas with Mollyanna at Longacres in 1990

Tarica claimed his most expensive horse for $16,000, because the late-breaking colt named Autumn Purchase reminded him of a famous Thoroughbred named Silky Sullivan. The proud owner remembers how the horse would settle in near the back of the pack in every race, and would then break into full stride rounding the last turn before the home stretch. Autumn Purchase earned more than double what the Taricas paid for him, winning five races out of 30 starts with purses that totaled $31,700 over his career. Their next horse, Loving Thought, accumulated $45,677 by winning nine starts and finishing in the money 36 times in 102 races.

The Taricas visiting their Thoroughbreds

David and Karen purchased the grandson of Autumn Purchase, and named the yearling Jake's Dream, in honor of their grandson. "Yeah, winning was just a dream for that horse," joked Tarica. The devoted family man named his stables Two by Two to represent the Taricas and their two daughters. Their riding silks included the image of two dice embossed on the sleeves with the number two on each.

Friends convinced Tarica to invest in shares of Emerald Downs. He can only laugh about that one too. "There is one investment that I may never get a return on," he said. "But my money did get me a lifetime pass for free parking."

The
Sonny & Gena Gorasht
Family

Sabrina Endres
Roosevelt High School
Swimming

Brett Endres
Ingraham High School
Football

Rebecca Endres
Gymnastics,
Dance

Ella Endres
Gymnastics, Dance

Jamie Merriman-Cohen
Garfield High School
Swimming

Jeff Merriman-Cohen
Yeshiva High School
Basketball

Jeff Merriman-Cohen - back row, 2nd from right

Sam Holland
Football, Basketball,
Baseball

Shaya Merriman-Cohen
NBA Prospect

Aaron Cohen
The Bush School, Tennis, Basketball

David Israel

David Israel galloping "Search for Roses," his 3-year-old filly at Longacres in 1983

A Jazzy Opener

A Jazzy Venture, with jockey Vicky Baze aboard, stays in front at the wire, outlasting favorite Banana Raspberry and Mike Allen to yesterday's $35,000 U.S. Bank Stakes on Emerald Downs' fourth Opening Day.

Owner makes his run in Opening Day feature

By Jay Muehori
Journal Reporter

AUBURN — David Israel started running with his filly A Jazzy Venture, along the rail with an eighth of a mile to go in the $35,000 U.S. Bank Stakes, yesterday's feature race on Emerald Downs' fourth Opening Day.

Israel didn't care how silly he must have looked. But despite his exuberance, Israel stopped far shorter than his winning 3-year-old filly, who covered that final eighth of a mile in 13 1/5 seconds.

But with her best effort, A Jazzy Venture, the 9-to-2 second choice, was good enough to win by three-quarters of a

"I never ran so fast. I was out of breath," the ecstatic co-owner said. "I couldn't tell if she won or not, but I knew she gave the best effort of her entire life. And that's all I could even ask."

The rest of the 11-horse field must have heard an inflection on the tote board as Israel slid on the rail. Right were at double-digit odds against the heavy favorite, previously unbeaten Banana Raspberry. Three fillies were off at more than 50-to-1 odds.

length under jockey Vicky Baze.

It was Baze's first victory with her new name. The former Vicky Aragon married Gary Baze, the state winningest rider, on April 1.

"I just let her get out of the gate comfortable and let her run," Baze said. "She's going to have some bananas and raspberries for dinner tonight."

During the race she ate up the field sprinting 6 furlongs. A Jazzy Venture took the lead at about the quarter pole on the final turn for home. Baze kept her rated

See EMERALD DOWNS, BB

A 20-Year Love Affair Continues

By DENNIS DODGE

LONGRACRES, Renton, Wash.—David Israel, who along with partners Michael Julian and Wally Cluphf will see his colors carried by Regal Vixen in Sunday's $30,000-added Renton Handicap, has been badly bitten by the racing bug.

It didn't happen all at once. Israel's fascination with the track has been growing for 20 years, ever since he took a summer job in the program office as a 17-year-old student at Seattle's Franklin High School. It had a distinct beginning, however, and he still remembers it vividly.

"I started selling programs in May and I made my first bet in July," he recalled. "I bet a $2 daily double from Egypt's Girl to Moon Tike, and naturally they both won. I ran from the eighth pole to the wire with Moon Tike, and if I hadn't been stopped by a security guard I would have dead-heated for the win. The double paid $140. It's still the biggest daily double I have ever hit."

Israel worked in the program office until he graduated from the University of Washington's school of pharmacy, when he began plying his profession at A and H Pharmacy in Renton, which just happens to be the nearest drug store to the track. He dispenses medicines rather than programs for a living these days, but horses are still his passion.

Israel got his first taste of horse ownership in 1974 as a charter member of the infamous Media Stables, which is a story in itself. The short version is that 20 press box types anted up $200 a piece to claim an ancient gelding named Rare Sunshine. The partnership got along swimmingly while campaigning Rare Sunshine and a succession of other runners with similarly limited ability, but it was undone by success. Media Stable's last horse, Mediately, won several good races before being claimed, swelling the stable's coffers to around $40,000 by 1979.

"We had a meeting to decide whether to cash in or buy another horse, and the vote was 19 to one," Israel reported. "I was the only one who wanted to keep racing."

He therefore took his Media Stables windfall and reinvested it in all ill-bred yearling named Ittle Do, who eventually won two of 90 outings and $11,309. He wasn't satisfied with his level of involvement in the sport, however, so he hit upon the idea of exercising horses as well as owning them. The only problem was that the life-long city boy was then 29 and had never been on horseback.

"I took riding lessons from (former jockey) Barbara Thompson," he said. "When I thought I was ready I came to the track in March of 1982 and my trainer, Bill Thompson, let me gallop a filly named Island Melody. The first day she ran off with me, then the second day she bolted through the gap and made Smitty (trainer Marion Smith) spill coffee all over himself. The third day I took her to the training track and she propped and threw me over her head, then when I got back on she bucked me off again. After that I went back to the farm for more lessons.

"I came back the next March and fell off horses for 13 days in a row. (Outrider) Jimmy Worth threatened to rule me off the track if I fell again, but I went the rest of the meeting without falling off.

"I kept galloping until 1985. I was riding one of my horses at Reber Ranch and the girth broke, so I was flipped under the horse and it really scared me. I threw my helmet in the trash and I haven't gotten on another horse since then. The amazing thing is that I never got hurt in all that time. Everybody said I had a nice way of falling."

Meanwhile, Israel's fortunes as an owner paralleled his career as an exercise rider, hitting rock bottom in 1987 when his two-horse stable consisting of Murphy and Michael S. went one for 25 before he gave both horses away. He was by no means discouraged, however.

"I figured my problem was that I wasn't spending enough money," he said. "I wanted to claim a horse for $16,000 instead of for $4,000, but I didn't have that much. I got Michael Julian and Wally Cluphf to be my partners, but the three of us together could only come up with $15,000 when we spotted Regal Vixen in for a $16,000 tag. I got a $1,000 cash advance on my Visa card and made the claim."

Israel explained that he wanted the 5-year-old son of Royal Chocolate because it looked like the gelding would be able to win for a $12,500 tag. He didn't mind losing money on the horse, but he didn't want to lose as much as he had become accustomed to losing.

As it turned out, however, Regal Vixen exceeded his new owner's expectations. Under the tutelege of trainer Bill Thompson at this track and conditioner Judy Goffus in California, the New York-bred has won seven races and over $94,000 since being claimed in June of 1988. His owners are therefore rolling in cash. Right?

"Not exactly," Israel admitted. "We have reinvested Regal Vixen's earnings in more horses. We claimed Prion (a 5-year-old gelding who ran third for a $16,000 tag on last Wednesday's card) and we bought two yearlings. One is now a 3-year-old maiden named Rockin Soul and the other is a 2-year-old Sharper One gelding named September Fire.

"We still don't have any money, but we have a lot of fun. To tell you the truth, I wouldn't have it any other way. I love owning horses and being able to come to the backstretch in the mornings and to the frontside in the afternoons. I think horses are the greatest animals and racing is the greatest sport in the world."

Israel's partners, both long-time friends, also enjoy watching their horses run. Neither is quite so wrapped up in the sport as Israel, however, so we wondered if they were satisfied with seeing their initial investment grow into a four-horse stable.

"I told them when we started that they won't see any money until we win the Kentucky Derby," Israel reported. "Right now, in fact, I'm trying to build the kitty back up so I can go to Kentucky this fall and buy a really nice yearling. If Regal Vixen can win the Renton, we'll be on our way.

So here is the scenario: Regal Vixen wins the Renton Handicap this Sunday and Israel takes the prize money to Kentucky and reinvests it in another yearling. That yearling grows up to win the Kentucky Derby and Israel, Julian and Cluphf, cash in their chips and retire from horseracing as rich men.

169

Herb and Fern Meltzer

Lovingly Honored

Patti Newby   Bobbie and Michel Stern   **Eric Meltzer**

Abby Stern and Tom Phillips
Kirbi and Mallory

Dana and Jay Azose
Mason and Molly

Tara and David Stern
Madeline, Nathan, and Zach

Eddie Sherman, far left, with Lilly Fa Pootz

Funding for Distant Replay was made possible, in part, by a grant from:

MACCABI

BUILDING JEWISH PRIDE THROUGH SPORTS

David Jack Funes

November 11, 1935 – April 29, 1995, Seattle

Former golfer takes aim at Maccabiah Games

There was nothing that David Funes did half-heartedly. He enjoyed skeet shooting so much that he served multiple terms as president of the Seattle Skeet and Trap Club. The Seattle native not only represented his country at two Maccabiah Games, but he brought back three gold medals.

As an active member of the Sephardic community, Funes was a fixture on the links at the Glendale Country Club until the twisting motion created too much strain on his back. A friend recommended that he focus his athletic energies on skeet shooting.

"David took to skeet shooting right away," his wife Eva remembers. "He loved the competitive aspect of the sport and the camaraderie it provided. He especially enjoyed excelling in a sport without straining his back."

Funes met his wife while shopping at the post exchange on the American base while he was stationed in post-war Germany. For years after, he insisted that Eva was the most beautiful souvenir he brought home from Europe.

The retired 46-year-old soldier was good enough at his newly adopted sport to earn a spot on the 1981 US Maccabi team. Funes' marksmanship earned him a gold medal in the individual competition in Israel. His love of the sport was so infectious that in 1985, when he returned to the Maccabiah Games in Israel, the US team included his wife and his son Jack.

David won a second individual gold and a third gold for his part in the team event. Eva earned her own gold medal in the women's individual competition.

David Funes, Maxie Kahan, shooting event organizer, David's wife Eva and their son Jack at the Maccabiah Games in Israel in 1981

"The Maccabi Games were a great bonding experience for the family. They reminded us of our roots," said Eva. "Being in Israel made us proud to be American Jews and proud to represent our country."

Funes was inducted into the Washington State Skeet Shooting Hall of Fame in 1994 and was honored by the United States Army Marksmanship Unit at Fort Benning in Georgia for his contributions to the sport.

Matt Grogan

January 23, 1954, the Bronx, NY

Softball league and Maccabi Games are legacy of kid from the Bronx

In 1988, East Coast transplant Matt Grogan and Terry Posner took on the challenge of recruiting and raising enough money to send 35 young athletes (ages 13-16) to the Midwest for the Maccabi Games. The team from Washington pitted local athletes against Jewish competitors from across the US and countries around the world in dozens of team sports and individual events.

"The parents were easy, but many times we had to make personal visits to the home of the athlete to convince them to spend several nights away from home to stay with a bunch of strangers," Grogan said as he thought back 24 years. "Most of these kids were barely teenag-

Terry Posner and Matt Grogan led the effort to send a Seattle team to the Maccabi Games in Chicago in 1988

ers and most of them had never even slept away from home for more than a slumber party."

In addition to his sales pitch to the families, Grogan teamed with his friend Terry Posner and volunteers Ruth Bunin and John Muscatel to raise enough money to send the local delegation to Chicago. "We did not want money to be an obstacle," said Grogan.

Grogan's involvement with athletics dates back to his undergraduate days at Springfield College in Massachusetts, where he received a degree in physical education in 1974. While walking across campus, he spotted somebody he had not seen since his freshman year who mentioned an opening in the physical education staff at the local Jewish Community Center. Grogan admitted that he had never heard of a JCC, and applied for the job.

His interview with the center's executive director — who had never hired a Jew — changed dramatically when Grogan mentioned something about playing on the basketball team at his own synagogue. The director's face lit up with a huge smile and, according to Grogan, he said, "Oh my God, you're Jewish!" Grogan was offered the position before the end of the interview.

During his tenure with Jewish Community Centers on the East Coast, Grogan was instrumental in the organization of Olympics-style events in the New England region and brought the same style program to the Northwest when he moved to the Seattle area in 1981. Grogan was prepared to put the necessary pieces into place when Posner proposed that the Seattle community send a team of athletes to the Maccabi Games.

In the years since that first team traveled to Chicago, the Northwest delegation has been represented in Maccabi Games held in Detroit, Cleveland, Sarasota, Los Angeles and Tucson in addition to staging its own regional competition in 1997. Grogan still smiles whenever he glances up at the plaque in his office that honors the 1995 basketball team from Washington. It was the first to beat the Israeli basketball squad at the Maccabi Games.

Grogan himself excelled in high school as a wrestler in the 169-lb. weight class, and has become a fixture at local meets in the Seattle area as an official. In addition to the multitude of responsibilities he has assumed since moving to the Northwest, the enthusiastic director used his expertise to boost the JCC-sponsored softball league from six teams in 1981 to the largest independent league in Washington, with more than 600 players on 35 teams.

In Grogan's opinion, the Maccabi Games and the competition are wonderful, but he went on to emphasize his own version of the 80-20 philosophy. "Eighty percent of Maccabi is just being there. The other 20 percent is playing the sport," he said. "Over the years, what's really gratifying is watching these young people realize they are part of something much larger than the activities they participate in. You can see it in their faces. The kids look around and realize they are among thousands of other athletes and are part of something exclusively Jewish."

Grogan went on to say the Maccabi Games and the SJCC Co-ed Softball League have probably resulted in more long-term relationships and marriages than any dating Jewish service. In his opinion, the traditions that have become part of Maccabi are every bit as inspirational as any Olympics he has seen. He described the opening ceremonies, the competition during the day, and the social activities at night as awesome, but ventured to say the best part of every Maccabi Games is the celebration held after the closing ceremonies.

"Friendships are made at the Maccabi Games that last a lifetime because the participants have more in common than a single sport," he said. "This is the history they share and the heritage they all have in common."

Leon Grundstein

June 30, 1947, Washington, D.C.

Sprinter continues physical fitness philosophy

Leon Grundstein still has the long, lean body of a sprinter, and his eyes reflect the same determination he had when he burst through the tape of an intermediate dash in college. The difference today is that the Seattle resident has traded his track shoes for the promotion of Whole Life Living, a philosophy that exercises the mind and body of seniors who live in one of his four GenCare facilities in Western Washington.

Raised in the outskirts of Detroit, Grundstein ran in the 200- and 400-yard intermediate sprints and was part of the 4x100 relay team at the University of Michigan during the outdoor season. During the winter months, he switched to the 300-yard race and the 4x400 relay team on an inclined track for indoor meets. At one time,

his 30.8-second mark ranked him as the second best in school history and the ninth fastest in the nation.

Grundstein's speed also earned him a spot on the US team that competed in the Maccabiah Games in Israel in 1969. He returned to the Holy Land again with the American contingent four years later. His memories of his trips to the Middle East are filled with a combination of camaraderie and anxiety.

"The massacre at the Munich Olympics was still on everybody's mind in '73," he recalled. "We had armed security at the athletes' village during our second visit. That was a complete reversal from the relaxed atmosphere we had the first time we traveled to Israel for the Maccabi."

Grundstein won gold medals at both Maccabiah Games for his contribution in the 4x400 relay, including the anchor leg of the record-setting foursome in 1973. He also brought home a bronze medal from the '73 Games for his individual effort in the 400.

Adrenaline, he admits, was an important element in his success. Grundstein said he "rose to the level of his competition," when he set personal best times at Michigan while competing at the Penn Relays and in the Big Ten Conference finals. He said there was something inspirational about running in front of 30,000 screaming fans.

"The inspiration at the Maccabi games was on the field," he said with a smile. "Just competing with thousands of other athletes was wonderful. But knowing that we were all Jewish was even better. That was truly an exceptional experience."

The Midwest transplant competed in Amateur Athletic Union events until a partially torn Achilles tendon ended his track career at the age of 27. Grundstein continues to lead by example by following the four-pronged approach to Whole Life Living for residents at his retirement communities. The plan emphasizes good nutrition, physical activity, mental stimulation and — the factor that binds them together — life with a purpose.

Recalling his days at Michigan track meets, Grundstein laughed thinking about the fact that he was often the only Jewish competitor among sprinters of various ethnic backgrounds.

"It was inspiring to realize that I represented a distinct minority within my own gene pool," he said.

Michael Morgan

April 21, 1949, Modesto, CA

Goalie led team to NCAA and Maccabi championship victories

In the eyes of Coach Pete Cutino, the 1970 water polo team at the University of California, Berkeley was at the lowest point of an unfulfilled season when his squad was thumped by UCLA. The talented team took the defeat as a wakeup and won its next eight games in a row, including victories over traditional powerhouses like USC and San Jose State, to find itself in the NCAA finals against the same bruin team.

Key to the winning streak, according to their coach, was the determined play of goalie Mike

Morgan, who got "tougher and stronger" as the games became more intense. The Bears from Berkeley lost the NCAA final match against UCLA — its third loss to the Bruins that season — but Cal bounced back in 1971 to win the national title.

Morgan was selected as an All-American while playing goalie for Beverly Hills High

School before accepting a scholarship to play water polo at Cal. He was also an All-American during college and the goalie for the US gold medal team at the 1969 Maccabiah Games in Israel. He moved to Mercer Island with his wife, Linda, in 1974 and is now an attorney with the Seattle law firm Lane Powell PC. The Morgans have two children and four grandchildren.

"Water polo is not as popular here as it is in California, so there are not as many places to play," Morgan said. "For now, I've taken up running so I can try to keep up with my wife."

Terry Robinson

July 20, 1973, Portland, OR

Marathon man captures Seafair Race and invitation to Maccabiah Games

Competition is more than participation for Terry Robinson. It's also about giving back to his community. The energetic father of four expects to finish first in whatever challenge he takes on. Tired of the emotional outbursts from players on the basketball court at the Jewish Community Center, Robinson replaced the pick-up games at the JCC with runs along the quiet shores of Lake Washington near his home on Mercer Island. But his first two-mile jog almost changed his mind.

"It was awful. I hated it," he said. "But I could not go back to the yelling and screaming on the basketball court. So I decided to give running one more try."

The second day of running was "tolerable." His third day was even better. By the end of two weeks, Robinson had learned to enjoy the solitude and satisfaction of running.

Later, he decided to challenge himself by entering his first race, the 2005 Swedish SummeRun & Walk for Ovarian Cancer.

"This 5K race definitely ignited my competitive spirit. It also motivated me to run for such a meaningful cause," Robinson remembers. "I was not just running alone. Participating in sponsored events allowed me to direct my efforts back to my own community."

Robinson never imagined taking part in a true endurance race until he was invited to be part of a co-ed team in the grueling Hood to Coast relay over Labor Day weekend that year. The race required him to run three six-mile legs over a 20-hour pe-

Robinson heads to the finish line

riod. Robinson ended up recording the fastest times on his 12-person team.

The relay inspired the 1991 Mercer Island High School graduate to test himself even further. He entered marathons in Boston, Chicago, New York and back home in Seattle and quickly became the favorite to win many of the shorter-distance community races.

In 2012, he finished first among 579 runners in the July event sponsored by Swedish Hospital, third in the Redmond Derby Dash 5K, second in the Spirit of Bellevue 12K and first (among 727 runners) in the Kirkland Half Marathon.

Running, according to Robinson, is 90 percent mental and only 10 percent physical. He explained that running allowed him to discover his true potential.

Robinson receives invitation to join Team USA

His personal highlight came in 2012 when he broke through the tape at the conclusion of the annual 5K Seafair Torchlight Run with a time of 17:23. The 39-year-old was especially proud of his 14-year-old son Aidan, who won his age division at the race along the streets of downtown Seattle. Robinson was quick to add that he is equally proud of his other children: Jordan, 16, Alexander, 13, and 8-year-old Elena.

"My times in the Seafair race had gotten better and better each year, but winning was an unexpected thrill," he said. "People are lined up 10-deep along the Torchlight Parade route. It's a smaller race, but the crowds are almost as in-tense as the Boston Marathon."

Robinson's improvement was also noted by the organizers of the American team for Maccabiah 2013. The Seattle native was invited to run as part of Team USA in the half marathon against Jewish competitors from around the world in Israel in July. "The Games in Israel have been on my radar since I began running," he said. "If I work hard and improve my times, there is no reason I shouldn't come home with a medal."

This will not be Robinson's first trip to the Holy Land. He first traveled to Israel for his Bar Mitzvah in the '80s. This will also be a repeat performance at the Maccabi Games. Robinson was part of the Seattle basketball team — along with high school teammate Aaron Wolff — that played in the 1988 Games in Chicago. He coached the Seattle girls' basketball team two years later at the 1990 Games in Detroit.

Robinson's upcoming invitation to run in Israel also earned him an invitation to be the guest speaker at Camp Solomon Schechter. His motivational message to the young audience combined his passion for his athletics with his devotion to Judaism.

As the great-grandson of a butcher who served as the reverend of the Sephardic Congregation in Seattle, Robinson said he grew up in an Orthodox home with a deep connection and sense of pride for his Sephardic heritage. Like many of his relatives, Robinson has traced his roots back to the Island of Rhodes. His grandparents set an example by playing an active role in their respective communities: Charles and Florence Robinson were involved with Temple Beth El in Tacoma, while Lazar and Katherine Scharhon were active at Sephardic Bikur Holim in Seattle. Katherine Scharhon continues to be Sephardic Bikur Holim's Ladies Auxiliary co-president.

Robinson credits his parents for encouraging him to learn about his faith. He attended both Seattle Hebrew Academy and Phoenix Hebrew Academy through the eighth grade. His mother taught first grade in the community for 40 years, and his father served as director of the JCC and continues to serve as the executive director of the Y Camps in New Jersey.

"Being Jewish is more than my religion," said Robinson. "It is truly who I am."

David Schiller

August 6, 1965, Denver, CO

Sports fan, player, coach, mascot, cynic

After coaching at the JCC for several years, in 1988 David Schiller and Harley Spring were asked to coach the boys' basketball team of Seattle's first delegation to the Maccabi Youth Games in Chicago. The experience left an indelible impression on everyone who participated.

"Walking into opening ceremonies for the first time at Northwestern Stadium was an emotional experience," remembers the Mercer Island High School and

University of Washington graduate. "First, to be representing the Seattle Jewish community, and second, to realize that I was surrounded by thousands of other participants...all Jewish!" Schiller went on to coach in four more Maccabi

1988 Seattle Maccabi Team Front row (l to r) Glen Caro, Aaron Coe, co-coach Harley Spring, co-coach David Schiller. Second Row: Russell Katz, Tim Wall, Steven Schwarz, Jason Burns, Terry Robinson, Michael Sichel. Back Row: Charlie Barokas (barely visible), Robert Starin, Aaron Wolff, Jonathon Rubinstein

games, winning a silver medal in Los Angeles in 1994. He later was a co-chair of athletic events when Seattle hosted the games in 1997.

Seattle Sounders mascots David Schiller with his brother Michael and friend Michael Hector

Schiller's lifelong passion for sports may be best exemplified by how far he went to show his support for the Seattle Sounders during their North American Soccer League years (1974-1983). During his bar mitzvah year in 1978, he and his brother Michael and their friend Michael Hechter had kid-sized soccer ball costumes made, then called the team's office and offered to be their mascots. The stunt earned them tickets to every home game, use of the players' entrance, and a sideline vantage where the three teens entertained the Kingdome crowd.

Schiller also grew up a fan of sports radio, listening to Wayne Cody on KIRO. "My passion for talking sports was reignited when I first called the Fabulous Sports Babe, an opinionated host on KJR sports radio," Schiller said. Over time in the mid-'90s, he developed a character called the "Sonic Cynic," who called in frequently, using poetry and banter to question the local team whose popularity was at its peak.

"The phones at KJR would light up with callers going crazy, which only drove me to call more," Schiller recalled laughing. His highlight though was when he lost a bet that the Sonics would make the Western Conference finals in 1996. "My debt: I had to have 'I Love the Glove' [Sonics guard Gary Payton's nickname] shaved in the back of my head. It was done in front of the Key Arena prior to one of the games in the final series and the crowd went nuts."

Schiller has participated in the Stroum JCC Co-Ed Softball League and has coached a team for nearly 20 seasons. In 2001, his team "Yo La Tengo" won the A division's championship. He also has played basketball at the J from Biddy Basketball through the Master's League, and continues to play every weekend today. David also played and coached in the BBYO basketball league and won titles in both roles.

Most recently, Schiller put a challenge out to the community to raise money for MS research, a disease that struck his brother Michael several years ago. Over the course of three and a half hours, David drained 1,000 free throws and raised nearly $3,500.

After losing a bet to KJR Radio's Fabulous Sports Babe, the "Sonic Cynic" gets his head shaved by barber Donna

Howard Shalinsky

October 18, 1960, Kansas City, KS

Maccabiah tennis player finds he's "not in Kansas anymore"

When Howard Shalinsky tried out for the adult tennis team for the 1997 Maccabiah Games in Israel, he didn't plan on facing an internationally ranked player.

Shalinsky began playing tennis at the age of ten in Kansas City, and continued to play as an adult in numerous matches and tournaments after moving to Seattle. In 1997, he tried out and made the Maccabiah tennis team giving him an opportunity to travel to Israel and compete with over 5,000 Jews from around the globe.

Playing in the 35 and older division he was seeded against Shlomo Glickstien, who had

Shlomo Glickstein and Howard Shalinsky outside the courts at the 1997 Maccabiah Games in Israel

been ranked as high as No. 22 as a singles player and No. 28 in doubles. He was also Israel's all-time leader in total wins. Shalinksy was hoping for an upset, but found himself on the short end of a 6-1, 6-0 match. Despite the loss, Howard enjoyed an incredible experience in these Jewish Olympics.

In 1998, he competed on the Seattle Tennis Center team that went to the national tournament. Over the next two years, playing in the 4.0 division, he won the local Avanti tournament and the Seattle City Tournament.

Shalinsky looks forward to trying out for another Maccabiah Games in the coming years in the Masters or Grandmasters division. He continues to practice hard and plays frequently at Green Lake and the Seattle Tennis Center. He feels a re-match with Glickstein is imminent and is determined to change the outcome.

Amy Posner Wolff

August 8, 1972, Seattle

"Noodles" cleared thousands of hurdles across the globe

Amy Posner Wolff has seen the world as a dedicated competitor in track and field. Her best event was the hurdles, but she was always available to compete in any of the field events. Eighteen years later, she still smiles at the thought of her best efforts at the javelin and shot put during high school. Despite more than two decades since track meets and smelly equipment bags, Wolff still remembers the people she met and the friendships she has maintained with athletes from dozens of countries.

Amy Posner Wolff, 3rd from left, at the Pan Am Games in Uruguay

Nicknamed "Noodles" because of her curly blond hair, Wolff said that her strongest bonds were created when she competed in the Maccabi Games. "My Maccabi experience probably brought me closer to my Jewish identity," she reflected. "The Games in Chicago [in 1988] were great, partially because we were the first-ever delegation from Seattle. But also because my dad helped organize it and that's when I first met my future husband."

The international Maccabi competition in 1991 in Uruguay impacted Wolff in a completely different way. She remembers being amazed by the number of athletes who had traveled from all over the world to compete in South America. "And they were all Jewish," she said.

Wolff played soccer and ran track at Lake Washington High School, where "there were not a lot of Jewish kids." She graduated in 1990 and ran the 400-meter hurdles all four years at the University of Washington, starting out as a walk-on.

While a broken foot cost Wolff her chance to run at the 1993 Maccabiah Games in Israel, since 2000 she has continued her connection to the sport by coaching hurdlers at Mercer Island High School. Wolff and her basketball-playing husband Aaron Wolff both grew up as members of Temple De Hirsch Sinai. They have two boys and a girl who all will be attending pre-school at the JCC.

THE STROUM JEWISH COMMUNITY CENTER

In honor of the first Seattle delegation to the
North American Maccabi Youth Games
In Chicago, from August 18-25, 1988, these young men and women
competed with enthusiasm and ability, and brought honor
to themselves and their community.

MACCABI SPORT ROSTER

BASKETBALL
Charlie Barokas
Jason Burns
Glen Caro
Aaron Coe
Russell Katz
Terry Robinson
Jonathan Rubenstein
Steve Schwartz
Mike Sichel
Robert Starin
Tim Wall
Aaron Wolff

*MEDAL WINNER
(Maiden Name)

KARATE
Sam Rosen*

PING PONG
Avi Tanners

RACQUETBALL
Ronen El-Ad

SWIMMING
Paul Chasan
Ashley (Cohen) Slater*
David Goodman
Julie Pease
Deborah (Schneider) Lurie
Rachel (Schneider) Schwartz

TENNIS
Adam Caplan
Amy (Clarfeld) Lavin
Tim Gottesman*
Dan Guralnick*
David Herrman*
Kim (Muscatel) Waldbaum
Ryan Tacher*

TRACK
Lisa Chasan*
Sam Chestnut
Daniel Ehrlich
Erick Goldman*
Karen (Pantilat) Rasmussen*
Amy (Posner) Wolff*
Stacy (Robinson) Ezrine*
Karen (Schwartz) Friedman*
Jody Shapiro

WRESTLING
Mark Bunin*
Ryan Elsemore
Mike Greenberg

Sponsored by:
The Posner/Wolff and Muscatel/Waldbaum Families

ARIEL SCHNEIER

TO OUR FAVORITE SWIMMER!

Seattle Summer Swim League
1990-92 All-City Butterfly Champ

Western State Finals and Maccabi Games, 1994

Love,
Mom and Dad

Ben Belur

Congratulations Ben
on making the
2013 USA Maccabiah
Men's Golf Team!

We are so proud of
you and can't wait to
cheer you on in Israel.

Jerry, Nancy,
Brianne, Jacqueline
and Brittany
(Your #1 Fans!)

Asher Lane

Enjoying the day cross-country skiing!

Matthew, Jeff and Josh Coopersmith

Our grandson, Asher Lane, doing a one-handed cartwheel!

Fil and Janet Rose

SOFTBALL

Junior Sephardic League

A league of their own

Sam Angel remembers fondly his days on the diamond playing on the Junior Sephardic League fast-pitch softball team. At 16, Angel, Mike Himes and Ray Moscatel were the youngest to play on a team of mostly 22 to 24-year old men. "We played against all sorts of teams, once or twice a week and we even won a couple of championships, " Angel remembered.

Originally named the Young Hebrew's Literary Club, the organization of young Sephardic adults changed its name to reflect the many social and sporting events the group staged. "The big event of the year was the Snowball Dance held at the Olympic Hotel," recalled Ike Baruch.

The softball team played games at Garfield High School, where many of the players also attended classes. "Our best pitcher," Angel said, "was Victor Alhadeff. He had great control and

speed." And while Angel thought shortstop Jerry Israel was the best player on the team, Baruch thought Ray Moscatel was the most talented. "He was a helluva third baseman with the softest hands I'd ever seen," said Baruch. Angel recalled being coached by Al DeLeon, who was "a natural leader and a great strategist."

Junior Sephardic League softball team, circa 1948

Back: Jerry Israel (C, CF), Ike Baruch (RF), Sam Angel (CF, SS, 2B), Myer "Mike" Himes (2B), Ray Moscatel (3B)
Front: Joe Peha (OF), Dave Calvo (1B), unknown boy, Bob Hanan (OF), Leon Alhadeff (OF), Louie "Jerry" Israel (SS)
Not pictured: Victor Alhadeff (P), Ike Hanan (P), Ed Bensussen (C)

Sam Angel, 1950

Victor Alhadeff, 1943

Ike Baruch, 1943

Joe Peha, 1944

Ray Moscatel, 1948

SJCC Co-ed Softball League

Diamond in the rough sparkles after 30 years

At one time the Stroum Jewish Community Center's Co-ed Softball League was billed as "The largest Jewish softball league in the United States." As the league's 33rd season came to a close in 2013, the softball league remains a popular focal point for Jews of all ages.

ACJS playing at Miller Field in 1982

The league began when Stuart Willner of Bikur Cholim Machzikay Hadath Congregation in Seward Park organized a softball team as part of their outreach program. Two doors down Morgan Street, Albert Angel from Sephardic Bikur Holim fielded a team as well. Shortly thereafter, the Jews on Call Co-Ed League (JOC) was formed with its mission of providing "a safe, family-oriented, social venue

for young people in the Jewish Community."

The 1981 inaugural season started with six teams, five of which represented local synagogues: Bikur Cholim Machzikay Hadath, Sephardic Bikur Holim, Temple De Hirsch Sinai, Herzl-Ner Tamid and Congregation Beth Shalom. The sixth team, the All City Jewish Singles, was organized by David Calderon, who culled together a team from the JCC's singles volleyball league. Games were played that first season at Miller Field on Capitol Hill, with the playoffs taking place at Dahl playground near Temple Beth Am.

Three years later, when Willner needed to find a new home for the league, the SJCC took over. Matt Grogan, SJCC Physical Education Director, served as league coordinator and was aided by a strong volunteer committee.

Part of what has made the league unique has been the "mishagas" rules, which have evolved over time as situations arose. In one instance, after Herzl's Mark Piezer had been injured in a serious motorcycle accident, an early league rule allowed a player who could hit but not run, to have a courtesy runner who would start with one hand on the backstop behind the hitter.

For many years, some of the toughest league meetings focused on the debate about who was eligible to play in the "Jewish" League. This issue often showed the depth of passion many of the early organizers had about this league and the philosophy behind its existence. A search of league records found letters from community members and rabbis discussing the impact of the league on their lives and that of their congregations. League chairpersons over the years included Charles Kapner, Ron Pergamit, Steve Kasner and Patty Willner, Jay Agoado, Lindsey Schwartz and Adam Stein.

After a few seasons at Miller Field, the games were moved to Genesee Field on Rainier Avenue. This was somewhat of an upgrade since the games would be played on grass fields rather than on Miller's all-rock diamonds. But Genesee Field had its own character. Local football practices or cricket matches often competed for space in the outfield. One evening, Dana Gold, coach of Beth Shalom, was trapped in a bathroom stall in the Community Center while a drug deal escalated into a fight. On another night, Brian Lurie was walking to where his car was parked and instead found only a lone screwdriver! It was one of about a dozen cars prowled that night. After that, the league paid for a security guard.

In 1988, the league moved to South Mercer

Randy Eskenazi pitches for Sir Plus in 1988

Playfields on Mercer Island, which could accommodate four games at a time. This became necessary as the six-team league grew to 30 in the 1990's. The league sprouted a complex genealogy of teams. Brackets resembled family trees as teams formed around siblings, cousins and in-laws. It's estimated that between 2,000 and 2,500 players have played in the league. As of this writing in 2012, one of the founding teams, Congregation Beth Shalom, is still led by its original captain, Stan Sorscher. Ron Pergamit is another player from the inaugural season who was still playing at this time.

The first two league champions were Temple De Hirsch and the All-City Jewish Singles. In the 80's and early 90's, the league was dominated by the likes of the Grizwalds (formerly All-City Jewish Singles), Kamas Realty, Ezzy Bezzy, TDHS and Sir Plus.

To accommodate different skill levels, the league created four divisions with some organizations fielding multiple teams. For a few years in the early 2000's, Yeshiva had an A, C and D team. As players "matured," (in both senses of the word) their teams moved up and down throughout the years. Only one team, the Bitewings, began as a D team and worked their way up to the A level. Over the 30+ years, half of the

Charles Kapner's 1984-1989 JCC Softball season records

current teams in the league have been around for at least a decade.

Yo La Tengo won the A-league championship in 2001

While the Seattle Mariners won an historic 116 games in 2001, Yo La Tengo, captained by David Schiller, took the A league championship. The 2004 season saw multiple teams run away with their divisions, at least in the regular season. Ten Plagues was 14-0-1 in the A division before falling to Daniel's Broiler in the finals. Top Katz went undefeated in C and captured the championship. And in D, Happy Hour lost only one game all season before dropping the winners bracket finals to Hobbytown. They came back to beat Hobbytown twice on championship Sunday in two close, hard-fought games. In 2005, Gordon's Bitewings ran the table in the C Division, the most recent champion to go undefeated. In 2006, for the third season in a row, C Division's Temple De Hirsch was undefeated in the regular season, but fell in the championship to Happy Hour 15-6 and 11-8.

One of the wildest playoff runs ever in the C Division occurred in 2007, when the eighth seeded Hebrew National team captured the championship over the number seven team, Jews on First. Hebrew National won as many games during the playoffs (5) as they had in the regular season. Two teams deserve special mention for sustained excellence. The Bulldogs, now the Mighty Ducks, captured the D championship in 2007, 2008, and 2009. And the Jewcers swept through the playoffs to win the A championship in 2010, went 14-1 in the 2011 regular season, and repeated as champions, winning an amazing 25 of 26 games in the top division.

For more than 30 years, the SJCC has provided the greater Seattle area with a wonderful annual ritual. Every spring, captains pull together teams with up and coming talent and diehards who want to extend their playing careers. While some players voluntarily "age-out" of a team, others reach the league's minimum age and join the squad. For Jews that have lived in Seattle for generations, the league offers a chance to connect with landsmen from different synagogues. For unaffiliated Jews and those who are new to the Seattle area, the league has been a means for many to gain a foothold in the Jewish community. All and all, the league has provided decades of fun while drawing our community closer.

The Jewcers won the A-league championship in 2011

The Grizwalds

Team motto: another game, another hero

When David Calderon fielded a team for a startup softball league, he had no idea that his effort would produce a multi-championship squad that would play together for more than a decade.

In 1981, Calderon learned that outreach coordinator for Bikur Cho-lim Machzikay Hadath Congregation Stuart Willner was forming a Jewish co-ed softball league. Willner had commitments from five synagogues, and if Calderon could put together a sixth team, no one would have a "bye" on their schedule.

At one of the open volleyball nights at the Mercer Island JCC, Calderon recruited a number of players who came together as the All-City Jewish Singles (ACJS).

ACJS finished in third place that first season, with Temple De Hirsch Sinai winning the first league championship. By the next season, the TDHS team had disbanded. In 1982, Charles Kapner joined David Calderon to co-coach the team with great success. ACJS completed an undefeated season, including an 18-2 victory in the championship game over Sephardic Bikur Holim.

Early in the 1984 season, one of ACJS' newest players, Sherry Caditz, was playing catcher when a Yeshiva player attempted to beat a throw home. The two collided and Caditz' knee was badly injured. When the ACJS players met for dinner after the game, the mood was somber, with all believing the collision could have been avoided with a slide. The incident prompted the league to add a rule the next season, mandating that every effort must be made to avoid collisions.

Caditz re-joined her teammates at a weeknight practice a couple of weeks later. Accompanying her was her one-eyed dog, Grizwald. The team had the perfect revelation - renaming their team the ACJS Grizwalds to pay tribute to Caditz. Because Grizwald had only one eye, the team joke was that his vision was "20" rather than "20-20," so uniforms were ordered with each player having the number "20" on the back and a dog with an eye patch on the front.

During that same 1984 season, The Grizwalds faced Temple De Hirsch Sinai in the championship game. The teams were tied 12-12 in the bottom of the final inning. ACJS had the bases loaded and one out. A ground ball was hit to the pitcher but the batter froze in

Page 8   The Jewish Transcript   September 2, 1982

TRIUMPHANT! — The Jewish Community Center's All-City Jewish Singles co-ed softball team wound up an undefeated season clinching all 15 games. In the championship, ACJS defeated Sephardic Bikur Holim, 18-2. Other teams in the synagogue league included Herzl-Ner Tamid, Bikur Cholim-Machzikay Hadath, Ezra Bessaroth and Beth Shalom. Shown with their first-place trophy are these members of the All-City Jewish Singles team, left to right: Rick Lindsley, Barbara Earle, Penny Freedman, Joel Saxe, David Israel, Charles Kapner, Sue Amira, Jim Meisner, David Calderon, Brian Lurie, Denise Bornstein, Ron Pergamit, and Jeanette Metzon. Other players not pictured, include Randi Lindsley, Robin Meyers, Howard Gorlick, Dena Brashem, Steve Kasner, Lenny Stochel and Steve Fantle.

1984

the batter's box. The result was a double play, sending the game into extra innings. The ACJS coach slammed the ball into the ground and was ejected from the game. TDHS capitalized on the change in momentum and went on to a 14-12 victory in extra innings.

The Grizwalds played for the championship every season from 1984 to 1991, winning the title in half of their appearances. During that eight-year stretch, The Grizwalds' collected 100 regular season wins, 13 losses and four ties.

The Grizwalds practiced often, and were serious about practicing hard. While the team wanted to have fun, they believed that winning was important and fun would be a by-product of winning. Team member Earl Caditz often reminded players, "the way you play in practice is the way you'll play in the games." His words lost a bit of cred-

Corey Goldstein of TDHS and Charles Kapner both played in the championship game with leg injuries

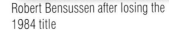
Robert Bensussen after losing the 1984 title

ibility when an umpire, who watched Earl slide into third base, told him that "Pete Rose had nothing to worry about". Earl, along with pitcher, Brian Lurie, kept the team in good humor. Most practices and games ended with the team going out together to eat.

There weren't any players that were physically imposing on the team, but when opponents arrived at the field, they often expected to lose. This was a team that was the sum of its parts, with many good players rather than one or two superstars. Everyone had a role and everyone knew how to do the little things that led to success. "Another game, another hero," was often heard in the dugout after games.

While Alan Wittenberg's combination of outstanding play at shortstop, clutch hitting, and speed, may have put him a step ahead of the other Grizwalds, an injury late in the season kept him out of the 1990 playoffs. Martin Goldberg stepped in at shortstop and elevated his defense beyond any level he had played the entire season. The Grizwalds again capped their season with another championship.

In addition to Wittenberg and Goldberg, Brian Lurie, Earl Caditz, Jeff Droker, Owen Lubin, Ron Pergamit and Charles Kapner were the key male

Dennis Richman in a close one at first base

Charles Kapner sprints home in 1985

be seeing her the most!

As the innings and the seasons stacked up, players got married, had children and less time to devote to softball. The inevitable decline of skills occurred as well. The Grizwalds moved down to the B league and eventually many players retired or made their way to other teams. Ron Pergamit is the last Grizwald player from the inaugural season who still plays today. The Grizwald players are still great friends today, all thanks to the Jewish softball league.

Melissa DeLooze fires one in to Judy Marx at first base

contributors over the years. Of the females, Melissa Lurie, Judy Posner, Miri Stern, Jana Moshcatel and Julie Schauffer were the standouts.

What also made this team unique was that there were five different head coaches during this eight-year period. Many of the teams in the league kept the same head coach from year to year, but The Grizwalds encouraged greater coaching participation. Since the team felt like a family, it was fine with rotating the alpha dog role (with apologies to Grizwald). A unique head coach dilemma came up for Earl Caditz in 1990 when he had to choose between his wife and his sister as the second baseman in the championship game. But Caditz was a true leader, deciding to go with his wife since he'd

	TEAM NAME	REGULAR SEASON FINISH	COACH	LEAGUE CHAMPION
1981	ACJS	3rd	DAVID CALDERON	DEHIRSCH def. HERZL
1982	ACJS	11-0 1st	CHARLES KAPNER / DAVID CALDERON	ACJS def. SBH
1983	ACJS	3rd	RON PERGAMIT	SBH (16-14) def. HERZL
1984	ACJS GRISWALDS	8-4 2nd	STEVE KASNER	DEHIRSCH def. ACJS
1985	GRISWALDS	8-3-1 1st	CHARLES KAPNER	GRISWALDS def. LOX
1986	GRISWALDS	14-2 2nd	CHARLES KAPNER	DEHIRSCH def. GRISWALDS
1987	GRISWALDS	14-1-1 1st	ALAN WITTENBERG	GRISWALDS def. SIR PLUS
1988	GRISWALDS	13-1-2 1st	LARRY BONSUSSEN / BRIAN LURIE	GRISWALDS def. SIR PLUS
1989	GRISWALDS	13-1 1st	KEITH DEGGINGER / JULIE SCHAEFFER	KAMAS def. GRISWALDS
1990	GRISWALDS	15-1 2nd	EARL CADITZ	GRISWALDS def. EZRA BESS.
1991	GRISWALDS	15-0 1st	KEITH DEGGINGER	DEHIRSCH def. GRISWALDS
1992	GRISWALDS	10-5 5th (tie)	CHARLES KAPNER	DEHIRSCH def. SEATTURST
1993	GRISWALDS	10-5 2nd (tie)	MARTIN GOLDBERG	DEHIRSCH def. CohenWoods
1994	GRISWALDS	8-7 4th	BRIAN LURIE	CucinaCucina def. Healthy Palate

CHAMPIONSHIP RECORDS IN THE 80's

ACJS/GRISWALDS	4 - 3	MOST CHAMPIONSHIPS - 4
DEHIRSCH	3 - 0	MOST APPEARANCES IN CHAMPIONSHIPS - 7
KAMAS	1 - 0	
SBH	1 - 1	ONLY BACK TO BACK CHAMPIONSHIPS: 1987 1988
LOX	0 - 1	
HERZL	0 - 2	ONLY UNDEFEATED TEAM: 1982
SIR PLUS	0 - 2	CONSECUTIVE APPEARANCES IN CHAMPIONSHIPS: 8 years

1985

1990

1986

1991

1988

1992

1989

2012

Grizwalds gather at the WSJHS sponsored softball reunion

The Maccabees

The Maccabees began playing softball in Spokane in 1971. Sponsored by several local Jewish-owned businesses, the Maccabees competed in fast pitch softball leagues for over 25 years, winning several championship titles. The team brought many young Jewish men and families to Temple Beth Shalom, strengthening the Spokane Jewish community. The most frequently asked question by opposing softball players: "Where is the Maccabees Tavern located?"

1981 Maccabees Softball Team

Back row: Ron Taitch, Roger Cohen, Mark Silver, Jay Weiner, Gene Elliot (coach), Mike Rubens, Mike Silver, Al Anders (coach) Becky Corigliano (score keeper)

Front row: Mick Soss, Mark Lax, Mike Denmark, Mike Mitchell, David Brenner, Larry Kuznetz, Jeff Morris, Mike Morris and Scott Morris (bat boys). Missing: C. Rogel

1987 Maccabees Softball Team

Back row: Mickey Cannon, Mick Soss, Gary Leva, Murray Huppin (Melissa), Mike Rubens, unknown, Mark Lax

Middle row: Carl Greenberg, Mike Morris, Jeff Morris, Scott Morris, Alan Rubens, Larry Kuznetz

Front row: Mark Shark, Sam Lax, Sam Rubens, Rachel Rubens, Elysa Kuznetz (Piha), Laura Kuznetz, Rebecca Rubens (Blunt), Stacie Suskin (Rottinghaus). Missing: C. Rogel and M. Mitchell

Brian Lurie enjoys a post game picnic

Ric Lindsley at shortstop and Brian Lurie on the mound for ACJS in 1984

The Grizwald's Earl Caditz in 1985

The Grizwalds walk away with a win in 1986

Todd Peltz swings away in the 1988 championships

Jeff Droker sprints from homplate in 1989

Steve Kasner takes a swing

Just Friends, 1991 B-League Champions

The Fishermen, 1995

Stephen Sadis, Curtis Knopf, 1995

Gary Forman, Rich Strauss, Kym Campbell, David Schiller (coach), Matt Turetsky

Dawn, Karli and Mike Schiller, 1995

Belltown Billiards, 1995 B-League Champions

The Misfits, 1996

Electroimpact, 1997 B2-League Champions

Seattle White Lox, 1997 C-League Champions

Seattle White Lox, 1997 C-League Champions

Seattle White Lox, 1997 C-League Champions

Morrie's Kids, 1998 B-League Champions

Rainier Moving, 1995 A-League Champions

Happy Hour, 2006 C-League Champions

SBH, 2008

Empty Pitchers, 2011 B-League Champions

Jay Berry's, 2011 C-League Champions

Hava Tequila, 2011 D-League Champions

2012 A League Champs – Bitewings

2012 C League Champs – The Mad Batters

2012 D League Champs – JFS

2012 WSJHS-SJCC Softball Reunion

Albert Israel, Bob Solomon, Earl Caditz, Jack Schaloum, Dave Roselle

Steve Kasner and Dave Roselle look through photos from the softball league's earlier days

Howard and Sue Robboy

Zach Duitch, Tiger Budbill and Josh Colwell

Michele Keller and Sylvia Angel

Albert Israel takes a swing in the home run competition

David Schiller serves 'em up

Rusty Federman and Mike Schiller

Warren Libman and Carla Barokas

Mickey Freidman, Nancy and Wayne Morse and Paul Burstein

On the Softball Title Page:

Front Row:
Craig Tall, Gerry Ostroff, Mark Rubin, Brian Kremin, Jim Rosenwald

Back Row:
Joe Franco, Irv Zonkin, Jimmy Taylor, Alan Naness, Mark Pass, Bob Mesher, Bill Schwartz

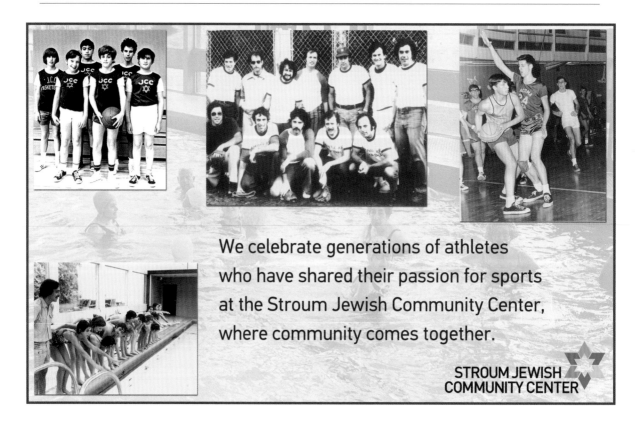

We celebrate generations of athletes
who have shared their passion for sports
at the Stroum Jewish Community Center,
where community comes together.

STROUM JEWISH COMMUNITY CENTER

SPORTS COLLECTORS & RETAILERS

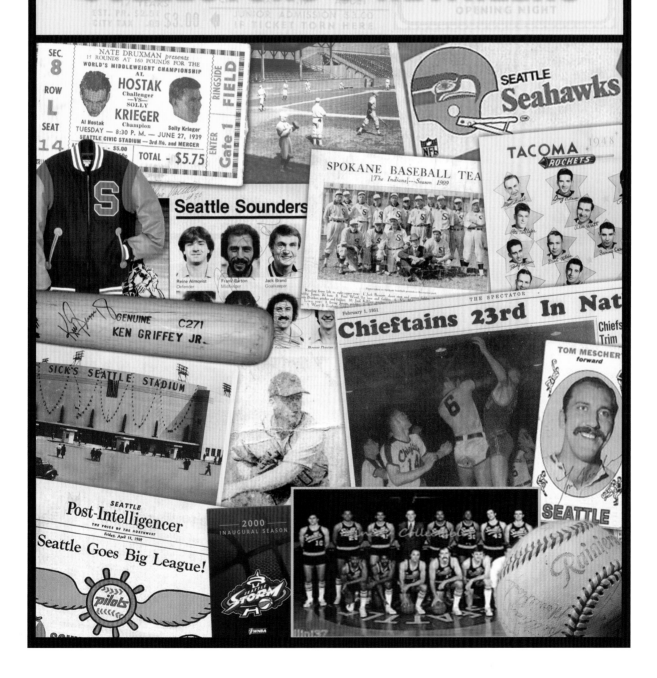

Marc Blau

May 14, 1951, Tacoma

Historian preserves Tacoma's rich sports heritage

A lifelong supporter of athletics in Tacoma and throughout Pierce County, Marc Blau is the executive director of the State of Washington Sports Hall of Fame and chairman of the Tacoma-Pierce County Sports Hall of Fame. A lifetime member of Temple Beth El in Tacoma, some of Blau's earliest and fondest sports memories include playing on an AZA chapter that faced the B'nai B'rith men's organization, and playing forward on the Tacoma chapter's two-time AZA regional basketball championship teams in 1966 and 1967.

The 1969 Stadium High School graduate spent time at both the University of Puget Sound and the University of Washington before earning his degree in recreation planning and administration in 1973. Blau served as the director of community

Marc Blau, back row third from left, with his Tacoma AZA teammates

centers for the Pierce County Parks & Recreation Department from 1973 to 2004, and was granted the Distinguished Service Award from the Washington Recreation & Park Association in 2005.

A member of the Tacoma Athletic Commission since 1989, Blau co-founded the Shanaman Sports Museum of Tacoma-Pierce County with longtime sportswriter and broadcaster Clay Huntington. Located at the Tacoma Dome, the museum opened in 1994 with the mission of educating the public about the community's sports heritage.

Blau served as co-chairman of the Tacoma-Pierce County Baseball-Softball Oldtimers Association for 14 years, and is a recipient of the Dill Howell Award, the Meritorious Service Award and the Gordon Waldo Award from the Northwest Oldtimers Baseball Association.

The Tacoma native has coached slow-pitch softball since 1972, guiding his team to a pair of men's 35-and-over state championships. He was elected to Washington's Slow Pitch Softball Hall of Fame in 2008. He also created the RAGE Sports Club for select girls' volleyball and fast-pitch teams, and established the RAGE Volleyball League, which has served over 6,000 girls and has contributed over $85,000 to local high school volleyball programs.

In addition to his duties as manager of the Sprinker Recreation Center — which included an ice arena where hockey, curling and figure skating were prominent activities — Blau also served a stint as the deputy commissioner of ice hockey for the 1990 Goodwill Games. He also supervised minor off-ice officials for the Tacoma Rockets hockey club from 1991-93. From 1983 to 1991, he was also a member of the statistical crew for the Tacoma Stars of the Major Indoor Soccer League.

But Blau's involvement with volleyball overshadows most of his activities. He began officiating high school volleyball in 1974 and has continued for 39 years. He currently serves as the supervisor of volleyball officials for the 10-team NCAA Division II Great Northwest Athletic Conference. During his volleyball career, Blau officiated six seasons of college ball, has

Blau presents plaques to former Seattle Mariners Edgar Martinez and John Olerud and daughter of columnist and former Seattle Rainier, Emmet Watson, to honor their induction to the Washington State Sports Hall of Fame

Blau officiating a volleyball match

refereed in six state high school championship tournaments and has served as the official's coordinator for 12 state tournaments. He was named Washington Volleyball Official of the Year in 1996, was a recipient of the National Federation of Interscholastic Officials Association Award in 2008, and received the Tom Cross Service Award in 2009 presented by the Washington Officials Association.

A sports historian with a passion for local history, Blau co-authored *Playgrounds to the Pros: An Illustrated History of Sports in Tacoma-Pierce County* in 2005 and wrote *Baseball in Tacoma-Pierce County* in 2011. He is a collector of area sports memorabilia and maintains the largest collection of Tacoma baseball memorabilia in existence.

Blau and his wife, Cheryl, have been married for 34 years and have two children — CJ is a kindergarten teacher in the Auburn school district and Chad is a strength and conditioning coach with previous experience in the St. Louis Rams and Oakland A's organizations.

Jerry Cohen

January 2, 1958, Brooklyn, NY

Ebbets Field Flannels pays homage to sports history

By the time Jerry Cohen was born, the Dodgers had moved out of the cozy confines of Ebbets Field in Brooklyn and had taken Major League Baseball to the West Coast. Though his father talked about the Dodgers on occasion, Cohen was 11 when the "Miracle Mets" won the World Series in 1969 and has always been a fan of New York's "other" team.

Thirty years after he was born — and 31 years after the Dodgers landed in Los Angeles — Cohen honored his hometown team and the stadium where they played by opening a store in Seattle that specialized in vintage baseball jerseys.

Growing up in Brooklyn and New Jersey, Cohen was fascinated with sports emblems and uniforms. As a youngster, he would purchase baseball cards to see the uniform changes and colors rather than the players. Later in life, when he was performing with his rock band and was unable to find an original Dodgers uniform to wear on stage, he became obsessed with the idea of vintage baseball shirts. Cohen finally had a few wool uniform tops custom-made to replicate the baseball uniform he had only seen in old photographs.

"When people literally wanted to buy the shirt off my back, Ebbets Field Flannels was born," said Cohen. "The original founders of Ebbets Field Flannels remain committed to bringing the quality, beauty and craftsmanship of mid-century American athletic garments to a 21st-century public."

The business took off in 1990 after *Sports Illustrated* magazine ran a full-page article about Ebbets Field Flannels. In addition to the retail store in Seattle's Pioneer Square, Cohen said the effort to honor teams and uniforms from the past now reaches out-

Jerry Cohen at his Ebbets Field Flannels store

side the state of Washington. In fact, he said, 95 percent of the business at Ebbets Field Flannels comes from out of state. "We started as a catalogue store, and then became a web-based business," said Cohen. "Now we're international. We do a lot of wholesale and brand collaborations as well."

The entrepreneur is adamant about one fact: the uniform tops sold by his store are not jerseys. "A jersey is a shirt from any sport, which is not what I am making. I am making flannel baseball shirts," Cohen explained. "The flannel is the same authentic baseball wool-flannel blend used in pro baseball until the 1970s."

Major League teams often order replica uniforms for turn-back-the-clock events during the regular season. Cohen said he was honored when Yankee legends Yogi Berra and Whitey Ford wore baseball shirts from Ebbets Field Flannels during the closing ceremonies at the old Yankee Stadium.

Ebbets Field Flannels has sold more than 20,000 replica baseball shirts since opening its doors, with a client list that includes David Letterman and Spike Lee. Over the years, celebrities and athletes have come into his store to browse the merchandise. "Mike Piazza [the 12-time All-Star who played for the Los Angeles Dodgers and New York Mets] came in once and I didn't even know who he was until he left."

When Cohen reflects on the thrill of witnessing the Mets take the World Series, he has his father to thank for his love of the game. And some 40 years later, he found a way to show his appreciation. Months before filming began on the story of Jackie Robinson, Cohen was asked by the producers to recreate all the minor and Negro League uniforms the film. When "42" premiered in Los Angeles, Cohen was thrilled to be there, but even happier to have his father at his side.

David Eskenazi

July 22, 1960, Seattle

Sports historian and collector shares his treasures with thousands

Seattle native David Eskenazi has amassed an extensive archive of Seattle, Northwest, and West Coast historic sports photographs, artifacts and ephemera. Eskenazi enjoys sharing his collection and zeal for Northwest sports history and has displayed

David Eskenazi with collection (Ben VanHouten)

his historical showcases at numerous museums, historical societies, and community events, including the annual Northwest baseball history display at the Mariners FanFest. His efforts also include working on baseball-themed fundraising events for the Fred Hutchinson Cancer Research Center.

Since the early 1990s, the Seattle Mariners have enlisted Eskenazi to help recognize and illustrate Seattle and the Northwest's 120-year baseball legacy. This collaboration has produced rich, colorful displays at Safeco Field, including seven 35-foot long historical storyboards throughout the main concourse, Fred Hutchinson seat-end stanchions, and classic early photographs on the suite level, all created for the opening of Safeco Field in 1999.

From its opening in 2007 to the present day, Eskenazi has provided thematic ideas, design elements, images, and scores of baseball artifacts for the Baseball Museum of the Pacific Northwest at Safeco Field.

Eskenazi has also contributed visual materials, historical consultation and on-screen interviews for documentaries on the Seattle Rainiers, the Spokane Indians and the Seattle Pilots, as well as images and consultation for a multitude of books, magazines, websites and other media focusing on Northwest sports history. He contributed extensively to *Rain Check: Baseball in the Pacific Northwest,* published by the Society for American Baseball Research, and *Pitchers of Beer: The Seattle Rainiers Story,* penned by local sports writer Dan Raley.

Currently, he and sports journalist Steve Rudman collaborate on "The Wayback Machine" column, for sportspressnw.com. Their colorful essays tell compelling stories that bring to life individuals and teams of a bygone era and are filled with evocative images, many of which have never been seen publicly.

It is not just that Eskenazi has spent decades and untold resources accumulating this treasure of sports artifacts, but it is his willingness to share them with so many organizations, publications and documentaries that has allowed this history to be retold and preserved for generations to come.

Above, David Eskenazi in front of display he created for Safeco Field and below with Seattle Mariner Mike Sweeney who is wearing a Seattle Rainiers uniform that was replicated with Eskenazi's help (Ben VanHouten)

Charles Kapner

January 24, 1956, Seattle

Kid collector becomes baseball historian

It was at a 1964 Seattle Rainiers exhibition game against the Boston Red Sox when 8-year-old Charles Kapner pulled a small black and white card of Rico Petrocelli out of his box of popcorn. Kapner held on to that card and that memory, adding to his collection of both over his lifetime.

Following the lead of his father Don, a philatelist specializing in Israeli stamps, Charles began collecting baseball cards at age 7, beginning with ones that appeared on the back of Post cereal and Jell-O boxes. The following year, he added Topps cards to the collection and found more Rainiers cards in popcorn boxes at Sick's Stadium.

As if it said "I knew him when…" Kapner was especially glad he kept the Petrocelli card when the Red Sox player was promoted to the Major League club and went on to become an All-Star shortstop. These early cards were the very beginnings of a baseball memorabilia collection that could easily fill a museum.

When the Rainiers became the Seattle Angels in 1965, Kapner continued to follow the team and took great pride in their 1966 PCL Championship, as well as enjoying the Major League careers of former Rainier players like Maury Wills, Vada Pinson and Jim Lonborg.

When Sick's Stadium became home to the Pilots, Seattle's first major sports franchise, in 1969, Kapner focused his attention on black-and-white photos of the Pilot players and promotional items and mementoes from the Pilots' inaugural season.

The teenager's collection became famous almost overnight when the Pilots were moved to Milwaukee before the start of the 1970 season. Memorabilia from professional baseball in

Charles Kapner's signed Seattle Rainiers bat is part of his vast sports collection (Mike Siegel/Seattle Times)

Seattle became a hot commodity as the Seattle Pilots became the focus of a prolonged lawsuit against Major League Baseball.

The most infamous member of the Seattle Pilots was pitcher Jim Bouton, who used his year in Seattle as the backdrop for his tell-all, ground-breaking book, *Ball Four*. For the last edition of the book, *Ball Four, the Final Pitch*, Bouton contacted Kapner to supply him with photos of Pilots players.

One of Kapner's most memorable collector moments took place in 1968, when Major League Baseball sent Jimmy Piersall and Mickey Mantle to Seattle Center to promote the con-

Some of Kapner's collection on display at the Evergreen State Fair

cept of a domed stadium. Since the event was not well publicized, Kapner recalled, "My father and I were pleasantly surprised to find only 200 people in the room watching a film on the World Series. When the film ended, the players made a few remarks and then signed autographs for everybody in the room."

When Charles first started collecting, he saw a display of 1964 Topps cards that a student prepared for Broadview elementary school. This inspired him to create his own displays for others to enjoy. Over time he has created displays for Sea-Tac Airport, Seattle University, SPORT Restaurant, MOHAI, the University of Washington, ESPN, Monroe and Puyallup Fairs, Key Arena, and the Summit.

A favorite acquisition was a collection of over 50 different 8x10 player photos that used to hang in the Rainier Brewery. These photos of Seattle Rainiers and Seattle Indians ballplayers wound up in the possession of a former Brewery employee who pitched for the Rainiers. Kapner had been friendly with the ballplayer and after he passed, his widow asked Kapner to make an offer on the photos.

"I've made many friends through collecting. And I'm lucky that some people have generously helped feed my passion for unusual Seattle items. I've received several of the popcorn cards, as well as the 'Old Woody' pitching contest cards from my friends in the hobby. Those are both favorite parts of my collection. I also enjoy recalling the stories that go along with items I acquire. For example, I was given an old Seattle Rainiers clubhouse shoe brush from a neighbor 40 years ago. Someone else contacted me with a 1940 Rainiers autographed serving tray. An Oregon collector friend traded me an 1894 Seattle baseball schedule. You just never know what item might be next."

When a Seattle Pilots DVD was being produced, and a Pilots reunion took place, Kapner was again enlisted to help. "I was given the opportunity to speak at the reunion and produce a display of Pilots and earlier memorabilia from the Seattle Indians, Seattle Rainiers and Seattle

Angels along one side of the hotel ballroom."

That led to another Pilots event at the Burbank Public Library, where Kapner sat on a panel with former players Bouton, Greg Goossen and Tommy Davis, and where he again loaned pieces of his collection for a display. "These retired ballplayers had so much fun together. The library was standing-room only and everyone attending had a great time. I couldn't believe I was actually a part of it."

Another favorite memory of Kapner's was during that one Seattle Pilots season:

Kapner getting an autograph from batting great Ted Williams

On a Friday evening in May of 1969, my father and I took the bus to Sick's Stadium to see the Pilots play the Washington Senators — interestingly, both teams survive today but in different cities [the Pilots became the Milwaukee Brewers and the Senators became the Texas Rangers]. The Pilots' Mike Marshall [who would go on to win the 1974 Cy Young Award with the Los Angeles Dodgers] pitched a remarkable two-hit shutout to defeat the Senators.

The legendary Hall of Famer Ted Williams (arguably the best hitter who ever lived) was the Senator's manager and was clearly frustrated by the loss. At Sick's Stadium, the only way for players and managers to exit was to leave through the same concourse that the fans used.

My father and I were waiting around for autographs when out of the clubhouse area walked the great Ted Williams, rapidly moving through the crowd. I quickly sorted through my cards until I came across his 1958 Topps baseball card. Ted stopped to sign an autograph for a little girl who was standing next to me. I held out the Topps card and asked Ted if he would also sign for me. Ted took my card and my father quickly snapped a picture. Ted returned my signed card and announced to the crowd, "That's it for tonight, folks."

In an instant he was out of the ballpark. I was speechless in my excitement and good fortune. We stayed to chase down a few more autographs and didn't get home until nearly 2 a.m., but for me, it was all worth it. It was an evening I'll never forget.

In addition to collecting, as a senior at Ingraham High School, Kapner's golf team won the state championship. He also spent 28 seasons playing in the JCC Co-Ed Softball League. His team, the ACJS/Grizwalds, were one of the most dominant teams in the mid-1980s. Kapner's baseball collection can be seen at the Helen M. Fuller Virtual Art Gallery at www.seattlepilots.com/imgindx4.html. He is always happy to discuss Seattle baseball history and collecting, and can be reached at ckapner@foxinternet.com or 425-749-6507.

Beau Sadick

January 23, 1951, Seattle

2nd Base owner gives used sporting goods second chance

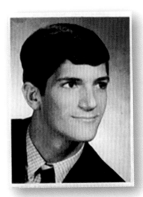

Growing up as the younger brother, Seattle native Beau Sadick learned how to recycle at an early age. In additions to receiving hand-me-down toys and clothes, Beau's father taught him that playing the games you love does not always require the newest or most expensive equipment. Brought up in the Montlake community near the University of Washington, Sadick learned to play golf at the Jefferson Park Golf Course with a set of clubs his father cut down to fit his swing.

Sadick brought his love of sports together with his passion for recycling when he opened 2nd Base, a vintage and quality used sporting goods store on Capitol Hill in 1988. The concept was simple: keep sporting goods out of landfills and in the hands of sports enthusiasts who can use them.

Walking through his retail location near the marina on NE Boat Street is like a tour of sports history. Besides dozens of bats, gloves and sea–soned footballs, there are classic jerseys in the back of the store, an eight-man crew shell hanging from the ceiling and every variety of used — or seldom-used — apparatus to help people lose weight.

Sadick's mission has always remained the same: to provide the right piece of equipment to the right person for the right price. He is committed to the important role of sports in the life of anybody who wants to play.

"What can I say? I'm just an old hippie working with the two things I love: sports and recycling," Sadick said with a proud grin. "It's just the right thing to do."

The name 2nd Base has multiple meanings to Sadick. Besides being the focal point on every baseball diamond, it also means base camp for mountain climbers and the second chance he gives used sporting goods. "I'm just the middle man in this equation," he explained. "Everything goes through second base in baseball. Whether it's a runner rounding the bases or an outfielder making a throw home, second base is central to all the action."

On any day, you can find baseball gear, bicycles, hiking and

Beau Sadick (86) played on Mercer Island HS's varisty squad in 1968

212

camping equipment, athletic wear, or even a kayak. Designers and prop masters scour 2nd Base for vintage sports items.

Like his father told him, quality used equipment can often outperform new gear — and for a lot less money. A used baseball glove is already broken in and ready for play.

Over the years, Sadick has routinely donated sports equipment to areas of the world where a used baseball glove or tennis shoes are considered a luxury item. Gloves, bats and balls from 2nd Base

Sadick sets up for another day of business at 2nd Base

have been shipped to dozens of underprivileged communities served by relief groups and private citizens. 2nd Base has even provided deflated soccer balls to pack sensitive medical equipment and medicine sent to third world countries by relief organizations, including Doctors Without Borders.

"In addition to keeping the supplies secure and protected," said Sadick, "the doctors and relief workers tell me that the soccer balls often provided the most powerful medicine: fun."

Marco Speer

1950, Wichita, KS

Collector's sports knowledge and inventory has earned a growing Eastside reputation

Sports enthusiast Marco Speer developed a passion for sports sitting at his grandfather's feet watching the Brooklyn and Los Angeles Dodgers on television. When questions arose about baseball, Jewish history, or history, Speer

always had his grandfather there to elaborate for him. Having spent his career as a US Army officer, Speer's grandfather could offer first-hand accounts of chasing Pancho Villa along the Mexican border, fighting the Germans in the muddy trenches during World War I, and defending the homeland during World War II.

While working as an assistant manager in the stamp and coin department at The Bon Marché during college, Speer had an inside track on what was available for him to add to his personal stamp and coin collection. He soon added classic comic books, vintage sports cards and memorabilia to his collections.

The sports nut found the perfect job when he managed merchandising, promotions and souvenirs for the Seattle SuperSonics during the team's glory years (including the 1979 championship). Speer put his collection on display in 2002 when he opened Kirkland Sports Cards, transforming a faltering business into the largest Hobby Edition sports card store on the Eastside. His store has grown in part to his strong reputation for fair prices, a variety of products, and his detailed knowledge of his inventory and the memorabilia market in general.

Marco Speer displays a Ken Griffey, Jr. collectible at his store

family in Seattle, Speer has also researched and developed a special focus and database on all four Sephardic players from Major League Baseball and Jews who have played in other professional sports leagues. "I pride myself on being a resource on other ethnicities in American sports, with an extensive collection of players' cards and collectibles," said Speer.

In 2008, the store owner was featured on the front page of *Beckett Sports Cards Monthly* magazine (the official reference guide to card collecting). His store in Kirkland was also the site of a historic card pull. During a promotion, one lucky buyer pulled the oldest original buyback card *ever* found out of a special Hobby Edition box: an 1887 Mike Kelly Allen and Ginter tobacco card valued around $5,000.

Speer also collects Jewish sports memorabilia, working with an elite national group of Jewish sports card collectors. His most prized possessions are an original Topps Vault prototype of a 1964 Sandy Koufax baseball card, and the original print plates for the cards of Hank Greenberg and Al Rosen.

Married into the pioneer Sephardic Calvo

Speer and his son Josh displaying a sampling of their collection

Marco lives on Mercer Island with his wife, Gail, and runs the store with his son, Josh.

The Warshal Family

Marksman hit bull's-eye with iconic sporting goods store

It did not take long for Polish immigrant William Warshal to turn his father's soft goods and fabric business at First and Union into a pawnshop in 1922. The downtown Seattle business became popular for buying and selling a variety of merchandise, including pistols and collector rifles.

The store thrived, and William reached out to his brother Adolph to join him in the family enterprise. Adolph had graduated from the University of Washington as a pharmacist in the late 1920s, but Jewish pharmacists had a difficult time finding work dispensing drugs, according to William's son, Dennis. "There was still anti-Semitism in Seattle at that time," Dennis explained. "So my dad invited his brother to join him in the sporting goods business." A third brother, Milton Warshal, was also involved with the business for a brief time.

By 1936, the Warsaw-natives moved Warshal's Sporting Goods into its location at First and Madison where it remained for 65 years,

eventually purchasing the building from their landlord, Longacres racetrack founder Joe Gottstein. The corner space became home to one of the largest outlets for firearms on the West Coast, as well as boots, fishing tackle, cameras and photographic accessories. Warshal's stocked practically everything local residents could ever need for camping. In those first years of business, Sam Angel, a prominent member of Seattle's Sephardic community, managed the camera department.

William was also his own best customer. He played golf, took hundreds of photographs of his family, skied during the winter months and competed in dozens of national and regional marksmanship tournaments. According to his daughter, Dr. Laurie Warshal Cohen, William was the only non-military member of

Warshal & Sons Sporting Goods in downtown Seattle

the National Rifle Team in the 1930s and won the highest civilian medal for shooting at competition with .22 caliber pistols. Cohen said her father was also an avid tennis player until the day he died. Warshal was ranked in his age category at the age of 85 by the Washington State Seniors Tennis organization. In addition, he earned his pilot's license in 1933 and made one of the first solo landings at night at Boeing Field.

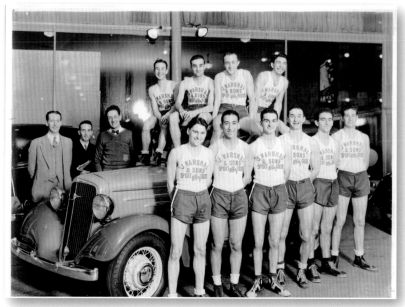

An early 1930s basketball team sponsored by Warshal & Sons Sporting Goods

Over the years, William became notorious for his ability to find and purchase large quantities of manufacturers' closeout items and pass the savings on to his customers. At one point, he bought up the entire production inventory of 8- and 10-foot fiberglass boats and thousands of discontinued sleeping bags from a bankrupt manufacturer. Another time, he bought a cave filled with bat guano. He packaged the droppings as fertilizer and sold them through the garden departments at Valu-Mart discount stores, which were owned and operated by fellow Jewish retailer Leo Weisfield.

Dennis Warshal recalled the time during the 1960s and early '70s when his father was worried about the number of Uzi-style military rifles with high capacity clips being sold. After some lengthy discussions with family and employees, the founders decided to discontinue selling the non-hunting firearms and focus sales on athletic clothing and footwear. "My father rationalized the move by asking, 'how many guns could one person ever want? Or need?'" said Dennis. "But they will always buy new clothes and need new shoes."

The office in the rear of Warshal's Sporting Goods was a regular stopping point for traveling Orthodox rabbis who passed through Seattle on fundraising campaigns for various Jewish causes over the years. "Employees knew that the gentlemen with the long beards, black suits and hats should be ushered directly into my father's office," said Dennis. "My father and uncle had a reputation as honest and ethical businessmen. They enjoyed business together for over 50 years and they always supported the Jewish community."

Dennis and his first cousin, (Adolph's son) Jerry Warshal, managed the store until 1992 when Dennis sold his interest in the family business to his cousin. The property was eventually developed into a hotel after the store closed its doors in 2001.

The Goldstein Family

Celebrating all sports in Washington through all seasons

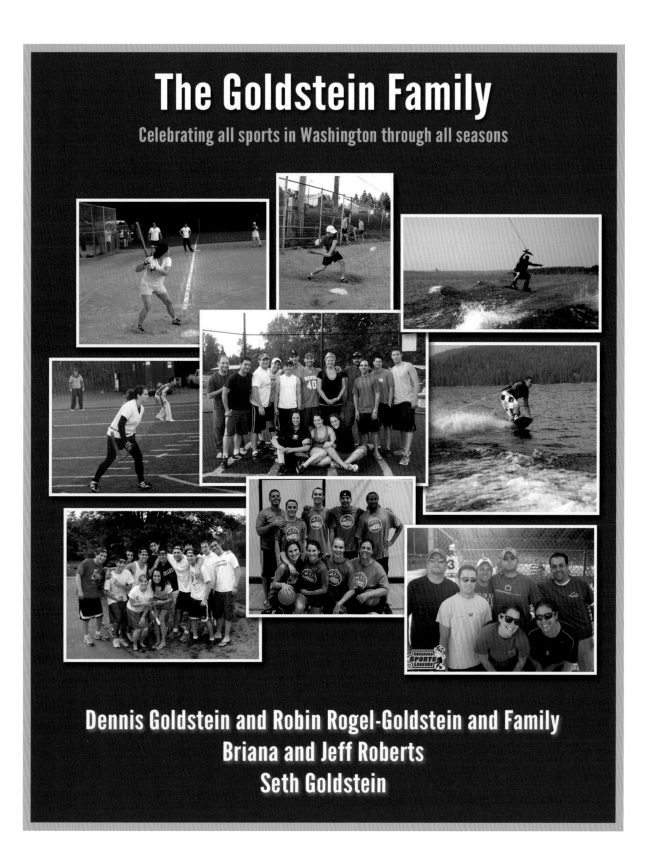

Dennis Goldstein and Robin Rogel-Goldstein and Family
Briana and Jeff Roberts
Seth Goldstein

Levi and Jordan Stoner

getting ready for a swim meet at
Newport Hills Swim Club

Proud grandparents,
Jane Isenberg and Phil Tompkins

The Kapner Family

Thanks WSJHS for a great book,

**Charles and Betsy Kapner,
Joshua and Julianna Mason and Velcro**

GO WSJHS!

Sydney Linkon

**Cheers,
Cindy and Steve Linkon**

MAZEL TOV TO ALL JEWISH JOCKS!

**Julie and Jeff Morris
Spokane**

SPORTS MEDIA

Steve Bunin

February 20, 1974, Seattle

Former Mariners batboy lives out his dream behind ESPN anchor desk

Moses was only allowed to view the broad panorama of the Promised Land from the top of Mount Nebo before his death. As a kid growing up on Mercer Island, Steve Bunin could only see his version of the Promised Land on TV. But in August of 2003, he was allowed entrance to that hallowed place when he was offered his dream job as an anchor with ESPN. In 2011, Sports Illustrated proclaimed Bunin "one of the most underrated talents in sports journalism."

Breaking into the broadcast field, Bunin crisscrossed the country reporting sports in small markets across Michigan, Arizona and upstate New York before landing at the 24-hour sports network in Bristol, CT. Best known for his interviews and anchoring coverage of major sporting events, Bunin admitted that his most

Steve Bunin, a baseball and "Boz" fan in 1988

difficult and rewarding assignment to date was attending the 2002 Super Bowl with 16-year-old Ari Grashin.

The two had met while Bunin was coaching the junior varsity basketball team at Northwest Yeshiva High School on Mercer Island while he was "between jobs" in broadcasting. Steve remembered Grashin as one of the best players on his team, but that the teenager suddenly began having difficulty with his balance. When the problem was diagnosed as a brain tumor, Steve reached out to the Grashin family. "He was our most dedicated player. The spindly sophomore guard could light it up from 23 feet," Steve recalled as if it were last week. "He usually didn't want anyone helping, but for some reason he let me in. We formed a bond — an undeniably strong one."

When Chai Lifeline granted the teenager's wish to attend the Super Bowl in New Orleans, he asked Bunin to make the trip with him. "Ari was starting to lose his hair from the latest round of chemo treatments," said Bunin. "I'll admit to being more than just a little nervous. His mom and dad gave me the names and locations of the five closest cancer centers and a long list of warnings about what he should or should not be allowed to do. Here was a kid who was strictly kosher. But he was also a typical teenager who was a picky eater, too."

The bond between Bunin and Grashin grew strong enough to survive Bunin accepting a position with a television station in Kalamazoo, MI. The sportscaster flew back to Seattle six times in the last six weeks of Ari's life to be with his friend until his death in September of 2002. "I was just so sad when he was in the final stages that I wanted to spend every possible second I could with him," Bunin remembers. "I was consumed with sadness. Flying across the country was something I had to do."

Bunin on the set of ESPN's Outside the Lines in 2012

The experience inspired Steve to give back, and he has mentored at-risk teenagers and coached basketball teams for the past 10 years. In 2010, his co-workers recognized these efforts by honoring him as the first anchor at ESPN to win the company's prestigious Game Ball award for character among employees in Bristol. Bunin admitted that he silently shed a tear for Grashin during the presentation. "Ari taught me about courage in the face of adversity," said Bunin. "He gave me the strength to appreciate my life. And the importance of sharing that lesson with others."

For Bunin, the Maccabi Games served as the highlight of his personal athletic career for more than a dozen years. He played basketball for the Seattle team at the 1990 Games held in Detroit and coached Team San Francisco at the 2001 Games in Atlanta. He also took a team from Hartford to the 2004 Games in Boston.

Bunin characterized his religious path as being anything but a straight line. Brought up in a Conservative Jewish home on Mercer Island, Bunin said his parents drove on Shabbat and did not prevent him from performing his duties as a batboy for the Mariners for night games on Friday or day games on Saturday. "They understood," he said. "My parents taught me about the importance of fulfilling my obligation." Bunin confessed that he consumed more than his share of shellfish in the years before he made the decision to follow traditional dietary laws.

Bunin graduated from Mercer Island High School in 1992 and is on the school's list of notable alumni. He went on to earn his undergraduate degree from Syracuse University before embarking on his climb up the career ladder. Between stints on the air, Bunin scrubbed floors, worked in construction, worked as a substitute teacher and a barista, and even did one night of stand-up comedy.

His responsibilities at ESPN ranged from anchoring "Sports Center" and "Baseball Tonight" to "NFL Live," "College Football Live" and the primetime slot on ESPN Radio. In 2012, after nine years at the sports network, Bunin took a position as the lead anchor at Comcast SportsNet in Houston, TX, the 4th largest city in the nation.

Bunin's workload means that he is often required to cover sporting events on Friday nights or Saturdays, and he is quick to point out that he takes full advantage of the rare occasions when he can be home to spend Shabbat with his wife, Viviane, and their 2-year-old daughter, Gabriela, as often as his hectic schedule allows.

"We try to do Friday night dinner together as often as possible," he said with a sigh. "We go to shul on Saturday mornings whenever we can. And nothing is better than a Shabbat nap in the afternoon." Eventually, Steve professed, he would like to get to a point in his life and his career that would allow him to shut off the television and his computer for Shabbat. "But I'm not quite there yet."

Stan Farber

November 22, 1941 – September 5, 2005, Tacoma

Tacoma sportswriter covered beat for 46 years

Stan Farber was a lifelong Tacoma resident and one of the area's top sportswriters. For 46 years he covered virtually every local sport for the *The News Tribune* and as a sportswriter for hire under the banner of Farber News Service. Farber's passion for sports writing first emerged during his time at Stadium High School. He served as the sports editor for the student newspaper while managing the school's 1959 state championship basketball team.

Enrolled at the nearby College of Puget Sound, he served as the sports editor for the

Farber interviews MLB Commissioner Bowie Kuhn in the Kingdome during its construction

in 2006. Three years later he was inducted into the Tacoma-Pierce County Sports Hall of Fame.

With a wealth of experience to draw from, Farber was known by many as the "King of Trivia" and enjoyed compiling local sports trivia questions that invariably would stump his family, friends and fellow sportswriters.

Farber was a longtime member of the Baseball Writers' Association of America and a member of the Baseball Hall of Fame selection committee. He also served on the University of Puget Sound's alumni board and athletic hall of fame committee, as well as the Pierce College athletic advisory committee. Farber passed away on September 5, 2005, in Tacoma.

school newspaper and the sports information director for the athletic department. While serving both these roles and earning degrees in journalism and English literature, Farber also began his professional sports writing career at *The News Tribune* in 1959.

Later at the *Tribune*, he became one of the most vocal supporters of the "Dome of Our Own" campaign to build the Tacoma Dome. For his efforts, the Tacoma Athletic Commission presented him with the President's Award on the Tacoma Dome's opening night in 1983.

After nearly three decades at the *Tribune*, Farber ventured out on his own, starting the Farber News Service in 1986. Working as a correspondent for numerous major news outlets, Farber had his articles published in countless national magazines. He received the Pacific Northwest Swimming Association Media Award in 1990 and was inducted into the Tacoma-Pierce County Old-Timers Baseball-Softball Association Hall of Fame as a sportswriter

Farber mugs for the camera

Adam Gordon

February 14, 1967, Seattle

Broadcaster brought hat trick of talents to teams

For Adam Gordon, learning to call a hockey game while following a high-speed puck around the ice wasn't enough. He also learned to design computer graphics and create software to track sports statistics; the ultimate hat-trick of hockey broadcast talents.

While earning his BA in Communications at Washington State University, Gordon was cutting his teeth behind the radio mic for the Spokane Chiefs of the Western Hockey League. After calling games there and hosting a weekend talk show from 1988-1990, Gordon was hired to call the radio play-by-play for the Tacoma Rockets and was the director of broadcasting.

Adam Gordon while broadcasting for the Everett Silvertips

Gordon recalled that his parents were very excited to hear that he got his first "real" broadcast job and came to Tacoma to watch him call a game from the booth. "I'm a bit of a pacer if I have to stand and call a game," he explained. "And as the night went on, my dress shirt started to slip out of my slacks. Without hesitation, my mother walked down next to me - while I'm on the air - and whispers into the open mic, 'Adam, tuck in your shirt.' It was a broadcast moment I'll never forget." While in Tacoma, he took it upon himself to design a statistics program that was ultimately used by the coaches and the general manager.

In 1994, he moved on to the Houston Aeros of the International Hockey League, where he was the team's TV and radio play-by-play announcer and the IHL's announcer for nationally televised games. He also began creating graphics for the Aeros' television broadcasts.

Gordon's shot broadcasting for the National Hockey League came in 2000, when was hired to call a game for the Nashville Predators. Later that year, he returned to the Northwest and designed a baseball database system, a real-time stats system for college football and basketball and a revolutionary interface that was used for the U.S. Olympic track and field trials in 2008 and 2012. In 2001, his graphics skills landed him work with NHK TV of Tokyo, where he designed all the graphics for their Major League Baseball telecasts.

From 2007-2012, Gordon was the broadcaster for the WHL's Everett Silvertips on Comcast TV. While Gordon designs graphics for the Pac-12 Network, he continues to look for opportunities to get back in the hockey broadcast booth.

Dave Grosby

August 3, 1960, Buffalo, NY

'The Groz' is synonymous with Seattle sports talk

Although it's been almost four decades, Dave Grosby can still remember, in detail, how nervous he was walking into the Deer Lake Training Camp in upstate New York for the chance to interview Muhammad Ali. The room was filled with Ali's entourage, including his trainer Angelo Dundee and his sparring partner, Larry Holmes. The young reporter was disappointed when it seemed that Ali was not in the room. Then Grosby heard the muffled champ's voice from under a mound of towels on the sofa: "I smell a reporter."

Ali emerged from the pile of laundry with a large grin on his face and introduced the star-struck teenager to the celebrities in the room. He was only 15 years old at the time, but Dave Grosby knew he had to make the most of his opportunity to interview the American icon. The People's Champion escorted the young journalist around the remote mountain facility while he shared stories, talked about his career and answered questions about his upcoming fight against Leonard Spinks. Grosby was so enthralled with the "one-sided conversation" that it took him 20 minutes to realize that he had forgotten to turn on his tape recorder.

The radio personality, known as "The Groz" to sports fans in Western Washington, helped pioneer sports talk radio in Seattle. In 1992, when he joined KJR 950, the former rock-'n'-roll station had just switched formats to become only the third radio station in the country with the interactive sports format. Grosby was recruited away from KFI in Los Angeles, where he had replaced the legendary Gary Owens during morning drive time.

Hiring Grosby and switching formats was part of an overall marketing plan by Barry Ackerley, who owned both the radio station and the NBA's Seattle SuperSonics. Grosby was such a sensation with sports fans in Seattle, KIRO radio recruited him 18 months later to replace longtime sports personality Wayne Cody on

Dave Grosby and Bob Stelton of 710 ESPN Seattle

Sportsline. That began an intense competition between the two stations for the on-air personality. Three years later, in 1996, he was back at KJR where he remained for 14 years. Grosby returned to KIRO in 2010 when that station switched to an all-sports format as part of the ESPN network. "It's very special and kind of weird at the same time to have influenced sports and the style the media uses to report on teams in Seattle," said Grosby.

As a young man, Grosby became a bar mitzvah in Akron, OH and was then confirmed after his family moved back to New York, to the Scarsdale community. "I am proud of my religion and my heritage," said Grosby, who grew up in a Reform congregation. "I did it all and it did not take much for my mom to convince me to attend Sunday school."

The Groz said he has been puzzled by the number of Jews in the Seattle media who cover sports, but guesses it may have something to do with an attraction to the entertainment side of the industry. Grosby said his religion has helped him create immediate bonds with sev-eral co-workers, and that true friendship often requires similar interests and common backgrounds.

Grosby is especially proud of the careers he's helped launch of several well-known radio personalities who began as producers for his afternoon show. The list of ex-producers nicknamed by The Groz includes Mike "The Gas Man" Gastineau, Dave "Softy" Mahler and his current co-host, Bob "Rock Star" Stelton.

In addition to his sports talk show five days a week, Grosby has served as Bob Robertson's play-by-play partner on Washington State Football broadcasts and handled both pre- and post-game duties for the Seattle Mariners and Seattle Seahawks from 1993 to 1996. His love of sports and gift of gab have given him the opportunity to provide play-by-play coverage of high school football games in Sacramento and color commentary for the NHL's Los Angeles Kings. In 2009, Grosby was named the new voice of Seattle University basketball.

"I never wanted to be anything but the lucky Jewish boy that I am," he said.

Mike Kahn

June 5, 1954, Ohio – December 17, 2008, Seattle

Sportswriter fell in love with Northwest, Super-Sonics and Seahawks

Mike Kahn grew up in Ohio, spending his early years in Cincinnati and Cleveland, and graduating from one of the nation's football powerhouses, Ohio State University. He began his career as a sports writer in the Midwest, covering high school sports in Jefferson City. Talented at his craft, he landed a job as a writer for the NFL's Indianapolis Colts. When the Colts played the Seattle Seahawks in 1984, he visited the Pacific Northwest for the first time and fell in love with the city.

Two years later, he moved to Tacoma, joining the *The News Tribune* sports department. His main assignment was to cover the Seattle SuperSonics and the NBA, but also to assist John Clayton, the senior ESPN.com writer. Kahn and Clayton teamed up with another *Tribune* writer, Bart Wright, to create a nationally renowned sports page.

Kahn made a name for himself with his unabashed enthusiasm for the Sonics. He held the Sonics beat for nine years before moving to Florida to work for CBS Sportsline. While there, he developed one of the first independent sports websites in the country, Sportsline.com.

"(Kahn was) an absolute pioneer in sports journalism. In the mid-1990s he saw the power and potential of the Internet and knew there was an audience for original, professionally-written sports content," wrote Steve Miller, Managing Editor of FOXSports.com. Sportsline was eventually bought out by Viacom in 2004, which led to layoffs, including Kahn's.

As a result, Kahn returned to the Seattle area, joining the Seattle Seahawks as their staff writer. He was with the team for five years, serving as their website and internet manager. With his legendary knowledge of pro basketball, he also covered the NBA for Fox Sports.com. At the end of 2008, Mike passed away at the young age of 54 from complications with lung cancer.

Les Keiter

April 27, 1919, Seattle – April 14, 2009, Hawaii

For 50 years in the broadcast booth, Les was more

From 1958 to 1960, Les Keiter never once saw an actual pitch during the San Francisco Giants' baseball season, but that didn't stop the broadcaster from calling the exciting play by play for WINS radio listeners in New York. From a broadcast booth in Manhattan, the Seattle native recreated entire ballgames from the minimal information he received from telegraph reports and his best guess as to what was happening on the diamond.

Throughout the broadcast, the University

of Washington graduate would knock a drumstick against a wooden block to simulate the sound of players like Willie Mays connecting on a hit, while his engineer triggered taped sound effects of an excited crowd, a regular crowd, or even booing.

In his 1991 memoir, *Fifty Years Behind the Microphone*, Keiter explained, "You might not know what kind of pitch struck a man out, but you remember what a certain pitcher's key weapon is." With Western Union only providing scant information, Keiter had to take a stab at describing the rest. "You can't see the

condition of a field after a rain delay, but you know from your preparation what conditions the stadium is usually in when wet. You use all this research and experience to create a broadcast that may not be correct in every detail but is certainly plausible."

On occasions when the telegraph failed to transmit or became gar-

Les Keiter interviews Joe Louis, legendary World Heavyweight Champion from 1937-1949. The "Brown Bomber" was 69 and 3.

bled, Keiter filled the air by inventing a pitcher-catcher conference on the mound or a batter fouling off pitch after pitch. Despite a sophisticated audience that knew the games were only recreations, Keiter's booming voice and excitable embellishments lured an average of 300,000 listeners to his broadcasts.

Keiter used the same colorful descriptions to explain his parents' escape "from Czar Nicholas II, who forced them to live in poverty in the Jewish settlements, just like *Fiddler on the Roof.*" The Keiter family settled in Seattle, eventually sending their son to the University of Washington. Keiter began his broadcasting career in Hawaii in the late 1940s, became a stadium announcer for minor league baseball teams, and was then promoted to play by play for the New York Giants at the Polo Grounds before they moved West. He also did play by play for the NFL's Giants from 1956 to 1959, the Knicks from 1955 to 1962, as well as many Rangers games during that period. He later hosted pre- and post-game shows for the Yankees as part of his duties as sports director at WINS-AM from the mid-'50s until 1963.

Keiter left New York in 1963 to broadcast games for the Philadelphia 76ers and Big 5 college basketball, where he coined the sign-on phrase, "Welcome to Panicsville, USA." Basketball fans loved hearing Keiter describe the ball swishing through the net as "tickled in twine," or a long-range off-balance shot as a "ring-tailed howitzer," or "in again, out again Finnegan" for a shot that rimmed the basket but failed to fall. The excitement and flourishes he brought to broadcasts during his seven years earned

Broadcasting legend Howard Cosell and Keiter cover boxing

him an induction in the Big 5 Hall of Fame in 2003. "I've never been able to contain my excitement," he once told the *Associated Press*.

During the 1960s, Keiter often sat beside broadcasting legend Howard Cosell to call some of the biggest fights in the history of boxing, including the 1964 victory by Cassius Clay (later Muhammad Ali) over heavyweight champ Sonny Liston. In the summer of 1968 in Mexico City, Keiter worked with former Olympian Jesse Owens to cover the Olympics for Mutual Radio, which included his play-by-play call for George Foreman's gold-medal boxing victory.

In 1970, Keiter and his wife moved to Hawaii, and he was hired as KHON's sports director, where he would stay for over two decades. After two guest appearances as a military officer on the television series "Hawaii 5-0," Keiter earned the nickname "The General," which stuck with him for the rest of his career.

Two weeks shy of his 90th birthday, in April 2009, Les Keiter passed away with his family by his side. Despite his incredible and varied career calling the live action of multiple sporting events, he was most remembered for the games he called using just the ticker and his imagination. When Keiter appeared on NBC's "The Today Show," Tom Brokaw asked him to reprise his baseball recreation. In his memoir, Keiter recalls, "Brokaw commented to Jane Pauley after my feature that 'Neil Armstrong didn't really walk on the moon…Les Keiter recreated the whole thing!' I took that as a compliment."

Aaron Levine

March 27, 1982, Tarzana, CA

From small-town cub reporter to top-15 metro sports anchor by 25

Growing up as a sports-crazed kid in Southern California, Aaron Levine combined his love of sports with his ability to tell an entertaining tale. His talent earned him the sports anchor job at Q13 Fox News in Seattle and as the host of "Q It Up Sports," the station's weekend wrap-up of local teams. But the road to his pair of regional Emmy Awards for best sports anchor detoured through thousands of miles of rural highways that bordered minor league ballparks and dozens of high schools in the San Joaquin Valley.

The always-smiling Aaron Levine describes himself as the product of "a unique set of Jewish parents." His Filipino mother converted to Judaism before she married his father. Together they raised Aaron and his three sisters with a strong Jewish identity that included attending Hebrew school three times a week and two vis-its to Israel before the age of 11.

His mother could have predicted her youngest child's career path when she witnessed him poring over the sports section of the *Los Angeles Times* before the age of five. Whenever possible, Levine would make the trek from his family's home deep in the San Fernando Valley to the outskirts of Los Angeles to watch his beloved Lakers and Dodgers play.

Throughout his high school and college years, he pursued his dream by working odd jobs at newspapers and radio stations. After graduating from Stanford University, he found work as a reporter with an independent television station in Bakersfield, CA, where he took on the challenge of covering five minor league teams, two dozen high schools and a Division I small college.

His two-and-a-half years of driving endless stretches of Highway 99 paid off in 2007, when Seattle's Fox affiliate offered him the opportunity to anchor the sports department. "I knew I had arrived when I walked through the tunnel and smelled the grass at Safeco Field," he said. "Before moving to the Northwest, I had been covering the Single-A Bakersfield Blaze. So I was extremely fortunate to be a media director of a top-15 market at the age of 25."

Levine does not consider himself "overly observant," but identifies himself as one who honors the customs and traditions of his Jewish ancestors. Because Rosh Hashanah and Yom Kippur almost always conflict with the busiest time on the sports calendar, he regrets that he cannot always spend the High Holy Days with his family.

"My heritage is an important part of who I am and who I have become as a person, so I try to spend as much time as possible at home with my family," Levine said. "But I never get tired of watching and reporting on every possible type of competition. And I'll admit that I usually sleep until late in the morning to make up for all the long nights

Aaron Levine proudly displays his regional Emmy for sports broadcasting

spent in the press box and delivering the late edition of the news."

Aaron's biggest thrill in sports came simply as a fan watching his alma mater defeat Virginia Tech in the 2011 Orange Bowl. Levine said it reminded him of just how much fun it is to just sit back and watch the action on the field without having to take notes or rush to the locker room after the game for an interview.

Currently in a committed relationship, Aaron's bachelor days may be numbered. In pondering this next step, he emphasized that Judaism will always remain a part of his life, wherever his next assignment may take him. "My life would not be complete if I did not pass on to my own children the vital lessons that Judaism has taught me," he said.

Ken Levine

February, 1950, Santa Monica, CA

Dodger fan inspired by legendary broadcaster to pursue dream

For Seattle Mariners broadcaster Ken Levine, the silky voice of Vin Scully was as much a part of growing up a Dodgers fan as Dodger Dogs and Chavez Ravine. More than just the extraordinary feats of players like Sandy Koufax, Don Drysdale and Maury Wills, it was Scully's broadcast that turned Levine's blood

Dodger blue and sparked a kid's dream to call big league games.

"One day, I made the decision that if I really wanted to broadcast baseball games on the radio, I had to dedicate myself to reaching that goal," he said. Over the next few seasons, Levine spent countless summer evenings sitting high above home plate on the 500 level of Dodger Stadium calling the play by play into a small tape recorder he had hidden in his backpack. He still laughs when he remembers the odd stares he received from drunken fans seated around him.

Ken Levine joined the Seattle Mariners broadcast team in 1992

He submitted his audition tape to dozens of minor league teams. After several agonizing months waiting for a reply, Levine received an offer to provide color analysis for the Syracuse Chiefs in upstate New York in 1988.

While he pursued his broadcasting dream, Levine was already living another. From the time he wrote his first script for the television show "The Jeffersons" in 1975, Ken had built a reputation as an Emmy-winning screenwriter. Over his 30-year career, he has worked in a variety of capacities on well over 200 television episodes for such shows as "M*A*S*H," "Cheers," "Frasier," "The Simpsons," "Wings," and "Everybody Loves Raymond." With his partner, he wrote the feature *Volunteers*.

After a few years broadcasting games for the Chiefs, executives from the Baltimore Orioles heard the unique personality Levine brought to the radio and invited him to join their Major League broadcast team. It was during his time with Baltimore that Levine's passion for baseball conflicted with his Jewish identity. When a game against the Red Sox fell on Yom Kippur, he didn't know how the Orioles management would react when he told them he would not be available for the broadcast. "The Orioles were fantastic," said Levine. "I was thrilled when management insisted that I observe the High Holy Day. The team paid for a replacement and flew him to Boston to fill in for me that one day."

In 1992, Levine joined the Seattle Mariners' broadcast team, and worked portions of each subsequent season with Hall of Fame announcer Dave Niehaus and his partner, Rick Rizzs.

"Working with Dave was like sitting next to one of the presidents on Mount Rushmore, only a lot more fun," he said. Niehaus was the voice of the Mariners from the team's inaugural game in 1977 until his unexpected death in 2010. "Dave was a great traveling companion, but he was a much better broadcaster," Levine recalled. "Many of the descriptions that we use in the booth today are vintage Dave." What Levine remembers most about Niehaus were the stories and the humor he injected into the game. During one-sided games when Seattle was behind by 10 or more runs (and there were many, according to Levine), Niehaus would ask Levine to join him for a duet of Johnny Cash's "The Wabash Cannonball."

As a Mariners broadcaster, Levine had an opportunity to meet his childhood hero when he interviewed Scully as part of a pre-game show. He admitted to being nervous before the interview, but remembered how the Hall of Fame broadcaster treated him as an equal from the moment they shook hands.

When someone asks Levine about his

Levine gets a chance to visit with boyhood hero Vin Scully

broadcast education, he explains that he received an advanced degree from the College of Niehaus and Scully.

As much as he is a die-hard Dodgers fan, Levine is quick to admit that Safeco Field is probably his favorite Major League ballpark and that Seattle is a great baseball town. He predicts that Mariners fans would be rewarded for their patience with a championship team in the next few years

Paul Lowenberg

November 15, 1942, San Francisco, CA

Stringer spins sports yarns for 30 years

Paul Lowenberg enjoyed a 30-year career as sports "stringer," a freelance writer who covers games for a publication, in this case for the *Associated Press*, *United Press International* and *SportsTicker*. From 1978 until 2009 he covered all of the home games for the San Diego Padres and later the Seattle Mariners, as well as the San Diego Clippers, San Diego Chargers, and the Seattle SuperSonics.

Born in San Francisco, Paul was not always a baseball fan. In fact, he was 15 years old before he attended his first Major League game. On April 16, 1958, he and his friends went to Seals Stadium to watch the two newly transplanted teams, the San Francisco Giants (from New York) play the Los Angeles Dodgers (from Brooklyn). With most of the same players moving with the team, the heated rivalry between the Giants and the Dodgers continued on the West Coast.

"My buddies and I had a front row seat — make that a bleacher seat — to history of a sort," recalled Lowenberg. "The second game for both teams in their new home, it was also the first Major League night game ever played on the West Coast. We were in the right-field bleachers, where we had ponied up 90 cents for our ticket. It was another sellout with 22,735 fans on hand on a cool, foggy night. Journeyman right-hander Ramon Monzant was on the mound for the Giants, facing 1955 World Series hero Johnny Podres, and the game wasn't close. The Dodgers avenged their opening day 8-0 loss with a 13-1 win. The only highlight I remember was Dodger Hall-of-Famer Duke Snider's long homerun over the stands in right field."

For Lowenberg, that was the first of many days

Paul Lowenberg and his son Aaron enjoy a SF Giants game

and nights spent at Seals Stadium and later the infamous Candlestick Park.

The UC Berkeley graduate started his baseball-writing career in 1978 when he was working in the news office at the University of California, San Diego. The Padres were hosting the All-Star game that year and he called the team's public relations office to see if they needed any help. The Padres said no, but mentioned that the *Associated Press* bureau needed someone to report the Padres' home games. Lowenberg called the *AP* and wound up spending the next 11 years in the press box. The cub reporter wrote stories, interviewed players and was even responsible for keeping what was then the official box score for the game.

"What a great job!" recalled Lowvenberg. "I earned 25 bucks a game, and frequently got home well after midnight while still having to report for work at my real job at UC San Diego."

Since this all occurred during the pre-computer age, Lowenberg banged away on his little Olympia portable typewriter and dictated his stories on the telephone. Dictating and rewriting his story as the game progressed, the goal was to hang up the phone with the box score and game coverage finished as the final out was made.

In 1989, he relocated to Seattle to take a position in the University of Washington news office. After a couple of years he resumed his baseball duties, covering Mariners home games for *United Press International* and then *SportsTicker*. "It was quite a change for me from San Diego — American League, designated hitter, indoor ballpark. But, hey," Lowenberg said, "it was still baseball and I had a front row seat for the Mariners' great pennant drive in 1995."

During his baseball-watching career he was lucky enough to witness:

- The West Coast debut of the San Francisco Giants

- 1959 All-Star game in the Los Angeles Coliseum
- Giants' Hall-of-Famer Willie Covey's sensational Major League debut (4-4 with two triples off Hall-of-Famer Robin Roberts at Seals Stadium)
- 1961 All-Star game at Candlestick Park, the seventh game of the 1962 World Series (Giants-Yankees)
- Final two games of the 1962 Yankees-Giants World Series
- Giants-Angels 2002 World Series
- Giants-Rangers 2010 World Series
- Willie Mays' 3,000th career hit
- 1984 NL playoffs and World Series (Padres-Tigers)
- 1984 All-Star game (San Francisco)
- The Dodgers' Orel Hershisher's record-setting 59-inning shutout streak
- Chris Bosio's no-hitter for the Mariners
- 1995 Mariners drive to the AL championship
- The 2001 All-Star game in Seattle

Although Lowenberg admits baseball is his favorite sport, his sports coverage wasn't limited to the diamond. He also spent six years covering the hapless San Diego Clippers of the NBA before they moved to Los Angeles, the San Diego Chargers during the "Air Coryell" era, the Seattle Seahawks for a couple of years, and the Seattle SuperSonics for about 15 years until they moved to Oklahoma City.

While Paul and his wife, June, have lived in Seattle since 1989, their son, Aaron, has carried his father's love of sports with him to Los Angeles where he is now a vice president with Fox Sports.

Dave 'Softy' Mahler

August 10, 1973, Seattle

Star-struck reporter a softy for sports heroes

Sitting down with Edgar Martinez and Ken Griffey, Jr. in the locker room at the Kingdome was more than Dave Mahler could ever have imagined when he joined the staff at KJR radio. "I was not prepared to sit down with my heroes at an age when I still had heroes," he said.

Thanks to a father who had played baseball

Dave Mahler chats with Lorenzo Romar, UW basketball coach

235

for Queens College in New York, Dave Mahler grew up with sports as the focal point of his life. He remembers watching his father play basketball at the JCC on Mercer Island with legendary members of the Seattle SuperSonics when he was only 6 or 7 years old.

"Softy," as he's known to sports fans in Seattle, played basketball and baseball at Bellevue High School while he honed his skills as a reporter by following the stories of other teams and individual athletes on campus.

Mahler began his senior season as a catcher and left fielder for the Wolverines' varsity baseball team. But his season was cut short when he refused to travel to an away game with the junior varsity squad because it meant he would not be home in time to attend High Holy Day services that night with his family. "The coach threw a fit because he thought I did not want to catch for the JVs," Mahler remembers. "He did not understand that I needed to be home before dark when services were scheduled to start."

The decision to walk away from the baseball field that afternoon was an easy one. In addition to his father's enthusiasm for sports, Mahler said he was brought up in a family that treasured religion and cherished the culture that comes from being Jewish. "Even as children, my parents made sure we knew where our family was from, and the sacrifices our ances-

Mahler interviews Mariner legend Ken Griffey, Jr.

tors made years ago that made it possible for us to live here today," he said. "Even at an early age, my parents made sure that we knew we had relatives who died in the Holocaust. We spoke about those family members often because they were killed and never had the chance to live in the freedom we enjoy now."

Mahler continued his connection to sports working the play by play on broadcasts for Bellevue Community College's radio station. His college work at the far end of the dial earned him an internship with KJR 950, the only all-sports radio station in Seattle at the time.

Mahler turned that part-time work experience for college credit into a full-time position, putting him shoulder to shoulder with sports stars and high-profile television and newspaper reporters. One of his first assignments was to travel around the country to witness the assault on Roger Maris' record of 61 homeruns. His media pass allowed Softy access to any game where Mark McGuire, Sammy Sosa or Ken Griffey, Jr. might be in a position to break the 40-year-old record.

As it turns out, Mahler was in the press box to see McGuire hit homeruns No. 61 and 62 on consecutive nights. He was also in Tempe, AZ in 1996 to see his beloved Washington Huskies come from 21 points behind Arizona State on the passing of Brock Huard, and in Detroit to witness the Seahawks' only Super Bowl appearance in 2006.

But none of those thrills, he fondly recalls, compared to the miracle run of the 1995 Seattle Mariners. "That was as good as it gets," he said with a faraway look in his eyes. "I had been with the station less than two years, and here I was drinking beer with Edgar, Tino, Griffey and Randy Johnson. "I was star struck."

Mike Salk

April 28, 1978, Boston, MA

Sports reporter witnessed grandfather's bar mitzvah and Red Sox World Series victory

Mike Salk grew up an avid sports fan in what he described as a "white bread" suburb of Boston. He tried his best to emulate Boston Celtic Larry Bird when he played on the neighborhood CYA basketball team, which was not allowed to advance in the playoffs, because there were not enough Catholics on the roster. Religion was never a barrier for Salk. Being Jewish was just another factor of his animated personality he used when he gave up his career as a stockbroker in his early 20s to follow his dream to host a show on sports radio where he could actually get paid to talk for hours about his favorite subject.

His mother was active in their synagogue, and Salk remembers proudly that he became a bar mitzvah with the same rabbi who married his parents and also helped his grandfather become bar mitzvah on his deathbed. "My grandfather did not want to die without being bar mitzvahed," Salk said. "He had spent much his life denying his faith and wanted to be sure he sets things right before he died. That taught me early in life — at about 15 or 16 — about the important role Judaism plays in our lives every single day."

Salk's first job in broadcasting was as a reporter for the ESPN station in Boston, where he covered the New England Patriots, the Boston Bruins and his beloved Boston Red Sox. "I was living the dream. Regular fans are not allowed free access to the locker room," said Salk. "With my press pass, I could walk into the dressing

Mike Salk brought his love for sports to listeners in the NW

room to talk with the same athletes I had just watched playing on the field."

He shared his greatest sports memory with his listeners when he wandered on the infield at Fenway Park in 2004 after the Red Sox had won their first World Series in more than 80 years, interviewing the likes of Johnny Damon, Terry Francona and Manny Ramirez. "It was unbelievable," he said with emotion. "Like every Red Sox fan, this was a moment we thought might never happen. My credentials allowed me on the field to share the moment with all the players and thousands of drunk people who had suddenly become my best friends."

Mike Salk with fellow 710 ESPN broadcaster and former UW quarterback Brock Huard

Salk moved to Seattle in 2009 to co-host "Brock and Salk" weekday mornings on 710 ESPN Seattle, where he shares the airwaves with former Washington quarterback Brock Huard. He also hosts "SportsCenter Saturday with Mike Salk" nationwide on the ESPN Radio Network.

Working side by side with Huard, the devout Christian and hometown hero, taught Salk to be tolerant of the beliefs of others and to watch his language at all times. "Faith is an important part of Brock's life. It's part of who he is, and I respect that.

"No town is free of anti-Semitism, mainly because some people are just not taught to understand that another person's faith and their beliefs may be different than their own," he explained.

Although he was raised on the East Coast, the young Salk chose to travel across the country to Pomona College in Southern California for a degree in liberal arts that he described as "truly liberal."

Salk settled in the Phinney Ridge neighborhood of Seattle with his wife, Heather, their daughter, Avery, and their French bulldog, Wendell. "Seattle was an easy place to feel at home right away," Salk said. "Both Heather and I made the comment that the green hillsides in Seattle make the area look like it was being broadcast in high definition compared to the black-and-white cities on the East Coast."

After four years at 710 ESPN, Salk left the #1 rated "Brock and Salk Show" to return to his native homeland. There he joined WEEI in March of 2013 to co-host the afternoon drive show, "Salk and Holley."

Mike Siegel

May 2, 1955, Seattle

Sports photographer has best seat in the house

Mike Siegel's passion for photography began when he was ten-years-old after he was given an Argus box camera. Looking back on a newspaper photography career that has spanned more that three decades, he remembers those early moments of discovery when he'd take his weekly trip to Pay-n-Save at Northgate Mall to see how his prints came out and to purchase more film.

Siegel's early skills earned him a spot as the photographer for his junior high school newspaper, where he later learned to process his own film and make prints in the darkroom.

While enrolled at the University of Washington, Siegel covered Husky football and basketball for the school newspaper, The Daily. After graduating in 1978, Siegel leveraged his UW sports portfolio to get a job as the Sonics team photographer from 1977 until 1981.

"There is really nothing more thrilling than experiencing the game from courtside. The in-

Mike Siegel high atop the Space Needle

Siegel captures his favorite Sonic Gus Williams scoring a layup

tensity of capturing a buzzer beating victory or seeing up close the agony of a last second defeat is unforgettable," said Siegel. To capture those moments, he explained, "the longer you shoot a sport, the more you're able to anticipate whose going to get the ball and what's going to happen. You become very knowledgeable about the nuances of the sport."

Siegel's time with the Sonics luckily coincided with the team's two trips to the NBA Finals in 1978 and 1979. "Growing up a Sonics fan, there was nothing better than having a courtside seat to watch 'Downtown' Freddie Brown sink winning baskets at the buzzer. Those memories will stay etched in my memory forever."

Siegel's work with the Sonics and United Press International led to newspaper jobs with The Bremerton Sun, The Bellevue Journal American, The News Tribune in Tacoma and his current job with The Seattle Times. "Working for the Times these past 27 years has been a great ride," said Siegel, "fulfilling the dream I had when I first started using that Argus box camera so many, many years ago."

Stan Tobin

October 27, 1920 – December 15, 2009, Seattle

Sports editor's lifelong love of the Huskies began in the press box

As an avid sports fan, Stan Tobin had the unique opportunity to watch his beloved Washington Huskies up close as the sports editor of the campus newspaper.

According to his wife, Goldie, the newspaperman never claimed to be an objective journalist. "Stan was always a sports 'wanna-be,'" Goldie remembers. "He wanted to play football. He wanted to play basketball. But he was just too small to play in college. So reporting on the teams he loved was the next best thing."

Tobin during his days as the UW Daily sports editor

Goldie said her late husband loved to play football, basketball, baseball and golf and was always ready for a pick-up game. While a member of his AZA chapter in BBYO, his basketball team won the regional championship in 1937 and 1938. He was most proud of the lineup of players formed by his brothers from the ZBT fraternity that dominated the intramural leagues at the UW campus during the '40s. Tobin also played on the championship softball team sponsored by the Jewish Community Center in 1954.

Tobin's wife said he began writing for the campus newspaper to become part of the athletic program at Washington. "He started out covering games and eventually became the sports editor of the *UW Daily*," she said. "And he remained a lifelong Husky fan."

Stan Tobin, front row far right, with 1938 championship AZA team

Hy Zimmerman

August 21, 1914, Zolkieka, Poland – April 22, 1989, Seattle

Yiddish-speaking journalist covered Seattle sports for three decades

Like every kid who grew up in Minneapolis, Hy Zimmerman developed a passion for ice hockey. While his obsession with sports grew to include the all-American game of baseball, nobody envisioned the awkward teenager, who was raised speaking Yiddish, would go on to become an award-winning sportswriter in his adopted language.

Seattle was a rough port town when Hy Zimmerman arrived to begin working at *The Seattle Times* in 1953. But the eager journalist walked into the middle of a union strike that shut down the newspaper for 94 days. By the time the strike was settled, his wife and two daughters had moved across the country to join him. "She supported her husband and two daughters on a new teacher salary until the strike was settled," said his son, David.

When the newspaper reopened, the newest reporter was put on the local news beat until he proved to the editors he was ready to cover the city's professional hockey team, the Seattle Americans. The sports assignment lasted more than three decades. Zimmerman is credited with suggesting the name Totems when the franchise was rebranded before the 1958 season. During his tenure with the newspaper, Zimmerman covered horse racing at Longacres and was also the paper's primary baseball writer, covering the Rainiers, the Seattle Angels and the one ill-fated season of the Seattle Pilots.

Zimmerman earned his journalism degree on the GI Bill after driving a tank in Europe for the Army for three and a half years during World War II. He

Hy Zimmerman covering the Thoroughbreds at Longacres

began his career with a newspaper in Iowa and went on to cover sports at the *Chicago Tribune*. After two years in the Windy City, he realized he wanted to provide a better life for his family and chose Seattle after sending out resumes to dozens of newspapers.

The Yiddish-speaking journalist became a fixture at the *Times* and an influential figure in Seattle sports for the next 30 years before retiring in January of 1982. "My dad always saw the potential of Seattle as a Major League city, and brought up the idea of a domed stadium way back in the '50s," David remembers. As a columnist, Zimmerman generated support for a domed stadium to attract professional sports teams, and took an active role in the legal battle that required Major League Baseball to award Seattle an expansion team.

Zimmerman was honored with various awards for his work over the years, including induction into the Seattle Hockey Hall of Fame. "He was always clear about his career," said David. "He was not a writer. He was a journalist.

My dad loved the smell of ink and was fascinated with the typesetters. Sometimes he would take me to his office just to watch the presses."

David remembers the 1972 season for the Rainiers when he was asked to carry his father's manual portable typewriter to the press box after his father had injured his back. The younger Zimmerman also recalled the night at Sicks' Stadium when he was allowed to run the hand-operated scoreboard.

Born into an ultra-Orthodox family, Hy Zimmerman lived a more secular life, marrying a non-Jewish woman. Ironically, his 50-year-old son, David, went through the complete Orthodox conversion eight years ago. David was always proud of his father's sense of tolerance and justice, traits he had learned from his own parents.

"There was never any doubt that we were raised in a Jewish home," said David. "My father identified himself as a Jew and was always proud of our heritage."

The Sternberg Grandchildren

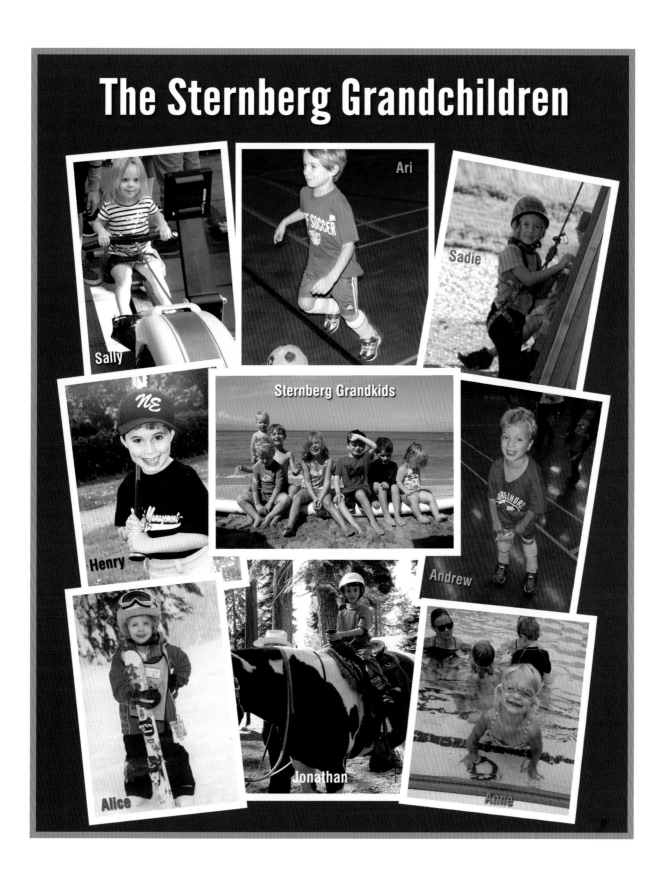

Sally

Ari

Sadie

Henry

Sternberg Grandkids

Andrew

Alice

Jonathan

Anne

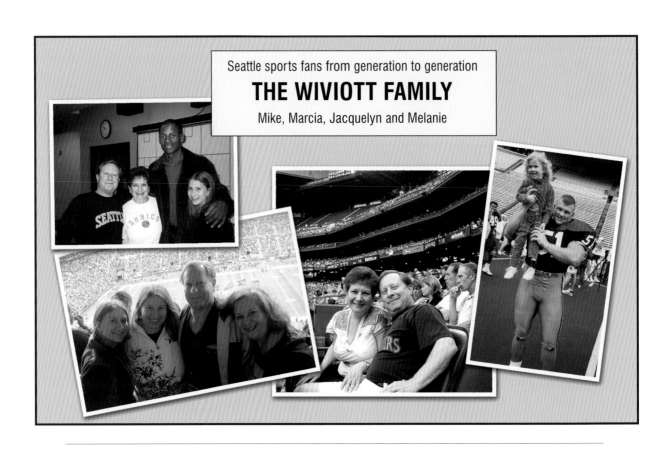

Seattle sports fans from generation to generation

THE WIVIOTT FAMILY

Mike, Marcia, Jacquelyn and Melanie

Congratulations to the Washington State Jewish Historical Society

From the **Muscatel** and **McLeod Families**

Thank you Eastside Dream Elite Cheer for instilling the love of sport, for teaching responsibility and respect towards everyone and for giving our girls many years of happiness and great memories.

The Brumer Family
Janice, Marshall, Megan, Jessica & Kayla

Joel Buxbaum

2001 Sitka Alaska Sportsman
Salmon Derby Winner

47 pounds 3 ounces!

In Appreciation

Eugene Normand
former President, WSJHS, Research Leader, Instant Replay program

As an early organizer of the Instant Replay program and a long-time WSJHS Board member, I was grateful for the opportunity to combine my love for both sports and history.

Having grown up elsewhere, my Seattle sports participation was evening basketball at the Seattle Hebrew Academy, racquetball, gym, fishing, etc. and being a die-hard local fan.

I strongly support Distant Replay as an opportunity to celebrate the achievements of our fellow Washington Jews in sports of all kinds. It provides a broad sweep of one small, but often very meaningful aspect in our lives, sports.

May these stories inspire and motivate us.

Eugene Normand
former President, WSJHS, Research Leader, Instant Replay program

TEAM OWNERS

Proudly sponsored by

HERMAN AND FAYE SARKOWSKY

Barry Ackerley

April 15, 1934 Des Moines, IA – March 21, 2011, Rancho Mirage, CA

Billboard baron behind Sonics' best years

Very little was written about the religion of Barry Ackerley during the 18 years he owned the Seattle SuperSonics. But all doubts about his faith were eliminated in 1994 when comedian Adam Sandler sang "Put on your yarmulke, it's time for Hanukkah; the owner of the Seattle SuperSonicahs celebrates Hanukkah!"

Seattle Post-Intelligencer sports columnist Art Thiel chose to use brevity to describe the long-time NBA franchise owner: "Cantankerous. Obstinate. Irascible. Litigious. Best owner the Sonics had."

California business mogul Barry Ackerley became a major player in the Seattle business community in 1975 when he brought his expertise with outdoor advertising to the Northwest. By 1983, The Ackerley Group was listed on the New York Stock Exchange and he had purchased the NBA franchise from the original group of owners led by Sam Schulman.

At the time, the Sonics may not have been his best business decision. Losses in 1984 jumped to $7.4 million from $769,000 the previous year. But Ackerley turned down three early offers to move the team to Florida and Southern California. "When we bought the Sonics, they were bankrupt," he said in 1985. "I don't think people realize that."

Ackerley was a courtside fixture over the 18 years he was at the helm of the team. During those years, the Sonics won four division titles, reached the conference finals three times and the NBA finals in 1996. They won a league-best 63 regular-season games in 1993-94 and topped that with a franchise high of 64 wins two years later. During Ackerley's tenure, the Sonics had their most successful run, with 834 wins versus 610 losses for a .578 winning percentage. About the only thing the Sonics didn't do under Ackerley was win an NBA championship.

"He was a guy that wanted perfection, wanted the team to do well," said Lenny Wilkens, Sonics coach when Ackerley bought the team. "He was excited when he got the team and was always very supportive." Ackerley was in the front office for the six consecutive seasons the Sonics won 55 or more games beginning with

Barry Ackerley reacts to ref's call at 1984 Sonics game
(Harley Soltes/Seattle Times)

the 1992-93 campaign, and was at the helm during the time the Seattle Coliseum was remodeled to become Key Arena. He sold the team in 2001 to a group of local buyers headed by Starbucks CEO Howard Schultz.

With his wife looking on, Barry Ackerley congratulates former Sonic Nate McMillan after his number was retired (Alan Berner/Seattle Times)

"The thing that I remember about him just from a business standpoint is he would spend the capital that was necessary to bring the talent in," said Kevin Calabro, who was hired to the Sonics' broadcast team under Ackerley. "He was a very tough, hard-nosed guy."

When Ackerley died in 2011 following a stroke, *Seattle Times* sports columnist Steve Kelley wrote that Ackerley taught the team and the city how to win. He was also not afraid to take a risk to make the team better, adding a teenager named Shawn Kemp, an opinionated player like Gary Payton, and a head coach, George Karl, who at the time had been relegated to coaching a team in Spain.

In addition to his impact on the city through basketball, Ackerley brought the Sonics to KJR in 1987, which was instrumental in its becoming the city's first all-sports talk radio station.

The Brotman Brothers
Tacoma's first family of sports

BERNIE, MORLEY AND HAL BROTMAN
The Brothers Are Boosters

Harold Brotman

September 6, 1906, Winnipeg, Manitoba – March 20, 1982, Tacoma

---

Harold Brotman was an outstanding athlete while attending Stadium High School and helped the school's athletic program make headlines in 1926. As a wrestler in the 135-lb. division, his team won the interscholastic championship. Playing on Stadium's football squad, he helped the team win Tacoma's interscholastic championship by defeating the Lincoln Railsplitters. In addition, Harold was a star on the basketball, soccer and baseball teams as well running the quarter-mile in track.

Harold Brotman, outstanding football player and wrestler, center

Originally from Canada, the Brotman family moved to Tacoma in 1923 where the boys got involved in rugby, hockey and many other sports. In 1929, Harold returned briefly to Regina to coach the Regina A.C. Tees to the Canadian junior rugby championship.

In 1939, Harold opened Brotman Brothers, a men's clothing store he operated in downtown Tacoma for 32 years. From the mid-'40s to the early '50s, the Brotmans owned the Tacoma Rockets of the Pacific Coast Hockey League, playing in the Tacoma Ice Palace and the Tacoma Arena.

Harold was a two-time president of the Tacoma Athletic Commission and a member of Temple Beth El, the Tacoma Elks Lodge and the Fircrest Golf and Country Club. He was a candidate for the Tacoma City Council in 1953 and was appointed vice president and general manager of the Tacoma Cable Company in 1971.

Morley Brotman

November 16, 1910, Regina, Saskatchewan – April 22, 1980, Tacoma

An avid sports fan all his life, Morley Brotman was especially proud when the baseball team he sponsored in 1956 advanced to the American Amateur Baseball Congress championship game in Battle Creek, MI. His team took the cup, and as a result, a bat bearing his name now resides in the Baseball Hall of Fame.

In 1941, Brotman founded Morley Studios, a photography business, and partnered with brothers Bernie and Harold in a clothing store in Tacoma. Friends knew them as "The Three Busy B's" who were very active sponsoring youth athletic teams. Morley was the official photographer for the 1962 World's Fair in Seattle and operated concessions in World's Fairs in New York, Montreal, San Antonio and Spokane.

Morley spearheaded the fundraising efforts on three separate campaigns to get public approval to build a mini-domed stadium in Tacoma. In the closing days of his life, the bill was approved, but Morley passed away a year before he could witness the groundbreaking of the Tacoma Dome.

Morley was past president of the Tacoma Athletic Commission and an active member of Temple Beth El.

Morley Brotman receives championship trophy in 1956

Bernie Brotman

August 24, 1912, Belgonia, Saskatchewan – August 23, 1996, Seattle

In 1930, Bernie Brotman won the Richard Graff Memorial Trophy, the highest honor presented to a graduating male student from Stadium High. In high school Bernie was a 440-yard speedster on the track team and was also on the mile relay team. Upon graduation, he earned a track and field scholarship to the College of Puget Sound.

Bernie joined the Brotman Brothers men's clothing stores in Tacoma, but struck out on his own to establish the popular Bernie's Men's Wear in 1950. In 1965, he moved his offices to Seattle and quickly clued in to the denim-wear trend for women, opening Bottoms, a store for young women in 1970. Also an owner of Seattle Knitting Mills, he helped invent the long, skinny, button-front "penguin sweater."

"He also was the originator of the Costco idea," said son Jeff Brotman, co-founder of Costco Wholesale, the world's largest warehouse club chain. "I wasn't even in retailing. But he convinced me it was the opportunity of a lifetime. He'd seen the Price Club wholesale operation in California and we expanded to wholesale and retail combined."

Bernie also joined with brother, Morley, to help pass a bond issue that built the Tacoma Dome.

A street running past the Tacoma Dome was named Brotman Way to honor the Brotman family's long record of civic activities. Bernie was on hand to unveil the sign for his brothers on June 30, 1983.

Brotman Way runs past the Tacoma Dome, honoring the three Brothers for their contributions to sports in the region

Stanley Golub

1913, St. Louis – 1998, Seattle

Jeweler invested in hometown diamond

In 1974, local newspapers called him one of Seattle's 10 most powerful people. Born in St. Louis, Stanley Golub moved to Seattle with his parents when he was eight. He graduated from Franklin High School in 1931 and earned his undergraduate and law degrees from the University of Washington. His sphere of influence changed dramatically during law school when he became best friends with classmate and future US senator Henry Jackson.

The young Golub's law practice was set aside when he went to work for his father's Seattle-based wholesale jewelry firm. At the outbreak of WWII, he left the family business to volunteer for the Army, eventually rising to the rank of captain. He returned in 1945 a highly decorated war hero, earning a Bronze Star, Silver Star and Purple Heart. He took over the small business in 1947 and by 1965 had turned it into a regional powerhouse, acquiring the Seiko franchise for the Northwest and eventually buying out his largest competitor.

A 1974 newspaper story described Golub as a "key fundraiser and idea-man for Senator Jackson and an influential behind-the-scenes resolver of ticklish community problems."

One of those "ticklish problems" was a lack of a Major League Baseball team in Seattle. He, along with entertainer Danny Kaye, Lester Smith, Walter Schoenfeld, James Stillwell and James Walsh, were the six original investors who brought the Seattle Mariners to Northwest baseball fans in the newly constructed Kingdome in 1977.

"Besides his love for Seattle, he got into it because our mom was a baseball nut, and it was a blast, even though it only lasted for five years," said his family. As the team struggled with attendance in its early years, Golub used to joke, "owning a baseball team added a new chapter to my life; too bad I didn't know in advance it might be chapter 11."

The original owners eventually sold the financially troubled Mariners to California businessman George Argyros in 1981; however, Golub always remained upbeat about the team.

SeattleMariners BASEBALL CLUB

Seattle Mariner partners James Stillwell; Walter Schoenfeld; James Walsh; Danny Kaye; Lester Smith; Stanley Golub.

We Can Do It Together!

Joseph Gottstein

July 14, 1891 – January 1, 1971, Seattle

The Laird of Longacres

An enigmatic character, at once blustery and brooding, cantankerous, conciliatory and colorful . . . Joe Gottstein, in the final analysis [was] an amazing human being.

– The Seattle Post-Intelligencer, 1970

It all began as the dream of one man. He was called the "Laird of Longacres," the "Aga Khan of the Green River Valley." Everyone who knew him called him Joe. For 25 years, wagering on horse racing had been illegal, bringing the equine industry -breeding, training, feed- to a standstill. But Joe Gottstein's love of the sport, perseverance and backroom negotiations brought Longacres Race Track to life in 1933. By the time he retired 30 years later, Thoroughbred racing was still the only professional sport in Seattle and horse breeding was the sixth largest industry in the state.

In 1902, the Meadows Race Track opened where Boeing Field sits today. Not only did it allow Seattle to become a player on the national racing circuit, it elevated the city's status as a major metropolitan area. But the luster soon faded when rumors of corruption prompted Washington State lawmakers to shut down the track and declare the sport illegal. Among those who took a loss was Meadows Race Track shareholder Meyer Gottstein.

Meyer and his bride Rosa had settled in Seattle in 1879 and established a wholesale liquor distributorship. On July 14th, 1891, Rosa gave birth to her only son, Vinson Joseph Gottstein. For his eighth birthday his parents gave him his first racehorse, Prince Liege. Joe recalled years later what his father told him, "Son, there are plenty of sports in this world, but damn few sportsmen."

Gottstein was an offensive lineman for Brown University

Ever since I was a small boy I have been active in athletics and all sorts of sports, but the Thoroughbred has always been closest to my heart.

–Joe Gottstein

At 5'-9" and weighing 200 lbs., Gottstein earned an honorable mention on the All-American college football team in 1912 as an offensive lineman for Brown University. The *Evening Tribune* reported in 1911, "Gottstein looks like a natural-born football player...Play after play shot at him was piled up in a heap. The fact that Gottstein has plenty of beef and is built broad and solid, together with his keen desire to play the game... will some day make a star of him."

While at Brown, he also won the New England heavyweight wrestling championship. His interest in sports was threaded throughout his

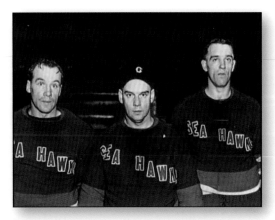

Gottstein's semi-pro hockey team, the Sea Hawks

life. Years later, he, along with a number of other Jewish golfers banned from private courses, established Glendale Golf Course in Seattle and was the club's first champion. Later, he owned a semi-pro hockey team called the Sea Hawks.

In 1914, Gottstein's years at Brown were cut short by the death of his mother, and he returned to Seattle to work in his father's liquor business. Talk of Prohibition laws forced the Gottsteins to rethink their business interests, and they decided to invest in a new form of en-

Gottstein and business partner Bill Edris

tertainment. It was called the motion picture, an invention created by accident while proving a bet on a racehorse. At the age of 23, Gottstein was put in charge of the $600,000 construction of the Coliseum Theater on 5th and Pike. Later, they would add the Liberty and Alaska theaters to their holdings.

After the death of Gottstein's father in 1917, he enlisted in the armed services and completed a tour of duty in Naval Intelligence during World War I. Returning home, he and his close friend William Edris became real estate partners and began to reshape the city's skyline. In July 1930, they closed a complicated $10-million real estate deal, the largest transaction in Seattle at the time. Gottstein proved again and again his knack for correctly reading the Seattle marketplace.

When the stock market crashed in 1929, Gottstein began to build his case to legalize horseracing, which would stimulate the economy and create jobs. His tenacity paid off in 1933 when lawmakers in Olympia approved House Bill 59. Gottstein quickly organized the Washington Jockey Club and outmaneuvered several other groups to obtain the racing permit for Seattle. But at the eleventh hour the Jockey Club's investors dropped out, leaving Gottstein and Edris to finance the track themselves. Armed with an

August 3rd, 1933, Gottstein opened Longacres Race Track, bringing the thunder of Thoroughbreds back to the Northwest

$85,000 personal loan and a slew of mortgaged properties, they signed a 10-year lease on 107 acres of the old James Nelsen farm in Renton.

Gottstein hired his friend and Coliseum Theater architect B. Marcus Priteca to design the track. Priteca, a Scottish-Jewish immigrant, had gained a reputation as one of the most prolific theater architects in the country, but had never designed a racetrack.

Gottstein then pulled off what stands as one of the greatest construction feats in the Northwest. In only 28 days, an army of 3,000 unemployed carpenters, gardeners and tradesmen working around the clock built the track, the grandstands, the clubhouse and the first set of stalls for what would become one of the fastest tracks in the country. He named the course Longacres as a tribute to the Longchamp Race Course in France he visited as a young man.

On Thursday, August 3, 1933, the grand opening was held under clear skies. A crowd of 11,000 people gathered to watch the first horse race in Washington in 25 years. The first race, a five-and-a-half furlong, $1,200 claiming race, went off at 2:08 p.m. John W. Marchbank's Vetsera, with Herbert Simmons aboard, won the $400 purse. The first day's mutuel handle (the total wagered) was around $13,000. The Seattle *Post-Intelligencer* reported, "Western Washington's gift to the turf empire, artistically set on the glorious greenery fringing the White River, blossomed forth with the first of its forty-day sessions of Thoroughbred racing."

In 1935, while the country was still recover-

The $10,000 Longacres Mile was the richest one-mile race in the country in 1935

ing from the Depression and Longacres had yet to turn a profit, Gottstein made headlines when he announced the Longacres Mile with an unheard of purse of $10,000. The event was the richest race of its kind in the country. Coldwater, a 20-to-1 long shot, won the inaugural race, beating Biff by a neck.

Despite the Mile's unprecedented national attention, the track suffered a number of lean years. Edris pulled out of the venture and Gottstein at times had to borrow money to pay the horsemen. At one point, he even asked his friend William Boeing, Sr. to chip in for a new tote board. Many of Gottstein's real estate friends bought stock in the track to help him through the financial rough spots.

When Longacres opened in 1933, there were only eight breeding farms in Washington. Gottstein knew that a successful track needed a strong supply of Thoroughbreds and helped organize the Washington Horse Breeders Association. He funded the fledgling organization by designating to it a percentage of the mutuel handle. He created stakes races exclusively for horses bred in Washington and voluntarily established breeders' awards for Washington-bred runners. No other racing track at the time had a voluntary awards program. His favorite stakes race was the Washington Futurity. Created to highlight the speed and talent of 2-year-olds, the future of local racing, the race was later named in his honor and continues its run at Emerald Downs today.

Over the years, there were dozens of instances in which Gottstein helped horsemen with funds to travel to the next track as well as assist local Thoroughbred breeders with a down payment on a farm. Forty-five years after the track opened, those eight Washington breeding farms grew to 1,500.

Gottstein's horses won the Longacres Mile three times

For Gottstein, owning a racetrack was merely a means to an end. His true passion was racing his own horses. Under the banner of Elttaes Farm ("Seattle" spelled backwards) he owned some of the fastest Thoroughbreds on the coast. Gottstein won his first Mile in 1942 with Lavengro, then 25 years later with King's Favor in 1967 and a year later with Steel Blade.

"There was nothing he loved more than

winning a horse race," remembers grandson Ken Alhadeff. When jockeys appeared on the track wearing Gottstein's lime and chartreuse silks, it became a tradition for race fans to boo. Ironically, the same fans that booed were the ones who bet on Gottstein's horses and won. When asked if it bothered him, Gottstein said, "I wish they would boo eight times a day, if I could win eight races." Making light of all the fuss, Gottstein was known to boo along with the crowd!

Gottstein was a man of great charm and influence, which he used to woo Seattle society to come to his track and then to become racehorse owners. Among the Jewish community, he convinced many to purchase their first horse, creating a respectable list of Jewish horse owners who captured the Longacres Mile:

1940	Al Rosenberg	Pala Squaw
1942	Joe Gottstein	Lavengro
1946	Irv Levine	Amble In
1948	Irv Levine	Amble In
1963	Boris Rubens	Full Regalia
	Elias Solomon	
1967	Joe Gottstein	King's Favor
1968	Joe Gottstein	Steel Blade
1972	Herb and Fern Meltzer	Red Wind
2005	Herman Sarkowsky	No Giveaway

Raised in an Orthodox household, Gottstein would not be at Longacres if the race schedule conflicted with a Jewish holiday. But Ken said that his grandfather knew that the track was the "only show in town" and would never cancel races.

Gottstein's daughter, Joan, married Morrie Alhadeff, who came to work at the track in

1947. By 1963, Gottstein passed down the reins of the day-to-day operation to his son-in-law. "He was a brilliant man," said Morrie in 1978. "Being around him was like going to college every day."

Gottstein at home on the turf was a true sportsman at heart

At the urging of his longtime friend Senator Warren Magnuson, Gottstein led a fundraising campaign in 1969, amassing over $1 million for the University of Washington to purchase a pioneering radiation cobalt machine for cancer research. Ironically, the same machine was used two years later in Gottstein's final battle against lung cancer. His death came in 1971 on January 1st — the universal birthdate for all Thoroughbreds.

The Laird of Longacres ruled Washington's racing with an iron fist — and a soft heart. Joe Gottstein would thunder. And roar. He scowled, cursed (but never obscene), threatened. Then, after assuming an unalterable position, he would ask for advice, listen, and as many times as not, do exactly what he had said 15 minutes ago he would not do.

-Bob Schwarzmann, *The Seattle Times*, 1971

John Ivan Haas

July 9, 1911, Berlin – November 16, 1993, Tacoma

German refugee becomes refuge for Tacoma soccer

Hans Haasz, later known as John Haas, led an exciting life that flourished once he and his family were able to immigrate to the United States after WWII. Like many refugees he was highly motivated, which led him to establish the Discount Mart, a successful business in the downtown Tacoma area. That, in turn, developed into an interest in promoting soccer in his newly adopted city.

Haas was born in Berlin prior to WWI. He married his childhood sweetheart Gerda Buchheim in 1935 and three years later their son Henry was born. With their infant son they fled Berlin, first to France and then, in July 1939 to Shanghai, China, a city that did not require a visa for entry. In December 1941, the Japanese army occupied the International Settlement of Shanghai, but this worsened in 1943 when the Japanese interned all 18,000 Jews into a small slum section of the city. The family endured, and following the end of the war, with the help of the Hebrew Immigrant Aid Society, they came to the US in 1947, arriving in San Francisco on a troop ship. They started their new life in Portland, OR, then Centralia, WA, finally settling in Tacoma in 1955.

As a boy in Germany, Haas loved playing soccer and was able to "get back into the game" as an adult by having his successful store sponsor a soccer team. During the 1950s his team became the B division champions in the Washington State Soccer League. During the 1960s, the Discount Mart team evolved into Tacoma's first professional soccer team. Later the name of the team was changed to the Tacoma Tides,

John Haas, back row far right, with one of the many soccer teams he supported

which Haas still owned and led for about five years. A decade later, the soccer team's name was taken over by a brand new team that was created to be a part of the American Soccer League.

Haas and his family were members of Temple Beth El in Tacoma.

Adrian Hanauer

February 7, 1966, Seattle

Childhood kicks prompt NW return of professional soccer

Adrian Hanauer's obsession with soccer began when he was first introduced to the game at the age of two and furthered when he saw his first NASL soccer game at eight. In his first year at Mercer Island High School, he was one of only two freshmen to make the soccer team. Despite his failure to make the varsity squad the next year, Hanauer continued to play in pickup games at community fields and on intramural teams while attending the University of Washington. While those final years in college could have been the final chapter in a boyhood love of a sport, it was actually just the beginning.

Hanauer began working in the family busi-

Co-owner and general manager Adrian Hanauer after Sounders victory

ness, Pacific Coast Feather Co., at the age of 13. The firm, which manufactures down pillows and high-end bedding, was originally founded in Germany in 1884, but is now headquartered in Seattle. With an interest in flexing his own entrepreneurial muscles, at 22 he founded Museum Quality Framing in 1988, which grew into a chain throughout Washington, Oregon, and Idaho. He also opened four Mad Pizza restaurants in the greater Seattle area. But it was his next venture that gave him the freedom to pursue his boyhood interest. As an early investor in aQuantive, an online-based advertising company, Hanauer turned a substantial profit when the company went public in 2000 and again when Microsoft purchased the company in 2007.

In 2002, his passion for soccer led him to become the managing partner of the Sounders of the United Soccer League. He inherited a club that had lost $1 million a season for five consecutive years, but reduced the losses to about $350,000 annually. Despite the losses, he was committed to building on the memory of watching the original Sounders in the North American Soccer League in the 1970s.

"I got a crash course in running a professional soccer team," recalled Hanauer in an article for *The Seattle Times*. "When I took over, it was more a philanthropic thing than it was managing a team that could sustain itself. That had to change." Under Hanauer's leadership, the team went 23-4-1 in his first season, the second best record in USL history, and made it to the league championships three times, winning it twice.

Hanauer began working on getting a Major League Soccer team in Seattle, making a $250,000 investment for a 15% stake in an English soccer team, Cambridge United FC, in May 2007. The Mercer Island grad was then introduced to movie executive Joe Roth after the MLS All-Star game in July of that year, and within six months the two had brought in Microsoft co-founder Paul Allen and comedian Drew Carey as investors. In a press conference on November 13, 2007, the group announced that the MLS had awarded Seattle an expansion team. It marked the return of top-level soccer to Seattle for the first time in 24 years. The Sounders FC became the 15th team in the MLS.

Serving as both an owner and as the general manager for Sounders FC was the realization of a dream come true for Hanauer. For Northwest soccer fans, their dream had also been realized as the Sounders quickly established themselves as one of the league's elite teams.

The Seattle Sounders celebrate after winning their second straight US Open Cup.

On March 19, 2009, in front of a sold-out crowd of 32,523, the Sounders FC played its inaugural match against the New York Red Bulls, winning 3-0. Seattle went on to become the first MLS expansion team to win its first three games and did so with a shutout in each. The club set a new MLS record for average attendance with 30,943 fans per match and sold out every league match.

In that inaugural season, the Sounders FC became the second expansion club in MLS history to win the Lamar Hunt US Open Cup, and the first ever to win it back to back. The history books were again rewritten in 2011, when the Sounders FC won their third consecutive Open Cup. In 2012, the Sounders went to their fourth consecutive open cup final, but lost on a penalty shootout when regulation time finished with a 1-1 score.

Hanauer has also taken the lead on "friendly" matches at Century Link Field, which have given fans a taste of soccer at the international level. The club set a state record for attendance at a soccer match on August 5, 2009, when 66,848 watched the Sounders play FC Barcelona, a record which was later broken when they hosted Manchester United in front of 67,052 fans. Perhaps a stronger indicator of the league's local support occurred on October 7, 2012, when the ever-increasing rivalry with the Portland Timbers attracted 66,452 to watch the Sounders blank their Northwest nemesis 3-0.

Just as 14,000 fans chose the name for their team in an online poll in 2008, season-

Hanauer gets doused by champagne after the Sounder's second straight US Open Cup in 2010
(Corky Trewin)

ticket holders and members of the Alliance (the Sounders' official fan association), took part in an unprecedented vote. From October 7th to December 7th, 2012 fans decided whether or not to retain Adrian Hanauer as the general manager. It was the first time in US pro sports history that a general manager's fate was in the hands of a team's fans.

"I'm very excited about what we're doing here in Seattle," said Drew Carey on the Alliance's blog. "Where else can the fans fire the general manager? I hope this becomes a model for every professional sports organization in America."

With fans voting to retain Hanauer, they not only got a dedicated GM, but one who does not draw a salary. "It allows me to do my job with more focus on what's right," said Hanauer to *The Seattle Times*. "I'm a minority owner, and for me, that's compensation enough. I don't have to worry about keeping my job or a contract extension or anything like that. I'm solely focused on what's right. If someone else could do the job better than me, I would gladly hand over the reins, and that would be fine with me. It's all about what's best for the franchise."

Beyond soccer, Hanauer is involved in many organizations throughout Seattle. He sits on the board of trustees for the Museum of History and Industry. He also donates his energy to the advisory board for The University of Washington Intercollegiate Sports master's degree program.

Danny Kaye

January 18, 1913, Brooklyn, NY – March 3, 1987, Los Angeles, CA

Comedian was serious about Seattle baseball

The son of Jewish Ukrainian immigrants, David Daniel Kaminsky grew up to become one of the most beloved entertainers in America during the 1950s and part of the ownership group that brought Major League Baseball back to the Northwest. Known as Danny Kaye to the rest of the world, the film and stage star never resided in Washington State, but has been given honorable mention in this collection of stories.

Danny Kaye throws out first pitch of 1979 MLB All-Star Game at the Kingdome with a group of children to celebrate the International Year of the Child (Cole Porter/Seattle Times)

The redheaded Kaye was probably most famous for sharing top billing with Bing Crosby in the classic film *White Christmas* in 1954. But off screen, Kaye was a regular at Ebetts Field as a fan of baseball and his beloved Brooklyn Dodgers.

Mariners coach Vada Pinson and Kaye in the dugout

The ardent baseball fan was there in the front row when the Dodgers moved to Los Angeles. And he was first in line when his friend and business partner, Lester Smith, put together the Seattle Mariners' original ownership group in 1977. With the exception of the film production company he owned along with Smith, baseball was Kaye's only connection to Seattle, but it was a strong enough bond to make him a frequent fan at the Kingdome.

In addition to being an owner for five seasons, Kaye's musical tribute to the Dodgers' pennant chase in 1962 was included on "Baseball's Greatest Hits," compiled by Major League Baseball.

The entertainer was well known to his friends for his encyclopedic knowledge of the game. His grave in New York is adorned with images of a baseball and bat. Smith's son Alex said the happiest days in the lives of his father and his friend Danny Kaye were opening day for the Mariners in 1977, the All-Star game in 1979, and when they sold the team in '81. "It was quite a ride," he said.

Anne Levinson

February 1, 1958, Topeka, KS

Saving the Storm was her 'tikkun olam'

While sports fans in Western Washington watched helplessly in 2006 when the Seattle SuperSonics were sold to an Oklahoma group led by Clay Bennett, former judge and Seattle deputy mayor Anne Levinson watched from a different angle. She saw that the WNBA's Seattle Storm was going to be taken as well. The two teams had been sold together as a package and it appeared that no one was stepping up to keep the Storm from blowing out of town.

Levinson was aware that the Oklahoma group had turned down every offer to sell the teams together or separately, so the chances of keeping the Storm in Seattle were slim to none. Undaunted, she reached out to three Storm season ticket holders who had the financial means to help and asked each of the women the same question: if she could convince the Oklahoma group to separate the Storm from the Sonics, get league approval and negotiate a long-term lease in Seattle, would they be willing to buy the team?

They all said yes. That was all she needed. Levinson, along with Dawn Trudeau, Lisa Brummel and Ginny Gilder, founded Force 10 Hoops, and then Levinson quietly began seven months of negotiations with the Oklahoma group and the city to keep the Storm in Seattle.

The path that led Levinson to save the Storm seemed more like destiny, beginning at the intersection of her long-time interest in athletics,

Storm co-owners Dawn Trudeau, Ginny Gilder, Lisa Brummel and Anne Levinson
(Karen Ducey/seattlepi.com)

her spirit of activism, and her success in her career. Growing up Jewish in Kansas, and then in suburban Massachusetts, gave her a unique perspective on both religion and justice. Her parents emphasized a love of learning, commitment to community, standing up for others and making a difference in the world.

Levinson's introduction to sports began when she played basketball, softball and field hockey during high school in Massachusetts. She continued to wield her field hockey stick as a freshman at the University of Kansas, but in her sophomore year the university announced that the women's team would be cut in order to focus on men's athletics.

Levinson quickly moved from athlete to activist. She started by lobbying the student senate and eventually worked her way up to the governor's office, where she succeeded in securing short-term funding to save the women's program. But Levinson didn't stop there. In her junior year, she filed one of the first Title IX challenges in the country. The final settlement mandated that the university provide parity to women across the board, including scholarships, facilities and travel.

Levinson credits those years struggling against the odds with helping her find her voice and inspiring her to go to law school. After graduating, she moved to Seattle and joined a field hockey team, where a chance introduction led to her first foray into politics. After working for two successive mayors, she was appointed by the governor to chair Washington's utilities commission. Levinson was later appointed to the bench and created one of the country's first mental health courts. Over the years, she served on numerous non-profit boards, where she met the women who would become co-owners of the Storm.

Working in the mayor's office, Levinson became intimately familiar with professional sports leases when the city negotiated with the former owners of the Sonics over the renovation of Key Arena. While deputy mayor, she

Levinson with then Governor Christine Gregoire and former Governor Booth Gardner

assisted the American Basketball League (ABL) with locating the first women's professional basketball franchise in Seattle, the Seattle Reign.

Although the ABL folded after its third season, the Reign proved that women's professional basketball could be viable in Seattle. In 2000, the Sonics were granted a WNBA team, the Seattle Storm. Levinson thought that from then on she could just enjoy being a season ticket holder. Then in 2007, when it looked like the Sonics and the Storm were on their way out, Levinson decided to step out of the stands and into the front office.

Aware of the acrimony surrounding the Sonics situation, Levinson knew her effort would only be successful if she could find common ground with Bennett and the ownership group in Oklahoma. After all, she was a long-time leader in the LGBT community and life-long Democrat, whereas they were conservative Republicans.

She began with their shared Midwest roots and determined they had several mutual colleagues. She eventually discovered that Bennett was a fan of women's basketball, had been raised by a Jewish mother and had even celebrated his bar mitzvah.

Levinson celebrating with Storm after winning 2010 WNBA championship

The financial benefit of professional sports was irrelevant, according to Levinson. What mattered was that the team remained a part of the fabric of the community. She wanted girls and boys in the Pacific Northwest to grow up seeing professional female athletes.

"It's important that girls see that women in today's society can reach goals that were out of reach in previous generations," she said proudly. "These players stand on the shoulders of so many, and they in turn will open new doors for those who follow."

On January 8, 2008, Levinson and her Force 10 Hoops partners presented themselves as the new owners of the Seattle Storm. "Through our extensive negotiations," said Clay Bennett when the deal was announced, "we have become convinced that their commitment to the community and passion for the game will result in a secure and promising future for the Seattle Storm. We knew the right thing to do for Seattle was to work with Anne's group to see if we could make this happen."

Two years later, in 2010, the Storm rewarded the city with its second WNBA championship. Levinson was there on the podium in Atlanta when the trophy was handed to the team from the WNBA commissioner. "It was a very special experience," said Levinson, "made all the more special by knowing that very few people really knew how close we came to losing the team and what it took to get there."

Levinson made it clear that she was not doing this to become an owner, but wanted to make sure the team could remain part of the Seattle community. "I wasn't against becoming an owner. I just never had that intention," said Levinson. "My focus was on saving the team however possible. Me becoming an owner came late in the process and was necessary to close the transaction."

Just two months following the Storm's championship run and with its future secure, Levinson decided to step down from the ownership group she formed. "The WNBA is extremely appreciative of Anne Levinson's contributions to the team's ongoing success," commented

WNBA president Donna Orender in a released statement.

From high school athlete to college activist, from civic leader to judge, from sports fan to team owner, the experiences of Anne Levinson all intersected at the moment she stepped up to save an emerging professional sports franchise.

Levinson's efforts ensured the continuation of a community asset that enables thousands of dedicated fans to witness and cheer the athletic abilities of women at the highest level. Keeping the Storm in Seattle was her way of repairing the world in her community.

Charlie Littman

January 21, 1939, New York, NY

Stickball bat and BlueJackets are prized possessions for New York transplant

Charlie Littman still considers his pink Spaulding stickball bat one of his most prized possessions. As a kid growing up in New York in the 1940s, playing stickball was a rite of passage. For Littman, baseball became a passion that would endure for a lifetime.

The Littman family moved to Denver in 1948, and at the age of 13 Charlie started selling peanuts and popcorn at Bears Stadium for the Double-A Denver Bears. As the stadium emptied, Littman would often hang around the dugout for a chance at getting a used or broken bat from one of the ballplayers. His collection grew and by the next summer he organized the Utica Street Bums, a street baseball team that played in a vacant lot on Sundays against the Grove Street Specials.

After attending Denver University, Littman went on to a career in sales, ultimately establishing a fine jewelry store. While he continued his lifelong love of the New York Yankees (particularly the teams from the '40s through the '60s), he became a Seattle Mariners fan after moving to Bremerton in 1973. The following spring, he began coaching a Little League team called the Chico Pee Wees. In his first three years with the team — 1974, 1975 and 1976 — he won three consecutive championships. During that run,

Littman was named the league's coach of the year.

In 2005, Littman was able to combine his passion for baseball with his interest in strengthening his community when he became one of the original owners of the Kitsap Blue-Jackets. Playing in what is now called the West Coast League, the BlueJackets are a summer, wood bat, collegiate league that attracts an elite group of players. As of 2013, 120 of the league's players have signed letters of intent with Major League clubs. The West Coast League offers many of these players their first opportunity to get comfortable hitting with a wood bat, while playing competitively over a 56-game season.

The West Coast League includes 12 teams from Canada to Northern California. Littman is now one of three owner-partners of the Blue-Jackets and is excited by the league's continued expansion, which will add four new teams in 2014 and become part of a two-division league.

Littman is especially proud that the team enriches the quality of local life by providing affordable, wholesome family entertainment. He is also a member of the Tacoma Athletic Commission, where he focuses on promoting sports to the youth of Pierce County.

The couple moved to Bremerton in 1973 to take over the family business, Goldberg Jewelers, a business they ran in three locations until consolidating the stores in 1993 and then retiring in 2001.

Herman Sarkowsky

June 9, 1925, Gera, Germany

Legacy of one man elevates Northwest to major player on national sports stage

Herman Sarkowsky is considered by many to be one of the most influential individuals in Northwest sports history. Over a period of 30 years, he brought the Trail Blazers to Portland, the Seahawks to Seattle, invested in the NASL Sounders, kept the Mariners from fleeing and helped resurrect Washington's horse racing industry.

After graduating from the University of Washington in 1949, Sarkowsky launched a career in home development, and by 1969 was the largest residential developer in the Puget Sound region. Sarkowsky first became a hero to Northwest sports fans in 1970 when he and two of his friends, Larry Weinberg and Robert Schmertz, "who happened to be Jewish," paid $3.7 million to secure an NBA expansion team for Portland. Seven years

Herman Sarkowsky as a student at the UW, 1947

267

later, the Trail Blazers delivered an NBA championship title to the Rose City. The team was later sold to Microsoft co-founder Paul Allen in 1988 for $70 million.

Later on in the '70s at a lunch with Ned Skinner, Sarkowsky and the shipbuilding heir came to the conclusion that they were both interested in owning an NFL team and later brought retailer Lloyd Nordstrom in to become the majority owner.

In a maneuver to endear themselves to Lamar Hunt, the head of the NFL expansion committee, who owned the Kansas City Chiefs and three soccer teams, the group bought the rights to a North American Soccer League franchise, the Seattle Sounders.

The strategy worked and the Sarkowsky-led group was granted an NFL franchise in the winter of 1974. On August 1, 1976, Sarkowsky

watched with pride as the Seattle Seahawks took the field at the newly built Kingdome. "There were more than 60,000 people who crowded into the building that day. Every one of them was excited. But I guarantee you I was the happiest guy in the place," recalled Sarkowsky.

Fast forward to 1992, when Mariners owner Jeff Smulyan was plotting to move the team out of Seattle.

Sarkowsky, Ken Easley, the Seahawk's 1981 first round draft pick and coach Jack Patera

Not wanting to be the mayor that lost baseball, Norm Rice appointed Sarkowsky to spearhead a last-ditch effort to save the team. Smulyan held the team hostage for $13 million, the amount of capital he needed to keep the team afloat. Despite Sarkowsky's efforts to raise around $5 million within months, Smulyan changed the rules and announced the team was for sale for $100 million. With a Kingdome lease that required Smulyan to first offer the team to local buyers, Senator Slade Gorton stepped in and got Nintendo aboard for the full nut.

But Major League Baseball resisted the non-North American ownership. Ultimately it was the investors Sarkowsky brought into the mix that made the difference in the minds of the MLB hierarchy. In the spring of 1993, Sarkowsky watched as the Mariners returned to the Kingdome, and was further rewarded two years later when the 1995 Mariners staged one of the most exciting season finishes and playoff runs in baseball history.

Sarkowsky with Seattle Mariners manager Lou Piniella

Sarkowsky's interest then returned to his first love, horse racing. The entrepreneur got his first taste of the sport of kings when he paid $1,200 for his first horse, Forin Sea, following a claims race in 1960. By 2007, Sarkowsky owned 37 Thoroughbreds.

Horses from his stable included Phone Chatter, which won the 1993 Breeders' Cup for Juvenile Fillies, and Mr. Greeley, which placed in the 1995 Breeders' Cup Sprint. But the race that eluded Sarkowsky, and one that he wanted most, was the Longacres Mile. After four attempts, his 60-1 long shot No Giveaway came from 20½ lengths behind at the halfway point and brought Sarkowsky the win.

In 1992, after Longacres racetrack in Renton had been sold by the Alhadeff Family, Sarkowsky stepped in as an investor in Emerald Downs, bringing Thoroughbred racing back to the Northwest.

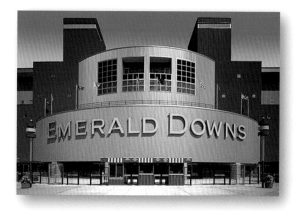

Herman Sarkowsky was only 9 years old when his family left Germany in 1934 to escape Hitler and the Nazis. Two years after arriving in New York, the family moved again to settle in Seattle in 1937. The teenager attended Broadway High School, where he became sports editor and wrote a column called "The Water Boy" patterned after journalism legend Royal Brougham. From "waterboy" to sports mogul, Herman Sarkowsky has been at the forefront of professional sports in the Northwest. His teams have galvanized entire cities and filled their stadiums with cheering fans for more than 40 years. Any sports fan who looks to the Seahawks with SuperBowl dreams or recalls the indelible memory of Ken Griffey, Jr. under a pile of teammates, should also remember that there was one man behind those dreams and memories.

Walter Schoenfeld

November 6, 1930, Seattle

Schoenfeld dressed up Seattle in major sports franchises

Walter Schoenfeld was born and raised in Seattle and it was likely that he learned to get dressed up at an early age. His father, Max, and his two uncles founded Fashion Craft Neckwear. After serving in the military in Korea, Schoenfeld joined Fashion Craft in 1954 as a salesman. By 1971, he had helped grow the business into the largest neckwear company in the U.S.

Over the years, the fashion executive was a strong supporter of many civic and cultural organizations, but for Schoenfeld, the city still lacked the amenities to compete on the national stage.

That all changed in 1966 when California businessmen Eugene Klein and Sam Schulman approached Schoenfeld to invest in Seattle's first modern professional sports franchise. Schoenfeld became the local anchor Klein and Schul-

Walter Schoenfeld was an original investor in three of Seattle's professional sports franchises

man needed to bring the Seattle SuperSonics, the NBA's newest expansion team, to the Northwest. Schoenfeld served as vice president and director of the Sonics' parent company from 1968-1979 and had to learn quickly on the job.

While watching rookies play in Everett in the 1970's, he witnessed one player score 47 points in just three quarters. He commented to coach Lenny Wilkens that he thought the rookie was destined to be an all-star. Wilkens replied, "I wish you hadn't said that. I'm going to cut him. You didn't see him at the other end of the court." Schoenfeld said, "It was a quick lesson for me as an owner that the coach knows more about the game."

In 1979, Schoenfeld watched as his city's team competed on the national stage, ultimately sprucing up Seattle's image with an NBA championship.

Schoenfeld's interest in sports continued, becoming a partner in the Seattle Sounders (NASL), which took root in 1974 and six years later won its first Western Division title.

Earlier, Seattle had landed a Major League franchise in 1969, but the Pilots' debut season would be its last, as Major League Baseball hijacked the team to Milwaukee. The following year, the City of Seattle, King County, and the State of Washington — represented by state Attorney General, and later U.S. Senator, Slade Gorton — sued the American League for breach of contract.

When a team was promised to the city, Schoenfeld organized a group of investors known as the Original Six, which brought Major League Baseball back to Seattle. On April 6, 1977, the Seattle Mariners played their first game to a sold-out crowd of 57,762 at the Kingdome, losing 7-0 to the California Angels. "We just wanted to bring baseball back to the city," Schoenfeld said.

In 1979, Jim Stillwell and Jim Walsh of the Original Six left the group, dividing the ownership into four equal shares. Following the 1981 season, the Mariners were sold to California businessman George Argyros. Schoenfeld and Stan Golub remained minority partners until 1984.

As an original investor in three professional sports franchises in Seattle, Walter Schoenfeld, the neckwear king, did his best to dress up his home town.

Sam Schulman

April 10, 1910, New York – June 12, 2003, Beverly Hills, CA

Rebel movie producer changed Seattle sports scene and the NBA

If he had been born during the second century BCE, Sam Schulman would surely have been a general with the insurgent Maccabee army that reclaimed the Holy Temple and witnessed the miracle of Hanukkah. Schulman was a rebel long before he helped secure Seattle an expansion franchise with the National Basketball Association and served as the first president of the SuperSonics.

Born in New York, the 1934 graduate of Harvard Business School began his career by going against the grain. He purchased a bankrupt publisher in

Brooklyn, which he quickly turned into a profitable enterprise.

He moved west to become successful in various business ventures that led him to become a producer in the motion picture industry. His financial stake in dozens of Hollywood films brought the East Coast native respect within the industry, but he rarely allowed his name to appear in the on-screen credits. In June of 1966, he entered the world of sports when he became a minority owner of the San Diego Chargers following the merger of the American and National Football leagues.

Six months later, Schulman teamed with an-

Sam Schulman and Sonics forward Spencer Haywood hit the courts in 1970 and changed the NBA forever (seattlepi.com)

other Jewish owner of the Chargers, Eugene V. Klein, to bring the NBA to Seattle. While Klein served as president of the football club in Southern California, Schulman took the helm of the NBA franchise as president and head of operations for the SuperSonics.

Schulman exposed his defiant character when he challenged the rules of the NBA by signing Spencer Haywood of the Denver Rockets. The Rockets were part of the upstart American Basketball Association, which allowed teams to draft players before they had completed their college eligibility. Haywood's signing with the SuperSonics in December 1970 was in defiance of the NBA rule that said a player could not be signed until four years after graduating high school.

Schulman's legal battle went all the way to the US Supreme Court, which ruled in Haywood and the Sonics' favor. The landmark decision sent shockwaves through every city in the league, forever changing the face of the NBA. "It was a matter of principle," Schulman told *The Seattle Times.* "I couldn't see any logical reason for keeping a man from making a living. I thought it was unconstitutional."

For the 1973-74 season, Schulman hired the legendary Boston Celtic Bill Russell, who coached the Sonics to their first playoff appearance two years later. The team, which starred Haywood, guards Fred Brown and Slick Watts, and rookie center Tommy Burleson, defeated the Detroit Pistons in a three-game miniseries before falling to eventual champion the Golden State Warriors in six games.

When Russell left the Sonics after the 1976-77 season, Bob Hopkins took over as coach, but the team faltered, starting the year with a bleak 5-17 record. Schulman acted quickly to stop the bleeding, hiring former Sonics player Lenny Wilkens as the new head coach. The SuperSonics won their next 11 of 12 games and finished the season 47-35. The Sonics went on to win the Western Conference title, and led the Washington Bullets three games to two before losing in seven games in the 1978 NBA finals. The following season, a Sonics team that included guards Dennis Johnson and Gus Williams, center Jack Sikma and forwards Lonnie Shelton, Johnny Johnson, and Paul Silas took the Pacific Division title for the first time, defeated the Phoenix Suns in the Western Conference series, and then shut down the Washington Bullets in five games to secure Seattle's first modern professional championship.

Schulman and Sonics coach Lenny Wilkens arrive in Seattle bringing with them the 1978-79 NBA championship trophy (Matt McVay/Seattle Times)

Four years later, the rebel sportsman returned to Hollywood after his ownership group sold the SuperSonics to billboard mogul Barry Ackerley. He continued to finance a number of feature films as president of SLM Corporation until his retirement in 1995. Schulman was awarded the Pillar of Achievement Award in 2003 from the Southern California Jewish Sports Hall of Fame. That same year, at age 93, Schulman died from complications from blood disease. His wife, Sylvia, told *The Seattle Times* that her husband never took off his Sonics championship ring until she did so for him during his final hospital stay.

Howard Schultz

July 19, 1953, Brooklyn, NY

Starbucks owner brewed trouble when he sold the Sonics

Under different circumstances, Howard Schultz could have become a beloved Seattle icon like Ivar Haglund, Fred Hutchinson and the Nordstrom family. But instead of admiration, the founder of Starbucks became the object of derision from loyal SuperSonics fans for selling the team to an owner who moved the club to Oklahoma City.

Born in Brooklyn and by raised by German-Jewish immigrant parents, Schultz learned about basketball on the outdoor courts of the New York borough. He earned a scholarship to play basketball at Northern Michigan University and became the first person in his family to attend college.

After graduation, he became a general manager for Swedish drip coffee maker manufacturer Hammarplast. During a business trip to Italy, the entrepreneur noticed there were coffee bars on practically every street. And they didn't just serve excellent espresso; they also served as local gathering places for business meetings and social occasions. The coffee bars were Italy's societal glue, and there were 200,000 of them in the country. Those street-side cafés in Italy became his model for Starbucks, which he purchased in 1987.

The exponential growth of Starbucks gave Schultz the notoriety and financial ability to become a fixture at Sonics games in the old Seattle Coliseum, which was remodeled in 1995 to become the Key Arena. The founder and CEO of Starbucks pulled together a group of local investors who were also avid basketball fans in 2001. He established the Basketball Club of Seattle and purchased the Seattle NBA franchise from billboard magnate Barry Ackerley. Basketball fans in Seattle were

Barry Ackerley, left, announces the sale of the Sonics to Howard Schultz in 2001 (Paul Kitagaki, Jr./seattlepi.com)

Schultz sells the Sonics to Clay Bennett in 2006 who moves the team to Oklahoma for the 2008 season

elated with the possibilities of the franchise being owned by an actual fan of the team.

But the honeymoon was over almost before it started. The new owner voiced his disappointment with point guard Gary Payton, whom Schultz described as selfish and self-absorbed. When Payton failed to show up on the first day of training camp in 2002, Schultz ordered that Payton be traded. When contract negotiations with forward Rashard Lewis fell apart, the owner took the failure personally. The CEO was especially angry over the fact that Lewis kept a baseball cap lowered over his eyes while they sat across from each other at the table. "In my business, that's not how we do things," Schultz said later, referring to the like-minded negotiations he regularly undertook as the head of Starbucks.

After the Seahawks and Mariners each had new stadiums built, Schultz demanded that his basketball team receive equal respect from local government. When his request to replace the aging Key Arena was rejected by lawmakers in February of 2002, the team began negotiations with Bellevue and Renton to build a new arena in those communities.

Frustrated with the apparent bureaucracy of government, Schultz sold the NBA franchise in July of 2006 to Clay Bennett and his group of investors from Oklahoma City for $350 million. Schultz had seller's remorse two years later and filed a lawsuit against Bennett in an attempt to rescind the sale based on fraud and intentional misrepresentation. Fans of the team dismissed the legal action as Schultz's last-ditch effort to reduce the damage to his local image for having sold the team to out-of-state owners. Schultz dropped the lawsuit four months later, which opened the door for the Oklahoma Thunder to begin play in time for the 2008 season.

Dick Vertlieb

October 7, 1930, Watts, CA – December 5, 2008, Las Vegas, NV

Vertlieb delivered Seattle to the national sports limelight

Shrewd, bold, volatile, loyal, passionate, innovative, competitive, charismatic: Dick Vertlieb created a trail of adjectives that followed him as he worked his way through the pinnacle and lowlands of a career in sports. Over a span of more than 30 years, his efforts as a team executive left his distinctive fingerprint on virtually every professional franchise in Seattle. According to one local sportswriter, who shared the opinion of many others in his field, "[Vertlieb] remains the person most responsible for turning our coastal outpost into a big-league city."

University of Southern California graduate Dick Vertlieb was itching to operate a professional basketball franchise. He had played freshman ball for the Trojans in the late 1950s and subsequently coached USC's freshman team before embarking on a career as a stockbroker for Merrill Lynch. As a bachelor, Vertlieb shared a rental house with actors Martin Milner and David Janssen, with Natalie Wood a frequent visitor.

In the spring of 1964, Vertlieb approached his friend and fellow USC alumnus Don Richman with the idea that the two should quit their

jobs to start an NBA franchise. Neither had any experience in professional sports nor any connections or clout with the NBA. They were simply fans of the game with a motivated entrepreneurial spirit.

Vertlieb's plan was to locate the best markets that did not have NBA teams, sell the idea to NBA commissioner J. Walter Kennedy, and then unearth investors to fund the operation. Vertlieb arranged a meeting with Kennedy in New York and also consulted with members of the league's expansion committee to learn more about the task that he and Richman faced. Kennedy told them that an expansion franchise would likely cost $3 million, a daunting sum, but encouraged Vertlieb and Richman with news that the NBA intended to expand by up to eight cities over the next few years. That meant a lot of markets would be up for grabs.

Bill Douglas, left, shows Sonics business manager Dick Vertlieb uniforms for the NBA's newest franchise

Vertlieb and Richman tested out several markets over the next year, finally settling on Cleveland as their No. 1 landing spot. They recruited entertainer Danny Thomas and singer Andy Williams as investors, but the deal ultimately fell apart. Recalling his experiences in Seattle from earlier visits, Richman suggested the Queen City (Seattle's original nickname). "The feel of the city for sports stayed with me," Richman said years later. "I just thought it would be an exceptional place for a professional basketball franchise."

Alone or together, Richman and Vertlieb made more than 10 trips to Seattle over the next couple of years in order to learn it thoroughly. They studied the city's demographics, its population-growth trends, and its entertainment industry. Everything they found convinced them that the NBA would work in Seattle, including the fact that the city sported a relatively new arena, the 14,000-seat Seattle Center Coliseum, built for the 1962 World's Fair.

Vertlieb and Richman had a difficult time making the NBA expansion committee buy into their enthusiasm for Seattle. While the NBA had teams in two West Coast cities, Los Angeles and San Francisco, the Pacific Northwest had no major professional franchises in any sport. Plus, several cities larger than Seattle, including Chicago and Houston, did not have NBA franchises. Finally, the NBA had never expanded into any market that didn't have a Major League Baseball or the National Football League team.

"NBA owners were also afraid by an attack from Indians or other unfriendly and hostile forces," Richman quipped.

On August 26, 1966, after nearly two years of combing the Los Angeles area for a financial "angel," Vertlieb read a story in *The Los Angeles Times* detailing entrepreneur Eugene Klein's record $10 million purchase of the San Diego Chargers from Barron Hilton, Richman's former employer. Vertlieb called Klein's secretary at National General Corporation to request a meeting, and got it.

Vertlieb explained to Klein that the NBA was looking to expand by as many as eight cities before the rival American Basketball Association — scheduled to begin play in 1967 — could claim them. Vertlieb suggested to Klein that the opportunity to strike was now while Klein still had his pick of potential cities.

Klein couldn't resist Vertlieb's pitch and told him he favored a West Coast location. With Congress on the verge of approving the NFL-AFL merger and vastly increasing the value of Klein's Chargers, Klein felt flush and informed the 36-year-old former stockbroker that if he and Richman could secure a franchise, Klein would become an investor and that Vertlieb and Richman could operate it. Klein even opened a bank account, allowing Vertlieb and Richman

SEATTLE SUPERSONICS / NBA OFFICIAL PROGRAM 1967-68 SEASON / 50¢

DESIGN: PAGET LOOMIS

to cover their expenses.

"Dick was a very bright guy who understood business and basketball, and had the nerve to approach people and get them involved," said Addis Gutmann, an original Sonics season ticketholder who became a close friend. "He had the vision to do it."

Vertlieb and Richman now had two pieces of the puzzle: an ideal expansion city (Seattle) and a primary investor (Klein). Now they needed to convince the NBA to grant them the expansion franchise. Over the next year, Vertlieb and Richman consulted with league officials in New York. (They often rented large hotel suites to impress league owners, and then ate sandwiches out of brown bags to conserve on expenses.) Armed with their research, they finally sold Kennedy on Seattle's merits, demonstrating with charts and statistics why an expansion team there could average at least 5,000 fans per game, the break-even point for almost all NBA franchises in that era.

On Dec. 20, 1966, it was official. The NBA granted the city of Seattle an expansion team. Vertlieb and Richman casually flipped a coin to determine who would be the business manager and general manager. At a press conference, Richman introduced himself as the team's general manager and Vertlieb as business manager, stating that Seattle's NBA team would begin play at the Seattle Center Coliseum in the 1967-68 season. Richman explained that the team was backed by Klein and another California businessman, Sam Schulman, who together purchased 70 percent of the franchise's stock for $1,750,000. The remaining 30 percent was held by smaller stockholders, including Richman and Vertlieb who had a "participating" stake in profits.

After Richman's introduction, Schulman declared to Seattle, "I have a dream for this great city. I intend to pull together some of the most talented men in this country. Together, we will bring the world championship to Seattle."

Nobody in Seattle knew much about Schulman, a native New Yorker and Harvard Business School graduate. Schulman had partnered with Klein on the purchase of the San Diego Chargers and various projects at National General Corp., whose subsidiary, Evergreen Theaters, distributed movies to Seattle theaters. Schulman would become the "active" partner with Seattle's new NBA team, while Klein would remain the "active" partner with the Chargers.

Vertlieb and Richman had come to Seattle at considerable financial and emotional cost. They had to uproot their families and abandon

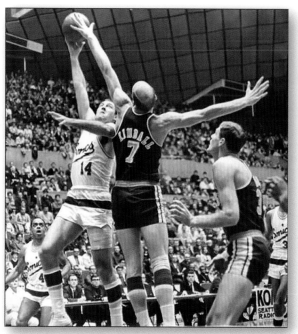

Tom Meschery stretches for the rim during the SuperSonics 1967-68 inaugural season

far more lucrative jobs. "I was making a lot of money," Vertlieb told the Seattle media, "but I found I just wasn't satisfied. We're both frustrated athletes and sports nuts, and the more Don and I talked about this, the more I knew we had to try it. If we didn't do it, we knew we'd spend the rest of our lives wondering why we didn't take the chance."

Vertlieb, Richman and Schulman soon became media favorites. Vertlieb was known for his garrulous personality and high emotion — he once twisted an ankle leaping out of his seat to protest a referee's call. Richman spouted a stream of one-liners, once referring to Seattle as a "24-hour car wash." Schulman was also not shy about offering lively and often inflammatory quotes to the media.

Names considered for the new NBA team included the "Miners," "Loggers," "Captains" and "Stevedores." With an eye toward landing that all-important first radio contract and sponsorship, Vertlieb's original choice was the "Olympians," with blue and gold uniforms. "We approached Olympia beer," Vertlieb recalled. "Richman says, 'You will have uniforms exactly the colors of an Olympia beer can. All over the United States of America, in New York, Los Angeles and Chicago, you'll have five Olympia cans running up and down the court.' That was the funniest pitch I ever heard. I thought it was hysterical. Hey, it's the water, the Seattle Olympians." The beer company wasn't interested.

Brainstorming later, the two picked up on the talk around town of Boeing receiving a contract to build the faster-than-sound Supersonic Transport. The name stuck. Vertlieb settled on green and gold, which represented Northwest trees and Alaska riches, with a stripe around the shorts.

Verlieb looks on as Lenny Wilkens is introduced as the newest Sonic and is given the unique role as player/coach

1968-69 Soncis team photo

The inaugural season began as promised in October of 1967, with the Sonics led by coach Al Bianchi, a former player for the Philadelphia 76ers and one of the last advocates of the two-handed set shot. Despite a Sonics lineup that included All-Star guard Walt Hazzard and NBA All-Rookie Team members Bob Rule and Al Tucker, Rod Thorn from the St. Louis Hawks and Bob Weiss from the Philadelphia 76ers, the expansion team was welcomed to the NBA with a 144-116 drubbing, finishing the season with a 23-59 record. Vert-

lieb remained positive, never letting his smile fade. "Basketball is one of the two most exciting indoor sports, and the other one shouldn't have spectators," he said.

That first season, Sonics fans witnessed Vertlieb's emotional commitment to the team when he rushed onto the court to defend Bianchi after the Sonics' coach had been decked by Gus Johnson of the Baltimore Bullets. Johnson turned and belted Vertlieb too. "I saw stars but I never went down," Vertlieb said proudly. NBA commissioner Walter Kennedy sent him a joking telegram that addressed the absurdity of a short, wide man challenging Johnson. "You're fined $500 for taking part in the fight," it read. "This fine will be rescinded if you seek psychiatric help."

Richman decided to call it quits after 16 months, turning over GM responsibilities to his fellow USC alumnus. Vertlieb's first move was to trade Hazzard to the Atlanta Hawks in exchange for Lenny Wilkens, who went on to average 22.4 points, 8.2 assists and 6.2 rebounds per game during the 1968–69 season. But the SuperSonics won only 30 games and during the off-season Vertlieb cut Bianchi, giving Wilkens the unique role as player/coach. "I loved being around him," Wilkens said of Verlieb. "He was very enthusiastic. He believed anything was possible."

But Vertlieb clashed constantly with Schulman, who wanted him to be "more business-like" and less emotional (Schulman was irked that Vertlieb changed seats constantly during games so he could hurl barbs at the referees from different locations in the Coliseum). The last straw was when he hired assistant coach Tom Meschery without consulting the owner. Vertlieb was let go during a testy 1 a.m. phone call to his Mercer Island home in 1969.

"I always expected the owners to read my mind and I wanted my way," Vertlieb said. "I never got mad, but if I didn't get my way, I'd just pout. I'd hold my breath until my lips turned purple. That's why I always got fired — because I was

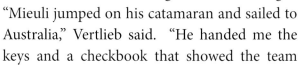

always smarter than the owners."

Based on his experience obtaining an NBA franchise, local Seattle developer Herman Sarkowsky brought Vertlieb into the mix as a consultant for the group who would ultimately bring the Trail Blazers to Portland in 1970.

Sarkowsky turned to Vertlieb again to help land the NASL's Seattle Sounders in 1974. The connection resulted in Vertlieb becoming a minority owner of the team. Landing the Sounders however, was all part of a calculated effort to obtain a pro football team for Seattle. Lamar Hunt, who owned three NASL soccer teams and the NFL's Kansas City Chiefs, also happened to be the head of the NFL expansion committee. Vertlieb and Sarkowsky gained Hunt's favor, making Seattle the proud home of its third professional sports franchise, the Seahawks.

The owner of the NBA's Golden State Warriors, Franklin Mieuli, had kept Vertlieb on his radar and in 1974 hired him as the team's general manager. "Mieuli jumped on his catamaran and sailed to Australia," Vertlieb said. "He handed me the keys and a checkbook that showed the team

Vertlieb's colorful personality and sports acumen lead to a long and varied career in professional sports (Seattle Times)

1974 Seattle Sounders

(Back Row, L-R) Walt Daggatt - Managing General Partner, Willie Penman, Hank Liotart, Tjeert Van't Land, Dave Landry, Barry Watling, Ballan Campeau, Roger Goldingay, Dave Gillett, John Rowlands, Pepe Fernandez, Jack Daley - General Manager.

(Front Row, L-R) Hal Childs - Public Relations Director, Roy Sinclair, Adrian Webster, Dave Butler, Jack Curran - Trainer, John Best - Head Coach, Jim Gabriel, Bernie Fagan, Alan Stephens, David D'Errico, Otey Cannon.

Vertlieb was a minority owner of the NASL Seattle Sounders

was $44,000 overdrawn and there was a payroll to meet." Vertlieb overhauled the Warriors with some creative bookkeeping, then outraged fans when he traded away their popular starting center, Nate Thurmond, leaving him with one superstar, Rick Barry.

Al Attles, who coached the Warriors, said he fought the trade "tooth and nail because I had been so close to Nate. Dick was very tenacious. He came in from the outside and could look at the trade more objectively than we did." In Vertlieb's first season, Golden State eliminated the Sonics in the Western Conference semifinals and swept Washington in four games to capture the NBA title. The 1974-75 season "was one of those magical years, and Dick was a very important part of it," Attles said, recalling the man who was then named the NBA Executive of the Year.

But championships and honors didn't seem to temper the GM's emotions. The following year, in a fit of anger over an official's last-second call that robbed the Warriors of a victory, Vertlieb kicked a police barrier and broke his foot.

With a white-hot reputation for success and volatility, Vertlieb was hired as the first general manager for the MLB's newest expansion team, the Seattle Mariners. Within months he was interviewing broadcast announcers and had settled on Dave Niehaus. When the two met to discuss salary, negotiations stalled when Niehaus asked for more than the new GM made. "I told my wife, 'There goes Seattle,' and then he called me back, blasted me and said, 'You've got what you want,'" Niehaus recalled. "He was a very dynamic person.... He was a jack of all trades. He was a Damon Runyon character. He was very nice to me, but you wanted to keep both hands in your pockets. I really liked the guy. I loved the guy."

Had Vertlieb gotten his way, Seattle's baseball team would have been named the Hustlers or the Pros

As general manager of the Golden State Warriors, Vertlieb, back row, far right, captured the 1974-75 NBA championship

Vertlieb was the Seattle Mariners first general manager

(short for Professionals). Vertlieb wanted something to set the ballclub apart from everyone else, something with impact, something with attitude. "I wanted the uniforms black," he said in a 2004 Seattle Post-Intelligencer article. "I wanted us to be the toughest sons of bitches in the world. I wanted a uniform where it looked like, when we slid into second base, you'd break the other guy's leg. The owners didn't agree with me on anything. "I said, now tell me what other nickname is the team going to be called? They said only M's. I said you mean they can't be the Men from the Moon? "They gave me a (lame) name with (lame) colors."

"He had some wild ideas," Niehaus said. "He had a little bit of rogue in him. He was a hustler himself."

Vertlieb and Mariners owners argued about everything and settled nothing. With the team losing and seats empty to start the second season, things came to a head. Jim Walsh, one of the primary owners, dressed down public relations director Hal Childs in front of the media assembled for a game one night, blaming him for the club's troubles and telling him that he should be fired. Childs was scheduled to have a heart procedure performed the next day. An incensed Vertlieb went to the owners' box, grabbed Walsh by the lapels of his coat and threatened to drop him over the ledge if he meddled again.

"The next day I got a call from Danny Kaye and went to see him," said Vertlieb, referring to the film actor and the baseball club's most powerful ownership member. "He said, 'You're going to have to fire Hal Childs.' I said, 'I'm not going to fire Hal Childs. It's in my contract.' Danny put an arm around me and said, 'You have more integrity than anyone I know. You're fired."

Having overstayed his welcome with every franchise in town, Vertlieb taught a post-graduate course in sports ethics at the University of Washington and later hosted a KVI radio sports talk show.

For the 1980-81 NBA season, he was hired as the general manager of the Indiana Pacers. With Vertlieb calling the shots, the Pacers enjoyed their first winning season since joining the NBA and earned their first trip to the playoffs. Fortune did not smile as fondly on the GM the following season and Vertlieb was again fired after the Pacers posted a 35-47 record.

Continually reinventing himself, Vertlieb became a player agent and represented Jack Sikma and Kevin McHale, worked on Seattle's Goodwill Games in 1990, and spent five years in the Netherlands as an executive for NFL Europe's Amsterdam Admirals.

The idea of spending the winter of his life in Europe appealed to Vertlieb, but a bout with

1980-81 INDIANA PACERS

Dick Vertlieb, Gen. Manager — Jack McKinney, Head Coach — George Irvine, Asst. Coach — David Craig, Trainer

Jerry Oliver, Director — Mike Bantom — Dudley Bradley — Johnny Davis

stomach cancer forced him to return to the United States. For the final few years of his life, Vertlieb lived with his only son, Adam, in Las Vegas until he succumbed to the disease in December of 2008. "His biggest legacy was his relationship with my mother," said Adam. "He was the best father and my best friend."

Vertlieb during his retirement years in Vegas in 2004 (seattlepi.com)

Dick Vertlieb's intense love of sports was both his passion and his undoing. He was a man with strong convictions and the emotions to make them heard or silenced. In today's world of suited sports executives and their glib responses to the media, it is hard to imagine one that will ever compare to Dick Vertlieb.

"He gave Seattle a complete sporting make-over," wrote Dan Raley in the Seattle P-I. "The guy was larger than life."

Commented Northwest sports promoter Bob Walsh, "He is a man that never really got the kind of credit he deserved for all the things that he did."

The man who wore his heart on his sleeve also carried permanent icons of his devotion and convictions. Tattoos of his wife's initials reminded him of the love of his life, facts and figures commemorated the Warriors' 1975 NBA championship, a butterfly symbolized the windfall from his Microsoft stock, and Hebrew words spoke of his Jewish faith and the acknowledgement that he was a lucky man. The last tattoo was a stern warning: "Don't Resuscitate."

As a fitting end to a man who brought so much excitement to the greater Seattle area, Dick Vertlieb requested that his ashes be spread over the Northwest.

TENNIS

THE SPORT FOR A LIFETIME

TENNIS

SPEED

David Haas

July 15, 1964, Tacoma

The son of Holocaust survivors, Dave Haas grew up in Tacoma where he attended the Charles Wright Academy. He and his tennis partner, Tim Davis, won the Washington State Class 2A doubles championship in 1982. The championship victory caught the attention of the University of Washington, which offered him a scholar athlete scholarship. He later transferred to the University of Puget Sound, where in his senior year he became the No.-1 ranked player on the tennis team and was also voted the most improved athlete within the entire UPS athletic program.

David Haas while playing for the University of Puget Sound

Lisa Coopersmith Kranseler

February 28, 1962, New York

'Lisa the Lobber' rattled her tennis opponents

At 5'-nothing and less than 100 lbs. dripping wet, Lisa Coopersmith (now Kranseler) did not strike fear into the hearts of her opponents when she arrived on the tennis court at her middle school in New York. But she was surprised when the coach told her she did not have the size or the strength to compete for the varsity squad. The coach — who was a member of the same Conservative congregation — apparently did not know who he was dealing with. Kranseler's mother demanded that the coach play her daughter to judge her abil-

Lisa Kranseler took to the courts in 1978

ity on the court. The diminutive dynamo beat the coach and earned a spot on the team.

In high school, Kranseler was forced to challenge the No. 2 player on the varsity squad to win a spot on the team. She not only defeated the ranked player, but beat her a second time in a rematch to prove her first win was not a fluke.

"My approach to playing tennis was not the most conventional," Kranseler said with a confident smile. "I was a consistent player, with the ability to hit harder shots. But in a match, I lobbed everything over all their heads. And I never missed." Her style of play frustrated other players and earned her the nickname "Lisa the Lobber."

At the county championships that year, Kranseler used her patient style to beat the No.-1 ranked player in the region. She went on to become the top-seeded player on her high school varsity team during her last three years of high school. The pint-sized player turned down scholarship offers from smaller colleges so she could attend the University of Pennsylvania and try to make the Ivy League team as a walk-on.

The scene from high school repeated itself when Kranseler showed up for tryouts at Penn. Only this time, she decided to take the coach's advice to join the varsity badminton team. "I had never realized badminton existed as a serious sport," she said. "But there was some serious competitions. It was really an amazing experience."

Kranseler paired up to play second-team doubles her freshman year and first team in her sophomore year against high-profile opponents. When badminton was demoted to a club sport on campus during her third year of college, the petite powerhouse continued to play both tennis and badminton on the club level.

Coopersmith nets tennis title

Lisa Coopersmith (left) of Clarkstown North returns a two-fisted backhand shot in singles title match

Kranseler's Ivy League education has taken her from the East Coast to Bellevue, where she lives with her husband Kenneth and their two teenage children. Lisa serves as the executive director of the Washington State Jewish Historical Society.

Now that she has her own children who compete in golf and tennis at Newport and Sammamish High Schools, Lisa better understands how her mother must have felt as she stood courtside to watch her play in high school.

"My son recently used my racquet from Penn in his high school gym class," she said proudly. "The other kids were impressed that he had his own racquet. He loves playing and is very competitive. Wonder where he got that from?"

Henry Prusoff

December 10, 1910, Cleveland, OH – May 3, 1943, Seattle

From Old Oswald champ to No. 8 nationally ranked tennis pro

One way to gauge the achievements of an athlete is to count how many times they appear in newspaper articles over their athletic career. In the Seattle Daily Times alone, tennis standout Henry Prusoff appeared over 700 times from 1923 to 1947. Born to Russian immigrants in Cleveland in 1910, Prusoff moved to Seattle with his family as a young boy and became a nationally ranked singles and doubles player in his late twenties. But Prusoff's athletic exploits began making headlines not for his tennis skills but as a local sports prodigy at the age of 12.

Henry Prusoff in his

In 1920, the Seattle Daily Times began two contests that became an annual tradition that attracted thousands of young boys over the years. During the spring at playfields around the city, boys lined up to compete in the Old Wooden Face contest, pitching baseballs through a wooden frame representing the strike zone. In the fall, the Times hosted the Old Oswald contest that included punting and drop-kicking for distance and forward passes through a large hoop.

Prusoff made his first headline in October, 1923, when the 12-year-old set a record by throwing seven consecutives passes through the "Old Ozzie" hoop at Garfield Playfield to win the preliminary round. A month later, he was on the front page of the sports section for winning the all-city championship in the Times' third annual Boys' Football Contest. In front of a crowd of over 10,000 at the University Stadium, which the Times called, "the greatest conclave of Seattle boydom ever seen," Prusoff's four passes through the hoop and 17 punts of 25+ yards were enough clinch the Old Oswald contest. After receiving a gold watch and gold football fob, the young Prusoff remarked, "I sure never expected to win. I'm mighty glad I did though. The other fellers deserve credit too. They certainly tried hard."

A year later, the 13-year-old began making news as a "Future Net Great," when he won the 1924 singles championship in the city's playfield tennis tourney. As a tall, bespectacled junior at Garfield High School in 1926, he and teammate Joel Staadecker both won their singles event in the city tournament. Prusoff won his match 6-3,

SEATTLE YOUTH CAPTURES PAIR OF NET TITLES

Henry Prusoff Is Winner of Tennis Laurels With Six Straight Sets Won in Two Tourney Events.

6-3 against Lloyd Nordstrom, whose father started a small shoe store in 1901. For the next several years, Prusoff and Nordstrom would meet again and again in tournament matches with Prusoff frequently edging out the retailer's son.

Prusoff's breakout year was 1928, beginning at the city championship held at the Seattle Tennis Club in June. In a three-hour, five-set marathon match, Prusoff beat Nordstrom, the previous year's winner, capturing the juniors' single's title. He then traveled to Vancouver in July to compete in the Pacific Northwest junior sectional tournament where he again defeated Nordstrom. A month later, the lanky Russian took the Western Washington junior title with another win over his Swedish rival.

It was at that tournament that Prusoff, though only 18 and still playing in the junior division, climbed his way through the men's division brackets to reach the finals. In a match that lasted two-and-a-half hours, Prusoff narrowly lost the men's crown in five hard fought sets. The feat earned him a No. 6 ranking in the Pacific Northwest's men's singles and a No. 1 ranking among junior singles.

In 1932, Prusoff teamed up with his long-time rival Nordstrom to win the city's doubles championship at Civic Auditorium. He followed that with singles championships in the Western Canada and the British Columbia tournaments.

The Seattle Tennis Club, which served as Prusoff's home court despite its reputation for barring Jews from membership, helped raise funds to send Prusoff to the Pacific Southwest tournament in Los Angeles, where he won the doubles championship. In June of 1933, Prusoff boarded a Milwaukee train headed for the Chicago city tournament and though he was fa-

PRUSOFF WILL ENGAGE IN TWO MATCHES TODAY

Former Garfield Star Meets Nordstrom for Title in Junior Singles; Tackles H. Langlie in Men's Event.

By KEN KAY KELSO.

THE first big upset of the Western Washington tennis tournament was registered yesterday when Henry Prusoff, city junior champion, rose to defeat Windy Langlie in the quarter-final round of the men's singles. Prusoff, who hits the ball harder than any other player in the city, had his drives working for him yesterday and Langlie went under in a bitterly contested three-set battle, 6-3, 1-6, 6-1.

Lloyd Nordstrom   Henry Prusoff

vored in the event, he lost in three sets. Prusoff bounced back in 1934, winning the men's singles crown in the Tri-State tournament in Cincinnati and the Ohio state tournament in his birth city of Cleveland. The victories allowed him to crack the 1935 national rank-

PRUSOFF IN CHICAGO CITY SEMIFINALS

SEATTLE YOUTH ADVANCES OVER EDWARD LEJECK

Prusoff Takes Tri-State Net Singles Crown

By Associated Press.

CINCINNATI, Monday, July 2.—Henry Prusoff of Seattle yesterday won the men's singles championship in the Tri-State tennis tournament here. He defeated Arthur Hendrix of Lakeland, Fla., 6-3, 6-2, 4-6, 6-4. In the women's singles Esther Bartosh of Los Angeles defaulted to Gracyn Wheeler, also of Los Angeles, because of illness.

Prusoff, in becoming men's singles champ, takes the crown worn last year by "Bitsy" Grant, Atlanta, who did not compete in

PRUSOFF WINS OHIO CROWN

By Associated Press.

CLEVELAND, Monday, July 16.—Henry Prusoff of Seattle is the new Ohio singles tennis champion.

Prusoff acquired his title yesterday by defeating Arthur Hendrix of Lakeland, Fla., 6-4, 6-3, 6-1, finishing his play in the tournament here without losing a set. Prusoff succeeds Gene Mako of Los Angeles as Ohio champion. Mako did not defend his title.

Prusoff and Hendrix, paired in doubles, lost to Leroy Wier and Andy Ingraham of Cleveland, 7-5, 6-4.

The rangy Prusoff, who won the tri-state tennis title at Cincinnati ten days ago, had little trouble in his match with Hendrix after the first set.

Prusoff aced Hendrix three times in one game.

PRUSOFF NOW NO. 13
* * *   * * *   * * *
Budge, Grant Get Net Promotions

By Associated Press.

NEW YORK, Friday, Jan. 10.—Wilmer Allison, despite his recent defeat by Arthur Hendrix, young Florida player, again led as a candidate for the United States Davis Cup team today after topping the national tennis rankings for the second year. The rankings, marked by a wholesale revision in the "First Ten," also placed the youthful Donald Budge of Oakland, Calif., and Bryan M. (Bitsy) Grant of Atlanta in the forefront of cup team prospects.

Budge, ranked ninth last year, his first time in the Big Ten, was advanced to second place, and Grant was moved from tenth to third. The 31-year-old Allison, conqueror of England's Fred Perry in the National championships, has been a "First Ten" player for eight successive years.

Prusoff Ranked No. 13

The others in the first ten: Frank H. Shields, Sidney Wood and Gregory S. Mangin, New York; Frank Parker, Milwaukee; J. Gilbert Hall, Orange, N. J.; Wilmer Hines, Columbia, S. C., and Berkeley Bell, New York.

Jacobs of Berkeley, Calif., as No. 1 woman player for the fourth successive year.

Her only rival for the place, Mrs. Helen Wills Moody, was unranked because of insufficient data. She played only in England last summer, winning the Wimbledon championship.

Mrs. Ethel Burkhardt Arnold of Los Angeles, another recent convert to the professional game, was ranked second, followed by Mrs. Sarah Palfrey Fabyan, Cambridge, Mass.; Carolin Babcock, Los Angeles; Mrs. John Van Ryn, Philadelphia; Gracyn Wheeler, Santa Monica, Calif.; Mrs. Mary Greef Harris, Kansas City; Mrs. Ary J. Lamme, Rye, N. Y.; Mrs. Dorothy Andrus, New York, and Catherine Wolf, Elkhart, Ind.

---

ings, landing at No. 20.

Off the court, Prusoff met his match in Dorothy Justham who became his wife in September, 1935 in a ceremony in Spokane. Three months later though, Prusoff's tennis hopes seemed all but shattered. While working as a salesman for outdoorsman Eddie Bauer at Bauer's Sport Shop, Prusoff severely injured his back in an elevator accident, landing him in a torso cast for two months. He was told his playing days were over. News of the injury hadn't traveled east, where the national tennis association moved Prusoff up to No. 13 in the national rankings.

In February of 1936, with his cast removed and thirty pounds underweight, Prusoff vowed to make a comeback. While he was recovering, he filed a $102,000 lawsuit against the owner of the building in which he was injured, but an editorial comment by The Post-Intelligenc-

NET FINALISTS . .

er's sports editor, Royal Brougham, caused a mistrial. After intense physical therapy, Prusoff was seen on the courts again in the spring of 1938 and began playing competitively in local tournaments that summer.

In August of 1939, nearly four years after being told he would never play tennis again, Prusoff pulled off an upset in a tournament in New York, which was followed by two more victories at the national tennis championship in Forest Hills in September. By year's end, Prusoff was the No. 10 singles player in the U.S. and climbed even higher the next year, ranking No. 8 as well as hitting No. 3 as a doubles player.

Seattle Times sports editor, Dick Williams, penned in his column, "Henry Prusoff is taken too casually by many people around here, when you consider he has not merely broken into the top bracket of his sport, but has done it twice, starting both times from scratch."

As the grind of the tournament season took its toll on Prusoff, an illness began to affect his play. The decision to quit professional tennis was forced upon him in 1941, when the United States Lawn Tennis Association was set to approve a rule that would bar any person from tournament play who was associated in any way with a sporting goods firm. Prusoff still worked at Eddie Bauer's Sport Shop and with a little girl on the way, he ultimately decided to give up tournament play for a more stable life in Seattle.

Tragically, the illness that began in 1941 took his life two years later at the young age of 31, leaving his wife and two-year old daughter, Stephanie.

Times sports columnist George Varnell

PRUSOFF, BACK IN ACTION, WINS

RYE, N. Y., Monday, Aug. 7.—(AP) —Henry Prusoff, of Seattle, who upset Bitsy Grant in the Meadow Club tennis tournament last week and then defaulted in the quarter-finals because of pulled stomach muscles, returned to action in the eastern grass court tournament here today and beat William Gillespie of Atlanta, 9-7, 6-2. Grant also is an Atlanta player.

Elwood Cooke, Portland, Or., upset Bernard Jacoby, New York, 6-0, 5-7, 6-1.

wrote of his passing, "The death of Henry Prusoff brought to an end the career of the man who surpassed all others who ever represented this city in national tennis. Prusoff was not only a court champion. He was a champion as a man and sportsman. He had the time and always the inclination to work with, and encourage youngsters interested in tennis, to the upbuilding of the game he loved. In passing he leaves his wholesome influence firmly imprinted on the game which to him in his playing days was his life."

In 1945, the Seattle Tennis Club added the Henry Prusoff Trophy, a perpetual award given annually to the men's single's champion.

Mickey Soss

July 16, 1939, Spokane

Spokane native was tennis ace

Tennis moved past baseball, basketball, and football on the list of priorities for Mickey Soss after starting high school. His decision to focus his energy on his serve and volley was not a decision he made easily, but it was his best choice considering that his 5'-0", 100-lb. frame was too small for contact sports. As it turns out, his decision to play tennis proved to be a life-changing experience. At Lewis and Clark High School, Soss earned his "letter" in tennis for three consecutive years, working his way up to the No. 1 single position on his team.

Soss played open-tournament competitions in Spokane after graduating high school in 1957. He and his partners won six city doubles titles starting in 1960, and Soss won the first of his two consecutive city singles championships in 1966. The singles titles completed a major goal for Soss.

While playing for Eastern Washington University, Soss held down the No. 1 singles and

Mickey Soss was the city singles champion in 1966-67

doubles positions all four years. He and his partners won two National Association of Intercollegiate Athletics regional doubles championships. "By the end of my senior year at Eastern, my singles game was peaking. I was determined that no one was going to stop me from becoming the conference champ," said Soss.

His big win came when he captured the 1962 Evergreen Conference singles title, defeating the only opponent who had beaten him during the regular season in the finals. In doubles, Soss and his partner upset the top-seeded team to win the league title during his junior year, and came in second the following year. He proudly pointed out that he also defeated the best singles players from the Division I programs at Washington State and the University of Idaho all four years at Eastern.

After moving back to Spokane from Seattle, Soss put his racquet in the closet for 20 years beginning in 1977, but did not sit still. He played golf, racquetball, and joined the Maccabees softball team with players from Temple Beth Shalom. "It was amazing to realize that there were enough Jewish athletes in Spokane to form a competitive team," he proclaimed. "The Maccabees always had a winning record and we won our league several times. The camaraderie among the team members and their families was the best part of the experience. My new teammates became close friends and helped me ease back into life at the synagogue." Soss is a past board member and volunteers on the cemetery/ burial committee.

When Soss got back into the swing of tennis, he lead a six-man "Super Se-

Soss, front left, and his Eastern Washington College teammates in 1969

nior" doubles team, which won the 2002 Northwest Senior Games doubles title in Sun River and an invitation to the national competition in Scottsdale. He also coordinated a Washington State Senior Olympics tennis tournament in Spokane in 2001, and was a volunteer assistant tennis coach at Ferris High School for two years.

"I feel very fortunate that I am able to continue playing and enjoying tennis through my senior years," said Soss.

Kim Muscatel Waldbaum

June 21, 1974, Mercer Island

Attorney was quick study on courts

Mercer Island resident Kim Muscatel knew she wanted to compete in Maccabi USA. Her only question was, which sport would she choose? Athletics came naturally to Kim as a teenager. After playing tennis for less than a year, she qualified as a player on the Seattle delegation that traveled to Chicago for the 1988 Maccabi Games. Admittedly, she surprised

herself by making it as far as the quarterfinals in her first major competition.

"My results far exceeded my expectations," said Muscatel. "Growing up on Mercer Island, I was accustomed to being around lots of Jewish people, but to have so many in one place competing against each other was amazing. I never realized so many were such good athletes."

The talented teenager went on to earn her letter in tennis all four years while attending Mercer Island High School, a school that had won more than 20 state titles. Muscatel reached the finals of the state Triple-A high school doubles championships in 1991, the same year she won the Sportsmanship Award by a vote of the other players.

On the soccer field, Muscatel played fullback on the team that finished second in the state during her senior season.

Muscatel retired her tennis racquet after she failed to make her college team at the University of Pennsylvania. She went on to graduate from the Ivy League school and law school before starting her own family with husband Alan Waldbaum. The proud mother of two girls and one boy has reduced her office hours to only one day per week to concentrate on her family. She also serves on the board of the Stroum Jewish Community Center on Mercer Island. Kim admits that her daughters have not picked up a tennis racquet yet, but excel at sports like gymnastics, dancing and swimming — sports their mother never even attempted during her youth.

Sidney Thal

July 15, 1909 Malden, MA - May 20, 2002, Seattle

Jeweler was a courtside gem and city champion

While many in the Northwest may be familiar with the image of Sidney Thal as the dapper, bowler-outfitted icon of Fox's Gem Shop, few are aware of his talent on the tennis court.

Born in Malden, Massachusetts, at the age of seven, Thal and his family moved in 1916 to Bellingham, Washington where he had numerous uncles and cousins. As a teenager, he and his cousin Myer Thal took up tennis and the two devoted hours to the sport honing their skills.

The two attended the Washington State Normal School in Bellingham (now Western Washington University)

Sidney Thal became a business icon

and both played on the school's tennis team.

In 1928, the Bellingham city tennis championship came down to a match between Sid and Myer. With the stands filled with several dozen family members, the two battled on center court with Sid capturing the singles title. There seemed to be no hard feelings as the two went on to win the doubles championship together in the same tournament.

Sid left the Normal School to attend the University of Washington

Thal during his playing days at WWU

the next year, but the Depression cut his studies short and didn't leave much time for tennis. He took on a variety of traveling salesman jobs and in 1934 married Berta, his high school sweetheart.

After WWII, Sid found work managing Fox's Gem Shop. By 1949, the Thals saved enough to purchase the business and went on to make a great success of it. Sid, in his bowler hat, became a well known man-about-town and an icon of the city. After years spent dedicated to growing his business, Sid was able to devote more time to tennis and was much in demand as a doubles partner.

Thal never lost his love for tennis

Gertrude Pearl Wolfe

November 1902 – July 25, 1982, Seattle

Sports were an outlet for 1920s tennis champ

More than 50 years before Billy Jean King made a statement for women's rights on the tennis court against Bobby Riggs, Seattle native Gertrude Pearl (later Wolfe) took home the sterling silver trophy for the women's singles championship from the 1920 Seattle Playfield Tournament. She repeated the feat again and again, wining the championship three years in a row. In addition to her singles trophy, Wolfe also added two doubles trophies to her collec-

Gertrude Pearl Wolfe was the women's singles champion of the Seattle Playfield Tournament three years in a row

tion during the 1920s.

Wolfe was the eldest of five daughters Morris and Jenny Pearl raised in Seattle. Her father ran the Pearl Brothers business in the same building where the 1889 Great Seattle Fire was rumored to have begun. Despite her father being one of the founding members of Chevra Bikur Cholim, Wolfe and her sisters attended Sunday school and were confirmed at Temple De Hirsch.

Wolfe was a three-sport atlhlete at Franklin High School

At the young age of 16, Wolfe graduated from Franklin High School in 1919, where she played for three years on the basketball and tennis team and all four years on the baseball diamond. She excelled at bowling and loved to cycle, swim and fish in the streams and waterways that crisscrossed the area south of Seattle.

According to her daughter, Joanne Sobel, the tennis champion was also an accomplished piano player and spent her hours indoors mastering bridge, poker, cribbage and dominos. "Mom was a whiz at crossword puzzles," Sobel said. "She was a capable

For Wolfe, "Sports became an important diversion in her life."

person and an extremely good soul."

Gertrude married George Emanual Wolfe in 1928 and had two children, Joanne in 1929 and William in 1931. Wolfe cared for her husband throughout his illness with multiple sclerosis and, as the eldest daughter, accepted the responsibility of caring for her elderly parents. Sports, and especially her ardent devotion to her beloved Seattle Rainiers, were an outlet for one so dedicated to caring for her family. "Sports became an important diversion in her life," said Sobel.

"My mother was always focused. She was a bright and warm individual who gave generously of her time and expertise." Wolfe served two terms as president of the Sisterhood at Temple De Hirsch and was vice president of the Council of Jewish Women until her husband's illness required more of her time. She was also a Sunday school teacher and principal at De Hirsch. Sobel said of her mother, "She was a loving daughter, wife, mother, grandmother and friend to all who had the good fortune to know her."

Alan Woog

May 29, 1924, Crestwood, NY

Forest ranger reinvents himself as a US Nationals tennis champion

The ice hockey team that represented Westchester County in 1942 was a proud reflection of the diverse neighborhood on the outskirts of New York City, with players treating each other like family. When an opponent greeted Alan Woog at center ice in the championship game with

bleachers and hung him over the edge by his skates. When play eventually resumed, Woog and McMahon teamed up to score both goals in a 2-1 victory to win the title.

Woog, third from left, played singles

Alan Woog, front row center, played hockey his sophomore, junior and senior year

an anti-Semitic slur, none of his teammates said a word. But during the first intermission, his teammate Tommy McMahon and his brother Brian dragged the opponent to the top of the

The big city never felt quite right to Woog. The bright-eyed young man looked past the tall buildings of Manhattan to an outdoor life out West. He served in the Army Air Corps during World War II and used the GI Bill to attend the University of Idaho, where he earned his degree in forestry and later became a forest ranger. As a student in Idaho, he made the Vandals tennis team. "Just like in football and basketball, the big schools like Washington and Oregon have Idaho on their schedule as a warm-up for conference play," Woog said with a smile. "And just like in football, Idaho usually does not put up much of a challenge for them. But it was fun."

His master's degree from the University of Michigan and a fellowship qualified Woog to spend even more years on the East Coast with the Academy of Natural Sciences in Philadelphia. As executive director of the Pennsylvania Forestry Association, he would often escort senators and congressmen through rugged backcountry out West, setting the groundwork for legislation for what would eventually become the National Wilderness Preservation Act. By the time his efforts became law in 1964, Woog had been living in the State of Washington for 13 years as a private consultant to preservation groups, including the American Forestry Association's Trail Riders of the Wilderness.

Although he had not played in 50 years, a friend urged the former forest ranger to take his tennis racquet out of retirement in 2009 to enter the NW Senior Games. Their goal was to qualify for the senior division of the US Nation-

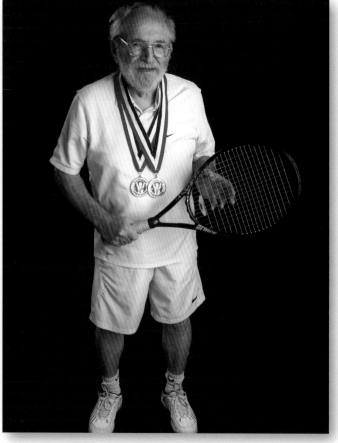

Woog rediscovered his love of tennis at 85

als Tennis Association (USNTA) tournament. Woog quickly determined that his birthdate would certify him as the youngest player in the competition for 85-year-olds.

Practice and determination helped Woog revive his serve and volley well enough to win gold medals in both the men's doubles and mixed doubles competition. The following year, when he submitted his entry for the 2010 NW Senior Games, he was surprised when it was returned. "The organizers said there was nobody in the 85-year old bracket willing to play against me," said Woog. "So I told them to just mail me my award."

Woog also won the US Tennis Association's national championship in an outdoor match in San Diego in 2009. The defending NW seniors champion works out three times a week at the Stroum Jewish Community Center on Mercer Island in preparation for turning 90, when he will be eligible to take on challengers in the 90-year-old division.

LIFELONG TENNIS PALS

Lou Lavinthal, Bob Silver and Howard Keller
(Howard played into his 90s!)

The Keller Family

Kranseler Family Going Places

Whether biking, hiking or playing tennis, sports are a great part of our lives.

Thanks to the WSJHS for preserving our history and the stories of our community.

The Kranseler Family

Congratulations to the committees and individuals who put together the events and collected the history for Distant Replay!

Mickey and Lyn Soss

SPORTS EXTRA

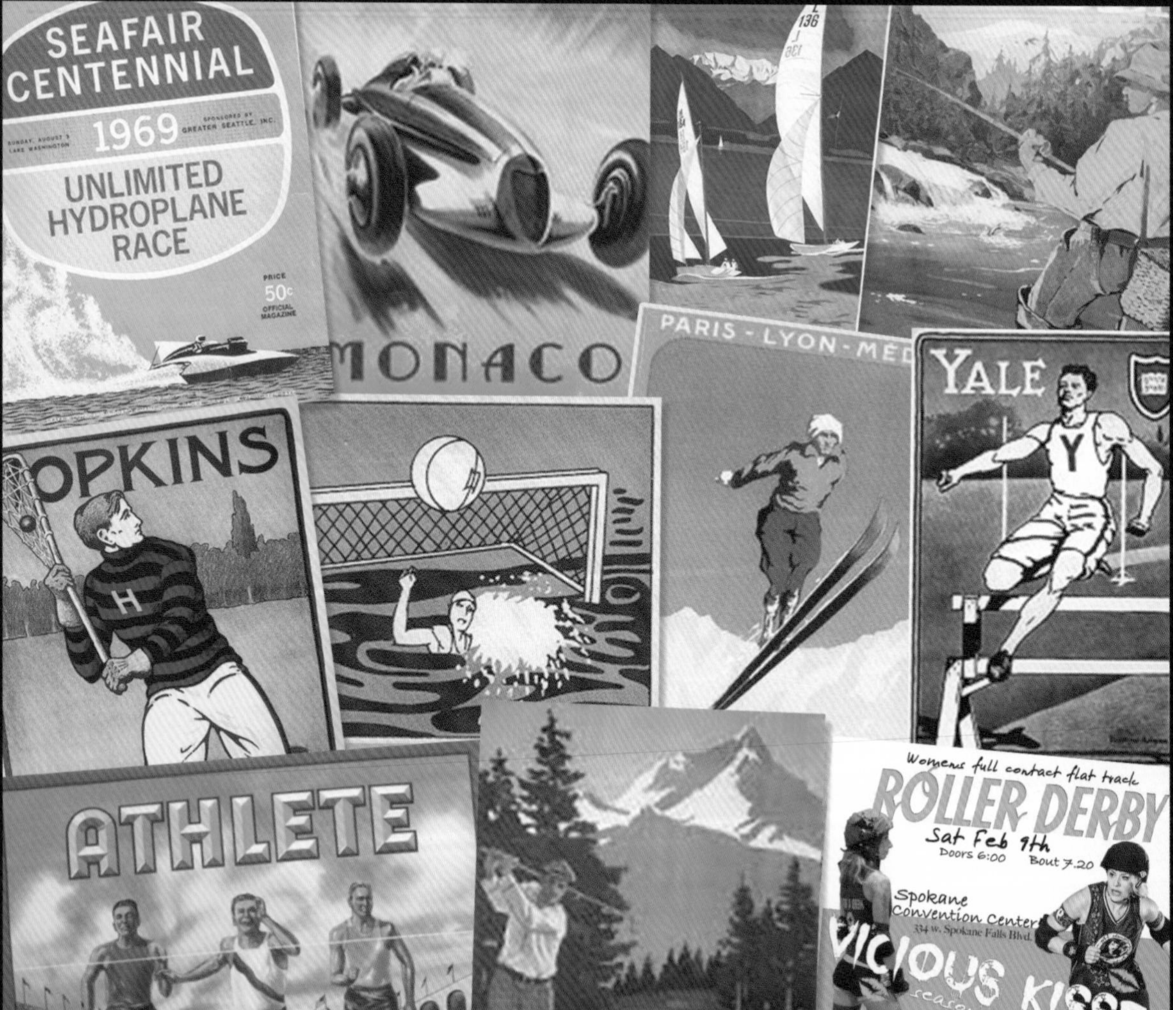

Leo Dobry

February 22, 1902, Tomsk, Russia – July 17, 1980, Tacoma

Auto parts dealer assembles "City of Tacoma" for Indy 500

Leo Dobry, a Russian Jewish immigrant, put the City of Tacoma center stage in the "Greatest Spectacle in Racing." A successful sprint car owner in the Puget Sound area before World War II, Leo's cars were well-known throughout West Coast racing circles. When wartime restrictions ended, Leo continued with the sprint cars, but harbored a bigger dream — to qualify a car for the Indianapolis 500.

Leo purchased the first of Frank Kurtis'

Leo Dobry at the wheel of the "City of Tacoma"

2000-series championship cars and prepared to fulfill his dream by entering the race in 1948. While the car was built in the California shop of driver Hal Cole, the crew consisted of Tacomans. After qualifying in the 14th starting spot, the unheralded "City of Tacoma Special" moved through the field, cracking the top 10 at the 350-mile mark and posting a solid sixth-place finish. Leo had become a credible Indy car owner.

The following year, a Spokane group offered Leo a $5,000 sponsorship for the race, but a Tacoma group pulled together enough support to maintain the car's Tacoma ties. Driver Jack McGrath qualified the car on the outside of the front row, but mechanical problems ended Leo's dreams of Indy glory in the 39th lap.

In 1952, George Hammond, a part-time racer and full-time tour bus driver, drove that

Dobry and the "City of Tacoma" at the Pikes Peak Hillclimb

same car to victory in the Pikes Peak Hillclimb, which was part of the national championship at the time. The car continued to campaign regionally in championship events until Leo sold it in the late 1950s.

Leo operated Standard Auto Parts, a supplier of new and used parts, on 21st and Pacific Avenue in Tacoma for many years. It was on the second floor of his shop that he built the majority of his cars.

CREW

Kara Schocken Aborn

November 1, 1972, Seattle

First female coxswain to lead UW men's crew

Freshman year of college was a near perfect experience for Kara Schocken. The only thing she missed was the physical exertion and camaraderie from being part of the lightweight crew she enjoyed for three years during high school at Lakeside. When she tried out for the Husky team her sophomore year, Schocken was told that they did not have a women's lightweight crew, and at 5'-4" and 115 lbs., she was too small to compete for a seat on the women's eight.

Schocken's sorority sister at Kappa Alpha Theta suggested she should try out as the coxswain for the men's crew team. She beat out four other applicants for the front seat in one of the freshman shells in her first season. Pulling an oar in high school, she said, helped her understand what to say to inspire the men in her shell. "Setting the pace takes more than a good set of lungs," she said.

In her junior year, Schocken was tapped to lead the junior varsity 8. Under her command, the UW crew swept UC

Kara Schocken Aborn at crew event

Berkeley on the Oakland Estuary. As a senior, the Mercer Island native became the varsity coxswain and the first woman to cox the Husky men's varsity crew. Schocken guided the men's V8 to victory at the annual San Diego Crew Classic that started each season. She was also the first woman to steer for a UW men's V8 crew in San Diego and was selected to the All-Pac 10 team in 1995.

Kara Schocken-Aborn with UW crew team

That same year she and her team earned the privilege of racing in the Henley Royal Regatta on the River Thames. Schocken became one of the first women to be part of the men's competition in England. "It was so amazing to race there," she said. "I missed my [graduation] march, but I was happy to experience one of the most famous regattas in the world."

Bob Moch

June 20, 1914, Montesano, WA – January 18, 2005, Issaquah, WA

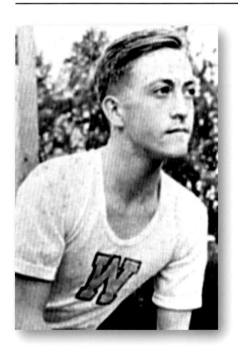

Jewish coxswain and UW crew denies Hitler Olympic gold

Reflecting on the athletic triumphs over the past 100 years, the Seattle Post-Intelligencer deemed it Washington State's greatest sports achievement of the century. In front of 75,000 German fans chanting, "Deutsch-land! Deutsch-land!" the University of Washington's 8-man crew came from behind to win gold in the 1936 Berlin Olympics. At the helm, was coxswain Bob Moch, who found out shortly before embarking on the trip to Europe that he was Jewish – a fact hidden by his father since immigrating to the United States.

Though the story has faded and resurfaced over the decades, the 2013 publishing of *The Boys in the Boat* has brought national focus to the Olympic feat, with a chance for even more attention with a movie on the horizon.

Born in 1914 in the town of Montesano, 30 miles inland from Grays Harbor and the Washington coast, Robert was the son of Gaston and Fleeta Moch. His father had emigrated from Switzerland and within years of arriving, married and opened a jewelry store in the small town of 2,500. Enrolled at the UW in 1932, Robert took up fencing and rowing, landing a spot on the 8-man crew coached by Al Ulbrickson. "I knew for years I was going to turn out to see if I could be a coxswain for the University of Washington crew...I was always interested in athletics and there was only one place I could go," remembered Moch in a 2002 interview.

At the start of the season, Ulbrickson had selected a different team as the varsity crew. Moch and his teammates were disappointed, knowing they were the faster team, but none of them had ever rowed before stepping onto campus and lacked the experience of the others. The eight oarsmen and the coxswain bonded over the slight and came up with a mantra, "L-G-B," that they would repeat quietly amongst them-

Front center: coxswain Bob Moch of the 1936 US Olympic rowing team. From left: Don Hume, Joseph Rantz, George E. Hunt, James B. McMillin, John G. White, Gordon B. Adam, Charles Day, and Roger Morris.

selves. If anyone asked, they explained it stood for, "Let's get better," when it really meant, "Let's go to Berlin." Inter-squad time trials eventually turned the tide, prompting Ulbrickson to name Moch's crew as the varsity team.

Since its earliest days, rowing had always been an elite sport with the nation's top teams crewed by the sons of the affluent from Ivy League schools. The Husky team, in contrast, was comprised of kids from working and middle class families - farm boys, fishermen, and loggers struggling to survive the Great Depression. Many of the oarsmen earned their tuition washing windows, scrubbing floors and selling tickets at football games. In addition to Moch, the team included, Don Hume, Joe Rantz, George "Shorty" Hunt, Jim McMillin, John White, Gordy Adams, George Day and Roger Morris. Moch was the only senior.

In June of 1936, after the Huskies beat UC Berkeley on Lake Washington, they traveled to Poughkeepsie, NY to compete in the Intercollegiate Rowing Association's Championship Regatta. Held on the Hudson River, the competition was viewed as rowing's national title event. Trailing by as much as five lengths at the midway point, they raised their stroke from 28 to 34 and their shell, dubbed, the "Husky Clipper," seemed to lift out of the water. "We took off...we just flew by them," said Moch. The wins by the UW freshman, JV and varsity crews combined for the first ever sweep of the rowing championship by a west coast crew. The victory also gave Coach Ulbrickson and the varsity eight the UW's first undefeated season.

Coach Al Ulbrickson lead his UW crew to its first undefeated season and Olympic gold

Ulbrickson's strategy of keeping the stroke count low in the beginning of the race and "mow 'em down in the finishing sprints," would be tested when the men traveled to Princeton in July for the Olympic trials. The crew trailed by as much as five lengths at the midway point, but in the final 400 meters, Moch called upon Don Hume - who set the pace for the seven oarsmen behind him - to turn the stroke up to 40. Again, the shell surged to the finish line, winning by a length.

Following the Huskies victory, the U.S. Olympic Committee contacted the UW to inform the team that they needed to come up with $5,000 for the trip to Berlin. Sports editors for both Seattle papers penned their outrage in editorials and enlisted newsboys to ask for donations while selling papers on street corners. Funds came in from all across the state and in three days enough had been raised.

Before taking up rowing, most of these young men had never traveled beyond Washington's borders. Now they stood on the deck of the S.S. Manhattan as it set sail for Europe. Also making the voyage was the designer and builder of the Husky Clipper, George Pocock. Pocock crafted his first shell for the UW in 1912 and while slowly growing his boat-building business, William Boeing walked into his shop and asked him to build pontoons for seaplanes during World War I. The Husky Clipper was specially designed for the 1936 Olympics, and after winning gold, Pocock's reputation soared. At one point, 80%

George Pocock's racing shells became the nationwide standard

The Husky Clipper hangs from the ceiling of the UW's Conibear Shellhouse on Lake Washington.

of all college crews were racing in Pocock boats, while US rowers returned to the Olympics in the Seattle-made shells, winning gold in 1948, 1952, 1956, 1960 and 1964. With Pocock's constant attention to its security, the Husky Clipper arrived in Hamburg undamaged; Hume and teammate John White however, became ill, while many of the others suffered seasickness.

Donned in uniforms now representing the United States, the boys from the UW would first face Great Britain, a team Ulbrickson and Pocock felt were their toughest competitors. The intense competition pushed both teams to their limits with the US taking the heat as well as setting a new Olympic and world record. Italy, Germany, Hungary and Switzerland also advanced to the finals. The brutal qualifying race

exacerbated Hume's illness, who passed out at the finish line and was revived by Moch splashing cold water on his face.

The regatta's final event and the final event of the 1936 Olympics was set for August 14th and would be broadcast live around the world. Seattle retailer Weisfield and Goldberg ran an Olympic special on Philco radios, offering home installation up to 8 o'clock the night before the 9am broadcast. With so many families having made donations to finance the crew's trip to Berlin, excitement for the race was pervasive throughout the Northwest. "People in the city felt that they were stockholders in the operation," recalled Gordon Adam, who rowed in the three-seat.

Up until the final race, Americans were

focused on the brilliance of African American athlete, Jesse Owens, who took four gold medals in track and field events. The victories were made that much sweeter as the US had earlier threatened to boycott the games after Hitler declared that Blacks and Jews would not be allowed to compete. While Owens and the American track team reigned on the field with 20 gold, 10 silver and 4 bronze medals, the Germans dominated on the water, winning five gold medals and one silver. Cesar Saerchinger,

75,000 packed the grandstand to watch the final event of the Olympics

The German crew is introduced prior to the final race

who, along with Bill Henry covered the rowing events for CBS, recalled later that with every German victory they had to, "stand up for the German anthem and 'Horst Wessel' [the Nazi party anthem] after every event, until we were nauseated."

On the morning of the race, Hume was shivering uncontrollably. He had lost 14 pounds. During warm ups that afternoon he could barely pull his oars. Ulbrickson considered an alternate oarsmean, but "Johnny White went to [the coach] and told him Don had to be in the boat," recalled Moch. "He said, 'Tie him in, and we'll get him across the finish line.'"

By 6pm, over 75,000 people gathered along

the banks of Lake Grunau. Hitler, Hermann Göring, Joseph Goebbels and a host of other Nazi officials watched from the grandstand. At the starting line, Moch looked over at Hume whose eyes were closed and his body listless. The Germans were in lane one, the Italians in two and the US at the end in lane six. Positioned farthest from the race official, the Husky crew didn't hear the starting commands, but managed a decent start nevertheless. Germany bolted for the lead, followed by Italy, Great Britain and the US. Millions listening by radio smiled apprehensively at Henry's broadcast;

Prior to the race, Moch noted, "Don's eyes were closed and his mouth was wide open. For all intents and purposes, he had passed out."

"We all know the Washington crew is probably the slowest-starting crew in the world. It gives everybody heart failure."

At the halfway mark of the 2000-meter race, Hume had kept the stroke down to 36, while the Germans and the Italians opened a boat-and-a-half lead. With 800 meters to go, Moch saw Hume's eyes pop open, his jaw clamp shut and he began to increase the stroke. Seattle listeners moved closer to their radios and clung to Henry's call:

"It looks as though the United States [is] beginning to pour it on now! The Washington crew is driving hard on the outside of the course. They are coming very close now to getting into the lead! They have about 500 meters to go, perhaps a little less than 500 meters, and there is no question in the world that Washington has made up a tremendous amount of distance. ... They have moved up definitely into third place. Italy is still leading, Ger-

At top, the US racing shell crosses the finish line edging out Italy

many is second, and Washington—the United States—has come up very rapidly on the outside. They are crowding up to the finish now with less than a quarter of a mile to go!"

In the final 200 meters, the crowd noise was so loud that Moch's megaphone was useless and the coxswain instead had to bang on the side of the shell to signal the desired cadence. Hume pushed the stroke to a near impossible rate of 44. Nearing the finish line, Moch called for "a 20" (20 powerful strokes) and the rowers thought those would be the last of the race.

"We hit 17 and 18, and then he said 20 more on top of that," recalled Jim McMillin, who sat in the five-seat. The US passed the Germans in the final 10 strokes and were drawing even with the Italians as they crossed the finish line together. The crowd's roar was deafening, but still none of the oars-

Germany's top filmmaker, Leni Riefenstahl, captures Moch being congratulated in her propaganda film, *Olympia*

U. W. CREW VICTORIOUS

THE WEATHER
Forecast for tonight and Saturday: Fair, but with morning fog or cloudiness; little change in temperature; gentle changeable winds, mostly northerly.
Temperature at noon today, 68.
Temperature during 24 hours ending at noon: Maximum, 71; minimum, 57.
Sunrise 5:00 a. m.; sunset, 7:25 p. m.

Today's Tides
First high ... 1:21 a. m. ... 9.9 ft.
First low ... 8:23 a. m. ... -1.1 ft.
Second high... 4:39 p. m. ...12.5 ft.
Second low ... 9:33 p. m. ... 4.5 ft.

Tomorrow's Tides
First high ... 2:27 a. m. ... 9.9 ft.
First low ... 9:29 a. m. ... -1.0 ft.
Second high ... 4:46 p. m. ...11.4 ft.
Second low ... 10:17 p. m. ... 4.8 ft.

TODAY'S NEWS TODAY

The Seattle Daily Times

7 Home Edition
COMPLETE
Final Markets

Published Daily and Sunday and Entered as Second Class Matter at Seattle, Washington. Vol. LIX, No. 127.

SEATTLE, WASHINGTON, FRIDAY, AUGUST 14, 1936.

PRICE THREE CENTS

men knew who had won. McMillin said, "I can still remember Bob saying in kind of a half-whisper, 'I think we won,' but no one was sure."

With the crowd now quieted in anticipation, the speakers above the grandstand announced that the US had won, followed by Italy and Germany. After racing for a mile and a quarter across the lake, the finishing times of the three nations were separated by just one second. Exhausted, the crew managed to row to the dock in front of the grandstand, where laurel wreaths were draped around the victors.

The next day, the nine men from the University of Washington gathered in the Olympic stadium to receive their gold medals. In front of the massive German crowd numbering 100,000, Bob Moch, the Jewish coxswain and his eight oarsmen stood proudly while the "Star-Spangled Banner" played and the American flag was raised.

Moch was credited with being the mind of the team, for pulling his teammates together and for getting them to respond to an unfathomable stroke count. "Bob got some things out of the crew that I didn't think were there," recalled Roger Morris, who rowed in the eight-seat. "We owe him a ton for helping win that race in Berlin," McMillin said. "We were in deep trouble, and he was able to pull us out of it."

Moch went on to help coach the Washington freshman and lightweight crews from 1937 -1939, then spent five years at M.I.T. as the head rowing coach. Moch graduated from the UW business school and partnered with the Seattle law firm, Roberts, Shefelman, Lawrence, Gay and Moch.

Starting in 1969, the nine crew members agreed to meet once a year— and did so nearly every year until they began passing away. In 2005, Moch died at his home in Issaquah. Roger Morris, who sat in the bow of the shell, had the distinction of being the first to cross the finish line, and after passing in 2009, was the last surviving member of the UW's legendary crew.

Moch was president of the UW Alumni Association in 1978-79 and was active for many years on the board.

With his crew behind him, Moch stands atop the Olympic pedestal

In a 2002 interview, Moch reflected on what he gained from the sport, "Crew has been a great influence on my life. It's one of the two greatest influences outside of my family that dictated what I did and how I did it. And this group of men I was associated with, they've been my best friends all my life – we were all like brothers… and I miss them."

Left: 1936 US Olympic rowing team: Don Hume, Joseph Rantz, George E. Hunt, James B. McMillin, John G. White, Gordon B. Adam, Charles Day, Roger Morris and Bob Moch in front. At the 40th reunion, the men gather again with an empty place for Charles Day who had passed away.

DIVING

Janet Leopold Esfeld

May 21, 1956, Seattle

Teen diver takes plunge into college athletics

Janet Leopold Esfeld splashed into Washington State's diving record books as a teenager. After years competing against local divers in her age-group, the Bellevue native broke onto the national scene in 1970 when she won the Northwestern Age Group Championships, a presti-

FACES IN THE CROWD

JANET LEOPOLD, a junior at Sammamish High in Bellevue, set a Washington State girls high school record with 427.90 points for 11 dives. In doing so she captured the one-meter diving crown, beating Terry Leonard, the defending champion, by one point.

gious event that attracted the best divers from ten Western states.

Esfeld's dedication to her sport meant practicing twice a day in the summer and once a day the rest of the year. "I attended many Bar Mitzvahs with wet hair!" Esfeld recalled.

In 1972, Esfeld won the Washington state high school championship with a record breaking score and was honored as a high school All-American. Her achievements were noted in Sports Illustrated's "Faces In The Crowd" column.

The timing of her achievement coincided with the passage of Title IX, which gave women equal access to sports, benefits and opportunities. Esfeld felt its impact immediately when she received an athletic scholarship to the University of Arizona. There she coached and competed in diving for four years, reaching the collegiate

Janet Leopold Esfeld receiving All America honors

national finals and was selected as a Collegiate All-American.

Esfeld stayed on another year after graduating to coach the Wildcats diving team. One of her team members, Michelle Mitchell, went on to win two silver medals at the 1984 and 1988 Olympics. Recognized for her leadership, work ethic and academic success, Esfeld was voted into the University's Arete Society.

Esfeld returned home to coach an age group team, high school team and the University of Washington's diving team. "It was a great source of pride to coach the Huskies," she said. "Even in the early 1980s, there were still very few women coaches at the collegiate level."

Esfeld is still active today skiing and golf with her husband, Jeff and children, Jordan and Josh.

ENDURANCE

Sylvia Azose Angel

November 9, 1943

Athlete hits stride at 60

It took a broken hip to slow down Sylvia Azose Angel. With the exception of the six months sidelined by an injury in 2008, the grey haired spitfire has gathered an impressive collection of hardware from her participation in triathlons, duathlons, long distance bike rides, mountain climbs, marathons, and endurance events for more than a third of a century.

She's always been a runner. In fact, she was the second fastest girl on the playground when she attended grade school at the Seattle Hebrew Day School (Talmud Torah). "Everybody knew I was the second fastest runner because there was only one person (my first cousin) at school who could ever catch me," Angel recalled proudly.

Athletics have always been a part of ths athlete's life. Beginning in her 20's, she took up downhill skiing and joined the B'nai B'rith Bowling League which she played on for several years. While living on an Indian Reservation in North Dakota in the 1960s, she bowled several days a week. After her family moved to New Orleans, she bowled a remarkable score of 209 - this while eight and a half months pregnant!

As a young mother in her early 30s, she took up racquetball, and became quite proficient. After winning several tournaments, she became an instructor/pro at the Mercer Island JCC, and later became the first racquetball pro at the newly built Bellevue Athletic Club.

At the age of 40, one of her racquetball opponents challenged her to focus her energy on the Seattle Marathon. Angel prepared for her first long distance event running for hours

Sylvia Azose Angel stands among her collection of trophies

a day, six days a week and completed the race in a respectable time. That same year, Angel climbed Mount Ranier and over the next two years conquered Mount Adams twice.

Later in her 50's she was an active participant in the JCC softball league for half a dozen years in the summer while becoming a proficient skate skier in the winter.

Requests from friends to help train for distance events have kept Angel in racing. She has completed six full marathons (26.2 miles) and is training for her seventh. She has participated in 25 triathlons, five of which have been half Iron Man races.

Biking is also a passion for Angel who has ridden in the Seattle to Portland event a dozen times over the past three decades.

In 2003 at the age of 60, Angel burst onto the world stage when she won the bronze medal in her age bracket in a duathlon competition in Switzerland. An event that combines running, cycling and running, this international competition was her greatest triumph and earned her All-American status. While most would be content to rest on these laurels, Angel still want to fulfill her ultimate goal, to compete in and finish a full Iron Man race.

Jim Brazil

October 12, 1965, Seattle

Brazil was first American to finish Ultra Iron Man competition

Marathon runners often describe the mental euphoria that overtakes their pain during long stretches of an endurance race. For Jim Brazil, the sensation he enjoyed while competing in the three-day Ultra Iron Man contest was closer to a sleep-deprived hallucination. The Seattle native became the first American to finish the grueling Le Defi Mondial de L'Endurance, or the World Endurance Challenge, held near Grenoble, France in 1997. The triple triathlon event covers 7.2 miles of swimming, 336 miles of cycling, and 78.6 miles of running.

"Not sleeping for three consecutive days is an element that sets the Ultra Man competition apart from marathons," said Brazil. "Your mind can play some really mean tricks on your body when you're deprived of sleep. The ratio of people who finish is relatively low. The year I raced, there were 52 people entered and only 31 made it to the finish line three days later." Brazil finished the extreme test of mind over body in 17th place. He admitted that becoming the first American was an incentive for him, but he finished the competition to reward his own hard work and dedication with a time of 46 hours and 26 minutes.

"There were some extreme highs and lows over the course of three days," he reflected. "My goal was just to finish and not hurt myself. The competition changed my concept of pain and how much one person — and one body — could endure. But once was enough."

The long-distance runner entered his first marathon at the age of 18 and competed in the first of four Iron Man competitions in Canada one year later. The standard Iron Man competition includes a full marathon (26 miles plus 365 yards) plus a 2.4-mile swim followed by a 112-mile bicycle race.

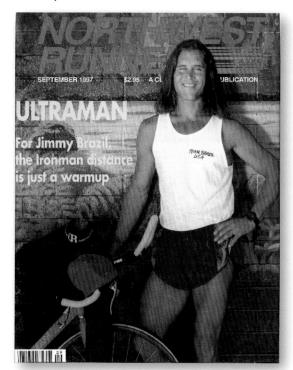

Jim Brazil graced the cover of NW Runner in 1997

Looking for additional ways to challenge his body, Brazil went on to compete in double and triple Iron Man events in Alabama, Europe, South Africa and Australia. "It was kinda crazy. My family understood that I needed to train five hours, six days every week," he said. "The commitment meant that I had to reduce my time at work from full-time to part-time. But it was worth the sacrifice."

His pursuit of challenges inspired him to look for additional events that included even longer and more challenging courses. Brazil firmly believes that his determination can be traced back to the ordeal Jews faced wandering in the Sinai for 40 years after escaping slavery in Egypt. He went on to say endurance events were a perfect match for his personal "desire for excellence." His Ultra Man trek around the world never forced Brazil to compromise his strong religious views. Instead, he believes Judaism provided him with an element of strength that other racers may have lacked.

Brazil took up mountain biking in his later years

"I grew up with respect for my ancestors and proud of the traditions that have been passed down for generations," he said. "My religion is the strength in my life that reaches beyond family and work. Being a Jew produces its own form of euphoria."

EQUESTRIAN

Trea Schocken Diament

November 5, 1976, Seattle

It all started with her big sister's $100 backyard pony and ended in consecutive national championships. Diament started at the age of nine, chasing around after her big sister. She began to compete several years later riding in competitions around small towns in Washington and Oregon.

Diament showed an aptitude from the start. She was a natural at communicating with her horse and intuitively understood how to organize and compete in a complex, challenging environment, skills that would serve her well later.

By the time she was 15, she got her beloved horse, Tex, and trained him to compete across the many different events.

A year later, she entered an intense five-day, well-attended national event in Oklahoma City and was crowned the 1993 national champion.

She returned the following summer and won the national championship again. Remarkably, the back-to-back championships were won with one horse.

At the national level, her primary competitors came from well-heeled families, who brought as many as seven horses, each trained for specific events. Diament competed with her one horse, Tex.

Having to contend with the people and personalities involved in a judged competition, Diament learned a great deal. Diament give a great deal of credit to her great coach, Sue

Trea Schocken Diament and her trusty steed "Tex"

Cummings Schultz, who has created a winning program, teaching life skills along the way.

After winning her second national championship, Diament was successful at a world level competition before her senior year of high school. After graduating, she said goodbye to Tex and went on to the U.S. Naval Academy for an intense competitive environment of a different kind. The organizational and leadership skills, as well as the discipline she learned as an equestrian competitor has been important in every aspect of her life.

FISHING

Lester Kleinberg

October 1, 1902, Ellensburg, WA – May 20, 1981, Seattle

Sportsman excelled on surf and turf

The name Lester Kleinberg dominates the record book of sports accomplishments in Western Washington, from golf courses around Seattle to the waterways of Puget Sound. Born just after the turn of the century at his family home in Ellensburg, Kleinberg was a second-generation Washingtonian who was raised to appreciate nature and spent his life as an enthusiast of outdoor sports.

He spent so much time fishing the waters around the state that The Seattle Times reported on the weekend catches of Kleinberg and his friend, Eddie Bauer, in the sports pages of the newspaper during the 1920s and '30s. Kleinberg still holds the unofficial record for the largest salmon ever caught in Puget Sound. The outdoor enthusiast hooked the 84.5-lb. king salmon in 1937 while fishing in a small boat close to Hat Island near Everett. A photo of Kleinberg and his salmon hangs on the wall of the Outdoor Emporium in South Seattle.

"My dad said the salmon was so big they had to beach the boat just so he could also beach the fish," said his son, Larry Kleinberg. "This was during the Great Depression. Times were tough. So my dad stored the fish in a rented frozen food locker and we ate it for months."

Larry said his dad excelled at golf and tennis as well as hunting and fishing. The Seattle Times reported his record round at the Lakewood golf course in 1931. His record low of 65 in 1929 at the Foster course near Tukwila was also reported, as were all five of his holes-in-one at Glendale.

According to his son, Kleinberg was put in charge of building the 18-hole course in Bellevue during the early 1950s to replace the original links in Riverton Heights. "The club de-

Lester Kleinberg displays his 84.5lb salmon caught in 1937

posited $450,000 into a new bank account and asked him to build the Bellevue course," Larry recalled with a smile. "He was not an engineer nor architect. But they trusted him to build the new course. And it turned out pretty well."

Longacres founder Joe Gottstein donated a number of three-foot fir trees to line the fairways of the new course. Some of those trees have grown as high as 40 feet. Besides the trees, Kleinberg left his own marks in the record books of both Glendale courses. His collection of trophies included first place finishes in the Captains Cup and the Presidents Cup at Glendale. Lester Kleinberg's father, Henry Kleinberg, helped establish the original Glendale club in 1925 and was also one of the founding members of Temple de Hirsch in 1899.

According to Larry, Kleinberg would also fly to Eastern Washington and into the wilderness of Canada with friends to hunt game before such hunting became politically incorrect. Larry still treasures the ashtray that his father had made from the hoof of a mountain goat that he shot during one of his expeditions.

Morris Miller

March 3, 1907, Philadelphia, PA – April 10,1985, Seattle

When it came to salmon, this angler was king

There was fishing. Then there was fishing the Morris Miller way.

The success of Miller's Seattle Quilt Company, which provided down blankets and sleeping bags to prospectors heading to Alaska, gave him the time to spend his life doing what he loved to do.

The king of comforters did not write the book on fishing, but he was quoted extensively in the 1956-57 edition of the *Pacific Northwest Fishing Guide*.

Morris Miller with his catch

Miller was the expert on the best places to catch the elusive king salmon in the waters around Hope Island, the closest fishing grounds to Seattle for the largest of the Northwest salmon runs.

"Some of the so-called fishing experts — including myself — couldn't catch the 60-70 pound Kings because they were fishing in only 30 feet of water," Miller wrote in an article, "The Hope Island Story." He urged serious anglers to always troll for the king, using large six-inch plugs with dodgers or herring to attract the largest catch.

His writing contained some basic suggestions that could make the difference between coming home with dinner or getting skunked. He urged fishermen to carry files to keep their hooks sharp and to only troll with two plugs to ensure a limit every time out.

"We have seen many large fish break through nets," he wrote, with recommendations to replace netting each season or to use a gaff for the dangerous transition from the water into the boat. The key to catching the really big fish (in the 50-lb. range), according to Miller, was to troll the channel adjacent to the island between June and Labor Day using lures at 600-800 feet attached to your normal tackle with stainless steel wire.

Miller with his daughter Bette

Diane Cohn said her father lived to fish. His skills were good enough to help him win a brand new Oldsmobile as the top prize in a salmon derby in the 1940s. "Like many of his friends, my father worked just so he could fish," she said.

Glendale Golf and Country Club

June 30, 1925, Seattle

Banned from other clubs, Jewish golfers built their own

There are few institutions that symbolize the transitional era of Jewish assimilation into Northwest life more than the golf course established in the Glendale neighborhood of South Seattle by a group of Jewish golfers.

In the late 19th century, the first wave of immigration to Seattle brought Jews fleeing poverty and violent anti-Semitism from Poland and Russia. Prejudices in the Mediterranean region prompted Sephardic Jews to leave their homelands as well, ushering in Seattle's second wave of immigration in the early decades of the 20th century.

Despite years spent establishing businesses, synagogues and philanthropic organizations,

Some of Glendale's early artifacts and ephemera

Seattle's Jewish population often faced prejudices in their adopted home. As Jews grew more affluent and wanted to experience the finer aspects of life, they found their admittance to local golf, tennis and social clubs was denied.

In an oral interview in 1988, Ralph Schoenfeld recounted his memories and knowledge of how a group of Jewish men started their own country club. The son of Standard Furniture owner, Louis Schoenfeld, Ralph recalled that shortly after World War I, a group of eight men would gather every day for lunch at a cigar store in the Savoy Hotel. The group, which included Ralph's father, Joe Gottstein, Joe Newberger, Marcus Lees, Arthur Cohen, Teddy Nesbaum, Mike Aronson and Sam Freeman, all loved to play golf but were limited to the municipal course at Jefferson Park.

"Let's be frank, these men were not the right religion [and the country clubs] didn't want them for that reason" said Schoenfeld. Undeterred, the group of men decided to take a stab at starting their own club. Schoenfeld recalled many Sundays spent in 1920 and 1921 with his father and mother caravanning with the other men and their families to properties north and south of Seattle as well as the rural community that would later become Bellevue.

After finding a site in Georgetown, the sobering matter of how to pay for it arose. Louis Schoenfeld and his two brothers pledged $2,000 (about $23,000 today). Alfred Shemanski, Nathan Eckstein and three others pledged $1,500 and on down to the $200 investors, which included Morris Rosen. "That was all he could afford in those days," Schoenfeld recalled. Though the property had only enough acreage for a nine-hole course, a group of ten men also put up $1,000 each to hold on to an adjoining property with hopes of expanding the course to 18 holes.

"Construction started in absolutely virgin woods," Schoenfeld said, "and in those days they didn't have the equipment to clear brush and virgin timber so it took them a long time - much longer than they expected - and all they did was clear out the fairways. They never thought of clearing out and making a rough. In those days, when you played and the ball went three to five feet outside the fairway, there was no chance of ever finding it in that heavy growth and underbrush."

On Tuesday, June 30, 1925, the 9-hole course at Glendale Golf and Country Club opened with an exhibition all-star professional-amateur match with several hundred guests in attendance. Guests called the course designed by Arthur Vernon Macon, "The Gem of Golf Courses." Macon, who also designed Broadmoor and Inglewood, was one of the Pacific Northwest's most prolific golf course designers of the day. Comparing it to the other courses in the area, John Dreher of The Seattle Daily Times reported, "...of the dozen [courses] here, none are more beautiful, more carefully thought out or better constructed than Glendale." Despite the lavish praise, Schoenfeld recalled that members initially had to make due with a rented house across the street as their clubhouse.

Originally, the course was named the Washington Golf and Country Club, "a name my father just picked out of the air," said Schoenfeld, but in short time it was changed to Glendale, the name local residents in the area called their community.

Several hundred guests were on hand at the opening of Seattle's 12th golf course in 1925

By August of that first season, plans were announced to build a $50,000 modern English clubhouse with a sweeping view of the fairways. On New Year's Eve 1926, hundreds from the Jewish community were on hand to celebrate its opening.

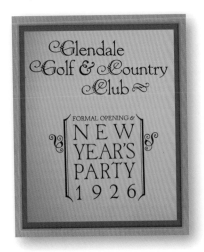

Ringing in the New Year became an annual tradition at the clubhouse which also served as the site of numerous weddings and B'nei Mitzvahs of its club members. "There were some great parties out there in the old days," said Schoenfeld. "It seemed like we had more fun then, but of course, we were younger then too! We had great dance bands and lots of food."

Work is finished on Glendale Clubhouse for New Years 1926

Club championships were also big events in the early years of the club. One look at Glendale's championship trophy and it is easy to understand why the eight men who founded the club were so interested in having a course of their own.

The trophy hangs in the Clubhouse of today's Glendale and lists the club champions from 1926-1951. Of the founding men, Gottstein won the first

Kermit Rosen
1948

two championships in 1926 and 1927, Aronson won in 1928, Lees in 1930 and Newberger in 1939. Other club champions included Lester Kleinberg in 1929, Joel Staadecker in 1937 and

Bud Burnett
1949

1938 and Sam Rubinstein in 1951. Kermit Rosen won six championships while Bud Burnett was Glendale's top golfer seven times.

Among the women golfers, Schoenfeld said that his mother and his wife were club champions and that his daughter, Nancy, had captured the title nine times. Other women golfers he remembered were Bobbi Leman, Rose Gottstein, Esther Block, Ruby Aronson and Dorothy Schupack.

While club membership reached a high of 92 units in the early years, according to Schoenfeld,

MARION ROSEN

"most of the members didn't play golf and used the club as social members. We didn't have a Jewish Community Center," he explained. "We just had the temples - but nowhere for people to socialize, so this became a primary reason to join."

Schoenfeld spent a good portion of his youth at Glendale, recalling the following story: "There were the four of us, Joel Staadecker, Kermit Rosen, Vic Staadecker and myself as young teenagers that played. When summer vacation came along, every day we'd drive out to the club in the morning and get there about nine o'clock. We'd play eighteen holes, go in and have lunch and shake dice to see who's father paid for it. Then we'd play eighteen holes in the afternoon. We played thirty-six holes every day, seven days a week. I remember one evening the four of us were together and we all remarked how our game wasn't so good. We all decided that we were all "over-golfed" and that we should lay off. So we did - for one day! We were back at it again and played thirty-six holes every day for the rest of the summer."

During the mid-1940s, gas rationing for the war effort caused membership numbers to fall to just 49 units. "People didn't want to use up their gasoline to drive out to Georgetown to play golf. They had better uses for their gas," Schoenfeld said. It was during this time that the men who held onto the adjoining property with hopes of expanding the course to 18 holes, lost faith in the future of the club and sold the land.

But the move proved to be premature. Ira Alexander, who served as the treasurer for the course, recalled that the post war years saw a steep rise in club numbers as returning servicemen were offered memberships at a nominal fee. "We had all these fellows in their 30's who wanted to play golf that we had never seen before," said Schoenfeld. "We had too many to accommodate on our nine-hole course. We

Mrs. William Warshal and Mrs. Rober Silver visit the new site of Glendale Golf and Country Club in 1953

had to turn down people." Golfers also began to find that the nine holes weren't challenging enough, prompting Glendale's board to consider expansion.

At the Club's entrance in its early years in Bellevue

Alexander said an exhaustive study in 1952 determined that expanding to 18 holes at the original site wasn't practical. The board asked John Schermer, Kermit Rosen, Joel Staadecker, Bud Burnett and Bob Leavitt to serve as the search committee for a potential new course.

The hunt for a new site took the search committee across Lake Washington to the suburban community of Bellevue. The board acted quickly on the committee's recommendation to approve a $1,000 deposit on an undeveloped piece of real estate bordered by Northeast 8th Street and 140th Avenue Northeast. The original course was then sold to a developer who wanted to build homes on the fairways. The plan never materialized and the original Glendale course continues to operate today as Glen Acres.

The Jewish community was again asked to rally its resources to construct a new course. Dozens of members, many of whom where the children of the original country club, contributed capital and labor to the project. Gottstein and his son-in-law, Morrie Alhadeff, donated 500 Ponderosa Pines from the nurseries of Longacres Racetrack.

In 1954, the first golfers teed off at the new course. "It was onward and upward," Alexander said. "Members used a shed to serve as the temporary pro shop." Envisioned as a family club, tennis courts and a swimming pool were added along with a new clubhouse completed in 1958.

In the early 1960s, debate soon arose as to who could become a member of the all Jewish country club. The turning point came when a well-known African American plastic surgeon, Dr. Walter Scott Brown, applied for membership. Alexander remembered very clearly how Club President Hy Wolfstone went out on a limb during his term when he proposed that

Glendale News

Published by
GLENDALE COUNTRY CLUB
Bellevue, Washington

VOLUME 13   NOVEMBER, 1958   NUMBER 9

WORK ON THE NEW CLUB HOUSE BEGINS

—Photo by Marvin Tipp
With golden shovels, four charter members of Glendale turn the earth. From left to right: Sol Spring, Joe Bernbaum, Joe Gottstein and Joe Newberger.

From the fairway of Glendale in the early 1960's

and tennis clubs adhering to unwritten policies of discrimination. In the last decades of the twentieth century, Jewish golfers and their families began to explore new courses and social circles, giving Glendale's membership greater diversity.

Today, with fairways lined with trees that have grown to maturity and a remodeled clubhouse, Glendale Country Club is considered one of the premier courses on the Eastside and continues to attract dozens of Jewish families who enjoy a round of golf, a dip in the pool as well as countless life celebrations in its clubhouse.

the club open its membership to people outside the Jewish community. "There was a strong feeling that if Jewish members wanted to see other clubs open their doors without prejudice, we should do the same," said Alexander.

Over time, as Jews became more and more assimilated into Northwest life, prejudices towards them began to fade as well. Less and less was heard of Seattle's private golf courses

Golfers Plan Field Day

Getting in the swing for the Glendale Women's Golf Association spring field day were Mrs. Stanley Sulman, left, club captain, and Mrs. Joel Steadecker, club champion. The event, to be held Tuesday at the Glendale Country Club, will begin with a day of golf. In the evening, nongolfing women members will join the players for dinner and the prize-giving ceremonies.

Glendale in 2013

Elliot Friedman

May 17, 1939, Seattle

Golfer put Jews on par at Broadmoor

It took Elliott Friedman three applications before the membership committee at the Broadmoor Golf Club agreed it was time to open its gates to all members of the community. But Friedman is quick to emphasize that the exclusive club, built in 1918, has abandoned its outdated membership policies and now reflects the various ethnic backgrounds of the community that surrounds the 18-hole championship course.

Growing up in a diverse neighborhood on Capitol Hill, Friedman was not accustomed to being excluded simply because of his religion, and remembers being the only white player on his Christian Youth Organization basketball team.

Friedman played golf with his father and brother while growing up on Capitol Hill. He was on the golf team at Garfield and played for two years for Washington State University in the late '50s. As a young officer, he was stationed at Eglin Air Force Base in Florida. During his four

Elliot Friedman wins at Sahalee

years there, he played on the base's golf course, improving his game dramatically. "The course had been built by Al Capone during the '30s as an escape for members of his 'crime family' in Chicago," said Friedman. "There was plenty of time for me to work on my golf game."

Returning home after his discharge, Friedman spent hours on the links with clients as a financial adviser with Charles Schwab. In 1980 when his wife, Susie, accepted an executive position with Rainier Bank and he assumed the duties of househusband, Friedman was on the golf course five days every week. His new lifestyle allowed him time to become a founding member of the Sahalee Golf Club on the Sammamish Plateau and join the Plantation Country Club in Palm Springs. Within five years, he had won the championship and the presidency at both country clubs. "My game had matured," Friedman said. "It shows you what a little practice can do. I was living my fantasy."

In 1996, Friedman qualified for the US Senior Open, where he lost to the eventual tournament champion. The next year he was invited to play in the British Senior Open. Ironically, the golfer who had worked his handicap

Friedman continues to refine his game

down to one stroke was twice denied membership to Broadmoor, a course that was literally two miles from his home in Madison Valley.

His third try was the charm. The membership committee at Broadmoor voted to accept Friedman's application in 1998. Within five years he had won both the club championship and the senior club championship. A few years later he was elected to the governing board and eventually became the club president.

Today there are 15 Jews among the 400-plus members at Broadmoor, as well as other minorities who had been excluded prior to the time Friedman became a member. The past president continues to hone his game on the course adjacent to the Washington Park Arboretum in Seattle.

Moe Muscatel

October 5, 1942, Seattle

City champion follows his bliss

"Follow your bliss," acclaimed scholar Joseph Campbell noted. Moe Muscatel seems to have followed this philosophy from the time he was thirteen, when he fell in love with the game of golf.

Born in 1942, Muscatel was the last four-year letter man in any sport at Franklin High School, and he has all four letters to prove it! He played in the prestigious All City Championship for three years, placing in the top ten his senior year. In college, he and Elliott Friedman teamed up to win the University of Washington Intramural Championship. "The team we beat were from Broadmoor and Elliott knew they were anti-Semitic. He made me practice every day," recalled Muscatel with relish. "We beat them four up with three to go." He then competed while serving in the Air Force Reserve.

Moe Muscatel during his Franklin High School days

Muscatel has continued to play golf throughout his life. He was an insurance broker for many years and felt golf was a good business resource. "Clients were more relaxed on the golf course," he said. "We could build a rapport and then work on business."

He played in many tournaments while living in Seattle and continues to play competi-

Moe Muscatel continues to love the game and coaches a high school team in California

tively in California and Hawaii, where he now spends most of his time. On his seventieth birthday, he hosted a tournament of friends. He shot his age the next day. In January of 2014, he will play in the Mitsubishi Electric Championship Pro-Am.

Muscatel feels golf has given him so much that he tries to give back to the sport by helping young players. When Coachella High School in California couldn't afford a golf coach, Muscatel volunteered. He taught the boys golf shots, but also the etiquette of the game and to have pride in themselves.

A father of two and grandfather of five, Muscatel is ecstatic that two of his grandsons are now playing the game. He travels frequently with his wife, Cindy, and plays golf wherever and whenever he can, from Australia to Zimbabwe. Campbell said that if you follow your bliss, you will live the life you ought to be living. Moe Muscatel can attest to that.

HANDBALL

Max Silver

October 11, 1894, Austria – May 23, 1990, Seattle

Max Silver moved to America with his family when he was six. From that point on, he strung together an astonishing list of accomplishments. Three feature articles in *The Seattle Times* and *P-I* list Silver's life experiences that range from his military service in World War I to running the Alaska Fur Company, to being appointed to President Franklin Roosevelt's National Labor Relations Board, as well as countless activities in the Jewish community. The focus of these articles, however, highlighted his enduring spirit and his love for handball, a sport he played for some 50 years. At 90, he was still playing once a week with friends Herb Bridge, Jay Jacobs and Harry Friedman.

A8 Seattle Post-Intelligencer, Saturday, June 13, 1981
T.M. KOORS/P-I PHOTO

Max Silver takes the court at the Washington Athletic Club for one of his twice-weekly handball games. Silver, 86, has been playing the game for 50 years and says he "can't afford" to stop playing it now.

Not a bad life at all for this 'young' man

Samuel 'Porky' Levine

1908, Toronto, ONT – 1970

Samuel "Porky" Levine was an All-Star goalie who played from 1927 to 1943. During that time, the 5'-8", 175-lb. Canadian played for 11 different hockey teams in five different leagues.

In the 1928-29 season, he played for the Seattle Eskimos in the Pacific Coast Hockey League and returned to the Northwest in 1942-43 to finish his career playing for the Lake Washington Shipyards. As the story goes, Levine was once invited to a roast pork dinner, but refused to partake. The nickname "Porky" stuck.

Levine is under pressure during an outdoor hockey game

notion around the Northwest that the Super-Sonics were the first professional team in Seattle to win a championship, the Metropolitans set that mark 62 years earlier.

"Porky" Levine stretches to save a goal

Side note: While many in the Northwest do not think of Seattle as a hockey town, it was once the best in the world. In 1917, the Seattle Metropolitans became the first American city to win the Stanley Cup. Despite the common

Seattle Metropolitans, 1917 Stanley Cup winners

Ken Muscatel

August 20, 1948, Seattle

Slo-Mo-Shun sparks passion and dream for Seward Park kid

Seven-year-old Ken Muscatel was with his family on vacation in Harrison Hot Springs in 1956 when he read a newspaper article that would change his life. The article detailed how the Slo-Mo-Shun IV unlimited hydroplane had hit a wake during a test run on the Detroit River, bounced into the air, and disintegrated in a spectacular accident. The youngster took the loss personally and joined the citywide tribute to mourn the passing of a local legend. He can still remember how people lined up for hours to walk past the broken hull on display. "It was like a viewing for the Queen of England."

By the middle of the 1950s, the Jewish population in Seattle had moved south from the area around Yesler Way to the Seward Park area. Hydroplanes had become a way of life for the generation of young people growing up on the shores of Lake Washington. Even as a young boy, Ken Muscatel would join his friends in Mount Baker to watch the boats roar past the shore. "It was a thrill for the senses," Muscatel

recalled. "This was way before the Seahawks and the Mariners. Seafair and the hydro races were like our own Super Bowl for the city every August. You couldn't escape them. The roar of the piston engines could be heard clear down to the Kent Valley."

Ken Muscatel, right, began driving hydroplanes in 1991

The lure of skidding across the surface of Lake Washington had become an attraction that fascinated every kid in the neighborhood. Muscatel also recalled that the hydros were usually the main topic of conversation among his friends during the High Holy Days.

While most hydroplane drivers spent their teens and 20s working on boats and working their way up the smaller circuits, Muscatel spent his youth buried in books to become a clinical psychologist. He has been called into action on more than 600 homicides since graduating in 1979 from the University of Washington with a Ph.D. and a specialty in forensic and neuro-psychology.

Muscatel began his racing career 12 years later when he had a little more time and some extra money. He earned rookie of the year honors in 1991 as a driver for owner Bob Fendler. Two years later, Muscatel started his own team and has been an owner/driver ever since.

His best year was 1998, when he finished sixth in the season points standings. Muscatel has finished first in numerous preliminary heats over the years, but has not yet won an overall race. His best finish was second place in Madison, IN during a race on the Ohio River.

In 2000, his hydro, Miss Freei, broke the world speed record by topping 200-mph. It was the longest held record in boat racing, established in 1962 by Miss USA. The Freei averaged 205 mph with a top speed at the end of the course at 221 mph. Over the years his biggest claim to fame as a hydro driver has been "the world's fastest forensic psychologist."

Muscatel's Miss Freei becomes the world's fastest propeller-driven boat in June of 2000

Muscatel's dedication to the sport and to his beloved Slo-Mo-Shun IV has never wavered. Six

years before he heard the news about its crash, the Slo-Mo-Shun IV set the straightaway speed record for propeller boats of 160.323 mph on a course near Sand Point in 1950. Two years later, the Slo-Mo-Shun IV team beat their own record by 18 mph. That record stood for three years.

With the Museum of History and Industry controlling the historic boat, Muscatel negotiated permission for him to restore the U-27 at no expense to the museum. Under the terms of the agreement, the Antique Race Boat Foundation (with Muscatel as president) retained the

Ken Muscatel was never happier than when he was driving in Slo-Mo-Shun

right to restore the boat to its former glory. Muscatel said the foundation had to get permission to cut a hole in the side of the museum just to get the hull outside. The agreement also gave the foundation the right to run the boat once it was restored, but never at speeds exceeding 100 mph.

In 1990, when the restored Slo-Mo-Shun IV made its debut exhibition at Seafair, George Woods, Jr. was at the wheel, and former driver 80-year-old Joe Taggart next to him. Muscatel, who had not yet qualified as an Unlimited driver, watched from the lakeshore as Slo-Mo-Shun IV skimmed across Lake Washington. It was a moment he will never forget.

As a child, Muscatel witnessed the spectacular flip of Slo-Mo-Shun V during qualifications

The thunder of Slo-Mo-Shun IV sent Muscatel and many other Seward Park kids to the banks of Lake Washington

for the Gold Cup on Lake Washington in 1955. Muscatel again took on its restoration, and 39 years later, now a licensed unlimited driver, he drove the boat in an exhibition performance during the 1994 Seattle Seafair Regatta.

Later, in 2000, Muscatel drove the Slo-Mo-Shun IV on the same mile record course off Sand Point that designer and driver Ted Jones had done 50 years earlier.

The forensic psychologist admits that he has survived his share of death-defying experiences as a hydro driver, including one race in Indiana when his boat lost its steering, leaped the shore and plowed into a grove of trees. When the boat finally came to a rest, it was right side up, but badly damaged with Muscatel trapped inside for several minutes until his crew and rescue workers were able to free him from the protective canopy. Miraculously, Muscatel has avoided any serious injury despite several violent crashes.

"The key to not breaking your legs and ankles is simply to pull your legs in, take your hands off the wheel and just relax," he said with a smile.

"Actually, remaining calm can help you avoid a great deal of pain. And not just when you're driving a boat that suddenly wants to become an airplane at 185 miles per hour." Muscatel says he'll continue to race boats, "until I can't or my wife tells me to stop."

Muscatel has spent countless hours and capital purchasing and restoring a good-sized fleet of vintage hydroplanes. For years, he served as president of the Hydroplane and Raceboat Museum in Seattle, and in 1998 he stepped in as the unlimited commissioner. Over the next two years, he is credited with turning around an organization that was badly mismanaged. As an owner, driver and hydroplane restoration expert, Muscatel was the perfect choice when he was selected as the consultant for the motion picture "Madison," about a hydroplane upset race based on a true story, in 1999.

Muscatel restored the Slo-Mo-Shun V and drove it 39 years after it crashed

Jordan Goldstein

October 26, 1990, Bellevue

Eastside athlete sticks to lacrosse

When all his teammates began to outgrow him, Jordan Goldstein had to rethink his committment to basketball. Beginning in the 7th grade, Goldstein took up lacrosse and developed a passion for the game that carried him through to his adult life.

His singular devotion to the sport, landed him a spot on Issaquah High School's varsity squad during his freshman year in 2006. During his four years on the team, the Eagles went to the state championships three times and won in 2008 and 2009. It was during those last two years, that Goldstein earned the honor of team captain.

As a senior he scored 68 points and was selected as a first team All-state midfielder. Goldstein was also one of only two lacrosse players from Washington State to be honered as a US Lacrosse National Senior Showcase selection.

In 2009, he enrolled at the University of

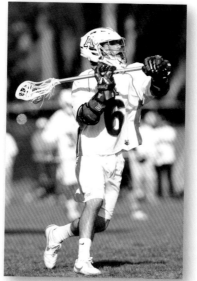

Arizona and by springtime he was playing for the Wildcats' lacrosse team, a Men's Collegiate Lacrosse Association Division I program.

"Playing lacrosse has given me so many great opportunities to compete and travel all over the West," said Goldstein. "The only challenge to being Jewish was trying to keep Passover while playing on the road," he added. "But my head coach was Jewish, so we had a couple of knowing looks while waiting in line at Subway."

Goldstein played all four years at Arizona and was selected as the team president and captain his senior year. The team advanced to the conference playoffs three out of the four years he played for the Wildcats and once went to the semifinals.

After graduating, Goldstein returned to the Northwest and found an opportunity to continue his involvement with the sport. While working a full-time job, he also works part-time as the youth director for the Issaquah Lacrosse Club, a program for kids from K-12th grade. "Lacrosse has given me so many great opportunities growing up, that this felt like the perfect way to give back," reflected Goldstein.

MARTIAL ARTS

Jacob Lunon

July 31, 1954, Toledo, OH

Tragedy inspired career in martial arts

Jacob Lunon brought his passion for martial arts and his strong ties to his adopted religion together at the martial arts studios he opened in Seward Park.

Lunon may have learned the importance of defending himself at the young age of three while his family was at a church picnic in Michigan. Members of the Ku Klux Klan arrived and began throwing rocks at his father who was swimming. He was struck by one and drowned.

Jacob Lunon demonstrates for his Macabee Martial Arts class

The heartbreaking memory never faded, but it wasn't until he experienced the Crown Heights riots in August of 1991 that he decided to start Masada Dojo, the first Orthodox kung fu school of its kind. Located at the Chabad House in Brooklyn, it's stated mission was to enhance the lives of Jewish youth through good health and community.

After moving to Seattle, the black-belt instructor taught yoga and kung fu at the University of Washington before founding the first of his three Macabee Martial Arts schools in Seattle. He continued to spread his message throughout the community through his involvement with the Friendship Circle, an organization that caters specifically to children with special needs.

Lunon said one unexpected benefit of the Macabee Martial Arts schools has been to bring adults and teens back to synagogues within their own community. "When I was growing up, I saw most of my friends leave Judaism after their Bar or Bat Mitzvah," he said. "A few would return after marriage, and then only if they had married someone Jewish. Macabee Martial Arts has given participants insight into the depths of our faith, which many may not have perceived. The result has been athletes who are fulfilled both spiritually and physically."

Naomi "Sweetart" Weitz

May 13, 1971, San Francisco

"Sweetart" is no sweetheart in the rink

If there is a commonly held perception of a Jewish woman, Naomi Weitz is not it. Nicknamed "Sweetart," Weitz spends much of her time adorned from head to toe in protective padding, muscling and fighting her way through a crowd of high-speed roller skaters. "In roller derby," Weitz explained non-chalantly, "I have had four hematomas, lots of bruises, strains, pulls, two minor concussions, but no broken bones."

Weitz describes herself growing up as a "rink rat" in the Bay Area, watching the sport on television and wishing for the opportunity to participate. After moving to Spokane in the early 1990s, she was thrilled when roller derby was introduced to the Inland Empire in 2006. Unlike the scripted roller derby seen on television 30 years ago, the sport today is very real and attracts women of all ages who have the desire to race and are not shy about lowering their shoulder or taking a hit.

The game consists of an oval track with two teams of five players. Each team has a jammer and four blockers. Only the jammer can score by passing the blockers on the opposing team. The job of the blockers is to prevent the other team's jammer from getting by. The players wear helmets and arm and kneepads, and are often adorned in fishnet stockings, short skirts and thin tops to add to the game's appeal. "If you are tired of the 9-to-5 routine," Weitz explained, "here is a really exciting way out."

Weitz was one of the original members of the Spokane Lilac City Rollergirls and served as

Naomi "Sweetart" Weitz, right, wears number 18 in the rink

coach and league president over a five-year period. With a strong vision and goals of her own, she left the Rollergirls in 2010 to start her own team, the Spokannibals. Weitz is very proud of how her team has developed into the best team east of the Cascades. "We have played and beaten all of the teams in our area. Our reputation is now starting to be known in Canada and on the west side. This is very exciting to me because it tells me my vision and my coaching strategies are on track."

Since starting the Spokannibals, she decided to go back to school to get a post-Master's certification as a sports psychologist. "You could say roller derby drastically changed my life; [but] it changed my entire career direction," she said. "I hope to work with individual athletes and groups to help them achieve their optimal performance." She also enjoys writing sports psychology articles and has been published in *Derbylife*, an online roller derby magazine, and *fiveonfive,* a women's flat-track roller derby print magazine.

Weitz appropriately picked 18 as her skating number (18 is derived from the numerical value of the Hebrew word "chai," meaning "life"). To Weitz this nod to her Jewish heritage also reflects her notion of living her life to the fullest. "Sure, roller derby is dangerous and not for everyone, but I have one shot at this life and I want to accomplish as much as I can. I originally chose the number 18 as a lucky token to keep me safe, but its meaning has evolved for me," she said.

"I am going to keep skating until I can't anymore and then concentrate on coaching full time. Women's flat-track roller derby is the fastest growing sport in the world — so that could be for the rest of my life."

SAILING

Howard and Martin Seelig

June 2, 1932, New York, NY   June 3, 1940, New York, NY

Brothers brought love of sailing to the NW

Young Martin Seelig learned to sail in the Thousand Islands region of the Saint Lawrence River in upstate New York in a 10-foot Moth-class dinghy his older brother, Howard, bought with his bar mitzvah money. It was convenient to have a brother with a boat, and in 1958 it was that same convenience that inspired Martin to join the sailing team when he was a plebe at the US Naval Academy.

As part of the sailing team, he would have access to an assortment of sailboats in the marina only a few steps away. The golf course was a 30-minute bus ride from the yard. It was a decision that Seelig has never regretted. "Golf is nothing but a lot of frustration," he said. "The Naval Academy was like living on an island, and boats seemed to be a natural part of the environment. Sailing was also better exercise and a lot more entertaining than hitting a little white ball with a stick into a hole in the ground."

The Seelig's sailboat with black, white and blue spinnaker takes the lead

The midshipman from New York City sailed a version of the two-person international 14 for the intercollegiate team during his four years at Annapolis, including an Inter-Collegiate Sailing Association's Dinghy National Championship race his junior year in 1961. Seelig and his teammates finished well behind the winner of that regatta, a crew from the University of Washington.

On his third tour of duty, Seelig served as the navigator aboard the USS Virgo in Seattle in 1965. While the cargo ship was converted to an ammunition supply ship to deliver bombs and rockets to Vietnam, Seelig lived in the bachelor officer quarters at Sand Point. He remembers his commute over the hill to attend Shabbat services at Temple Beth Am when he was off duty. At the synagogue, the young officer was introduced by a mutual friend to his future wife, Annice.

Seelig resigned from his commission in 1967 and settled permanently in Seattle, but he did not give up his love for sailing. He began racing with his brother Howard on Lake Washington in their three-person, 17-foot Thistle-class sailboat. The wives of Howard and Martin rotated in as the third member of the crew.

When they started sailing their Thistle, the Seelig brothers joined the Corinthian Yacht Club and began racing under the CYC burgee. Martin remembers their first races on Lake Washington as agonizingly long for his crew. "It was the first races — not the first wins — that were the most memorable," said the younger brother. "We finished 90 minutes behind the winning boat in our very first race. The winning team's captain was already on the float and packed up by the time we made it to the finish line." Despite an initially slow start, the Seelig team continued to sail their second Thistle and a third one, "Cecilia" (a gift from their mother and named in her honor), to events on waterways from Florida to the Midwest and the Northeast.

The Seelig crew captured its first of two West Coast championships in an exciting race at Huntington Lake in the High Sierras near Fresno. Although they had won numerous district championships, in their maiden race aboard Cecilia the Seelig crew lost the regional title on the last leg of the very last race held at the Ice Harbor Dam. Martin took full credit for that blunder. Another highlight was a very close third-place finish behind two professional sail-maker teams in a national championship in Westport, CT.

According to Martin Seelig, racing sailboats takes tremendous preparation. "When we practiced, we had confidence that we could handle the boat in the varying conditions encountered in a regatta," he said.

Martin credits Howard's flair for design and engineering for creating numerous rigging innovations to improve their Thistle's racing performance. Beatrice was credited for her design of padded "hiking pants" that significantly improved the comfort level when the crew's backsides were hanging over the windward side of the hull.

Sailing is not a sport that normally attracts a large number of Jews, so race dates are often scheduled without regard for major dates on the Hebrew calendar. Martin recalls attending Shavuot services in Victoria, Canada one year while he competed in a Laser-class regatta.

In addition to their boating partnership, the Seelig brothers were also partners in a commercial real estate firm that managed properties on both the East and West Coasts. They also managed a student dormitory built by Howard and Beatrice in Eugene, OR.

SKIING

Joel Brazil

December 29, 1967, Seattle

US Ski Team member began heading downhill at age two

Seattle native Joel Brazil was barely out of his teens when he raced to victory in three downhill events in Jackson Hole, WY in 1988. His best day on the slopes moved him into the top 10 skiers in the country, raising his hopes of representing

the US at the Winter Olympics in Calgary.

"It was pretty humbling to realize that it didn't matter how much I practiced, there always seemed to be a bunch of guys out there who were better," he admitted. "Only four skiers qualify for the Olympics in each event. It was a tough lesson, but one that helped me to be successful in both college and in business."

Brazil was a member of the US Ski Team for three years. He was introduced to winter sports at the age of two when his parents moved from Seattle to Packwood near White Pass.

Joel Brazil won three events at Jackson Hole in 1988

"I stuck with skiing despite not being very good for a long time, but I improved dramatically when I filled out at 15 or 16," he said. "But my success was only a flash in the pan. The reality was I had to either achieve greatness or throw in the towel."

Brazil finished among the leaders in the downhill competition and the giant slalom at the World University Games Bulgaria as well as the Western Region Ski Championships in '88 before retiring his racing skis. Brazil transformed the commitment he learned on the slopes to excel as a competitive bike racer. He reached the national championships between 1992 and 1997 and continues to race road and mountain bikes in the 45-year-old Masters Division. Dedication to his new sports includes 10-12 hours of roadwork every week near his home in Sun Valley.

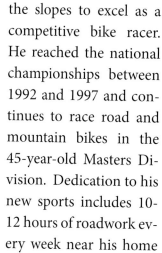

The avid Nordic and backcountry skier is a 1993 graduate of the University of Washington. His career with Microsoft moved him from Seattle to Ketchum, ID. He admits that he enjoys the fitness side of sports these days more than the quick-thrill of downhill skiing, though he says "skiing on fresh powder never gets old."

Julie Brazil

April 19, 1969, Seattle

College gave skier education on the slopes

Exhausted from a long season on the slopes with the ski team at Whitman College, Julie

Brazil made the decision to relax and simply enjoy the final run of the regional competition during her senior year. It turned out to be the best race of her career. "It was one of those fluke races when everything went right," she said with a smile. "Everything changed. I was able to let go of the tension from competition while

I took in the beautiful scenery and the thrill of where I was. But of course, that all changed and the tension was back before our next race."

Like her brother Joel, Julie Brazil grew up in a family that loved to ski. She learned to ski at the tender age of three on the slopes 20 minutes from her family's home near Packwood. By the time she turned seven, she was an Alpine skier and on her way to earning a full scholarship to Whitman. "College was all about skiing," she recalled. "The education provided me a great foundation for my life and I still keep in contact with many of my friends from Whitman, but I was there to ski. I was a very serious skier." Brazil was part of Whitman's first-ever national championship team in 1988. Individually, she finished third overall that year and was named an All-American in the NCSA division.

Brazil stays busy despite the fact she only

Julie Brazil was part of Whitman College's first national championship ski team

straps on her boots and skis five or six times a year. She teaches second and third graders and stays active coaching the volleyball and track at the local middle school.

Jerry Cohn

May 19, 1927, Seattle

Jerry Cohn began skiing in 1937 at age ten. His first trips were to Paradise Lodge at Mt. Rainier, which had the first rope tow in the Northwest. Cohn's introduction to downhill skiing began with wooden skis, bear claw bindings and leather boots. While in high school at Garfield, Cohn played guard for the football team from sophomore to senior year and lettered in track as well.

In the 1960's when his children attended middle and high school on Mercer Island, Cohn started and ran the ski school, which he did for ten years. "I've skied around the globe in Colorado, Utah, Idaho and Europe and have always had the time of my life," said Cohn. "I am now a member of the Ancient Skiers and am still downhill skiing at age 86."

Ralph S. Eskenazi

October 3, 1913, Seattle - October 17, 2011, Seattle

Ralph Eskenazi was the oldest of five boys born to Isaac and Estherina, who immigrated to Seattle from the Turkish island of Marmara in the early 1900s. With a household filled with four brothers, Ralph escaped to the outdoors, becoming an avid skier, hiker and climber.

The Garfield High School and University of Washington graduate spent countless hours exploring the area's natural wonders. He and his friends enjoyed a relatively new recreation called ski mountaineering - climbing mountain peaks then skiing down to the base. He and his friends were among the first to ski mountainier many of the peaks in the Olympic Mountain Range, establishing a number of record firsts along the way.

Sigurd Hall, Ralph Eskenazi and John James enjoy skiing on Mount St. Helens in 1938

He was an early member of the Mountaineers Club and is credited with teaching legendary mountain climbers, Jim and Lou Whittaker, how to ski in their early years. He skiied until his 80s and continued his long love of hiking and tennis for years later.

Ralph Eskenazi, back row, far right, and members of the Sephardic Young Men's Hebrew Association (YMHA) on a hike in the mountains, circa 1927. Front row: Judd DeLeon, David "Rah Rah" Alhadeff, Albert DeLeon, Ralph Israel, Sam Caston, Tom Cordova ?. Back row: Isaac Ovadia, Gordon DeLeon, Albert Levy, Sam Alhadeff, Max Bensal, ?, Ralph Eskenazi.

Harry Pruzan

January 24, 1912, Seattle - January 5, 2009, Seattle

Six decades spent on the slopes kept WWII vet active and fit

In 1912, the year Pruzan was born, the Titanic sank, Arizona and New Mexico were admitted to the Union, William Taft was president and the Boston Red Sox won the World Series. Pruzan, the son of a Lithuanian immigrant tailor, has been an athlete almost all of his life.

Harry Pruzan at Garfield, 1930

Growing up in the heart of the largely Jewish Central area neighborhood of Seattle, he tested his athletic abilities at an early age, racing home from Horace Mann Elementary School. At the end of his run he met a daily obstacle: "Our yard was surrounded by a hedge row," he says, "and I would leap it every day on the way home. That's how I learned to hurdle." When Pruzan reached Garfield High School he already was pegged for the 220-yard low hurdles and the long jump.

After four years on Seattle's high school champion track squad, he enrolled at the University of Washington and excelled under the coaching of "Hec" Edmundson. As a junior in 1934, he was the conference champion in the low hurdles, running his best time of 23.6 seconds that year. Pruzan and two teammates earned a trip to the national collegiate meet at the Los Angeles Coliseum.

Pruzan made it to the low hurdle final, but the sight of 35,000 people in the stands had a chilling effect. "I was so nervous I was shaking in the blocks," says Pruzan. "The starter's gun went off and I was still down there shaking. But I ran my heart out and caught up to finish sixth."

Pruzan graduated from UW with a degree in journalism and found work at the Post-In-

Pruzan and Max Gurvich at Chinook Pass on Mount Rainier on December 7, 1941

telligencer and as a city clerk. During this time, friends introduced him to the joys of downhill skiing at Mount Rainier. "It was a four-mile hike up a steep road with a pack on your back and all of your equipment," Pruzan says. "During that trudge I was sore as hell and I kept saying 'I'm never going to do this again.' But they taught me the fundamentals and I picked it right up."

Barely a year after he started skiing, Pruzan became a founding member of the first ski patrol at Paradise Park in 1937. It was a relationship that lasted 40 years. The service eventually expanded and came under the National Ski Patrol System, with Pruzan as the director at Stevens Pass from 1980-82.

Pruzan enlisted in the Army in 1942

In his late 20s, Pruzan took off one Sunday to ski with friends at Chinook Pass on Mount Rainier. When they returned to their cars for lunch and turned on the radio, they were stunned when they heard the news of the Japanese bombing at Pearl Harbor. It was December 7, 1941. "We just stopped skiing," he says. "It was very depressing knowing that we would be going to war."

In April of 1942, Pruzan enlisted in the Army. He filtered through the 10th Mountain Division and the 87th Mountain Infantry Regiment, the elite ski troops of World War II,

before he was shipped to Europe as a replacement officer.

When he returned stateside in 1946, Pruzan held a few jobs and even went to Honolulu for a three-month stint as "a beach bum." When he returned to Seattle in 1956, he put his journalism skills to work as a writer/editor at Boeing, where he stayed until he retired in 1982.

But retirement did not slow Pruzan down. During the spring and summer months, to stay in shape for skiing, he could be seen biking across the East Channel Floating Bridge on his way to any number of parks that dot Lake Washington. He continued this daily regimen into his 80's, which was often followed by 45 minutes of swimming at the Stroum Jewish Community Center. Twice a week during the winters, he would hitch a ride to Crystal Mountain with the Krazy Ladies bus tours, an Eastside group of mostly women skiers - anything it took to get to the slopes. *(Story adapted from Mercer Island Reporter article, 4/8/1992)*

Pruzan at 80 staying fit biking, swimming and skiing

Jerry Belur

August 23, 1953, Seattle

Sephardic track star clears hurdles and records

Seattle native Jerry Belur dominated high school sprints and intermediate hurdles in the early 1970s. As a junior at Renton High School, Belur captured the state championship in the 180-yard low hurdles and set four school records that have held up for more than 40 years.

The future track star became a bar mitzvah as a mop-haired teenager at Sephardic Bikur Holim Congregation in Seward Park. "I began to realize I might have the gift of speed when I would always win the running races at the Lag B'Omer picnics every year," he said, flashing his patent smile.

As a senior in May of 1971, Belur's time of 18.7 seconds in the intermediate hurdles was the fastest time in the nation and stands as the fastest time in the event in state history. At the state championships a week later, he broke his foot hitting a hurdle in his first event, ruining his chance for consecutive state victories.

Belur still holds the Renton High School record in the 120-yard high hurdles (14.1), 180-yard low hurdles (18.7), 100-yard dash (9.8) and mile relay (3:20.7). Belur was inducted into the inaugural class of the Renton High School Athletic Hall of Fame in 2011.

Following his record-setting prep career, Belur joined the track team at the University of

Jerry Belur was a blur on the track at Renton High School

into the UW Husky Hall of Fame in 1988 with teammates Billy Hicks, Keith Tinner and Pablo Franco.

In 1976, Belur was one of only 20 Division I athletes in the country to receive a post-graduate NCAA scholarship, which he used to study law at Seattle University.

After 20 years of practicing law and serving as a municipal court judge in Tukwila, Belur moved into the private sector in 1999 as president of EPK & Associates in Bellevue. He lives with his wife Nancy and their three children in Issaquah. Belur and his family have been active members of Temple B'nai Torah in Bellevue since 1986.

Belur, third from left, and his UW teammates won the one-mile relay at the 1975 nationals

Washington and was part of the 1975 mile relay team that went to nationals and won their event with the fastest collegiate time in the nation that year at 3:05.1. Their time set a UW record that stood for 30 years.

Belur served as team captain in his junior and senior years, setting the school record in both the 60-yard indoor dash (6.1) and the 300-yard dash (30.4). The sprinter was inducted

Jonathan Hurst

February 20, 1951, Tacoma

Tacoma native Jonathan Hurst enjoyed a successful athletic career in track and field from junior high through college in the 1960s and early '70s. He was a three-year letter winner at Mason Junior High and earned three varsity letters at Wilson High School prior to graduating in 1969.

While at Mason in 1966, Hurst set the national age-group record and the Tacoma city record for the 110-yard low hurdles. These feats earned him Mason's Most Inspirational Award. He lettered as a freshman at Pomona College and was a member of the school-record 400-meter relay team before transferring to the University of Washington where he earned his degree in 1973.

Hurst competed in sprints and jumps, where he posted personal bests of 23 feet in the long jump, 45 feet in the triple jump, 10.1 seconds in the 100-yard dash and 12.6 seconds in the 110-yard low hurdles.

Off the track, he played center field for the Retail Clerks Union baseball team, and in 1966-67, he was a member of Tacoma's two-time AZA regional basketball championship team.

Philip Sulman

1925, Seattle

Sulman's speed brought victory to Garfield

It was a bright, sunny day at the University of Washington stadium on May 28, 1943 when Philip Sulman took the baton from his team-mate and sprinted his leg of the 880-yard relay for Garfield High School. The victory was one of two that clinched the All-City track meet and all-sports trophy. After an 11-year drought, The Seattle Times reported, "The Garfield Bulldogs were kings of Seattle high school trackdom."

Sulman was a standout in the 440-yard dash and surprised even himself with a time of 49.9

seconds to beat out the favored Queen Anne runner by inches. Sulman had been clocking more than 52 seconds on Garfield's uneven pot-holed cinder track, but at the superior UW track he sprinted as if on winged feet. That day, he took home a gold medal in the 440-yard dash and a team gold for his role in the 880-yard relay, a fitting culmination to his two-year track career at Garfield.

Sulman, who was president of Aleph Zadik Aleph, Seattle chapter 73 in 1943, also played on its basketball team and bowled for B'nai B'rith.

Philip Sulman ran track at Garfield in 1943

Little did he know on that beautiful day in May, that after graduation he would be training for the US Army Coast Artillery and going overseas to France in 1944. When his division went ashore in Cherbourg, they were the first group to land directly in France, bypassing the usual stopover in England. Sulman and his division spent 195 consecutive days in combat fighting the Nazis in France, Belgium, Holland and Germany. Sulman was one of the lucky ones who survived the European campaign unscathed. As a member of the 104th Infantry Division, called the Timberwolves, he had orders to report to the Pacific theater when the war was suddenly halted by the atomic bomb.

Sulman lives in Bellevue and has continued his love of sports. At the age of 88, he still golfs regularly with Betty, his beloved wife of 38 years, and meets often with the "Garfield Lunch Bunch," a group of fellow graduates from the same era.

VOLLEYBALL

Danny Jassen

May 28, 1976, Seattle

'Kid from Seward Park' was multi-sport star

It was a dilemma of monumental proportions for a teenage boy. Danny Jassen a graduate and star athlete at the Seattle Hebrew Academy, where activities were always scheduled around Shabbat. That was not the situation when he entered Mercer Island High School.

During his first year playing basketball for the Islanders, Jassen excelled under the tutelage of Former Sonic "Downtown" Freddy Brown, who coached Jassen's sophomore team to a perfect 22-0 season. "I could justify playing basketball on Shabbat, but traveling on Shabbat was something I wasn't mentally prepared to do." There were several weekends where I would stay at my Aunt's or friend's

house which were within walking distance of the school so I wouldn't have any conflict. According to Jassen, Coach Brown and the team were very supportive and it was never an issue. "It was important for me that my situation wouldn't be a distraction to the team," Jassen recalled. "Coach told me to do whatever I needed to do to feel comfortable, just show up ready to play," But Jassen was ultimately forced to make a choice after his sophomore year, when he started playing varsity, which would require him to travel on Shabbat.

His friends and family encouraged him to try out for the baseball team when springtime games are almost always finished before sunset. "Playing baseball was an intriguing option, but I had never played before," he said. "Not even Little League."

Jassen showed up to tryouts, with the glove

Danny Jassen (at the net) played volleyball for Yeshiva University and keeps fit running with his wife Shiri Levy

his Nona had bought him a few years earlier and within a couple weeks he was promoted to the varsity's outfield. "Defense and sunflower seeds were the natural and easy parts of the game for me, but hitting live pitching was a different story, it was something I had never experienced before."

Known to his teammates as "The Kid from Seward Park," Jassen continued to play through his senior year. After graduating in 1994, Jassen spent a year of study in Israel. During that time, he played in the Jerusalem Football League, where his team advanced to the championship game. He later enrolled at Yeshiva University and competed on the university's volleyball team while earning his degree in business management.

After graduating, Jassen continued to play in various basketball, volleyball and softball leagues in New York and Seattle. At one point, his SJCC softball team won the championship four out of the five years he played. "People hated us because we were like the Yankees." Married to Shiri Levy, a combat fitness instructor in the Israeli Army, they began to run in 10K and 20K races so they could spend more time together. Jassen currently serves as the Director of Sales for an Israeli software company.

Dr. Benjamin F. Roller

July 1, 1876, Newman, IL - April 19, 1933, New York

"The Pride of Seattle"

With a medical degree and natural athletic talents, Dr. Benjamin Roller was a sportsman extraordinaire. While generally acknowledged by sports writers as the second best heavyweight grappler in the country, he also played college and professional football and was even a world record discus thrower.

On a farm near Newman, Illinois in 1876, Benjamin Franklin was the fifth of six children born to Phillip and Emily Roller. Growing up he enjoyed playing sports and early on knew he wanted to be a physician. While his father believed in the value of physical labor farming their land, Roller's mother encouraged him to pursue his education.

Benjamin Roller takes time out for publicity shots

In 1894, he attended De Pauw University, working at a dry goods store to pay for his tuition. Standing a little over 6' and weighing 200 pounds, Roller was captain and coach of the track and football team and was considered by newspapers in Indianapolis and Chicago as the best football player in the central states. While a team member for the Chicago Athletic Association, he broke the world's record in discus throwing.

True to his dream, Roller went on to enroll in medical school at the University of Pennsylvania, earning an income playing football in a professional league. The National Football League in 1902 was comprised of three teams in Pennsylvania, owned by Major League Baseball franchises; the Philadelphia Phillies, the Philadelphia Athletics and the Pittsburgh Pirates. Playing fullback for the Phillies, after Roller's team beat Connie Mack's Athletics 17-0, the Philadelphia Inquirer reported that he was, "a bull in line plunging" and a "credible punter."

He graduated from the medical department with the highest honors and the prestigious Saunder's Prize of $100 in gold. Early on in his medical career, Roller received national attention in newspapers for his use of formaldehyde, water and methanol to treat patients with tuberculosis in February 1903. Within a year, he was offered and accepted a position at the University of Washington as the professor of physiology. He also served as the supervisor to the school's athletics and as an advisor to the Seattle Athletic Club.

Roller is credited with founding the wrestling program at the UW and established an annual wrestling tournament that attracted over 100 athletes.

Having arrived in Seattle with very little money, Roller quickly turned things around. He was active in women's health issues, specializing in surgery and disease, and started a private practice on the side, earning more than $1,000 a month. After investing much of his income in property, he was faced at one point with needing to raise $10,000 or lose everything.

After hearing about a wrestling challenge with a $1,600 prize, Roller entered the competition and defeated Jack Carkeek with two falls

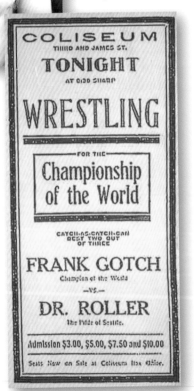

1906 newspaper ad

in a period of 17 minutes. Carkeek's manager saw the doctor's potential and began setting up matches around the Northwest.

Tagged with the moniker, "The Pride of Seattle," he next wrestled Frank Gotch, the three-time heavyweight champion, in an exhibition match and received $4,000. After the bout, Roller quit his work at the university and decided to use wrestling as tool for traveling the world.

Over the span of his career, Roller was a top draw in New York and other major cities throughout the country. He was a constant headliner and a fan favorite, defeating many of the top wrestlers of his day, including Farmer Burns, Fred Beell, Ed "Strangler" Lewis and Joe Stecher. From 1906-1918, Roller posted a record of 39 wins, 26 losses and 4 draws in 69 matches. Roller won the American Heavyweight Championship in 1911, 1913 and 1914.

Roller passed away in the spring of 1933 in New York City at the age of 57. Paying heed to the virtues of hard labor taught by his father and his mother's insistence of a solid education, the poor son of a farmer used his brawn and his intellect to amass an estate worth over a million dollars (around $18 million today).

YELL KINGS

Morrie Alhadeff
November 14, 1914 – November 8, 1994, Seattle
Garfield High School

Rudy Spring
November 17, 1920 – May 7, 2000, Seattle
Garfield High School, University of Washington

Louis Sternberg
January 1, 1928, New Rochelle, NY
Roosevelt High School, Oregon State, Utah,
University of Washington

Joey Mayo
October 13, 1937, Seattle
Garfield High School

Bruce Glant
February 16, 1948, Seattle
Franklin High School, University of Washington

Kenny Alhadeff
August 15, 1948, Seattle
Franklin High School

Yell king royalty inspired school spirit from the sidelines

Neither snow nor rain nor sleet nor gloom of night could stay these dedicated yell kings from the energetic completion of their appointed cheers. Jewish yell kings inspired crowds all across Seattle and were often forced to lead their cheers in the face of ugly weather and lopsided scores.

"We stood outside during the fall and winter months, and then moved into the humid gymnasiums for the basketball season. Many of us were also in the stands in the spring for baseball games and track meets too," said Ken Alhadeff, who led the student body in ovations for Franklin High School during the 1965-66 school year.

Ken Alhadeff lead cheers for Franklin High School

Bruce Glant got his Franklin classmates fired up

Fellow Franklin yell king Bruce Glant remembers one night when he did the splits before kickoff for a Franklin football game at Memorial Stadium and ripped the seam in his trousers. "There was a very cold wind that night and I spent the entire game miserable and embarrassed," he said with a smile. "Being selected as yell king was a position of honor that we all took very seriously. Our job was to fire up the crowd, even if it was the fourth quarter and our team was behind by 30 points."

Glant said the five guys and six girls who made up the spirit squad at Franklin were in constant motion from the time the fans started to fill the stands until the final whistle. "We had to keep moving or we'd freeze our asses off," he said. There were not a large number of Jews trying out for sports when he was in high school. Glant chose to lead cheers so he could be closer to the action. Of the five Franklin yell kings in that 1965-66 school year, three of them, Glant, Alhadeff and Sam Piha were Jewish.

Despite the many hours of practice and faithfully attending most of the high school's athletic events, yell leaders were not honored with varsity letters like the athletes. "We worked just as hard and practiced just as long as the players on the field, but we were not recognized as athletes," said Alhadeff.

Alhadeff petitioned the Metro Conference to give recognition to the members of his squad and as a result he became the first yell king to earn a varsity letter for yell in school — or conference — history. The change started a ripple. Since 1965, yell kings and cheerleaders have qualified for the same recognition as members of other sports teams.

Alhadeff was proud to show off the large "F" on the front of his jacket at every dance and school-sponsored activity. "We worked hard to earn our letter. It was an accomplishment that I look back on with pride just like every other

Bruce Glant, middle left, Sam Piha, middle right, and Ken Alhadeff, bottom right, were part of Franklin's yell squad in 1965-66

varsity athlete," he said. "But, I'll admit, sometimes I would hold up my right arm to hide the little megaphone when the pretty girls walked by."

Alhadeff became a yell king at Franklin 30 years after his father — Morrie Alhadeff — had fired up the crowds at Garfield with an oversized megaphone.

Joey Mayo tried out for the squad at Garfield because he was told he was too small and too light to play football or basketball. "Garfield had some great teams at that time and I wanted to be part of the excitement," said Mayo.

"Those stories about high school quarterbacks getting all the attention were only partially true. The best looking girls were always on the lookout for the guy with the megaphone," he said with a grin.

Mayo was at Garfield when the Bulldogs finished in second place behind Franklin for the city football championship in 1954, but he was courtside when the Garfield basketball team captured the state basketball title later that year. Mayo remembers

his role in front of the crowds when the rival high schools met the next year in the traditional Turkey Bowl.

"The game was always a sell-out. But that year there were probably 8,000 people in the stands [at Memorial Stadium]," he said. "The basketball games were moved those years from the campus gymnasium to the Hec Edmundson Pavilion at the university."

Mayo added that his squad performed their routines at pre-game rallies, as part of the halftime show and during timeouts, then went to all the dances to celebrate with the other students after each game.

Deb Srebnik never confirmed her theory with members of the family, but she is confident that her father, Louis Sternberg, became a yell king so he could be around all the pretty girls. According to his daughter, Sternberg was one of two yell dukes at Roosevelt during high school, and then joined the cheer squads at three separate colleges before joining the Army in 1951. "Our dad was the leader of the cheer

Morrie Alhadeff, 4th from right, with 1932 Garfield High School yell kings

Joey Mayo, far left, with 1954 Garfield yell kings

Louis Sternberg cheered for Roosevelt High School in 1944 and Oregon State in 1946

squad during his first year at Oregon State in 1946. Then he started the GDCs — the Good Dancer's Club," said Srebnik. "He was always ready to do something new and exciting.

And have fun!"

Srebnik said her father was never much of a sports fan, but was an avid skier who shared his love of the sport with his friends and family. Sternberg transferred to the University of Washington in 1948 and quickly organized a winter carnival for his fraternity brothers at Zeta Beta Tau. Craig Sternberg, the past president of the Washington State Jewish Historical Society, described his "Uncle Louie" as the kind of uncle all of his friends wished they had. "Everybody knew that he was passionate about skiing and that he had been a yell king," his nephew remembers fondly. "But Uncle Louie was also a cheerleader for life. It did not

matter what activity anybody in the family was involved with, he was always there with moral support and a big hug."

Rudy Spring wore his white letterman sweater with the purple W proudly to homecoming activities at the University of Washington every year until his death in the spring of 2000, according to his widow, Lucy. "He would lead his ZBT brothers in a performance of the same yells and hand motions he had used at Garfield and later at the University of Washington," she said.

Spring excelled in track and field while he was in high school, competing for Garfield in the 440 and the 100-yard dash. Lucy was quick to point out that her husband also honed his skills on the links and had a handicap of seven and was the club captain at the Glendale Country Club. In the late 1950s, Rudy had a hole-in-one off the second tee. Not to be outdone, Lucy was the Glendale women's club captain and in 1981, knocked in a hole in one from 145-yards away off 15th tee.

Rudy Spring, front right, and Dave Alhadeff, back right, were yell kings in 1938 at Garfield High School

Jerry Belur

Father, Husband, Friend, Husky with a Coug Son,
Optimistic, Generous, Passionate and Compassionate,
Lucky Poker Player and Smokin' Fast!
Not just words on a page
but examples of how you live your life.

Thanks for the inspiration!
Nancy, Bri, Ben and Jacqueline

ABO INVESTMENTS

Congratulations to the

WASHINGTON STATE JEWISH HISTORICAL SOCIETY

for preserving the history and memories
of our Jewish culture

Gerry and Sandra Ostroff
Dick and Marilyn Brody

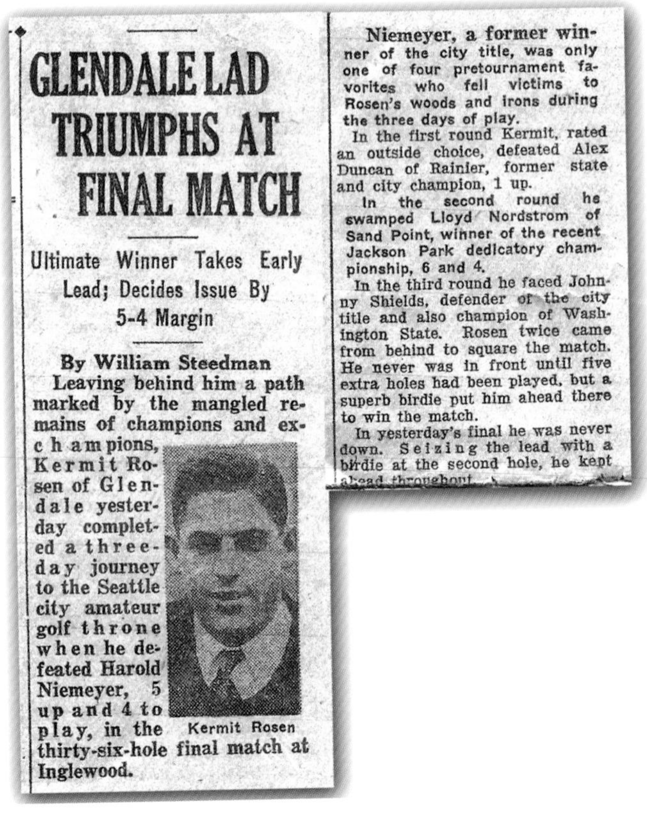

GLENDALE LAD TRIUMPHS AT FINAL MATCH

Ultimate Winner Takes Early Lead; Decides Issue By 5-4 Margin

By William Steedman

Leaving behind him a path marked by the mangled remains of champions and ex-champions, Kermit Rosen of Glendale yesterday completed a three-day journey to the Seattle city amateur golf throne when he defeated Harold Niemeyer, 5 up and 4 to play, in the thirty-six-hole final match at Inglewood.

Kermit Rosen

Niemeyer, a former winner of the city title, was only one of four pretournament favorites who fell victims to Rosen's woods and irons during the three days of play.

In the first round Kermit, rated an outside choice, defeated Alex Duncan of Rainier, former state and city champion, 1 up.

In the second round he swamped Lloyd Nordstrom of Sand Point, winner of the recent Jackson Park dedicatory championship, 6 and 4.

In the third round he faced Johnny Shields, defender of the city title and also champion of Washington State. Rosen twice came from behind to square the match. He never was in front until five extra holes had been played, but a superb birdie put him ahead there to win the match.

In yesterday's final he was never down. Seizing the lead with a birdie at the second hole, he kept ahead throughout.

KERMIT ROSEN WINS SEATTLE AMATEUR GOLF CHAMPIONSHIP!

August 30, 1930

A loving tribute,
Helen Stusser
Kermit Rosen, Jr.
Judy Rosen

Al "Big Al" Halela

Dad loved bowling. He was on many leagues throughout the years and bowled into his 80s.

The Mosholder Family
Mark, Maggie, Joey and Rachelle

Mary Alhadeff Halela

Mom and Dad met at a bowling alley. They both loved bowling and enjoyed the many friends they made.

The Mosholder Family
Mark, Maggie, Joey and Rachelle

Rachelle Katherine Mosholder

Rachelle has been riding and competing since she was 9-years-old. She is jumping her horse "Beeker" at her workplace in the San Francisco area.

With love,
Mark and Maggie Mosholder

Joey, Mark, Rachelle, Maggie Mosholder and Oz

Attending Rachelle's competition at the Prix de Villes at Lake Erie College in Ohio, 2012.

A Lifelong Love of Golf and Friends

Back: Stan Sidell, Bruce Backer, Joey Mayo, Harold Sadis, Harris Sprincin, Michael "Monk" Weinstein, Marty Levy, Bernie Wolfin
Front: Harold "Buzzy" Coe, Marty Lotzkar, JD Stern, Edward "Socco"Stern, Kenny Waldbaum, Gary Schwartz, Eddie Sherman

HAROLD SADIS

"My love of golf began when I was 11-years old and over the years I have enjoyed the sport with so many lifelong friends."
- Harold Sadis

Garfield High School golf team 1957, 1958

Best Friends Forever

Sue Waldbaum, Carol Backer, Esther Sadis, Pauline Stern

"Twenty years of playing golf with best friends. I love this special time we spend together - talking, laughing and "trying" to play golf."
- Esther Sadis

Cheers to
Stephen Sadis
(bottom of pile)
dedicated Little League coach, devoted dad of backyard baseball and champion of our community's sports heroes.

Love, **Cherie Singer**

THREE CHEERS FOR WSJHS!

Bina Alhadeff 2013

Dave Alhadeff 1938

Jordan Goldstein

We are so proud of your many
accomplishments in the field of lacrosse.
We love you.
Nana and Papoo

Kathy and Morgan Barokas

"Finished!"
Dave and Marcie Stone

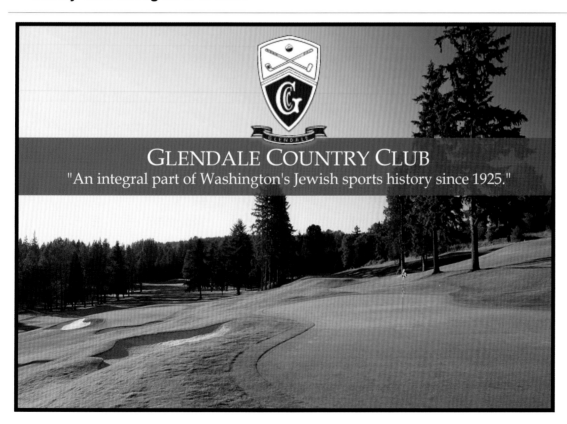

GLENDALE COUNTRY CLUB
"An integral part of Washington's Jewish sports history since 1925."

PHOTO CREDITS

The WSJHS is very grateful to al the individuals, organizations and companies who gave their permission to us to use the photographs that appear in this book. As colorful as these profiles are, the images help bring these stories to life and we truly appreciate everyone's contribution to preserving this slice of history. Photographs are credited in the order as they appear in the profiles from top to bottom, left to right.

KEY

ALH - Alhadeff Collection
CK - Charles Kapner Collection
DE - David Eskenazi Collection
ED - Emerald Downs
FHS - Franklin High School yearbook
GHS - Garfield High School yearbook
HRM - Hydro and Raceboat Museum
LK - Linda Krivosha
MB - Marc Blau Collection
MIHS - Mercer Island HS yearbook
PD - Public Domain
SJCC - Stroum Jewish Com. Center
PI - seattlepi.com
ST - Seattle Times
SU - Seattle University yearbook
SHS - Stadium High School yearbook
SMS - Stephen Sadis
UW - University of WA yearbook
WSJHS - WA State Jewish Hist. Soc.
WSU - WSU yearbook

BASEBALL

Chapter title page: David Eskenazi collection, DE, WSJHS Collection, **Steve Altaras**: Bellevue HS yearbook, **Morrie Arnovich**: source, Marc Blau collection, source, **Dave Azose**: source, source, **Michael Block**: MB **Joel Buxbaum**: source all, **Al Federoff**: Charles Kapner collection, **Joe Ginsberg**: source, CK, **Bob Goldstein**: source, **Dave Goodman**: MB, **Addis Gutmann**: source, **Sol Israel**: MB, **Herb Karpel**: DE, **David Kosher**: DE, **Rob Kraft**: source, **Barry Latman**: source, **Jack Levy**: Mark Brunke, **Bob Melvin**: Meryl Schenker/PI, **Lee Mezistrano**: source all, **Lipman Pike**: public domain all, **Jimmie Reese**: source, CK, **Jaden Sadis**: SMS **Charles Schwartz**: DE, **Larry Sherry**: CK all **Norm Sherry**: Everett Giants, **Jeff Solam**: source

BASKETBALL

Chapter title page: GHS, Esther Sadis, GHS (8) Louie Soriano, Roosevelt High School yearbook, SJCC, GHS, GHS, **Sue Bird**: Scott Engelhardt, **Jed Davis**: source all, **Albert DeLeon**: Esther Sadis all, **Warren Fein**: source all, **Marv Gilberg**: WSU all, **Ari Grashin**: source all, **Israel Halfon**: DE, **Ben Harris**: GHS, Molly Sherer, **Mark Maimon**: source, **Jack Meyers**: source all, **Al Moscatel**: MIHS, UW, **Neiso Moscatel**: source, MIHS, **Ray Moscatel**: source, DE, SU, **Don Richman**: DE, **Nate Ross**: SJCC, CK, **Todd Rubin**: source all, **Stan Sidell**: GHS, **Mike Silver**: GHS, **Louis Soriano**: source all, **Zollie Volchok**: DE, PI, **Rod Waldbaum**: source, **Todd Warnick**: source, **Harry Werbisky**: SHS, **Aaron Wolff**: source, **End Photos**: CK (2) MB

BOXING

Chapter title page: DE (2), **Intro photos**: PD all, **Herb Bridge**: UW, **Ely Caston**: LK all, **Jackie Caston**: LK, MB, **Sammie Caston**: LK all, **Nate Druxman**: DE all, **Abie Israel**: DE, DE, **Oscar Levitsch**: Harold Levitsch, Spokand Daily Chronicle, **Sid Nelson**: source, pd, **James Rosenwald**: source all, **Harry Weinstone**: MB

FOOTBALL

Chapter title page: GHS (6), Greg Rosenwald, SHS (2), GHS (2), **Louis Baroh**: GHS all, **David Baroh**: GHS all, **Hymie Harris**: source, source, **Joe Israel**: Albert Israel, **Sandy Lederman**: The Arlington Times, **Ben Mahdavi**: Enid Hammer all, **Taylor Mays**: Laurie Black, **Jamien McCullum**: source,

FOOTBALL

source, **Justin McCullm**: source, **Sam McCullum**: CK, private collector, **Jay Posner**: source, **Harry Scheiderman**: Paul Schneiderman, UW, **Abe Spear**: UW, UW, **Bill Tone**: SHS

HORSE RACING

Chapter title page: Ken Alhadeff, ALH, **Ken Alhadeff**: Alhadeff collection, ALH, Thoroughbred Times, Emerald Downs, **Mark Alhadeff**: source, **Michael Alhadeff**: ALH all, **Morrie Alhadeff**: ALH all, **Sonny Gorascht**: source all, **Alex Grinstein**: ALH, Grinstein Family, **Irv Levine**: ALH, ALH, Spokesman Review, ALH, **Perry Levinson**: Levinson Family all, **Herb and Fern Meltzer**: Meltzer Family all, ALH, **Herman Sarkowsky**: source all, ED, **Abe Sherman**: Sherman Family, **Eddie Sherman**: source all, **Elias Solomon**: Malakoff Family all, **Phreda and Joel Staadecker**: Staadecker Family, **Dave and Karen Tarica**: Alise Tarica all

MACCABI

Chapter title page: Terry Posner all, **David Jack Funes**: Funes Family, **Matt Grogan**: source, **Leon Grundstein**: source, **Mike Morgan**: source, **Terry Robinson**: source, **David Schiller**: source, **Howard Shalinsky**: source, **Amy Wolff**: source

SOFTBALL

Chapter title page: SJCC, **Junior Sephardic League**: Leon Alhadeff GHS all, **SJCC Softball League**: CK (3),SMS, SJCC, CK all, SJCC, **The Maccabees**:

PHOTO CREDITS

SOFTBALL

Jeff Morris all, **SJCC**: CK (7), SMS (4), SJCC (16), **WSJHS-SJCC Reunion**: SJCC all

SPORTS COLLECTORS / RETAILERS

Chapter title page: DE (2), SMS, Ebbets Field Flannels, Seattle Sounders, Spokesman Review, MB, DE (2), CK, SU, SMS (2), Seattle Storm, SMS, DE, **Marc Blau**: source, **David Eskenazi**: Ben VanHouten, source, Ben VanHouten, **Charles Kapner**: Mike Siegel/ST, source, source, **Beau Sadick**: MIHS, source, **Marco Speer**: source all, **Warshal Family**: Warshal Family all

SPORTS MEDIA

Chapter title page: ST, CK, **Steve Bunin**: source all, **Stan Farber**: MB all, **Adam Gordon**: source, **Dave Grosby**: 710 ESPN, **Mike Kahn**: Seahawks/Sounders, Les Keiter: Keiter Family all, **Aaron Levine**: Q13, Teamphotogenic, **Ken Levine**: source all, **Paul Lowenberg**: source, **Dave Mahler**: source, **Michael Salk**: 710 ESPN all, **Mike Siegel**: source all, **Stan Tobin**: UW, source, **Hy Zimmerman**: CK

TEAM OWNERS

Chapter title page: Herman Sarkowsky, **Barry Ackerley**: Harley Soltes/ST, Alan Berner/ST, **Brotman Brothers**: MB all, **Harry Brotman**: MB all, **Morley Brotman**: MB, **Bernie Brotman**: SHS, MB, **Stan Golub**: Carol Harris, DE, **Joseph Gottstein**: ALH all, **John Haas**: Franco Marchio, **Adrian Hanauer**: Seattle Sounders, Sounders, Corky Trewin, **Danny Kaye**: Cole Porter/ST, unknown, **Anne Levinson**:

TEAM OWNERS

Karen Ducey/PI, Seattle Storm, Seattle Storm, **Charles Littman**: source, **Herman Sarkowsky**: UW, source, Sounders, source, source, source, ED, **Walter Schoenfeld**: source, **Sam Schulman**: DE (2), Matt McVay/ST, **Howard Schultz**: Paul Kitagaki, Jr./PI, unknown, **Dick Vertlieb**: DE (3), unknown, DE (2), ST, unknown, unknown, Indiana Pacers, PI

TENNIS

Chapter title page: PD, **Dave Haas**: source, **Lisa Kranseler**: source all, **Henry Prusoff**: source, ST all, **Mickey Soss**: source all, **Kim Waldbaum**: source, **Gertrude Wolfe**: source, FHS, source, **Alan Woog**: source all

SPORTS EXTRA

Chapter title page: PD, Lilac CityRoller Girls, **Leo Dobry**: MB all, **Kara Schocken Aborn**: source all, **Bob Moch**: source, UW, PI (2), Vince Stricherz, ST, public domain (3), UW, public domain, ST, UW (3), **Janet Leopold Esfeld**: Sports Illustrated, source, **Sylvia Azose Ange**l: WSJHS, **Jim Brazil, Jr**: source, **Trea Schocken Diament**: source, **Lester Kleinberg**:Larry Kleinberg, **Morris Miller**: Diane Cohn all, **Elliot Friedman**: source, **Moe Muscatel**: FHS, source, **Max Silver**: Mike Silver, **Samuel Levine**: DE all, **Kenneth Muscatel**: Hydroplane and Raceboat Museum, source, HRM, unknown, Stephen Lane, **Jacob Lunon**: source, **Naomi Weitz**: Cathy Flora, **Martin and Howard Seelig**: source, **Joel Brazil**: source, **Julie Brazil**: source, **Jerry Cohn**: source, **Harry Pruzan**: GHS, source, WSJHS, source, **Jerry Belur**: source all, **Jonathan Hurst**: source, **Philip Sulman**: GHS, Benjamin Roll-

SPORTS EXTRA

er: PD, **Danny Jassen**: source all, **Kenneth Alhadeff, Jassen**: source all, **Kenneth Alhadeff, Bruce Glant**: FHS all, **Morris Alhadeff, Joey Mayo**: GHS, Louis Sterberg: Craig Sternberg all, **Rudy Spring**: GHS

TRIBUTES

All photographs included in the tribute pages have been obtained through their respective sources or family members thereof.

MOE EPSTEIN
First Base

HAROLD JAFFE

ANCHEL GOLDBERG

Laurie Sadick, Garfield HS, 1943

HARVEY FUSON